Discovering the
WONDERS
of our
WORLD

Death Valley, California, USA

READER'S DIGEST

Discovering the
WONDERS
of our
WORLD

A GUIDE TO
NATURE'S SCENIC MARVELS

Published by The Reader's Digest Association Limited
London • New York • Sydney • Montreal

Tabletop Mountain, South Africa

FOR 2005 EDITION

EDITORIAL
EDITORIAL DIRECTOR
Julian Browne

MANAGING EDITOR
Alastair Holmes

PRE-PRESS ACCOUNTS MANAGER
Penelope Grose

PRODUCTION EDITOR
Rachel Weaver

PROOFREADER
Kevin Diletti

ART
ART DIRECTOR
Nick Clark

ART EDITOR
Julie Bennett
Artworker: Martin Bennett

COVER DESIGNER
Melanie Young

FOR ORIGINAL EDITION

EDITOR
Noel Buchanan

ART EDITOR
Joanna Walker

WRITERS
Bernard Dumpleton
Anne Gatti
Anna Grayson
Derek Hall
Tim Healey
Tim O'Hagan
Peter Leek
John Man
Antony Mason
Geoffrey Sherlock
Keith Spence
Jill Steed

ILLUSTRATORS
Geoffrey Appleton
Phil Bannister
Will Giles and Sandra Pond
Peter Goodfellow
Gary Hincks
Pavel Kostal
Janos Marffy
Malcolm Porter
Polly Raynes
Peter Sarson
Gill Tomblin
Raymond Turvey
Contents map:
Rod and Kira Josey

FEATURES PHOTOGRAPHY
Vernon Morgan
Stylist: Penny Markham

Pinnacles Desert, Australia

SPECIALIST CONSULTANTS

Robert John Allison, BA, PhD
Department of Geography
University of Durham

Michael Bright, BSc
Managing Editor
BBC Natural History Unit

Sara Churchfield, BSc, PhD
Division of Life Sciences
King's College London

Chris Clarke, BSc, PhD
Department of Geography
Sheffield University

Barry Cox, MA, PhD, DSc
Division of Life Sciences
King's College London

Professor Ian Douglas, BA, BLit, PhD
Department of Geography
University of Manchester

Roland Emson, MSc, PhD
Division of Life Sciences
King's College London

Professor Andrew S. Goudie
MA, PhD (Cantab), MA (Oxon)
Department of Geography
Oxford University

A.T. Grove, MA

Peter Minto, MA, BEd
Blyth Ridley County High School

Peter Moore, BSc, PhD
Division of Life Sciences
King's College London

Bill Murphy, BSc, PhD
Department of Geology
University of Portsmouth

Sarah O'Hara, BSc, MSc, DPhil
Department of Geography
Sheffield University

Henry A. Osmaston, BA, MA,
DPhil, FICF

Dick Phillips
Specialist Icelandic Travel Service

John Picton, BSc
School of Oriental and
African Studies
University of London

Tom Spencer, MA, PhD
Department of Geography
Cambridge University

Robert Talbot

David S.G. Thomas, BA, PhD
Department of Geography
Sheffield University

Prof Claudio Vita-Finzi, BA, PhD,
DSc (Cantab)
Department of Geological Sciences
University College London

Tony Waltham, BSc, PhD
Civil Engineering Department
Nottingham Trent University

Grace Yoxon, BA
Skye Environmental Centre

Discovering the Wonders of Our World
was edited and designed by
The Reader's Digest Association Limited,
11 Westferry Circus, Canary Wharf
London E14 4HE

Printed in China by Leo Paper Products Ltd.

*Front cover: Mount Roraima, Venezuela;
insets (right): Anak Krakatau, Indonesia;
(left): Giant's Causeway, Northern Ireland
Back cover: White Sands, New Mexico, USA*

For more Reader's Digest products and
information, visit our websites at:
In Canada: www.rd.ca
In the U.S.: www.rd.com
In the U.K.: www.readersdigest.co.uk
In Australia: www.readersdigest.com.au
In New Zealand: www.readersdigest.co.nz

CONTENTS

The World's Greatest Natural Wonders

VOLCANOES AND DESERTS, GLACIERS AND
WATERFALLS – ALL THE WORLD'S
CONTINENTS CONTAIN LANDSCAPES THAT
INSPIRE AWE IN THE BEHOLDER

Forces That Shape the Earth

THE COMBINED POWER OF CONTINENTAL DRIFT, THE SUN AND GRAVITY THROWS UP MOUNTAINS AND THEN ERODES THEM INTO WEIRD SHAPES

Features

WILD LANDSCAPES HAVE ACTED AS MAGNETS FOR ADVENTURERS AND ARTISTS. THEY ALSO SUPPLIED STRONGHOLDS FOR ANCIENT CIVILISATIONS

Each site is located on the map by a reference number.

Africa

Europe

The Middle East and Asia

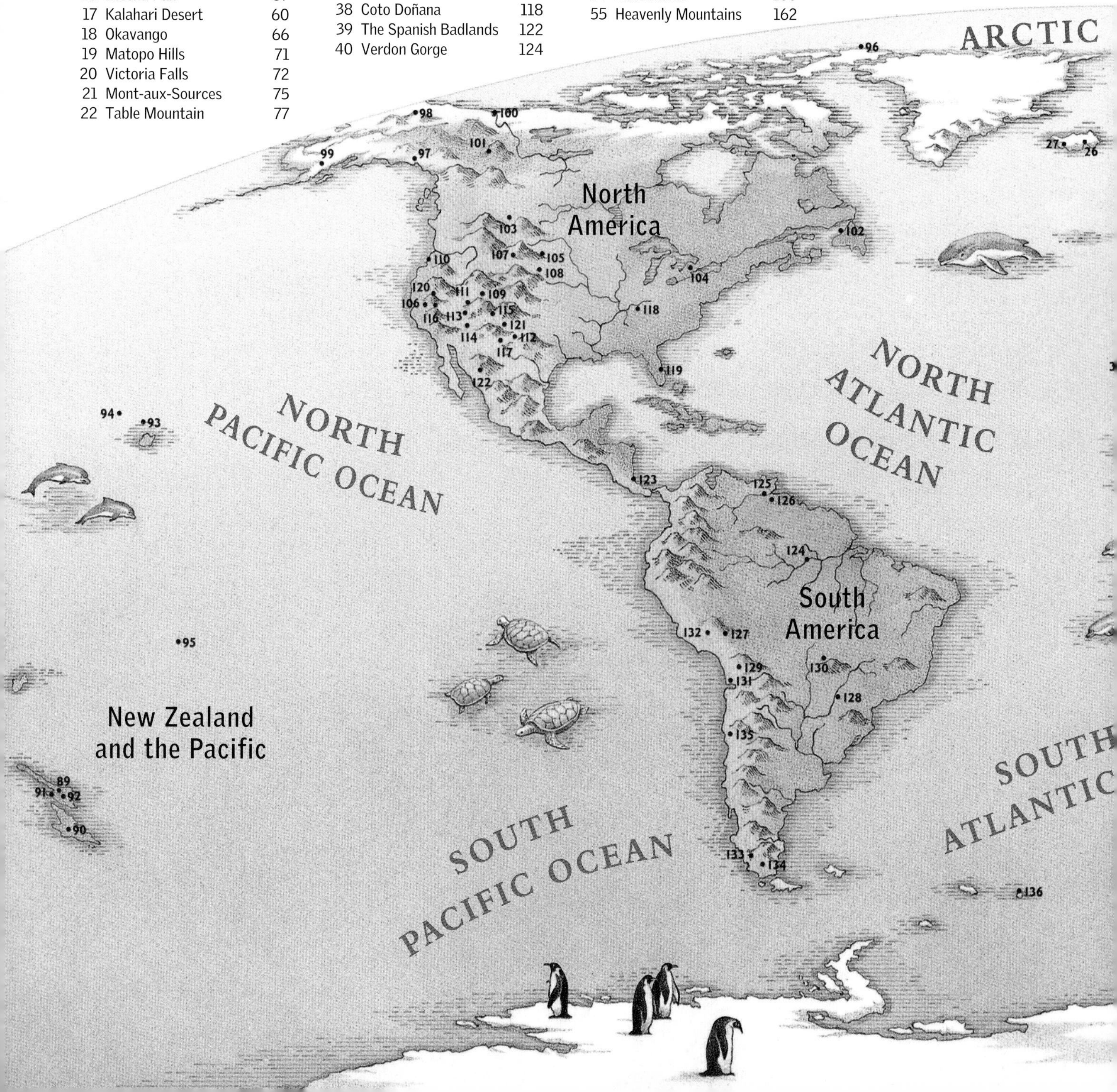

ARCTIC
North America
NORTH PACIFIC OCEAN
NORTH ATLANTIC OCEAN
South America
New Zealand and the Pacific
SOUTH PACIFIC OCEAN
SOUTH ATLANTIC

OCEAN

Europe

Asia

28 33
30 32
31
35
34
53
45
41 42
37 40 43 44 47
38 46
39 51 49
48
3 50
4
1
Africa
2
The Middle East
5
57
55 65
58
56
59 60
62 63
66 64
67
NORTH PACIFIC OCEAN
52
54
61

7
6
8
9 11
12 10
14
13
70
68
69
71

25
20
16 18 19
15 17
24
21
22
23

INDIAN OCEAN

72
80
76
Australia
74 77
79 78
81
73 82
75
83
87 85
86
88

OCEAN

SOUTHERN OCEAN

Antarctica

138 137

Africa

Tassili N'Ajjer

AT THE HEART OF THE SAHARA, LAND ALMOST DEVOID OF LIFE HAS MYSTERIOUS PAINTINGS OF ANIMALS AND HUNTERS

The well-heeled come by light aircraft. The less so, or the more adventurous, approach the great bulwark of Algeria's Tassili mountains by four-wheel-drive truck, crossing gravel, rock and shifting sand where the air shudders above a ground temperature that can reach 70°C (158°F).

Their destination is not a mountain range in the usual sense, though it rises

FANTASTIC PINNACLES *Water carved Tassili N'Ajjer's strange rocks when the Sahara was a land of rivers and lakes.*

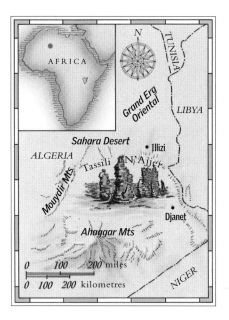

up to 7400ft (2250m) above sea level. Rather, it is a 400 mile (640km) long sandstone plateau, dissected into separate massifs which are themselves split and divided again by numberless ravines and wadis into a chaos of cliffs

ONCE FERTILE LAND *Below Tassili an archipelago of tumbled rock stretches far into the sandy ocean of the Sahara.*

and pinnacles of naked rock. It is a place of strange beauty that has few equals.

Best, perhaps, to see it first at dawn, when its twisted buttresses are touched by fire, rose and purple, and throw indigo shadows across the intervening sand. Then, with only a touch of fancy, the eroded rock turns into skyscrapers and cathedrals, spires and chimneys.

Though sand-laden wind was the artist that carved the softer rocks into shapes for the imagination to seize upon, the principal architect was water. Rushing torrents gouged out ravines, isolated bluffs from stacks and monoliths, split seams and fissures and excavated shallow caves.

The area now known as the Sahara once had a wetter climate. Many of the dry, sand-filled wadis and ravines on the desert's southern margin were then rivers or occupied by lakes. What is now desert was once green grassland.

AIR-COOLED NEST

An enterprising desert dweller, the white-crowned black wheatear builds a nest with a cooling system. If the sparrow-sized bird nested on bare rock, its eggs would cook in the fierce heat. So it builds a mound of pebbles in the shade of a boulder, then makes a nest of twigs in a hollow on the top.

The pebbles provide insulation from the ground's heat, and cooling winds blow between them. What is more, they are porous sandstone and soak up the dew that forms in the cold desert night. The dew evaporates by day, cooling the nest.

ANCIENT PAINTINGS THAT TELL OF A LAND OF PLENTY

In the most vivid and immediate way, paintings and carvings on rock faces and in caves tell the story of the life and death of Tassili N'Ajjer. The nomadic Tuareg people of the Sahara have always known about Tassili's art, but the outside world knew little of it until the French explorer and ethnologist Henri Lhote, with his assistants, spent two years making thousands of tracings and photographs during the 1950s.

Though most of the paintings share an immense vitality, economy of line and brilliant colour-sense, their style and subject group them into fairly distinct periods. The earliest, perhaps painted between 6000 and 4000 BC, show men of negroid appearance hunting elephants, buffaloes, hippopotamuses and wild sheep with huge horns – the animals of a greener Sahara – or wearing ceremonial dress for some tribal rite. Among them are huge, white creatures, half-animal, half-human, perhaps representing gods.

The second group, executed perhaps between 4000 and 1500 BC, shows a pastoral people tending large herds of long-horned, piebald cattle with giraffes and ostriches among them. There are scenes too, of banquets, a wedding, children asleep beneath animal skins, a woman pounding grain to make flour.

By the third period, however, about 1500–300 BC, the Sahara has become as dry as it is now, and a new people has arrived. They appear to be armoured soldiers, driving two- and three-horse chariots, but whether they are invaders, allies or a Mediterranean army fleeing the wrath of Pharaoh is uncertain. Gradually, around 200–100 BC, the horses disappear and childlike drawings of camels take their place. After that, there are no more drawings.

What is left is an almost unbearable curiosity. What became of the people who painted the pictures? Did they migrate south as the land grew arid, or did they simply die out? Perhaps we shall never know.

MURALS *Unknown people used ochre and other oxides to decorate rock walls with paintings of huge beasts, and of people going about their daily life, like the hunter above.*

Drying was a slow, slow process; the very name Tassili N'Ajjer translates as 'plateau of the rivers', though it has been arid since long before the beginning of the Christian era.

Staunchly surviving from this wetter time are small groups of gnarled cypress trees whose roots burrow into the rocks in search of water. They are reckoned to be 3000 years old and are the last of their line, for although they produce viable seed, the ground is too dry for it to germinate. Another survivor from a livelier past is the wild mountain sheep with immense curved horns that shares its arid habitat with jerbils, and with a wheatear which builds a nest that can cope with the desert climate.

Once, however, the plateau supported a very different fauna. There were giraffes and antelopes, hippopotamuses, lions and elephants – even men and women who lived by herding cattle and goats. Some of this is known from ancient animal bones dug out of the sand, but far more evidence comes, irrefutably and uniquely, from rock paintings (see above) found among the towering cliffs and wondrous rock formations of Tassili N'Ajjer.

Ahaggar Mountains

DEEP IN THE SAHARA IS A COUNTRY WHOSE LANDSCAPES, LEGENDS AND PEOPLE MIGHT HAVE ENHANCED THE ARABIAN NIGHTS

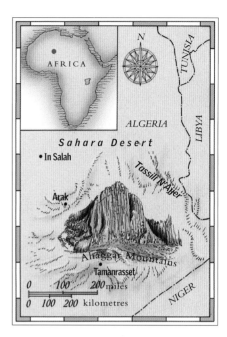

In the Sahara, at least when the sun is high, there are no horizons – only a milky vagueness whose bounds might be either near or far. Driving south though, from the oasis of In Salah towards the centre of the great desert, you slowly become aware of a distant hardening in the opacity, a darkening that reaches far to either side.

Gradually this resolves into the towering and seemingly endless cliff that is the outermost bastion of Algeria's Ahaggar massif. Astonishing even among Africa's formidable list of astonishments, Ahaggar is a huge island – roughly the size of France – set in the ocean of the Sahara. Bounded on three

LANDSCAPE OF ETERNITY *The fluted volcanic peaks of Atakor stand like banners over Ahaggar, a vast empty plateau about the size of France.*

sides by beetling cliffs, on the west it slides off into the Tanezrouft, the Land of Thirst, in which, in the old days, a traveller left behind by a caravan would simply compose himself to die.

Though it is known as a mountain range, Ahaggar – also called The Hoggar – is a high granite plateau. At its heart, in the region called Atakor, lava flows have covered the granite with 600ft (180m) of basalt, splintered and broken like the surface of a huge slag heap.

Out of this, rising to a height of nearly 10,000ft (3000m) is a fantastic array of towers, stacks and needles composed of phonolite, another volcanic rock. As it cooled, the rock broke into long prismatic shapes, generally likened to organ pipes, though in fact some resemble nothing so much as gigantic bunches of asparagus stood

on end. In one 300sq mile (777km²) area of Atakor there are more than 300 of these monoliths, adding unexpected shapes to a landscape already stark beyond imagining. The Tuareg, nomadic people associated with the Ahaggar for at least 2000 years, call this place Assekrem, 'the end of the world'.

MEN OF AHAGGAR *Although many young Ahaggar Tuareg now work on oil rigs, at festivals they show that they have lost none of the skills of their warrior forebears.*

Among the mountains there is no vegetation at all, and little enough throughout the entire Ahaggar massif. Rainfall is sporadic and brief, yet here and there in steep-walled canyons that delay evaporation, it collects in pools that encourage a little greenery and offer an illusion of coolness in their depths. Few though they are, the pools are of immense importance to the herds of the Tuareg.

PEOPLE OF THE VEIL

The Ahaggar Tuareg are a striking people. Tall and fair-skinned, the men wear veils from puberty onwards, some say to prevent evil spirits entering through the mouth. They carry long swords and daggers, and shields made from white antelope hide. According to some authorities, they are the descendants of mysterious charioteers who swept down out of Libya from about 1000 BC, and are depicted in the rock paintings of Tassili.

Their name, Tuareg, is an Arabic term meaning 'abandoned of God', for they were late in their conversion to Islam, and still show some divergences from

the strictest beliefs. The women go unveiled and have a powerful influence in family affairs, and Tuareg families are usually monogamous.

Until the late 19th century, the Ahaggar Tuareg ruled much of the desert from the oasis towns of Tamanrasset and In Salah, where they dealt in ivory, gold and slaves, supplementing their income by extracting protection money from the caravans that passed by.

On hearing, in 1881, that these aspects of their livelihood were under threat from French plans to build a trans-Saharan railway, they responded by massacring almost the entire expedition that had been sent to reconnoitre the route. Though the expedition had been both ill-organised and ill-led, and the tribesmen armed only with medieval weapons, the verve of the Tuareg charge and their sinister appearance earned them a reputation for invincibility in French eyes.

The Tuareg had a profound effect on the French, who invested them with all kinds of legends the Tuareg had never heard of. Most powerful was that

DESERT PRIEST

On a visit to the Sahara in 1883, a rich young Frenchman, Charles de Foucauld, was captivated by the desert and its peoples. Renouncing his money and former position, he became a priest, and in 1902 built a mission station at Tamanrasset.

There, in considerable privation, he devoted his life to the Tuareg as doctor, provider in times of want, and friend. He drew his serenity from the loneliness of the desert and the mountains, finding it especially among the high rocks of the Assekrem, where he made himself a hermitage.

De Foucauld was killed, probably unintentionally, during a Turkish-inspired rising at Tamanrasset in 1916. His eyrie on Assekrem still exists, and visitors scramble up there before dawn to see the curious, twisted peaks turn purple, then violet, then palest rose, as the sun climbs over the rim of the desert.

FRIEND IN NEED
De Foucauld made no converts among the Tuareg but is remembered among them for his kindness.

encapsulated in Pierre Benoît's novel *L'Atlantide*, written in 1919. It tells of Antinéa, a beautiful queen of Atlantis, who lives in a castle in the Ahaggar Mountains and there seduces and murders young French officers. Then, in 1925, archaeologists announced the discovery of the skeleton of a woman who had been buried with royal honours. In the popular press, she was at once translated as Antinéa.

The result was electrifying. French officers scoured the mountains for further evidence, and even the great explorer Henri Lhote was not immune from the legend. In 1928, in a remote cave, he discovered a rock painting of a woman whose breasts were daubed white, and claimed her as Antinéa, siren of the unforgettable Ahaggar.

Dadès Gorge

WINTER TORRENTS CARVED OUT THE SHEER-SIDED RAVINE THAT CUTS THROUGH THE HIGH ATLAS MOUNTAINS OF MOROCCO

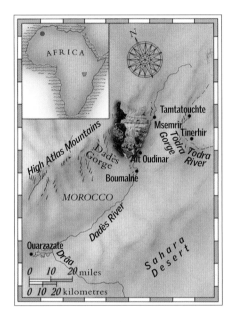

DIFFICULT PATH *High above the fast-flowing Dadès, a man treads warily along a path cut through the gorge. Above him multicoloured cliffs tower to 1600ft (500m).*

Where the Dadès River cuts between the forbidding peaks of the High Atlas Mountains, a narrow gorge winds a hairpin course between walls towering to a dizzy 1600ft (500m). As the sun climbs higher and sunlight seeps down the walls, the rocks change from black through greens and reds to brilliant yellow, depending on the season and time of day.

Around 200 million years ago these rocks were coral reefs at the bottom of the sea, but within the last few million years, movements in the Earth's crust heaved them up and folded them to form the High Atlas Mountains, whose geological history is now displayed in the multicoloured layers of sandstone, limestone and marl (clay) that pattern the walls of the gorge.

Thousands of years of winter storms have carved the river's course. From November to January or March, blinding downpours of rain bombard the High Atlas, turning the river from a trickle or a dried-up bed to a raging flood that subsides again after only a few hours. In this short while, the torrential rains can swell the river's flow twentyfold. In Arabic, these ephemeral rivers are known as *wadis* or *oueds*.

When the waters of the Dadès are at their fiercest, debris carried down from the mountain heights tears at the soft rock of the riverbed and cuts it steadily deeper. In one part of the valley, this erosion has worn the rocks into forms that take on the shapes of table tops, pyramids and jagged peaks, as well as strange, man-like shapes known locally as the 'Hills of Human Bodies'.

FROM SNOW TO SANDS

The High Atlas Mountains are a 460 mile (740km) chain of the Atlas range that splits Morocco in two. The Dadès rises in the mountains, where the highest peaks are capped with snow, then runs south-west for 220 miles (350km) to join the Drâa River at Ouarzazate, an oasis and former French fortress town on the northern edge of the sand-swept wastes of the vast Sahara Desert.

In its lower reaches, the river flows between groves of palms and almonds and fields divided by hedges of roses, grown to make sweet-scented rose-water. Figs are grown in summer, and in autumn left to dry on the flat roofs ready for selling at the *souk* (market).

The Dadès Gorge lies about 15 miles (24km) upstream from the market town of Boumalne. Between the town and the gorge the river banks are lined with ancient *kasbahs* (citadels) and *ksour* (fortified villages), and there are fields of rich red earth shaded by walnut and almond trees. The 'Hills of Human Bodies' are about 9 miles (15km) out from Boumalne. As the gorge narrows, the road runs at water level, the precipitous walls providing welcome shade from the fierce heat of the sun.

The road crosses a bridge at the village of Aït Oudinar, and beyond lies the narrowest and most spectacular part of the gorge. A gravel track climbs to the little town of Msemrir, beyond which the going gets increasingly rough as the rocky hills of the Atlas crowd down to the river.

TODRA GORGE

To the north-east of Dadès Gorge is the spectacular Todra Gorge. From Tinerhir a road leads there beside the crystal-clear waters of the Todra River. Along the way, tall date palms cast a protective shade over vines, olives, walnuts and pomegranates. Where the valley narrows into the gorge, the cliffs rise sheer to a height of 1000ft (300m), and at its narrowest point the ravine is hardly 30ft (9m) wide. African crag martins wheel

round their rock nesting-holes, and majestic Bonelli's eagles soar overhead.

Near the gorge is a clear spring, revered by the Berber people of this region because it is said to work miracles – they believe that if a barren woman wades across while calling the name of Allah, she will become fertile. The road peters out at the Todra Gorge, although lorries and four-wheel-drive vehicles may lurch onwards into the heart of the High Atlas.

From the village of Tamtatouchte, north of the gorge, it is possible to drive west over treacherous mountain roads

to Msemrir, above the Dadès Gorge, and from there south to Boumalne down the Dadès Valley, completing a circuit through some of North Africa's most spectacular scenery.

THE MOUNTAIN PEOPLE

The Berbers lived as migratory shepherds in this region for centuries before the Arabs arrived. They are believed to be the descendants of invaders from western Asia who spread across North Africa. They reached Morocco some time after the 10th century BC and were converted to

traveller Walter Harris described life in a Berber village as 'one of warfare and gloom … every family had its blood feuds'. Yet there was joy as well, with celebrations such as harvest festivals, and songs and stories by troubadours.

A wound was dealt with in an unusual way. The skin was pinched together and a live red ant put beside it. Once the ant closed its mandibles on the skin its head was snipped off, leaving the mandibles as a clip that fell away once the wound had healed.

Then as now, Berber women were freer in their behaviour than their Arab sisters. Mountain women went about unveiled, and were far more likely to marry for love. Girls still make the running in a Berber marriage. Regular *moussems*, or fairs, are held on a hillside outside the town of Imilchil, north of Tinerhir. Girls of 14 or 15, heavily made up and jangling with silver, approach potential husbands and haggle over their bride-price. If they agree, the parents arrange the wedding.

LAST STOP *Beyond the village of Aït Ameur (left) in the High Atlas, the valley road is impassable to traffic.*

RITE OF ISLAM *The women of his family escort a Berber boy (below) to the ritual surgeon for circumcision: this enrols him as a follower of the Prophet.*

Islam early in the 8th century AD. These people kept to the mountains, building highland fastnesses where, however harsh the conditions, they were free to live in their own way, far removed from the seductive pleasures of the towns.

Courage in battle was their highest virtue. A Berber man suspected of cowardice was forced to wear a skull-cap and allowed to eat only after the women had finished. The laws of hospitality were strictly observed, and once two Berbers had broken bread together they would defend each other to the death. Writing in the 1920s, the British

Oulad Said Oasis

TREES FLOURISH AND WATER FLOWS IN A POCKET OF FRUITFULNESS WITHIN THE SAHARA'S BARREN WASTES

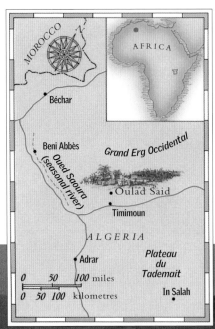

Water is the lifeblood of the desert, and the hundreds of oases scattered across the Sahara stand like fertile islands in a desolate sea. The popular image of an oasis is a romantic picture – waving palms beside a crystal-clear pool where nomads replenish their water supplies before moving on. It is an idyllic but not entirely true vision, for some oases, such as Oulad Said in Algeria, have long had permanent farming communities.

With its groves of palm trees and plots of vegetables, Oulad Said is a remarkably attractive place, where the

women's robes add splashes of colour to streets lined with red, mud-built houses. It stands in stark contrast to its surroundings – the Grand Erg Occidental. There, great dunes rise like the waves of a rolling sea of sand, and the relentless sun raises the summer daytime temperature to 49°C (120°F) or more. A traveller stranded without shade or water would die of heat stroke and dehydration within 48 hours. The people who have settled in Oulad Said are mostly market gardeners. They cultivate plots of irrigated land, growing vegetables, grapes, figs, peaches and

oranges, as well as the desert's most treasured crop, the date palm. Within the palm groves, pillars still mark the site of the ancient slave market, whose hapless merchandise once toiled to create the irrigation channels, or foggaras, that bring about all this fertility. The foggaras tap water held underground in a vast sandy 'sponge', up to 6000ft (1800m) thick in places (see below).

The date palm, it is said, likes to stand with its head in fire and its feet in water. Like the camel, it is essential to life in the desert, and because of its

importance it is treated with reverence, and almost as a near relative. It is also the subject of myths and legends.

One legend about the date palm says that Allah made the tree from the clay left over after he had created Adam. Another claims that after Adam had been driven out of Paradise, God commanded him to cut his hair and nails and bury them, whereupon a tree grew bearing a juicy fruit.

TREE OF LIFE

It is said, too, that the date palms develop close relationships with each other. If one tree dies, its nearby 'friend' mourns and produces no more fruit. A female tree will die if its lover is felled. The fruit of this precious tree is a staple food, and as well as being eaten fresh, dates can be dried and ground into flour. No part of the tree is wasted. Its trunk is used for timber and fuel, the rough fibrous bark is woven into rope, the stalks are used for fences and roofs, and the leaves are woven to make baskets, brooms, bags and sandals. The juice of some varieties makes a sugary syrup, and the juice of young palms can be fermented to make a palatable, though highly intoxicating, wine. Even date stones are put to use – they are roasted and ground to make date 'coffee', an alternative to the hot tea enjoyed on cold desert evenings.

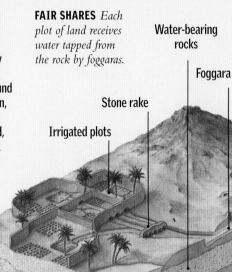

NIGHT AND DAY *A fire eases the cold of darkness, when temperatures can fall to −10°C (14°F). Day brings burning heat to dunes (inset) at the oasis edge.*

FLOW OF THE DESERT'S LIFEBLOOD

For centuries desert people have tapped underground water supplies by digging tunnels, known as foggaras, that channel the water down to oases. The tunnels may extend for as far as ten miles (16km), and can lie as deep as 100ft (30m) below ground level. They were dug by huge gangs of men, many of them slaves, using simple tools. Upkeep is a problem: channels get blocked, or have to be extended to tap more water.

The water emerges from the foggara near the irrigated land, minimising water loss by evaporation. A 'rake' across the stream directs water to the individual plots.

FAIR SHARES *Each plot of land receives water tapped from the rock by foggaras.*

Water-bearing rocks

Foggara

Stone rake

Irrigated plots

Ténéré Desert

LIFELESS SAND DUNES WHERE VEILED 'BLUE MEN' TRADE IN SALT LIE AT THE VERY HEART OF THE SAHARA DESERT

Land so devoid of life that it has been called the 'desert within the desert' lies just about as far from the sea as is possible in the Sahara. In the Ténéré Desert of land-locked Niger, rolling oceans of sand dunes, some as high as 800ft (244m), flow towards the horizon and lead to still more dunes in a seemingly endless progression.

But like the Sahara as a whole, there is more to the Ténéré than just sand. In an area the size of California, there are also gravel-covered plateaus blasted by the desert wind, and fantastic rock formations likened by one traveller to goblins, ogres and demons.

On the eastern edge of the Ténéré, the oasis village of Bilma is the starting point for the camel caravans of the Tuareg who trek for 350 miles (560km) across the desert carrying salt to trade in the market centre of Agadez. Bilma has given its name to the Grand Erg of Bilma – a vast expanse of sand extending eastwards for 750 miles (1200km) from Niger into Chad. The Erg's southern half consists of seif dunes – enormous parallel sand ridges – as much as 100 miles (160km) long and 1000 yards (1km) wide. The troughs between the dunes are known as gassis, and are used as routes by the caravan traders.

The nomadic Tuareg who roam this hostile environment are known as the 'Blue Men', from the colour of their faces. Unlike other Muslims, the Tuareg men cover their faces – a custom that may have evolved as a protection against days spent on camel back in the searing Sahara sun and wind. The blue dye of the cloth which swathes their heads and faces rubs off on their skin – hence their nickname.

SALT OF THE EARTH

The Tuareg's source of salt lies around Bilma, where naturally occurring salt deposits dissolve out of the ground when specially dug pits are filled with water. Crusts of salt crystals form on the water's surface; they are skimmed off and shaped in wooden moulds into

cones that each weigh about 40lb (18kg). For the journey across the desert, the Tuareg load the rock-hard cones onto camels, each animal carrying about six blocks.

Caravans of camels, strung together tail to nose, set off across the blistering Ténéré at a steady walking pace, and travel for 14 to 18 hours a day without stopping. Landmarks are few, and one, a single acacia known as the 'Tree of Ténéré', was the only tree that travellers might see for several days until it was mysteriously destroyed in 1973. It guided them to one of the route's few wells, where precious water can be found for the next leg of the journey.

It takes 15 days or more of arduous travel to reach Agadez, a hub of commerce and the site of a huge camel market in the Aïr Mountains. But camel trains with blue-stained drivers are becoming a thing of the past, for today's Tuareg are turning more and more to four-wheel-drive vehicles, cutting the trek across the desert to a few days.

In contrast to the parched desert, the Aïr Mountains, which border the north-western edge of the Ténéré , are far from being universally barren. Around Mount Bagzane there are springs that enable farmers to grow dates, olives and other crops on hillside terraces.

The mountains, which rise to 6400ft (1950m), are rich in wildlife, with gazelles, ostriches, baboons and antelopes among the larger species. Earlier inhabitants of the Aïr have left their mark in the form of rock paintings and carvings, some of which may be 5000 years old. Drawings of elephants, rhinoceroses and giraffes suggest that the central Sahara once provided grassy routes for its trade caravans, rather than burning sands.

SCORCHING SUN *Barren hills rise from the softly undulating sea of the Ténéré Dunes. The temperature drops sharply at night, and day and night readings can differ by as much as 33°C (59°F).*

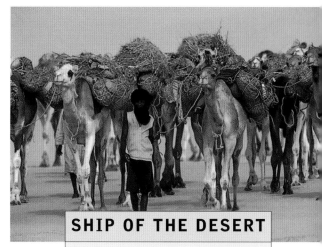

SHIP OF THE DESERT

Tuareg dromedaries - the one-humped camels of North Africa and the Middle East - carry blocks of salt wrapped in straw matting across the Ténéré Desert. They are well suited to the desert. A camel can, at one go, gulp down 30 gallons (136 litres) of water which its body then conserves - its dung is dry, it produces little urine, and its sweat glands only begin to work when its body temperature rises by 6-8°C (11-14.5°F) above normal.

Camels can also cope with erratic food supplies, storing fats - not water - in their humps, and finding nourishment in dry, thorny vegetation. In addition, camels' splayed feet do not sink into the sand, and their nostrils can close tight to keep out flying sand.

Lake Assal

EARTH'S SALTIEST BODY OF WATER LIES IN A LAND WHICH MAY BE SPLITTING OPEN TO DIVIDE AFRICA IN TWO

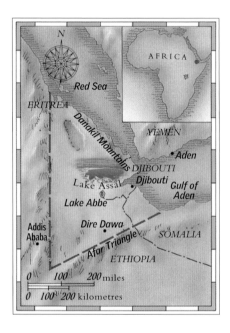

There came a time when the ancient Romans became so sated with the cornucopia of Africa's marvels that they greeted the latest travellers' tale with a polite 'Well, there's always something new out of Africa'. The truth was, of course, they had taken no more than a few tentative sips of all the continent had to offer, and even now, not even the most experienced of old Africa hands would be rash enough to say that its surprises were at an end.

Lake Assal makes the point well. Though not visited by Westerners until the late 1920s, nor properly explored or understood for years after that, it has already established new parameters in our knowledge of the world. For example, it is now recognised as the lowest point on the surface of the

ESSENTIAL TRAFFIC *A camel train, carrying salt to the Ethiopian hinterland, casts long shadows as it crosses Lake Assal's moistureless, glaring boundaries.*

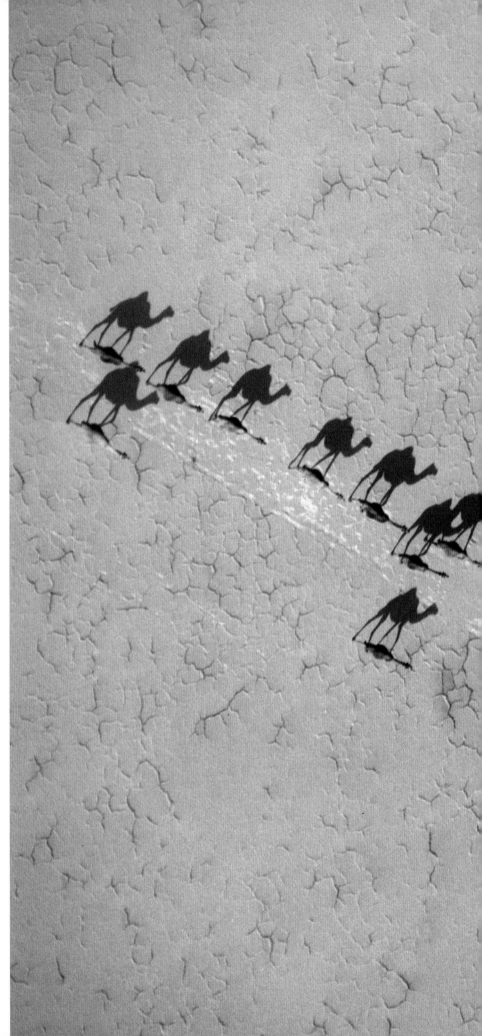

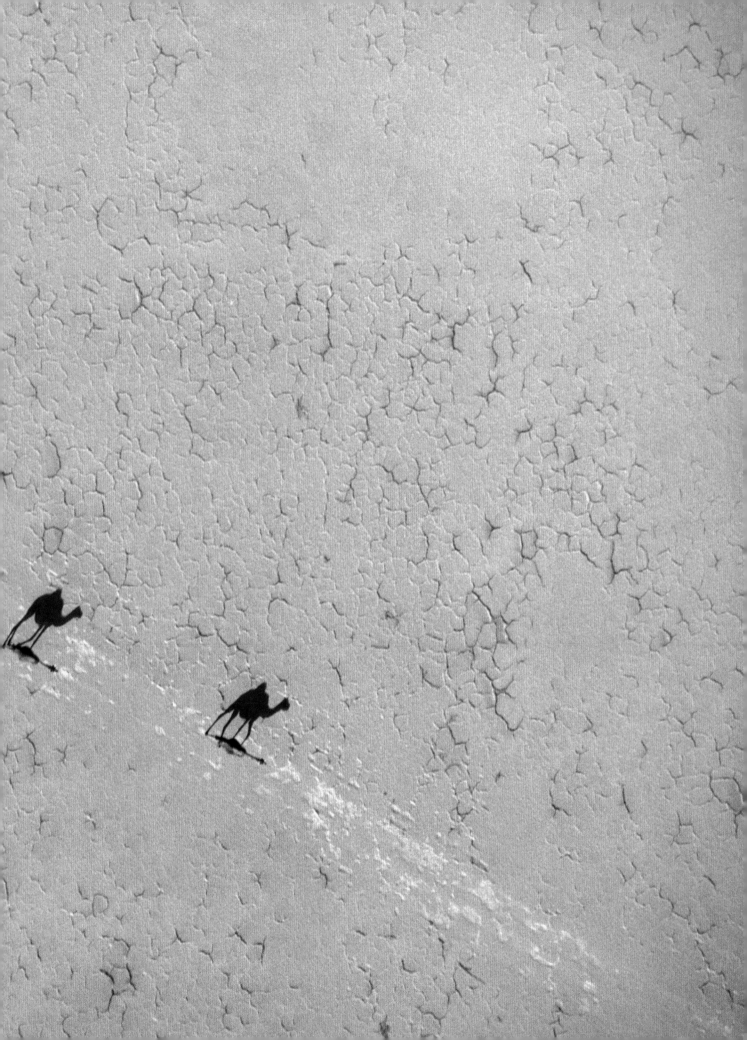

continent – 510ft (155m) below sea level – while its summer temperature of 57°C (135°F) makes it also one of the hottest. Both these factors contribute to its other claim to the record books, that of being the saltiest body of water on Earth, 10 times saltier than the ocean and far saltier even than the Dead Sea. Statistics apart, Lake Assal is also one of the planet's least hospitable spots. Backed by black, cindery hills of lava, parched by the sun, hardly a shred of vegetation grows there beyond an occasional pioneering thorn. No birds sing; nothing, not even a lizard, moves by the shore. It is a landscape of death.

PALETTE OF COLOURS

But it possesses, too, an unearthly beauty. The immediate surroundings are salt flats of a glittering white, while the clear, shallow waters are iridescent blue, shading to turquoise. Delicate fans and fronds of salt break the surface, painted by minerals in all manner of colours from pale green to violet to umber. The shoreline is dotted with the lake's self-created sculptures – grotesque, cabbage-like shapes formed of deposited salt.

Lake Assal owes its peculiarities to its position. It is situated in Djibouti, a tiny state that looks over the Gulf of Aden and the mouth of the Red Sea, and in a corner of the Afar Triangle, geologically one of the most disturbed areas on Earth. Here, three great fissures in the planet's foundations – the East African Rift, Red Sea and Gulf of Aden – meet, and earthquakes are commonplace.

Volcanic eruptions in the Afar Triangle are also commonplace, and for millions of years molten rock has been welling up to the surface as the jigsaw pieces making up the Earth's surface move apart. Such phenomena usually take place on the seabed, as in the Atlantic, whose floor is constantly being renewed along its mid-ocean trench. In fact, the Afar Triangle would also lie under the waves, were it not for the coastal barrier of the Danakil Mountains denying entry to the Red Sea. Instead, the area presents the rare spectacle of the type of crust normally found at the bottom of the oceans forming on dry land.

Nevertheless, despite the mountain barrier, most of the water in Lake Assal comes from the sea. It percolates

SHAPING EAST AFRICA

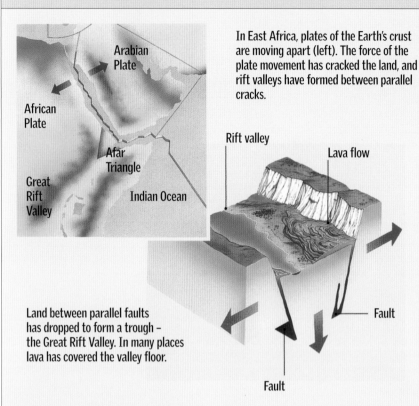

In East Africa, plates of the Earth's crust are moving apart (left). The force of the plate movement has cracked the land, and rift valleys have formed between parallel cracks.

Arabian Plate

African Plate

Afar Triangle

Great Rift Valley

Indian Ocean

Rift valley

Lava flow

Fault

Fault

Land between parallel faults has dropped to form a trough – the Great Rift Valley. In many places lava has covered the valley floor.

If a wedge is driven into the upper edge of a plank of well-seasoned wood, stresses and strains are set up down the entire length of the plank, causing cracks to open at various places along the grain of the timber, far from the original point of impact. In the simplest of terms, this describes the effect that the geological happenings in the Afar Triangle are having on the landscape of East Africa.

What occurs there is the planet's most dramatic and readily observable confirmation of the theory of plate tectonics, which postulates that the Earth's crust, or lithosphere, consists of half a dozen separate plates that float upon the molten inner asthenosphere, or mantle. The plates carry the granite foundations of the continents, surrounded by the constantly renewing basalt floors of the oceans.

At certain points on the globe, the plates slide under one another, and at others, pull apart. This last case has happened at the junction of the African and Arabian plates which, some 20 million years ago, began to drift apart, so creating the Red Sea and the Gulf of Aden. Proof of this movement is

satisfyingly provided by a glance at the map, which shows how neatly the opposite shores would fit into each other, were they to come together again.

Only at one point do they not fit, and that is at Djibouti and the Afar Triangle. The driving force that pushes the crustal plates apart is the upwelling of molten rock from the mantle, pushing upwards and outwards, and filling the central gap to create new ocean floor. At one time, the Triangle was part of the Red Sea, but with the uprising of the Danakil range of coastal mountains, it was cut off and slowly dried out. Nevertheless, it remains subject to the same forces that shape the bed of the sea. The lava continues to push out through fissures and volcanic cones in a vast, inexorable spreading of lava that for millions of years has been shouldering the sides of the Triangle farther and farther apart.

The same processes have created the Great Rift Valley system of East Africa and Arabia. For 4000 miles (6400km), from the Dead Sea to Mozambique, this trench slashes down one-seventh of Earth's circumference. Its entire length is an area of

SPLITTING CONTINENT *On Djibouti's coast, a sullen landscape of fissures and volcanic cones is being created as molten rock wells up from the planet's core. This is where Africa is splitting apart under the force of continental drift.*

volcanoes and earthquakes. It may even have contributed to such folk memories as the closing of the Red Sea and the destruction of the towns of Sodom and Gomorrah.

In both Ethiopia and Kenya, upwelling of molten rock has raised and thinned the continental crust, resulting in great mountainous plateaus, and it is there that the Great Rift has achieved its most dramatic forms. Unable to withstand the stretching, the Earth has split along lines of weakness into gaps 25–35 miles (40–56km) wide, leaving the land between them to drop. The depth of the subsidence is not always obvious, since in many cases it has refilled with a deep flow of lava, but even so the height of the escarpments on either side of the rift valleys can be breathtaking.

For some reason not yet understood, the Great Rift system in Africa has taken two separate courses. Due to the disturbance of ancient river systems, its western branch, curving through Uganda, Tanzania and Zambia, is filled with vast lakes, such as Albert, Tanganyika and Malawi. The eastern rift however, through Ethiopia, Kenya and eastern Tanzania, has shallow, alkaline lines like Lake Natron, and towering volcanoes such as Mounts Kenya and Kilimanjaro. There, too, is the great wildlife reserve of the Ngorongoro Crater, while some of the volcanic debris in the valleys, as at Olduvai, has been found to contain the remains of man's earliest known ancestors, dating from perhaps 2½ million years ago.

But perhaps the most intriguing thing about the Great Rift is not its past, but its future. If the Rift Valley turns out to be a plate boundary in the making, the Horn of Africa may eventually hive off and go voyaging into the Indian Ocean. But some geologists say this won't happen. In fact, as the Atlantic Ocean grows wider, they believe that Africa will be forced over against Arabia, and the Red Sea may close up again.

TOKEN OF MANHOOD *An Afar tribesman's most prized possession is a curved dagger (right), which is presented at adolescence and equates with masculinity. The dagger lies among a salt-gatherer's belongings. Salt from Lake Assal is packed into bags (inset), which are laced with palm fronds.*

through the rocks and down into the lake's deep bowl, there to be supplemented by water running off the hills during the brief winter rains. Salts from the sea water and minerals washed off the hills are added to those bequeathed through the ages.

But the area was not always so spectacularly arid as it is now. Some 10,000 years ago, the climate was considerably wetter, and the surface of the lake stood 260ft (80m) above its present level, as can be seen from the tide mark of freshwater mollusc shells on the surrounding hills. But what was the larger part of the bed of the lake is now a glaring white plain, where the

only sign of life is perhaps an Afar tribesman, who has come with his camels to dig salt, as his forefathers did before him, to sell in Ethiopia.

LAKESIDE JEWELLERY *Much of Lake Assal's water seeps in from the Red Sea. The sun burns off the moisture, leaving delicate patterns of salt flats.*

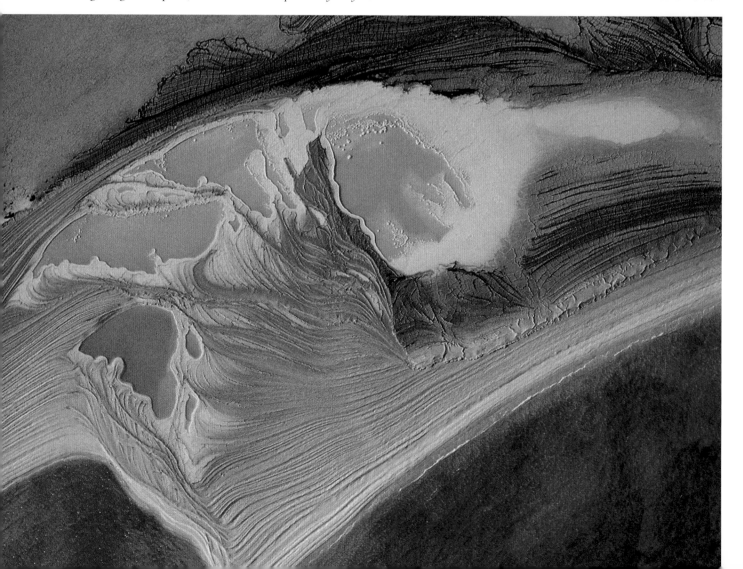

Erta Alé

A CURVE OF VOLCANOES RISES OUT OF THE DANAKIL DEPRESSION – 'A LANDSCAPE OF TERROR, OF HARDSHIPS, OF DEATH'

The British explorer Ludovico M. Nesbitt wrote in 1934: 'Perchance our grandchildren will discover means of journeying to the stars, and then will smile at the strivings of ourselves, who crept painfully over the unknown places of the earth.' With other dedicated travellers of his generation, he shared the conviction that Earth's last unexplored regions should not be won without matching them with Man's utmost endeavours.

CRATER AT NIGHT *Runnels and fountains of molten rock glow red in the dark in the seething lava lake of Erta Alé, one of five 'fuming mountains'.*

The motor car and the aeroplane, he felt, were too sealed off to be part of their surroundings. For himself, he was happy 'to employ the ancient, slow methods of exploration, by which the very taste and smell of remote and primitive territories is forced, even though it be painfully, on the observation of the traveller'.

And these were the methods used by his expedition of 1928, when he and his two Italian companions became the first Europeans to see the great company of volcanoes called Erta Alé.

The object of the venture was to make a 400 mile (640km) march from

south to north across the Danakil Depression, part of the Great Rift Valley that slashes down through East Africa. Prospects were not encouraging. Much of the terrain was alkaline desert, sunk well below sea level, where temperatures soared to a furnace-like degree. Water was next to non-existent, and the local tribesmen, the Afars, were reputed to be cruel and bloody-minded. Some half a dozen parties of Europeans,

BRINY LAKE *Lake Karum lies at the lowest point of the Danakil Depression. After rains, it is briefly filled with mineral-charged water that soon evaporates.*

venturing into the same area during the previous 50 years, were believed to have been slaughtered.

From the jumping-off point at the Aussa Oasis on the Awash River, Nesbitt's route lay ever deeper into the desert. Day by day, the sun grew hotter, and the expedition took to marching by moonlight and dawn. As the sun rose, the sky and desert became one, without horizon, form or distance. The sun's glow was at furnace heat. But if the open desert was hot, it was as nothing compared with the ravines of the Danakil Depression. There, the ground itself seemed to be on fire,

MEN AND ANIMALS CRAWLED UNDER ROCKS LIKE INSECTS TO ESCAPE THE HEAT

burning through the soles of boots. Water holes became ever scarcer, and even the camels began to die. In the glare of the sun, the temperature climbed to 75°C (167°F), and in the tents was only a few degrees lower. Men and animals crawled under rocks like insects to avoid the heat. But whatever the conditions, they could always see in the distance the tall, white-clad figures of Afar warriors, implacable as the land itself. To them the expedition, especially its rifles, represented riches untold.

One evening, as the haze lifted, Nesbitt and his companions suddenly beheld a wondrous sight. There before them, ranged in a curve 50 miles (80km) long, were five great volcanoes, rising sheer from the level white plain. The guide whispered their name – Erta Alé, the 'fuming mountains'. Closest was Ummuna, with a flattened cloud of smoke attached to its flank. Next was Erta Alé itself, exquisitely symmetrical, surmounted by a smoky plume climbing skyward. Over all hung a pall of smoke that, as dusk fell, was lit up on its underside by a pulsating red glare.

Next morning, the explorers set out to get closer. But far from being smooth

as it appeared from a distance, the land surrounding the volcanoes was a rolling lava field like a frozen black sea, each of whose wave crests was razor-edged. The troughs were filled with clinker that shattered like glass underfoot, tearing boots and skin. Defeated, and nursing their injuries, the little band marched west, past the reeking mouths of Mount Alu, and climbed a lofty escarpment. It overlooked a glaring plain of rock salt.

With the eternal fires behind and the bitter plain before, it seemed to the explorers a land devoid of pity, unique and frightful. Nesbitt called it 'a landscape of terror'. But with their water exhausted, they had no choice but to advance into it, hoping that their guide was correct in his promise of a well. With endurance almost at an end, they did indeed come to a water hole, but found their way barred by a large group of tribesmen. These, to the explorers' enormous relief, revealed themselves to be not warriors, but salt miners, who made them welcome and helped them to a camping place by sweet water. Several days later, the expedition began the last stage of its journey north to the Red Sea. Its total march, through some of the worst terrain in the world, had taken three and a half months.

WORTH THEIR SALT

The Danakil Depression, inhospitable home of the volcanic peaks of Erta Alé, is one of the least compromising landscapes on the face of the planet. For a large part of the year, it is a parched, salt-encrusted plain. Much of it lies below sea level, and it was in fact a branch of the Red Sea until movements of the Earth's crust raised the Danakil Mountains to the north, so cutting it off from the main body of the sea. The trapped water evaporated, leaving a layer of salt as much as 2 miles (3km) thick over the former sea bed.

Occasionally, rain washes more salt off the higher ground and carries it to the lowest point, Lake Karum. This shallow stretch of mineral-charged brine lies some 400ft (120m) below sea level. Briefly each year, it may swell to 45 miles (72km) across, with scalding springs erupting round it – caused by water seeping down to meet molten rock welling up from the Earth's centre.

WANDERERS IN HELL

DANAKIL EVENING *Backed by eroded mineral spires, an Afar shepherd boy guards the flock that is his family's only means of livelihood.*

Despite the nightmarish conditions of the Danakil Depression, it is the home of nomadic tribes known as the Afars – or Danakils, as the other people of the region call them. In the dreadful heat and parched landscape, they survive on two main activities – nomadic farming and salt gathering.

For centuries the salt of Lake Karum has provided a living for local Afar tribesmen, who use poles to lever blocks out of the thick salt crust and shape it into bricks. The salt is then transported to places all over North and East Africa. Many Afars, however, still follow the farming traditions of their ancestors, moving from place to place with their herds of goats, sheep and camels.

The Afar people are a handsome people – tall, slim and sinewy. The women are beautiful, and manage their long, brown skirts with grace. The men wear white cotton loincloths and togas and each is armed with a long, broad-bladed dagger and either a spear or a rifle.

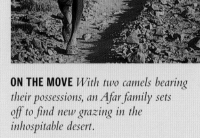

ON THE MOVE *With two camels bearing their possessions, an Afar family sets off to find new grazing in the inhospitable desert.*

The women and children tend the herds of animals as the family groups wander from one patch of sparse grazing to the next. The Afars' diet consists of little more than milk and meat – a lengthy drought, therefore, brings starvation and death to animals and people.

Lake Turkana

A RIVER THAT FLOWS
ACROSS THE SURFACE OF A
LAKE IN NORTHERN KENYA
HAS CREATED ITS OWN
'HIGHWAY' OF SILT

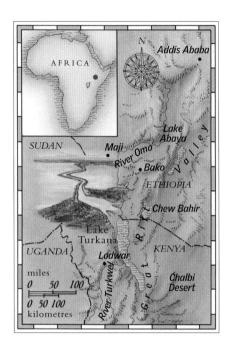

SELF-MADE RIVER BANKS *Between built-up banks, or levees, of its own creation, the River Omo snakes out into Lake Turkana. Count Samuel Teleki von Szek (left) visited the lake in 1897.*

Across the broad, flat surface of Lake Turkana, a 'river highway' snakes its way between silt banks so regular that they appear man-made. More than 3 miles (5km) from the lake shore, the highway ends in a dramatic, sprawling delta, shaped like the foot of a giant bird.

This is the end of its journey for the River Omo, which rises 400 miles (640km) away in Ethiopia. The river hurls itself southwards, through dramatic gorges and over waterfalls, until at last it winds its way through rolling scrublands and dry bush to flood – sediment-laden and orangey-brown – into the brilliant green expanse of Lake Turkana in northern Kenya.

But the river water, laden though it is with silt and debris collected on its journey, is still lighter than the water of the lake, which is dense with dissolved volcanic deposits. So the fast-moving river water flows over the lake's surface, gradually slowing its pace and depositing its silt and debris. As it does so, it creates its own banks. When its momentum at last expires, it spreads out to produce a delta and finally becomes one with the lake.

Lake Turkana, 195 miles (312km) long, is fed by several rivers, but has no outlets. Long ago, when the rivers were much fuller, the level of the lake was probably about 600ft (180m) higher than it is now. It used to drain into the Nile through a gorge in its north-western end, but severe changes in the climate have lowered the water level, and the gorge is now completely dry.

Over the centuries, great quantities of ash and lava have erupted from the

volcanoes which surround the lake, and have been washed into the water, building up thick deposits of mineral salts, including sodium carbonate, better known as washing soda.

Lying in the barren north-west of Kenya, right against the border with Ethiopia, Lake Turkana is so remote that only more adventurous travellers and dedicated anthropologists ever go there and share the experiences of the scattered tribes that live around it.

Their efforts are well rewarded, because the lake supports a breath-taking array of crocodiles, hippopotamuses and water birds.

About 12,000 crocodiles live in and around Lake Turkana. Although they are among the biggest in the world – up to 18ft (5.5m) long – they are not generally a threat to men and animals because they feed on the huge Nile perch which thrive in the lake. On a still night, a visitor standing by the water may hear the gnashing of great jaws, as the crocodiles work as a team to pen the fish against the shore, working slowly inwards and gorging as they go.

The main breeding ground of Lake Turkana's crocodiles is Central Island, a small cluster of volcanic craters near the western shore. Here they have multiplied, almost unchanged, for 130 million years. Crocodiles increase in size with age, and their large size and apparent docility may be due to a lack of predators combined with a good food supply. Perhaps as a result of the soda content of the water, they have horny nodules on their bellies so their skins are unsuitable for making into shoes or handbags, which may have saved them from human attention.

A DISPLAY OF TEAMWORK – BY PELICANS

Also living off the rich harvest of fish are vast congregations of birds – ospreys, spoonbills, herons, ibises, cormorants, ducks and geese, as well as great white pelicans. The pelicans appear to imitate the crocodiles' fishing techniques. They form a line and swim forward together and then, as if at a signal, they all plunge their bills into the water together and scoop up fish.

Until the early 1970s, Lake Turkana was known as Lake Rudolf. The first European to see it was Count Samuel

Teleki von Szek, in 1897, who named it after the Crown Prince of Austria. Count Teleki was a wealthy Hungarian sportsman and geographer who, with a large and well-equipped caravan of 450 porters and six guides, cut a swathe through the area, shooting everything from small wildfowl to elephants, hippopotamuses and leopards.

The lake provided the final piece in a 'jigsaw' being put together by Edward Suess, a Viennese geologist. He saw a pattern formed by the lakes and rivers stretching from Lake Nyasa in southern Africa to the River Jordan in the Middle East, and recognised the fault in the Earth's crust now known as the Great Rift Valley. Lake Turkana has its own special fascination, for it is here that decades of work by

ON A STILL NIGHT, VISITORS MAY HEAR THE GNASHING OF GREAT JAWS

anthropologists, including Mary and Louis Leakey and their son Richard, has uncovered some of the oldest fossil remains of modern man's ancestors.

They have shown that early people roamed this area 2 million years ago, walking on two feet – footprints have been found, preserved in the 'plaster cast' of volcanic deposits. Stone hand axes that were used for hunting litter the ground in places.

The richness of the fossil finds in the area is the result of thousands of generations of bones being buried, and turned into fossils, in successive layers of sediment and volcanic lava. Later upheavals of the land exposed the layers, creating a laboratory for the study of man's earliest years around the jade-coloured lake.

REAPING THE LAKE'S HARVEST

Of all the tribes living near the lake, only two, the Turkana and the El Molo, benefit from the plentiful fish.

Night fishing with the Turkana is dramatic and exciting. Standing in shallow water at the lake's edge, a fisherman waves a smouldering bunch of dry reeds, whose light will attract the fish to the surface. Then, holding an openwork basket made from bound saplings in the other hand, he deftly traps the fish on the lake bottom. The Turkana, who live on the lake's western shore, also fish with stone-weighted hand

lines to land the giant Nile perch, which can weigh as much as 200lb (90kg).

The El Molo people's name means 'the people who live by catching fish'. These skilled fishermen, living at the southern end of Lake Turkana, spear or net fish – and also crocodiles – while balancing on rafts made from palm logs bound together.

BASKET-WORK NETS *Trapping fish with openwork baskets, the Turkana use a technique which has been tried and tested over many centuries.*

The Ruwenzori

THESE SNOW-CAPPED PEAKS ON THE EQUATOR ARE CONSIDERED TO BE THE 'MOUNTAINS OF THE MOON' OF THE ANCIENT GREEKS

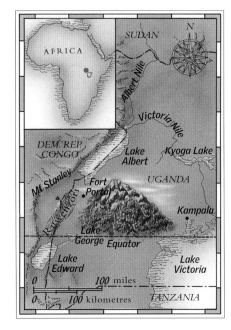

Here are veiled wonders: East Africa's Ruwenzori, also called the Mountains of the Moon. They hide their summit splendours behind an almost permanent mantle of cloud and it is only when veering winds tear back the curtain of mist that their snow-capped grandeur is revealed.

The explorer Henry Morton Stanley – who found Dr Livingstone – reached the mountain range, previously unrecorded by Europeans, in 1888. He noted that for 300 days of the year the peaks were concealed by brooding cloud, but when it parted the views were stupendous. 'Peak after peak

SEETHING TORRENTS *Waterfalls pour from the Ruwenzori. Ptolemy, the Greek geographer, believed the range to be the source of the Nile. It is not – but it stands exactly where his map shows it.*

struggled from behind night-black clouds,' he wrote, 'until at last the snowy range, immense and beautiful … drew all eyes and riveted attention.'

Ruwenzori means 'rainmaker', and it was Stanley who applied the Bantu name to these glittering snow mountains that are less than 30 miles (48km) from the equator. Their craggy mass sprawls for some 60 miles (96km) along the border of Uganda and Democratic Republic of Congo. Towering mountains, with glaciers creeping down their valleys, rake the sky at the heart of the massif. Margherita, one of Mount Stanley's peaks, rises to 16, 765ft (5110m).

The Italian Duke of the Abruzzi, Luigi di Savoia, first scaled, mapped and photographed the mountains in 1906. But a dim awareness of their existence has a much more ancient pedigree. More than 2000 years ago, Greek

geographers had spoken of mysterious mountains whose snows and torrents fed the headwaters of the Nile. Aristotle referred to a 'silver mountain' in central Africa in the 4th century BC, and Ptolemy called them the 'Mountains of the Moon'. Ptolemy's mountains are now thought to be the Ruwenzori.

ROCK THAT SPARKLES

When the mists clear, the peaks seem to glow with an eerie brightness that has to do with more than the snow. The rock itself sparkles, for the underlying granite is topped by mica schists – glittering, coarse-grained rocks trans-formed by the heat and pressure of mighty earth movements. The Ruwenzori were not shaped, as were Kilimanjaro and Mount Kenya, by volcanic action. Instead, an immense block of land was lofted heavenward and tilted in a drama that took place less than 10 million years ago – not long in geological time. And this comparative youthfulness contributes to the jagged vigour of the mountains' profiles.

Probably the most wondrous sight in the Ruwenzori is the weird vegetation which creates an eerie and improbable landscape on the mountain's slopes.

AFRICAN SNOWSCAPE *Vegetation persists high on the north-eastern flank of Mount Stanley (right), around the Irene lakes. But snow can prevent the rosettes of giant grounsel from closing.*

SECRET CORNER *Run-off from the Ruwenzori rains and glaciers has created many quiet lakes enfolded by soggy green forest. Bananas grow wild among the tree ferns and creepers.*

NECTAR EATER *The malachite sunbird, which is about the size of a blackbird, uses its long curved beak to feed on nectar from giant lobelias.*

The weather plays a major part in the stage-setting. Ruwenzori's clouds, descending to about 9000ft (2700m), have created an extraordinarily humid climate, and in the wettest month – November – there is as much as 20in (510mm) of rainfall.

Continual mists maintain a sodden atmosphere that fosters luxuriant growth. Plants grow to bizarre sizes amid the dank smell of fungi, the spongy mosses and the incessant dripping of water. The lobelias are astonishing. Species such as *Lobelia wollastonii* and *L. bequaertii*, which are related to the familiar garden lobelias, reach three times the height of a man, and sprout yucca-style spikes. Groundsels (*Senecio*) grow to the height of telephone poles, and species of heather reach 40ft (12m).

These prodigies grow chiefly above the tree-line – and it is absence of competition from true trees that has helped them to achieve phenomenal sizes. Another factor is the acid soil, rich in humus, which has also nurtured earthworms as long as a man's arm.

With such peculiarities, it is small wonder that superstition clings to this equatorial fairyland. The local Banande people long believed that the Ruwenzori harboured spirits that would roll rocks at trespassers venturing into their domain. Not long ago, a naturalist who cut down a giant lobelia spike found that none of his porters would carry or even touch it for fear of death. Nor will local tribesmen touch the rare chameleon (*Chameleo johnstoni*), one of the forest's oddest denizens. With three horns protruding from its forehead, the baleful-looking reptile is shunned as a creature of ill omen.

There are other forms of animal life. Sunbirds use their downcurving bills to sip nectar from the huge lobelias. Black and white colobus monkeys live in high branches, feeding on leaves and rarely coming to the ground, and leopards prowl the forest almost to the snow line. The most extraordinary creature is the tree hyrax which resembles a rabbit and shrieks like a guinea pig – but is related to neither. The hyrax has hoof-like nails instead of claws and is more closely related to the elephant than to any other animal. True elephants frequent the Ruwenzori, too, though only in the foothills. They move ponderously through thick stands of reed and papyrus in low swamps and marshes, like sentries patrolling this weird mountain kingdom.

Ol Doinyo Lengai

TO THE MASAI PEOPLE, A RUMBLING VOLCANO IN AFRICA'S GREAT RIFT VALLEY IS KNOWN AS THE 'MOUNTAIN OF GOD'

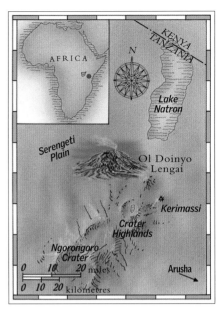

Amid the dusty, searingly hot Crater Highlands of northern Tanzania, in a region spattered with hot springs and steaming sulphur jets, stands a grey mountain known as Ol Doinyo Lengai. This is a Masai name that means 'Mountain of God'.

The bleakness of the surrounding scenery is relieved by little more than a few twisted umbrella thorns and stunted baobab trees. Dust devils whirl over the fissured earth, and what little grass there is turns to straw in dry weather.

An active volcano, Ol Doinyo Lengai is hardly a scenic attraction – it is only 9370ft (2856m) high, and not far away there are much more majestic

INSIDE THE CRATER *By moonlight, Ol Doinyo Lengai's crater takes on an eerie glow as patches of glimmering greyish-white ash stand out against the black slick of emerging lava.*

mountains, such as Kilimanjaro. But instead of belching fire and smoke like other volcanoes, Ol Doinyo Lengai spits out washing soda! Its extraordinary lava eruptions are formed of ash and carbonatite – which becomes washing soda (sodium carbonate) on contact with moisture in the air. It is the only active carbonatite volcano in the world, and what may sometimes look like snow on its summit is actually whitish ash from its remarkable eruptions.

But the molten rock in the volcano's core is black, and although it seethes menacingly enough within the crater, it comes out only about half as hot as normal lava – hardly even glowing as it spews from the volcano's vent. Once it reaches the air, the lava changes colour and transforms chemically to soda – the type used for cleaning and bleaching, which can be strong enough to scorch.

Ol Doinyo Lengai erupted in August

1966, and in 1967 there was another explosion. Today, the volcano still rumbles disquietingly. A climb to its rim takes six hours, and when visitors enter the crater, which is about 1000ft (300m) across, they look down into a hissing vent where lava bubbles like boiling tar. A visitor, Professor Curt Stager, wrote in 1990: 'Every few seconds the ground rocks; a fountain of lava bursts through the vent and crashes against its walls. As I approach, I realise that this tar pit is

DECEPTION *Pale streaks round the crater of Ol Doinyo Lengai are not snow but ash – it spits out ash and washing soda.*

actually a hole in a congealed crust. Beneath my feet seethes a lava lake.' The Professor described how one of his companions put his foot through the thin crust: 'Amid a puff of smoke he yanks it free … His shoelaces are gone. His pantleg is charred. I smile to myself as we retreat; "the Mountain of God" is a dispenser of justice.'

SACRED MOUNTAIN

To the west of Ol Doinyo Lengai sprawls the Serengeti Plain. This whole area is floored by layers of alkaline ash, which may have been discharged from Kerimassi, a now-dormant neighbouring volcano. The alkaline soil, along with the long dry season from June to October, does not favour many types of tree growth. But grasses flourish when the rains come in November, and the grassy plains abound in grazing animals

SMOKE SIGNAL

Billowing smoke clouds signal the coming eruption of the active volcano Ol Doinyo Lengai, in Africa's Great Rift Valley.

On August 9, 1966, after ten days of ominous simmering while the ground shook and rumbled, the volcano exploded, hurling black ash 33,000ft (10,000m) into the air and over the surrounding plains.

Within 48 hours the ground was coloured dirty white – the ash changes colour as it cools. It was three weeks before the eruption subsided.

– gazelles, wildebeests, zebras – as well as the animals that prey on them, such as lions and wild dogs.

Below Ol Doinyo Lengai's northern slopes is Lake Natron, whose shallow soda-filled waters overlie a bed of rank black mud. There are few fish here, and no plants of any size. But blue-green algae (minute water plants) abound in the alkaline soup, alongside the tiny creatures that feed in the evil-smelling mud. There is an exceptional bird that relishes this environment – the flamingo. Shimmering pink multitudes of more than a million flamingos often cover the lake surface while they feed on algae or tiny organisms.

The Masai cattle-herding nomads of Tanzania and Kenya believe that their god, Engai, thunders at its cratered summit. One of the central figures of their religion is an Eve-like figure called Naiteru-Kop. She was the first Mother, and lived in paradise with many children but no male partner. She often gazed in rapture at the moon, and one day Engai asked her to choose between the moon's survival and the survival of one of her own children. Because she could have more children, she chose to keep the moon. In this way, the first mother created human mortality.

Traditionally, the Masai measure a man's wealth and status by the size of his cattle herd. The Masai eat meat, but rarely their own cattle, except on ritual occasions. The humpback zebu cattle are kept for their milk and blood – drawn through a reed from the jugular vein of a living animal and drunk while still warm, or mixed with milk and stored in gourds. The Masai believe this diet gives them strength – their warriors were once lords of all the grazing lands in and around the Rift Valley.

Some Masai still follow a wandering lifestyle, herding their cattle to the best grazing according to the season. But advances in medicine have resulted in a large population increase. Now pasturelands are overgrazed and many Masai have drifted into the towns.

In times of drought, Masai herders have for centuries made a pilgrimage through the parched, ash-grey landscape to the base of Ol Doinyo Lengai to pray for rain. '*Eng kare! eng kare!*' is their eternal plea to Engai for water to restore the grass for their starving cattle.

WARRIOR RITES

Adult Masai living in traditional style, both warriors and women, are decked with massive earrings, colourful bead necklaces and bracelets of wrought copper, and women also wear anklets. Warriors wear orange-red cloaks knotted at the shoulder, and dye their tall, slim bodies with ochre clay and fat. Men and unmarried women wear their hair ochred and braided right up to the skull, but married women have their heads shaved and polished with red clay.

Every stage of life is marked by ritual. Naming ceremonies for infants, for example, and circumcision rites for older girls and boys. And once every 15 years at a full moon, the *E unoto* graduation ceremony for warriors takes place – the main one is at Mukulat in Tanzania.

Warriors, some wearing lion's-mane, ostrich-feather and leopard-skin headdresses, gather for the four-day event, which includes traditional dancing and sacrificing bullocks, as well as ritual shaving of the head. The young men cannot marry until they become senior warriors.

HIGH FLYERS *These traditional Masai dancers leap upwards to the accompaniment of rhythmic singing.*

East Africa's Soda Lakes

A CHAIN OF SHALLOW, SIZZLING, SODA-SATURATED LAKES IS STRUNG OUT ALONG THE SOUTHERN END OF THE GREAT RIFT VALLEY

Pea-green, pink or blinding white, East Africa's shallow soda lakes are dotted along the Rift Valley like a broken bracelet. Some glint in the equatorial sunlight, their soda baked to a hard crust at the water's edge. Others, such as Lake Bogoria, bubble and steam with the hot-water springs scattered along their shorelines.

It is the microscopic plants and animals that thrive in the water that give the soda lakes their predominant green or pink colours, but the colours change according to fluctuations in their numbers and to local conditions. There are billions of algae (minute water plants), and tiny grazing animals such as brine shrimps are so abundant that the water fizzes with air bubbles.

The white of the lakes comes from dried, encrusted soda where the water has evaporated. This soda, chiefly sodium carbonate (washing soda), is washed in from the soda-rich surrounding soil and the soda-ash spewed out by local volcanoes. The amount of soda in the water varies from lake to lake. Lakes Magadi and Natron, at the inhospitable southern end of the valley, neither of which has a water outlet, are the deepest and hottest and have the greatest concentration of soda.

Lake Magadi lies in remote, semidesert surroundings where the daytime temperature rises to 38°C (100°F), and is thick with soda. Natron, which often glows blotchy pink, is marginally milder but larger – 40 miles (64km) long and 10 miles (16km) wide. The heat causes more water to evaporate from these lakes than they get from rainfall, which is as little as 16in (400mm) a year. Scorching soda sludge rings the lake shores; at midday it can be as hot as 65°C (150°F) to the touch.

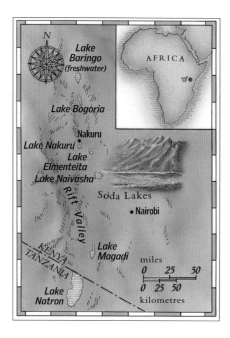

TINY GRAZING ANIMALS MAKE THE SODA WATER FIZZ WITH AIR BUBBLES

Other soda lakes, such as Bogoria, Nakuru and Elmenteita, are milder and more hospitable to wildlife, largely because of the river outlets that keep the water moving and limit the soda. But they also shrink from evaporation. During the 1950s Elmenteita and Nakuru almost disappeared, leaving the air filled with throat-searing dust.

Scientists believe that underground spring water, forcing its way up through the soda layers in the bed of the Rift Valley, is forever enriching the soda content of the lakes. On Magadi, soda has been commercially extracted since early in the 20th century without the supply diminishing. The hot springs and steaming geysers are heated by the volcanic rocks. At Bogoria, the scalding water overflows onto the grass, a hazard to visitors. In Natron and Magadi the hot springs are the only relatively fresh water available, and are the home of a

dwarf species of tilapia – a local fish that has adapted to live in hot water. After rain, when the soda is diluted, the fishes spread rapidly and breed. Millions gather in the shallows, causing the water to erupt with their movement.

In the 1950s, Leslie Brown, a British naturalist who was chief agricultural officer for Kenya, went to Lake Natron to find out if the flamingos seen from the air were able to breed there. To get close enough to observe them, he had to approach on foot for 7 miles (11km) or more. Starting at dawn, he walked from his camp to the lake edge and set out across the soda crust. The going was firm at first, but after a while the surface crumbled beneath each step. He began sinking in soft, foul-smelling mud. Walking became harder, every step an exhausting effort. To add to his miseries the drinking water in his canvas bag became soured with soda dust.

Despite Brown's powerful build and experience as a wildfowler in Scotland, his progress became so hopeless that he had to turn back. Intense heat, dehydration and exhaustion made the return journey almost fatal. Once he reached a solid surface he took off his boots, which were filled with soda crystals, and his legs, badly blistered, turned black as they were exposed to air. After the long walk back to his camp, Brown collapsed and was semiconscious for three days in hospital. It took six weeks and a period of skin grafts for his legs to recover.

FLAMINGO HAUNTS

Although the lakes are hostile to man and much wildlife, they are home to around 3 million lesser flamingos and about 50,000 greater flamingos, which feed on the waterlife; the pigments from their diet give the birds their pink

FLAMINGO LEGIONS *Thousands of milling lesser flamingos congregate on Lake Bogoria, one of the milder soda lakes. They have come to wash soda from their feathers in the hot springs.*

plumage. They feed in whichever lake has the most abundant food – this varies from time to time. The birds usually breed on the remoter lakes such as Natron, the soda-encrusted shores deterring marauders such as jackals.

The flamingos feed on algae or insect larvae with heads bent as they filter water and mud through their beaks, held upside-down in the water like ladles. They feed mostly at night when the wind has dropped down. Breezes by day can ripple the water and swamp their beaks, but sometimes they form a tight bunch, creating a calm central area between them where they can feed.

FAMILY LIFE

Flamingos breed at any time of year, but particularly after rains. They strut stiff-necked in courting displays that last for weeks, then build huge colonies of hollow-topped mud nests. The one or two eggs hatch a month later. After about a week in the nest, the fluffy grey chicks join huge crèches, where their parents find them to feed them red 'milk' from their crops. Until they can fly at about 11 weeks old, the chicks are at the mercy of predators such as fish eagles.

Congo River

THE MIGHTY CONGO
RIVER, ONCE KNOWN
AS THE ZAIRE, ARCS
THROUGH THE HEART OF
AFRICA TO THE ATLANTIC

NEAR THE RIVER MOUTH *Mangroove swamps line the banks of the lower Congo River, which was first visited by Portuguese in the late 15th century.*

Countless tributaries swell the great Congo River on its long curve to the Atlantic from grasslands on the border of the Democratic Republic of Congo and Zambia. They drain an area of rainforest and high grassland roughly the size of India. On its 2920 mile (4700km) journey, the river meanders through mangrove swamps and dense jungle, thunders over rapids and cataracts, and gathers such force that it spills about 41,700 tons of water a second into the sea. Its discharge is second only to the Amazon's.

When the Portuguese explorer Diogo Cão discovered the river estuary in 1482, he was unable to navigate the roaring rapids a short distance upriver (now known as the Livingstone Falls). So the mighty river remained unknown to most of the world for nearly 400 years. To 19th-century Europeans, this was 'darkest Africa'. According to the

novelist Joseph Conrad in 1899, in his *Heart of Darkness*, it was 'a country of nightmarish horrors'. Originally named the Zaire, the river was renamed the Congo by European explorers in the 17th century, after the Kongo people. In 1971 the former Belgian Congo was renamed Zaire, and the river also took that name. Since 1997, both country and river have reverted to Congo.

David Livingstone, the 19th-century Scottish missionary and explorer, thought that the Congo was the head-stream of the Nile, or perhaps the Niger. But horrific tales of cannibals

living in the forest depths deterred even the intrepid Livingstone from trying to prove his theory. Not until 1876–7 did the Welsh-born American explorer Henry Morton Stanley venture along the river to establish its true identity.

The headwaters of the Congo are known as the Lualaba River, only parts of which are navigable. It flows north-wards at first, through rocky gorges, then meanders through reed-fringed swamps and marshes to enter Lake Kisale, the haunt of egrets, ospreys, kingfishers and local fishermen. At Kongolo the ever-quickening river

Henry Morton Stanley (1841–1904) decided to explore the Congo River when he heard of David Livingstone's death in 1873. He had admired Dr Livingstone ever since their famous meeting in the Congo in 1871, when Stanley, a correspondent for the *New York Herald*, had been commissioned to find Livingstone.

Stanley set off from the east coast with a party of 350 in November 1874. They went first to Lake Victoria, carrying a small, single-masted boat, the *Lady Alice*, in sections. Stanley circumnavigated both Lake Victoria and Lake Tanganyika in the boat, establishing that they had no outlets to the Congo River.

When the party reached Nyangwe on the Congo in October 1876. Stanley enlisted the help of Tippu Tib, an Arab slave trader, and set off northwards with a party of around 1000. Progress was slow and difficult, and the Arabs left in December, after they had travelled 200 miles (320km).

Stanley acquired some canoes and continued by river and by land, on the way shooting rapids and fighting some 30 battles with local tribesmen. Only 114 of Stanley's original party eventually reached the sea in August 1877.

ACE EXPLORER
Sir Henry Morton Stanley (knighted in 1899) put the Congo River on the map. His party travelled on foot and in canoes.

has spread its girth sixfold to 1600ft (500m), and the bridge spanning the river is the only one for the next 1740 miles (2800km). Beyond lies a steep gorge with waterfalls and seething whirlpools – the Portes d'Enfer (Gates of Hell). Onwards there are some navigable stretches interspersed with rapids before Nyangwe, where the river enters the fearsome jungle that daunted David Livingstone in 1871 – he ventured no farther north. It was from Nyangwe that Stanley began his trip down the Congo in October 1876, after a two-year journey from the east coast of Africa. From Nyangwe it took Stanley nine months to reach the river

mouth, and on the way his party fought battles with people living in riverside villages.

Stanley was engaged in battle when he heard the sound of a waterfall ahead. It proved to be the first of seven that together dropped the river 200ft (60m) in about 56 miles (90km). It took the party nearly a month to get round them. Stanley named the falls after himself, but they are now called Boyoma Falls. They have the greatest discharge of any waterfall in the world – around 166,850 tons a second. Beyond the

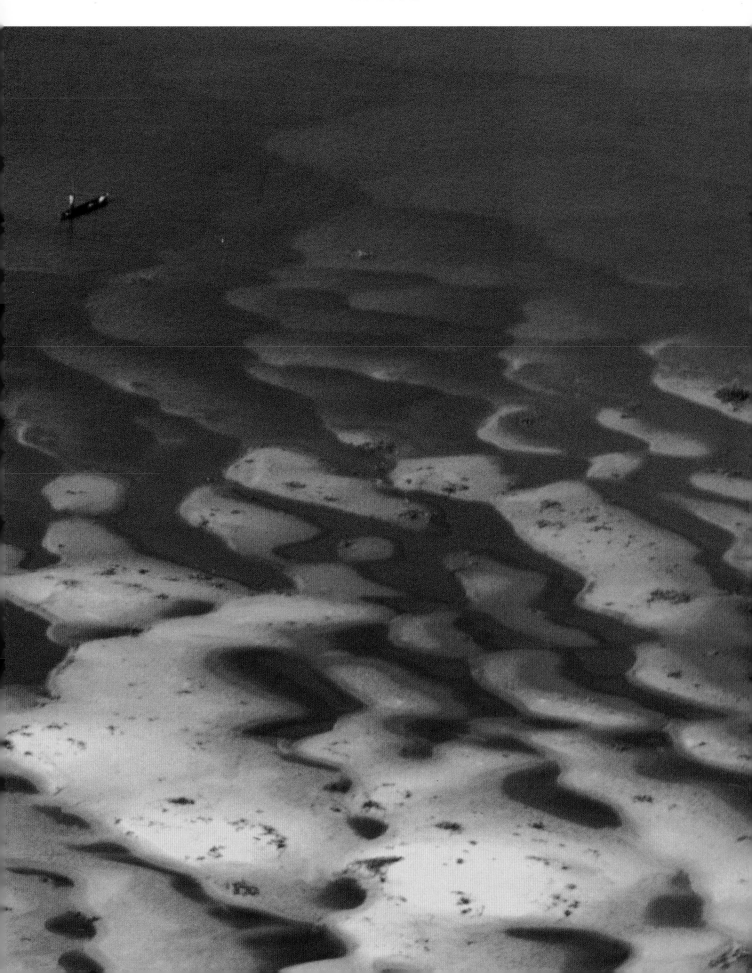

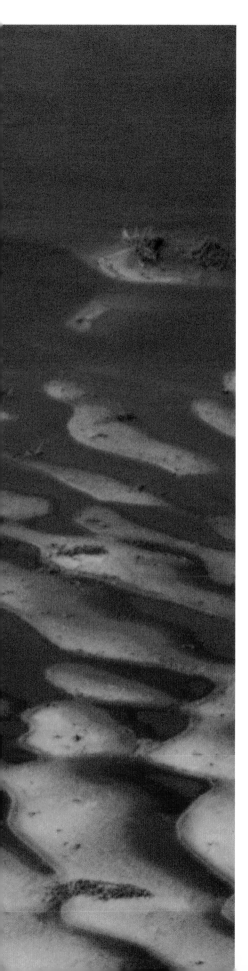

TRANQUIL WATERS *Malebo Pool near Kinshasa is 15 miles (24km) across, and dwarfs the tiny craft that ply its waters.*

falls Stanley founded a settlement, which he also named after himself – Stanleyville. He noted that the local fishermen caught large numbers of fish by means of poles and conical wicker baskets. They still do, for Stanleyville is now Kisangani, a busy fishing, manufacturing and tourist centre, and the end of the line for ships taking goods upriver.

From Kisangani, where the Congo curves westwards, the river is the main traffic route to Kinshasa, the nation's capital, just over 1000 miles (1600km) downstream. On the way it turns south-west, winding through dense rainforest alive with the chattering of monkeys and the screech of colourful birds. This stretch of the Congo River takes in more tributaries, including the Lomami, Aruwimi, Tshuapa, Oubangui and the Sangha – all contributing to the already vast volume of the Congo.

West of Kisangani, where it joins the Aruwimi, the river widens and then winds down to Mbandaka, with thousands of silt islands breaking its passage into a maze of waterways, an eerie network of dark lagoons choked with water hyacinths and overhung with trees laced with giant cobwebs. In *Heart of Darkness* Conrad described the river journey 'like travelling back to the earliest beginnings of the world, when vegetation rioted on the earth and the big trees were kings: an empty stream, a great silence, an impenetrable forest'.

One of the strangest crafts in the world plies the river between Kisangani and Kinshasa – it is a steamer known as the Big Pusher. This ungainly craft, a

'LIKE TRAVELLING BACK TO THE EARLIEST BEGINNINGS OF THE WORLD'
Joseph Conrad

floating village of travelling traders, pushes a large collection of barges, rafts, pontoons and canoes, all lashed together and crammed with as many as 5000 people, some in tiny cabins and others packing the decks and gangways.

The 'pusher' calls only at the larger trading ports. Elsewhere it merely slows down, and in midstream canoes and dugouts surround it like swarms of insects. Tying up alongside is a precarious undertaking, and trading exchanges have to be brisk. Within minutes boat decks are piled high with goods such as dried fish, antelope, fruit and smoked monkey carcasses. The floating village moves on until the next flotilla arrives.

Beyond Mbandaka, just over half way to Kinshasa, the forest thins out and the river gains momentum for its final rush to the sea, spreading to 10 miles (16km) wide with marshes reaching far into the distance. It is so wide just before Kinshasa that Stanley named it Stanley Pool, but now it is called Malebo Pool.

Kinshasa, on Malebo's south bank, is the sprawling capital city of the Democratic Republic of Congo. The Pool's tranquil waters are merely the calm before the storm. Just west of Kinshasa, the Congo enters its final stage – the awe-inspiring Livingstone Falls – and becomes unnavigable. These falls, with cataracts and rapids thundering through a deep gorge in the Crystal Mountains, descend 853ft (260m) in 220 miles (350km) and end about 90 miles (145km) from the sea. They were the last obstacle on Stanley's long journey downriver. He described them as 'a descent into a watery hell'.

HEALTH CARE *This chest was designed by Stanley for his journey. Medicines such as quinine for malaria were in glass phials.*

Ngorongoro Crater

ISOLATED FROM THE PLAINS BELOW, THE VAST
VOLCANIC CRATER IS A HIGH-RISE WILDLIFE HAVEN,
ABUNDANT IN ALL KINDS OF ANIMALS

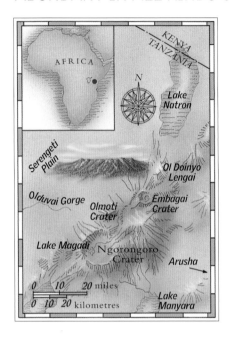

Cloaked in a tangle of ragged vegetation, the steep flanks of this ancient extinct volcano in northern Tanzania give little indication of what lies within its crater's walls. The silence of the thin air some 6000ft (1800m) above sea level is broken only by the rustling of leaves as warm breezes rise in the updraft from the surrounding plain, and chase over the rim into the watery blue African sky.

At the crest of the crater's rim, there is a breathtaking change of scene. The land plunges into a hazy void, sloping down to form a huge, pastel-shaded dish. At first it is hard to adjust to the giddying immensity of the space. The only points of focus are the filigree lines of the watercourses some 2000ft (600m) below, winding to glittering, pink-smudged pools.

Dark flecks pepper the crater floor; only when these begin to drift cloud-like into ever-changing formations does

THIS NATURAL NOAH'S ARK IS A HAPPY ACCIDENT

it become clear what they actually are – thousands of grazing wildebeests and zebras. Suddenly a wave of movement stirs the pools as the pink smudges take to the air, wheel, and then resettle on the water. They are immense flocks of flamingos, which congregate in the shallow crater lake.

One of the highest concentrations of wildlife in Africa – an estimated 30,000 animals – is to be seen on the crater's 100sq mile (260km^2) floor. Naming Ngorongoro's animals sounds like reading a check-list for photographers on safari. There are some 50 different species of large mammals, including lions, elephants, rhinoceroses, hippopotamuses, giraffes, various antelopes such as elands and impala, vervet monkeys, baboons, warthogs and hyenas. There are also more than 200 species of birds, including ostriches, ducks and guinea fowl. Effectively, the crater is a small-scale version of the wildlife of East Africa, raised to the heavens as if in the palm of some smiling god's hand.

CRATER HIGHLAND

This natural Noah's Ark is a happy accident of geology. Ngorongoro lies on the eastern spur of the Great Rift Valley, a fault in the Earth's crust curving through Africa from Mozambique to Syria. At various times over millions of years, enormous pressures at the Earth's core have exploited the weaknesses in the fault, and molten rock has been forced to the surface in the series of volcanoes now forming East Africa's 'Crater Highland'.

Ngorongoro is one of these volcanoes. Once it was cone-shaped and about twice its present height. But when the power of its last eruption was eventually spent some 2½ million years

DRAMATIC DAWN *Dark clouds roll across Ngorongoro Crater as sunrise brings a silvery sheen to the lake and swamps. Water available in the dry season sustains large numbers of animals.*

ago, and all the molten rock beneath its cone had been spewed out as lava, the top of the cone sank into the cavity. All that remains of it today is Round Table Hill in the crater's north-west sector.

Technically, a volcanic crater that is produced by a volcanic explosion or collapse is known as a caldera. Ngorongoro is the world's sixth largest caldera – about 11 miles (18km) across and roughly circular. But it is the largest caldera with an unbroken rim. The

crater's African name, however, takes little note of such statistical niceties. Ngorongoro simply means 'big hole'.

A rough and bumpy road built in 1959 leads down to the crater floor, dropping 2000ft (600m) in just 2 miles (3.2km). Only vehicles with four-wheel-drive are allowed in the crater. They bring thousands of visitors a year in a steady trickle.

Unlike the animals of the Serengeti Plain to the west, which migrate annually in search of water and fresh pastures, most of the Ngorongoro animals stay in the crater throughout the year – water is always available. Two springs and two rivers – the Munge and

GRAZING HERDS *In the vast arena of the crater floor, the striped zebras show up starkly among their wildebeest companions. But when they are on the move or grazing in the blur of a heat haze, their outlines merge with their surroundings.*

TREE OF LIFE

HOME MAKER *A male masked weaver bird weaves a grass nest, using an acacia thorn as a hook. He must attract a female before the grass browns, or she will reject it. Then he must start again.*

Acacia trees and bushes of several types dominate the East African grasslands. Although they have sharp and painful thorns, many animals feed on them – small antelopes such as dik-diks and Thomson's gazelles eat shoots, larger ones such as impalas browse on bushes, and elephants and giraffes strip full-sized trees.

As well as food, acacias provide look-out posts, larders, sunshades, umbrellas, scratching posts and homes. Leopards sit high in the branches to spot their prey, and after a kill lodge the carcass in a fork between branches, out of the reach of marauding hyenas. Lions rest beneath the leaf canopy in the heat of the day, and tiger snakes search among the branches for weaver-bird nests and a feast of chicks.

The silk cocoons of bagworm moths hang from branches. During mating, the female moth is inside the cocoon but the male stays outside, where he risks attack from ants living in tiny galls at the base of thorns. The ants guard the tree against leaf-eating insects, but not from invaders such as vervet monkeys, which pluck the curly seed pods and eat the seeds.

Mature seeds eaten by animals such as impalas and elephants are softened by the animals' digestive juices – without this they would not germinate. Dung beetles bury the seeds when they scavenge droppings. In this way, a new acacia comes to life.

HEARTY EATER *Among the mists of Ngorongoro Crater, an elephant feeds on an acacia. Elephants stripping off leaves and bark can kill stands of trees.*

Lonyokie – feed a series of swamps and the main lake, a shallow soda lake known as Magadi.

With no outlet, the lake water has a high salt content resulting from centuries of evaporation, and this gives it an intense blue colour in some lights. Only algae and some crustaceans, such as shrimps, can survive in the water, but this suits the millions of flamingos that feed there. There are two species – the greater flamingos stalk the lake margins with long-legged grace, heads bent as they dredge crustaceans through their bills, and the lesser flamingos filter for algae in deeper water. Neighbouring swamps provide muddy pits where hippos wallow, as well as watering holes for elephants and black rhino, with their attendant tickbirds or oxpeckers. These birds feed on parasites scratched from the leathery hides.

RAIN AND RENEWAL

Every year following the 'long rains' from December to April or May, the crater's grasslands are emerald green and awash with pink, yellow, blue and white flowers flourishing in the rich volcanic soil – they include petunias, lupins, daisies and rare blue clover. As the May–November dry season progresses, the crater gradually changes colour from green to yellow then fawn and biscuit brown, and the animals gather near the Munge Swamp. As grass covers about two-thirds of the crater, nothing breaks the smooth uniformity of the colours save for scattered clumps of acacia trees and outcrops of rock.

Virtually walled off from the outside world by the crater rim, the Ngorongoro animals have all they need to survive. Grazers such as zebras, wildebeests and gazelles make the most of the grasslands, and are preyed upon by carnivores such as lions, leopards, cheetahs, hyenas and jackals. They prowl round the grazing herds like nonchalant highwaymen, waiting to pick off a straggler. The grazers mostly give birth in January and February when the grass is greenest, and the predators do the same while there are plenty of calves and foals to provide food for nursing mothers and weaned youngsters.

So all is not paradise in this Garden of Eden. The agitation that runs through the wildebeest herd at the sight of a

SOCIAL SECURITY *Most of the crater's 15,000 wildebeest (or gnus) stay all year, and keep loosely together as a herd. Stragglers fall prey to predators.*

prowling lioness, the darting leap of a startled Thomson's gazelle, the whirring of flamingo wings as they launch themselves from the path of an opportunistic hyena – all speak of the constant alertness essential for survival in this tightly programmed community. And the soaring vultures spiralling over some distant kill mark another conclusion in this daily ritual of death.

LIVING LABORATORY

Ngorongoro's self-containment is a boon to the international scientific community, and for many years zoologists and others have come to study the wildlife here and its uniquely poised

ecosystem. But there is a cloud on the horizon – the cause for concern is inbreeding. Scientific analysis of the lion population, for example, has revealed that all the 100 or so lions in the crater are descended from just 15 individuals. These either survived a devastating wet-season plague of biting flies in 1962, or strayed into the crater shortly after. This means that the genetic pool of Ngorongoro's lions is very low, threatening both their ability to resist disease and the fertility of future generations.

A few animals leave the crater each year along the ancient tracks leading over the rim. They join the dry-season migrations on plains below the crater, and later return. These migrating animals are only a small percentage of the total, but they do expose Ngorongoro's wildlife to the genetic pool of the world beyond. But agricultural development

in the surrounding region threatens to encroach on these migratory routes, and to isolate the crater more than ever.

Once Ngorongoro was part of the nearby Serengeti National Park, where farming is not permitted. This put the Masai people of the region, who herd cattle, at a disadvantage, so in 1959 the crater and the area round it was made a conservation area covering some 3200sq miles (8300km^2). But cattle numbers within the crater are strictly limited, and no building is permitted.

The graceful, dignified Masai, with their reddened hair and rust-coloured robes knotted at the shoulder, are part of the magic of Ngorongoro. The soft footfall of a Masai herder-warrior, the rustle of sun-bleached grasses, the acrid scent of animal life, all contribute to the air of timelessness that hangs over this age-old landscape.

Virunga Mountains

EIGHT VOLCANOES – TWO OF THEM ACTIVE – RISE INTO THE CLOUDS AT THE JUNCTION OF THREE EAST AFRICAN COUNTRIES

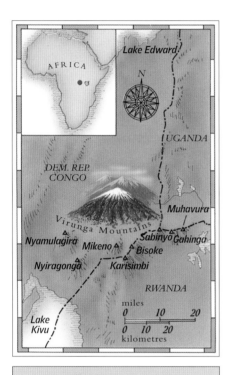

NIGHT CALLER

Loud whistles ring through the night on the forested Virunga slopes – the territory of the rabbit-sized tree hyrax. These noisy animals emerge from their short burrows mainly at night, and their vocabulary includes danger signals, contact calls, and territorial 'keep out' calls. Despite their small size, their closest relative is the elephant.

Seen from afar, the peaks of the Virunga Mountains stand in awesome magnitude in a mist of clouds. Rising sharply to dominate the plains of Rwanda, Uganda and the Democratic Republic of Congo, these mountains evoke a spine-tingling awareness of the Earth's origins. Eight volcanoes spread over 36 miles (58km) make up the Virunga range. Six of them are mute and extinct; the other two are active, forever smouldering with the threat of eruption.

Nyamulagira, meaning 'commander', is one of the world's most active volcanoes. Europeans first witnessed an eruption in 1894, and since then it has erupted several times through cracks along its sides. During a spectacular eruption in 1938–40, lava from a pool on the volcano's flank ran down to Lake Kivu, 15 miles (24km) away. An observer noted that the lava glowed 'like slag from a furnace' as it flowed, and that 'enormous clouds of steam were generated where the lava met the waters of the lake'. The loss of so much lava led to the collapse of Nyamulagira's summit, leaving a massive crater over a mile (2km) across.

An impressive crater also crowns the neighbouring active volcano of Nyiragonga. In 1977 its near-perfect cone split in five places, spilling out molten lava which destroyed everything in its fiery path as it moved downhill.

LAKE DAMMED BY LAVA

Spills of lava from the Virungas have helped to shape the surrounding landscape. The mountains lie in the western branch of Africa's Great Rift Valley. At one time the rivers of this branch drained north towards the Nile, but lava flows from the volcanoes are thought to have dammed the rivers to produce Lake Kivu. With its deeply indented shore, Lake Kivu is regarded by many as the most beautiful of Africa's lakes, but despite the sleeping beauty of the water the lake is a time bomb.

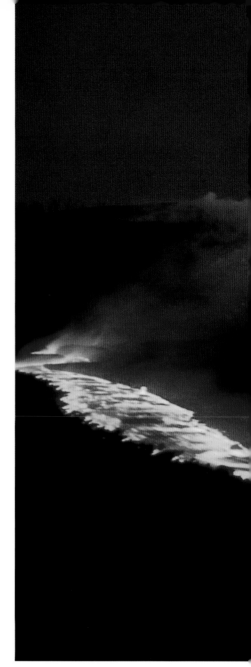

FIERY STREAM *During a burst of activity, scorching gas and a stream of golden-red lava pour from one of the Virunga range's active volcanoes.*

Carbon dioxide seeps through the bed of the lake and accumulates there, trapped by the enormous pressure of the water above – the lake averages about 600ft (180m) in depth, but in places is as deep as 1300ft (400m). When the same conditions arose in Lake Nyos in Cameroon in 1986, a deadly cloud of carbon dioxide suddenly burst through the water and settled like a suffocating blanket over densely populated valleys, killing more than 1700 people.

At Lake Kivu the consequences could be even more devastating, for bacterial

action is converting the carbon dioxide into methane. Human interference with the lake, such as pumping up methane to use as fuel, could cause the gas to bubble to the surface of the water. Once there, contact with a naked flame would turn the flammable gas into an explosive fireball, incinerating the surrounding area.

Upheavals in the Earth's crust pose no threat elsewhere in the Virunga Mountains, for the other volcanoes have long been extinct. Karisimbi, the highest point at 14,787ft (4507m), takes its name from *nsimbi* – meaning 'white cowrie shell' – an allusion to the snow which often covers the top of the mountain. The slopes of nearby Bisoke are the home of the mountain gorilla. Sabinyo, near the eastern end of the Virunga

range, is crowned by several peaks, on the highest of which the boundaries of the Democratic Republic of Congo, Rwanda and Uganda meet.

The Virunga Mountains played a part in the search for the source of the Nile. Speculation about the origins of Egypt's great river dates back to the heyday of the ancient Greeks. Ptolemy, the geographer, astronomer and mathematician of the 2nd century AD, believed that the waters arose in the 'Mountains of the Moon'. In 1862 the British explorer John Hanning Speke suggested that the Virungas, with their 'bold sky-scraping

AT PEACE *A light mist swirls round the jagged summit of Sabinyo, one of the Virunga range's extinct volcanoes. Conical Gahinga rises in the foreground.*

VOLCANO'S MOUTH *The inner sides of Nyiragonga's gaping crater fall almost sheer from its rim — a perfect circle more than two-thirds of a mile (1.1km) across.*

pretending to feed on vegetation, scratching, beating her chest and belching. After three years' work with them she made a remarkable breakthrough while 'munching' vegetation. She extended her hand towards a gorilla and the animal touched her fingers with his own – the first known incident of a wild gorilla touching a human.

LIFE'S WORK

To protect the animals, a Mountain Gorilla Project was set up by international conservation organisations. The aim of the project was to increase understanding of the gorillas, and to encourage tourism which would create jobs and reduce the need for poaching. The plan did not win Fossey's approval – she wanted patrols set up, with the authority to shoot poachers on sight.

Late in 1985, Fossey was found dead in her bed – murdered by an unknown assailant's single blow to the head. She was buried behind her cabin on the mountain, but her life's work has borne fruit, for the number of mountain gorillas in the forests of the Virunga Mountains is now increasing.

cones', were Ptolemy's mountains. Now the Ruwenzori to the north are generally thought to be the Mountains of the Moon.

Speke only saw the mountains from afar, but had he climbed them he would have found a striking succession of plant types. Now much of the lower land has been cleared for agriculture, but remnants of the original forest are still there. Dense bamboo grows further up, and higher again is an open patchwork of spreading trees, shrubs and grassy glades. Above 10,000ft (3000m) are spectacular giant forms of heathers, lobelias and groundsels, while above 13,000ft (4000m) little more than mosses, grasses and lichen survive. In this varied flora live 180 species of birds and more than 60 species of mammals, including leopards, civets, hyenas and jackals, as well as buffaloes, wild bush pigs, elephants and tree hyraxes.

THE LAVA GLOWED 'LIKE SLAG FROM A FURNACE'

The forests of the Virunga Mountains are also the only home of mountain gorillas. During the 1960s and 70s their numbers fell from an estimated 400–500 to about 250 – the gorillas faced competition from grazing cattle, and were captured for zoos and trapped by poachers who cut off their hands and heads to sell to tourists. Attention was drawn to their plight by Dian Fossey, an American occupational therapist who had worked with handicapped children.

Fossey settled in Rwanda on the slopes of Bisoke in 1967 and studied the gorillas at close hand for 18 years. With infinite curiosity and patience she won their trust. She sometimes spent days on end crawling around the rain-soaked forest on knuckles and knees imitating their everyday actions –

GENTLE GIANTS *Mountain gorillas live in family groups of 5–20 members. They are vegetarian, feeding off foliage, wild celery, stinging nettles and thistles.*

Skeleton Coast

THE BONES OF WRECKED AND BROKEN SHIPS LITTER ONE OF THE WORLD'S MOST DANGEROUS AND DESOLATE COASTLINES

A wilderness of white sand lies between the ancient Namib Desert, and the cold waters of the Atlantic Ocean. 'The coast of hell' Portuguese seafarers called this stretch of Namibia's shoreline. Now it is known as the Skeleton Coast.

Stretched out as if on a rack, the 300 miles (500km) of sun-tortured shore is infernal, unforgiving, and in its pure desolation, extraordinarily beautiful.

When the Swedish explorer and naturalist Charles John Andersson visited the coast in 1859, 'a shudder, amounting almost to fear' came over him. 'Death,' he exclaimed, 'would be preferable to banishment in such a country.'

From the air, the Skeleton Coast is furrowed by a million golden dunes that sprawl north-eastwards from the Atlantic to the gravel plains of the hinterland. Between the dunes, shimmering mirages rise up from bleak pavements of desert rock, the last remnants of a land surface buried by sand that can travel up to 16yds (15m) a year. Around the mirages, the restless dunes rumble and roar in an extraordinary symphony conducted by the wind.

All along the Skeleton Coast, treacherous crosscurrents, gale-force winds, creeping fog and reefs whose jagged fingers reach deep into the sea have taken a devastating toll of ships.

JOURNEY'S END *Broken bones of ships litter the coast. Winds, currents and reefs threaten any ship that ventures too close.*

Stories are legion of wrecked survivors staggering ashore, joyful to be alive, only to become victims of a slow, sandblasted death. The wreckage of ocean liners, tugs, gunboats, galleons, trawlers and clippers lies strewn from one end of the Skeleton Coast to the other.

Twelve headless skeletons lying together on the beach, and the skeleton

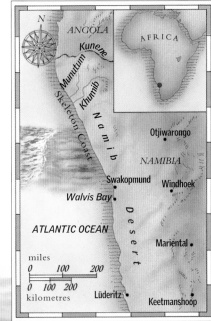

of a child lying in a nearby abandoned hut, were discovered on the coast in 1943. A weatherbeaten slate nearby bore the message: 'I am proceeding to a river 60 miles north, and should anyone find this and follow me, God will help him.' The message was written in 1860.

To this day no one has discovered who the tragic victims were, how they came to be wrecked on the coast and why they were headless when found.

In November 1942, the *Dunedin Star*, a British cargo boat carrying 21 passengers and 85 crew, foundered on rocks 25 miles (40km) south of the Kunene River. All the passengers, including three babies, and 42 of the crewmen were put ashore in a motorboat.

In one of the most difficult rescues ever staged, it took nearly four weeks for all the castaways and crew to be found and taken safely back to civilisation. The rescue involved two overland expeditions from Windhoek in Namibia, three Ventura bombers and several ships. One of the rescue ships itself ran aground and three of its crew were drowned.

The Skeleton Coast received its name when a Swiss pilot, Carl Nauer, crashed somewhere along the coast in 1933 while he was flying from Cape Town to London. A journalist suggested that his bones might one day be found on the 'Skeleton Coast'. Nauer's remains were never recovered, but the name stuck.

SCULPTED BY THE WIND

Beyond the coastal dunes, outcrops of rocks, honeycombed and hollowed into fantastic shapes by the wind over 700 million years, rise phantom-like from the desert floor. Some look like giant molten toadstools. Others, such as Skull Rock in the lower reaches of the Munutum River, have skeletal features and hollow 'eye' sockets which peer across the sandy wastes.

In the south, inland mountain chains produce streams that more often than not dry up before they reach the ocean. These parched riverbeds persist like desolate carriageways through the desert, until most of them are swallowed up by the dunes. Other rivers, such as the

Hoarusib, which flows through a steep-walled canyon of clay, occasionally make it to the sea when heavy downpours inland briefly transform them into an avalanche of chocolate-coloured water.

Scientists call the dry riverbeds 'linear oases' because their underground waters feed an astonishing variety of plants and animals. It is here that the mammals of the Namib come to feast on grass and shrubs sustained by the moisture. Elephants dig deep into the sand with their tusks to find water. Gemsbok cleave the dusty surface with their hooves for any trace of moisture.

Down at the coast, where desert and sea collide in a landscape of thundering surf and sloping beaches, the waves bring colour to the shore in the form of millions of tiny stones. Pebbles of granite, basalt, sandstone, agate, cornelian and quartz are hurled up onto the beach in a geological extravaganza.

Southerly winds blow in off the sea. To the early wrecked seafarers who broiled alive in the sun, or doomed adventurers who lost their way in blinding sandstorms, the winds served as a ghostly funeral song.

The San hunters of the Namib named the winds 'Soo-oop-wa', to describe their sound, and they are one of the desert's most extraordinary manifestations of nature. When 'Soo-oop-wa' blows, the slip-face, or exposed part, of the sand dunes collapses, causing friction between the crumbling quartz grains so intense that the dune 'roars' with the sound.

At night, when the wind subsides and the desert cools, nature looks down on this tortured land with compassion and sends a ghostly fog rolling inland. The

> 'DEATH WOULD BE PREFERABLE TO BANISHMENT IN SUCH A COUNTRY'

FALSE HOPE *A full moon casts an eerie reflection in a lagoon (right) on the edge of the coastal desert. Such lagoons, and the shimmering mirages around them, offer false hope to shipwrecked seamen.*

LIFE-GIVER *Fog creeps over the Namib sand dunes (inset) almost every day, cooling the ground and bringing life-giving moisture to plants and animals.*

HOW FOG SUPPORTS LIFE

At night, a ghostly fog creeps over the dunes of the Skeleton Coast. A black onymacris beetle climbs to a dune summit where the fog is densest, angles its head to the ground and waits as the fog starts to condense on its sloping back. Eventually, enough moisture gathers to form one drop, which rolls down to the beetle's mouth.

A lepidochora beetle collects the fog's moisture by digging a trench, edged by slight ridges, at right angles to the approaching fog. Water droplets condense on the ridges and collect in the trench, ready for the beetle to lap up.

The fog sustains larger animals, too. The sidewinding adder slides its mouth across its scales to suck moisture off its body. And stranded human beings have survived by licking droplets of fog from the metal wings of aircraft.

A plant that looks like a science fiction monster, the welwitschia, also catches the night fog. Its broad leaves, sprawling up to 10ft (3m) over the ground, absorb moisture through millions of pores.

FOG DRINKER *To quench its thirst, the black onymacris beetle (above) lowers its head, and water condensing on its back runs down to its mouth.*

FOG ABSORBER *Only two tough leaves sprout from the welwitschia's root (right), but both may be torn into ribbons that curl like wood shavings.*

White onymacris beetles keep their body temperature as low as possible by reflecting the sun's heat with their white topsides. This enables them to move about on the sun-baked sand long after their black-backed relatives have had to dive for cover.

As the day advances, a searing east wind whips across the dunes, bringing living and dead organic matter from the hinterland, which provides a feast for the specialised desert creatures. Suddenly, the sun-boiled sand comes alive as lizards, beetles and other insects emerge, scurrying after dehydrated morsels brought in by the wind.

DANCING LIZARD

When their body temperatures rise to dangerous levels, the desert creatures dive back below the sand in a frantic see-saw of hurried motion. They leave behind a sole companion: the sand lizard, which beats the heat by performing a strange dance, alternately lifting its feet two at a time to cool them off. Poised like some reptilian ballet dancer above the sand, the lizard keeps its tail and opposite fore and hind legs arched motionless in the air.

In contrast to the heat of the sand, the sea is cold, for the Benguela Current sweeps northwards along the coast from Antarctica. The chilly waters churn with pilchards, sardines, anchovies and mullet.

---

fog gropes across beaches and rocks bringing sustenance and renewal to sun-scorched plants and animals.

Nowhere is this more marvellously illustrated than in the explosion of colour and life in the gravel plains behind the dunes. During the day each tiny piece of hot gravel is covered by lichen that appears dry and lifeless. Caressed by the fog, the lichen comes to life in a sea of colour.

As night advances and the fog penetrates into the dunes, the tiny creatures of the Skeleton Coast emerge from the sand to gather water from the fog – the only moisture they will ever receive (see above).

When the new day arrives the miracle of desert life continues. Grant's golden mole, little longer than a finger and totally blind, swims deep into the sand, pouncing on crickets, beetles or geckos as they seek refuge from the sun. A cauricara beetle starts unfolding its stilt-like limbs to bring its body as high as possible off the ground, which protects it from the scorching ground temperatures, and exposes it to the relative coolness of the desert breeze.

COOLING POSTURE *The sand lizard raises opposite legs clear of the hot ground.*

They attract squadrons of sea birds, as well as hundreds of thousands of Cape fur seals that breed on the islands and bays of the desolate Skeleton Coast.

Etosha Pan

IN THE NORTHERN PLAINS OF NAMIBIA LIES THE SKELETON OF A GREAT LAKE THAT DIED OF THIRST MILLIONS OF YEARS AGO

This eerie wasteland of salt-encrusted clay stretching away to distant horizons is known to the Ovambo people who live there as Etosha – 'the lake of mirages' or 'the place of dry water'.

Seen from the air it appears as if Nature, in some unaccountable fit of rage, had banished the spirit of the land, leaving only its carcass draped lifeless across the subcontinent.

CEASELESS SEARCH *Game trails criss-cross the salt-encrusted surface of Etosha Pan during the dry season. Water holes and islands of green vegetation are the focal point of the ceaseless search by thousands of animals for water and food.*

The earth is blistered and cracked, gaping forlornly at dust devils and whirlwinds that scurry across its surface. A capillary network of game trails criss-crosses the pan, converging in the distance on various scattered oases – incongruous islands of green.

These oases in the salt desert of Namibia are the permanent springs and life-sustaining water holes for one of the largest concentrations of wild animals on Earth. In the dry season, which stretches from May to November, great herds of wildebeests, zebras and antelopes must run the gauntlet of lions and other predators to reach them.

The pan is part of a much larger phenomenon – the Etosha Basin, which, together with the Okavango Delta in Botswana and numerous other smaller pans and lakes, once formed what geologists believe to have been the largest lake in the world.

Millions of years ago, the rivers that fed this lake dried up. Deprived of its lifeblood, and continually exposed to evaporation and seepage, the lake itself eventually disappeared. Today Etosha survives as a small sample of its former self – a white salt pan 80 miles (130km) long and 30 miles (50km) wide. Lying at the heart of the Etosha National Park,

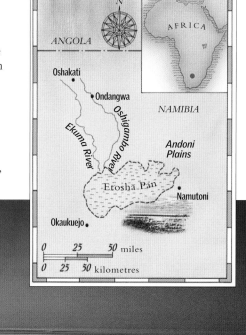

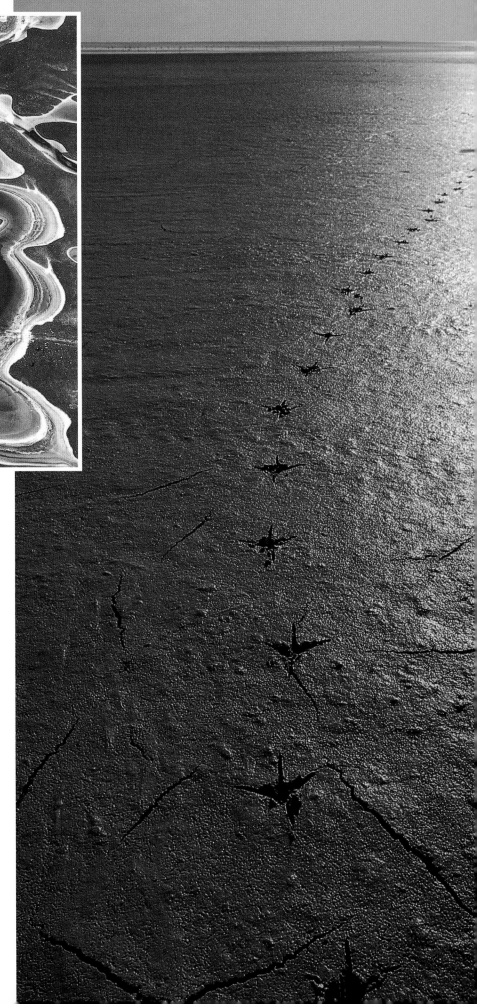

HAVEN IN THE SALT *Efflorescences of salt on the fringes of Etosha accentuate the curves of the shallow waterways. The waters attract tens of thousands of flamingos and other birds.*

one of Africa's greatest game parks, it is a landscape that undergoes phenomenal changes every year.

Scorched, dusty and dispirited in the dry season, the Etosha Pan undergoes an extraordinary transformation when the rainy season starts in December. Towering clouds mass along the eastern horizon, then roll in with their cargoes of water.

Sheets of rain descend on Lake Oponono in the north, filling it up and sending life-giving water along the Ekuma and Oshigambo rivers to the parched perimeters of Etosha.

VAST AND TRANQUIL LAKE

The baked earth steams as millions of tons of water pour in, transforming the pan into a vast and tranquil lake whose ephemeral waters spread away to the far distant horizons.

Nature celebrates with a series of extraordinary events. Millions of grass

END OF THE RAINS *Filled briefly with life-giving water in the rainy season, the pan soon dries up, its surface resembling a damp canvas of footprints marching off to bleak, empty horizons.*

seeds, which have lain dormant for months in the dry earth, suddenly spring to life, covering the land with a coating of luxuriant green.

Inspired by the smell of rain, one of the great animal migrations of Africa begins. Tens of thousands of zebras and wildebeests stream in from their winter feeding grounds on the Andoni Plains to the north-east. As the migration begins, the primitive sounds of Africa start to fill the air. The rallying bark of the zebra joins in with the mournful bawling of the wildebeest and the snorts, wheezes, whinnies and whines of 15 different species of antelope, large and small. Giraffes seesaw along with their turret-top eyes continually scanning the vast plains for predators, and elephants lumber along patiently in single file.

Large herds of springboks, the small brown and white antelopes of southern Africa, also join the massive animal migration. The springboks are famed for their athletic ability. In the face of danger, they first execute a series of balletic, stiff-legged high leaps known as 'pronks'. They then take off at a gallop. Springboks are capable of bounding a distance of 16yds (15m) in one jump, and reaching a speed of almost 56mph (90km/h).

Stalking in the wake and around the perimeters of these long, migrating columns of grass-eating animals, come lions and hyenas, cheetahs and wild dogs – overlords in a land of plenty.

Above them, pink skeins of flamingos also head towards the mineral-rich waters of the pan. Joining them in this great fly-in is a multi-coloured variety of birdlife: Egyptian geese, crimson-breasted shrikes, lilac-breasted

LIONS, HYENAS, CHEETAHS AND WILD DOGS – OVERLORDS IN A LAND OF PLENTY

rollers, hawks, eagles, doves, plovers and larks.

An American trader named Gerald McKiernan described such a migration in 1876 as 'the Africa I had read in books of travel ... all the menageries in the world turned loose would not compare to the sight I saw that day'.

In days gone by, the San people (or Bushmen) hunted freely on this plain, and together with the Herero and Ovambo peoples left a legacy of beautiful names to the area. A low range of hills on Etosha's southern boundary was known as the Ondundozo-nanandana, meaning 'the place where the young calves used to go and never return'. One of the tourist camps in the Etosha National Park is called Namutoni – Ovambo for 'high place which can be seen from afar'. Another camp name, Okaukuejo, means 'place of women'.

In 1907 the San hunting ground was proclaimed a game reserve – the Etosha Game Park. At one time it covered an area almost the size of Iceland and was the largest natural game reserve in the world. In 1967, however, the reserve was reduced in size to make room for tribal homelands, and became the Etosha National Park.

PRONKING *When danger threatens, the springbok makes a series of vertical leaps – a technique known as pronking.*

Kalahari Desert

A PARCHED
WILDERNESS OF SAND,
SALT AND DRY GRASS
IS HOME TO ONE OF
THE WORLD'S MOST
REMARKABLE PEOPLES

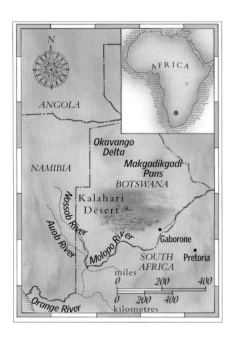

Just beyond the grey gravel plains of north-western South Africa, the land tilts gently down to reveal one of Nature's timeless masterpieces: an ancient sea of apricot-coloured sand that rolls on apparently for ever.

This is the Kalahari, an enormous plain on the African plateau. It is the longest continuous stretch of sand in the world, uninterrupted by areas of stone and gravel as the Sahara is.

Hauntingly beautiful in its immensity, prehistoric in its moods and culture, the Kalahari covers almost all of Botswana, reaches west into Namibia, and continues northwards into Angola, Zambia and Zimbabwe.

To the people who live there it is known as Kgalagadi, meaning 'wilderness'

KILLING GROUNDS *Cautiously observed by two groups of guinea fowl, a lion slakes its thirst at a water hole in the Kalahari. Water holes are favourite killing grounds. Predators pounce on their victims when they come to drink.*

– a region so vast, so impenetrable and so old that it holds untapped secrets of vanished civilisations dating back 500,000 years. Its sands are home and hunting grounds to the world's oldest people, the Bushmen or San, whose lives have been

lived virtually unchanged for 25,000 years. Their astonishing adaptations to scorching heat, lack of water and scarcity of food has enabled them to survive where others would inevitably perish.

Although there are only a few thousand Bushmen surviving in the Kalahari wilderness today, their ancestors have left a legacy of rock art, painted on exposed rock faces and in caves throughout the region.

The ragged cliff faces and caves of

BURNING PLANT *The thick-stemmed Bushman's Candle burns because its tarry juice contains wax, fat and a gum-like substance.*

Well adapted to the sun and sandstorms of the Kalahari and Namib Deserts is the plant known as the Bushman's Candle. It was given its name because its resinous stem is flammable, and will blaze furiously when it is set alight.

The succulent plant grows to about ankle height, and has a thick stem covered with long spines. It bears delicate rose, pink or purple cup-shaped flowers.

When the dried-out leaves of the Bushman's Candle are burned they give off a pleasant aromatic smell, similar to incense. One species of the plant was used as a diarrhoea remedy by Hottentot people in southern Africa during the 19th century.

Tsodilo Hills, in the remote north-western Kalahari, carry no less than 2750 works of art on 200 sites. The subjects vary from simple geometric designs to groups of animals and men.

Many of the San lived in the southern Kalahari where four ancient dry rivers, the Molopo, Kuruman, Nossob and Auob, snake towards a sandy grave just short of the Orange River. In these desolate watercourses, water only flows in years of exceptional rain.

Around these phantom riverbeds, Nature has sculpted sinuous dunes tinged copper and red by iron oxide in the grains of sand. In this sweltering environment meerkats and other burrowers emerge from their tunnels only to forage – ever alert to the danger of aerial attack from birds of prey, such as eagles, or a ground assault by Cape cobras. Gemsboks, hartebeests, duikers and other small antelopes forage on the long grasses between the dunes where

temperatures often exceed 50°C (120°F) in midsummer.

The Kalahari is one of the world's great monuments to the extraordinary powers of fire, wind, water and sand. About 65 million years ago great convulsions shook the earth, and massive outpourings of volcanic lava spewed out over central southern Africa. These undulating seas of lava, up to 5 miles (8km) deep in places, formed high ridges and deep river valleys.

Then over 50 million years, the action of the wind and rain gradually flattened the jagged landscape, wearing down the mountains and filling the valleys with clay and gravel. Finally, huge quantities of sand blown in from the coast were deposited to create a flat, multicoloured plain the size of modern South Africa.

The aridity of the Kalahari is caused by the cold Benguela Current which flows up the west coast of southern

DESERT RIVERBED *The Nossob River (left), a dry carriageway of sand, snakes across the Kalahari. The dunes support an extraordinary community of creatures that live in the sand.*

DANGER *Buffaloes (below) form large herds in the northern Kalahari. If they become aroused they are among the most dangerous creatures on Earth.*

Africa from the Antarctic. The icy sea water chills the prevailing winds, preventing them from absorbing enough moisture to create rain in the interior.

During the dry season in August and September, the Kalahari is almost devoid of surface water, and the struggle for survival is intense. The San of the central and southern Kalahari survive by digging below the surface of dry riverbeds and pans to find water, and storing it in ostrich shells. When these subterranean sources of water dry up, the San extract water from the stomach contents of antelopes they kill. Tsamma melons are another source of water – they eat up to 6¼lb (3kg) of them a day. After a rare downpour the San use reeds to suck up water from hollows in trees and rocks.

GREAT TREKS

In spite of its aridity, the Kalahari is home to a huge and diverse family of animals – no less than 46 species of mammals larger than a jackal roam the plains and grasslands.

Less than a century ago, herds of springboks, whose numbers were estimated at between 50,000 and several million, undertook great migrations or 'treks' across the Kalahari. One herd stretched for over 130 miles (210km) on a 13 mile (21km) front, causing havoc to farmers' lands, and trampling to death animals and people in its path.

Today large herds of springboks still march along the dry waterways of the Auob and Nossob rivers, sending plumes of golden dust spiralling into the sky. On the banks of these rivers prides of lions laze under the canopies of camel thorn trees, waiting for the night and the beginning of the hunt.

The gemsbok, a powerfully built antelope, can survive without ever drinking water – thanks to a natural air conditioner that keeps its body temperature under control.

During the sizzling heat of day, the rapid inflow and outflow of air created by its panting passes over a delicate network of blood vessels, cooling the flow of blood to the brain. At the same time, however, the body temperature is allowed to rise – eliminating the need to perspire, and thus conserving water.

IN HARMONY WITH THE KALAHARI

START OF THE HUNT *Armed with a spear, bows and poison-tipped arrows, three Bushmen set off on a hunt. Having wounded their quarry they have the stamina to outrun it.*

Nomadic hunter-gatherers known as the San (or Bushmen) were once widespread over most of southern Africa. But outside influences have encroached on the Kalahari, the San's last refuge, and taken their toll. Today there are only about 55,000 of them left, of whom fewer than 2000 live solely as hunter-gatherers.

These desert dwellers are probably the world's greatest conservationists. They believe that if they misuse their environment, they will incur the wrath of the Supreme Being.

Consequently the San gather and hunt just enough food to keep themselves alive, and no more. Similar in size to the pygmies of central Africa, they have abnormally large, protruding buttocks and fatty thighs which act as larders for the large amounts of food they consume in times of plenty.

The women and children spend much of their time gathering moisture-bearing plants and small animals for food. A San child is able to recognise and name 200

END OF THE DAY *The Bushman diet includes many animals and plants. A python, killed during a hunt, will be supper for the hunter's family.*

different plants. The San men are exceptionally skilful hunters. The arrows that they use are tipped with a powerful poison made from the pupae of flea-beetles.

VENTURING 'BEYOND THE GARDEN GATE'

Explorers risk life and limb to seek out the world's remotest regions

From the age of five, wrote the French traveller Alexandra David-Neel, 'I craved to go beyond the garden gate, to follow the road that passed it by, and to set out for the Unknown'. This deep desire to explore the unexplored filled many adventurers. Others, including the Swedish geographer Sven Hedin, were inspired by the writings of earlier travellers. Yet others are driven by an unslakeable thirst for knowledge of the natural world. Whatever the motive, the passion to explore seems to be all-consuming, enabling men and women to risk the most extreme physical hardships.

DINOSAURS IN THE GOBI
When the American naturalist Roy Chapman Andrews (above) led scientists into the Gobi Desert in Mongolia in the 1920s, their interest in eagles led to a major find. Near an eagle's nest, they found dinosaur eggs 95 million years old – the first proof that dinosaurs were egg-layers.

ASCENT BY YAK
A Swedish geographer, Sven Hedin, spent 40 years mapping central Asia, often on a camel (right). In 1894, he climbed the Pamir Mountains to more than 20,000ft (6000m) – on a yak.

PIONEER IN TIBET
A Parisian woman, Alexandra David-Neel, journeyed on foot through the mountains of Tibet in 1924 to become the first European woman to enter the forbidden city of Lhasa.

ANTARCTIC WINTER
Ernest Shackleton's plan to cross the Antarctic on foot with 27 men in 1914 was foiled when his ship was crushed by ice. After spending two winters in the bitter cold, the party was rescued when Shackleton sailed in a boat to South Georgia (below) and brought back help.

Okavango

THE LARGEST INLAND DELTA ON EARTH EXPANDS AND CONTRACTS TO THE HEARTBEAT OF THE MARCH FLOODS

In the parched heart of southern Africa lies an oasis that once a year grows larger than Wales, and brings pulsating life to the surrounding desert.

This is the Okavango Delta, a wilderness of waterways, swamps, islands and emerald reed beds that forms the largest inland delta on Earth.

From the air, the Delta – in northern Botswana – looks like some huge, skeletal hand whose fingers spread out across the sands of the northern Kalahari. Geologists call it an 'alluvial fan' – referring to the millions of tons of flood-borne sediment that have been laid down over the ages.

HAVENS OF LIFE *The waters of the Okavango Delta glide past islands of green – havens of life for the smaller animals of the delta.*

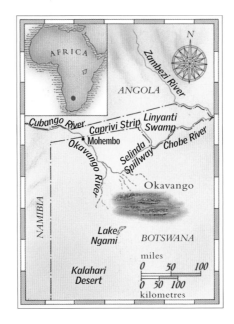

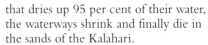

The 'wrist' of the hand is a floodplain 50 miles (80km) long and 10 miles (16km) wide called the Panhandle, which acts as a conduit for more than 10 billion tons of water that flows into the delta every year.

The 'fingers' are four large channels that stretch southwards, groping into a wilderness of ochre sand, salt pans and thorn scrub. There, after a journey of 160 miles (260km) under a blistering sun

that dries up 95 per cent of their water, the waterways shrink and finally die in the sands of the Kalahari.

The pulse of life in this extraordinary delta beats to the rhythm of the Okavango River, which rises in the Angolan highlands as the powerful Cubango River.

FLOODS THAT HERALD A REVIVAL OF LIFE

In March, the Cubango comes down in flood, charging over rapids and waterfalls to Angola's southern border. Now called the Okavango, it enters the Kalahari on the border of Botswana.

Channelled by two ridges 9 miles (15km) apart, the Okavango pours into the Panhandle. The gradient here is slight and the river meanders back and forth through a green sea of reed-like papyrus, touching the banks near small thatched villages.

At the village of Seronga, it disgorges its liquid treasure into a labyrinth of major channels which together form a broad, fan-shaped delta of papyrus-lined waterways, swampland and sandy islands.

The effect of the rising water level is spread over the entire delta as the maze of channels starts to bulge and then trickle onto the surrounding floodplain. Breaching ramparts of papyrus and reeds, streams flow over the surrounding grassland, circle palm-fringed islands and merge in a blue mosaic of radiant pools.

In years of heavy rain the fingers of the delta bulge out over 8500sq miles (22,000km²) of the Kalahari, transforming bone-dry wastes of sand into an oasis of shimmering water.

As the water creeps across the dusty floodplains, it refills stagnant pools and disperses thousands of animals which used them as water holes during the drier months of the year.

The waterways and islands of the Okavango Delta now become a paradise for an incredible variety of plants and animals. Here, species adapted to the aquatic life rub shoulders with animals from the Kalahari Desert.

More than 400 species of birds inhabit the delta – the only place in the world where slaty egrets are known to breed. Fish eagles perch proud and silent on tall trees flanking the waterways, waiting for tell-tale ripples on the glassy surface that will send them swooping

DUSK ON THE DELTA *Three mekoro, which are dugout boats hollowed out of trees, lie unmoved by the gentle current.*

down with outstretched talons to scoop up one of more than 65 species of fish found in the delta.

Tiger fish, with razor-sharp teeth, race through the lazy channels, while on the surface the leaves of waterlilies serve as stepping stones for jacana birds and frogs.

On a floating bed of papyrus, a tiny crocodile basks open mouthed in the strong sun, oblivious of the periscope eyes and impatient 'harrumphs' of submerged hippos nearby.

As dusk falls on the Okavango, the sounds of the wild drift from the islands across the waterways: the graveyard moan of a lone hyena, the deep grunting

GIANTS OF THE OKAVANGO DELTA

The slothful pose of the hippopotamus basking in the waters of the Okavango Delta can be misleading. Provoked in the company of cows or calves, an enraged bull may spring from the water, exposing huge jaws and curved, tusklike teeth capable of snapping a person in half.

BaYei tribesmen crossing the waters of the delta in their mekoro dugouts are careful to avoid confrontations, as hippos have been known to capsize boats in the delta.

Hippos play a vital role in keeping the delta's channels open – they trample pathways through the narrow watercourses during their night-time foraging expeditions. On these outings they consume up to 330lb (150kg) of the grass growing in the swamp.

Most of the hippos' day is spent partially submerged in water, with their massive heads protruding just above it. When hippos submerge they close their slitlike nostrils and disappear, staying under for up to five minutes. They move easily on webbed toes as they walk underwater along clearly defined paths on the bed of the river.

About 10 or 15 cows and calves live in a hippo bull's territory – a pear-shaped area up to 5 miles (8km) long.

HIPPO HERD *(overleaf) A herd of hippos, some partially submerged, moves along the Savuti Channel.*

of a lioness, the drawn-out barks of sitatunga antelopes and the insect-like prrp ... prrp ... prrp of a Scops owl merge with the muted wash of the water.

In the distance, the drums of the baYei tribesmen and river Bushmen beat a rhythm, eerie and ominous. The Bushmen, known also as the Banoka, were in the delta centuries before the baYei arrived in 1750. They specialised in hunting game by digging deep pits, lined with sharp-pointed stakes, and disguised with leaves and grasses.

The baYei, on the other hand, are aquatic hunters who take to the water in flimsy dugout boats, called mekoro. They originally journeyed into the Okavango in their mekoro, poling them like punts along the waterways of the Zambezi and Chobe Rivers and the Selinda Spillway.

HIPPO HUNTING

The baYei went hippo hunting in their mekoro, using crudely fashioned harpoons attached to ropes. Gliding silently into a group of hippos, the hunters would plunge the harpoon into an animal and then be towed through the waterways by the enraged and wounded hippo until they had a chance to close in and despatch it with spears. Often the hippo would overturn one of the mekoro and set upon its occupants with lethal jaws.

Today mekoro are the taxis of the delta, and some families specialise in making them. Each craft is trimmed and carved out of a single tree.

Another delta tribe, the Hambu-kushu, fish with funnel-shaped reed baskets which they line up side-by-side across the river's current. The women then form a line upstream and wade towards the baskets, driving fish into them. Lurking crocodiles have been known to seize unwary Hambukushu women, dragging them to lairs built just above the level of the water.

Each spring, the water swiftly starts receding from the swamps, signalling an urgent migration of reptiles, amphibians and fish from the flood plains back to the deeper channels. Some terrapins and toads burrow into the drying floor of the swamps, to sit it out in subterranean silence until the flood starts again in April.

But many of the smaller animals are beaten by the rate of evaporation: hundreds of fish, terrapins and frogs are left struggling in almost empty pools.

This state of emergency among the aquatic animals is the signal for a massacre of huge proportions. Great flocks of herons, storks, ibises and egrets fly in to feast on their stranded victims. The waterways, now filled with refugees, become corridors of plenty for aquatic carnivores such as the clawed and Cape clawless otters.

The extraordinary cycle of life in the delta continues unabated, sustained by a pristine wilderness that has no equal on Earth. To the Swedish explorer, Charles John Andersson, the first European to see the delta in 1853, it was a place of 'indescribable beauty'. To countless others who followed him, it will remain as one of Africa's magical places.

DEATH AND LIFE IN MOREMI RESERVE

The greatest concentration of game within the Okavango Delta is in Moremi Wildlife Reserve. Forests of mopane trees, islands of tall fan palms, huge strangler figs and kigelia sausage trees combine to create a paradise for birds such as rollers, hoopoes, kingfishers, owls and woodpeckers.

Crocodiles glide along Moremi's channels, ever alert to the chance of a meal – often a hippo calf that has become separated from the herd. To protect their young, adult hippos form a tight circle round them, a strategy that crocodiles sometimes counter by dashing across the backs of the hippos to reach the calf.

Deep in the grasslands and woodland of Moremi, ostriches congregate in the company of antelopes, elephants, buffaloes and baboons. This vast concentration of game attracts predators – leopards, lions, cheetahs, hyenas and Cape hunting dogs – which also roam the other grassland regions of the vast Okavango Delta. Lying within Moremi is Chief's Island, which is one of the few sanctuaries where humans may not live or camp.

BIGGEST BIRD
The world's largest bird, the ostrich, is flightless. But its powerful legs can carry it at more than 40mph (64km/h) as it flees from predators. Male birds help to raise the chicks.

Matopo Hills

AN EERIE BOULDERLAND IN ZIMBABWE IS THE RESTING PLACE OF A WARRIOR CHIEF AND A DIAMOND MAGNATE

Like building blocks piled up by some gigantic infant, granite boulders perch perilously one on top of another. Giant granite marbles poise on smooth granite domes as if a gentle push would set them in motion.

This astonishing boulderland is the skeleton of a landscape born more than 3300 million years ago, before the Earth had even developed an atmosphere. Seas of molten rock cooled and solidified, cracking as they did so to create joints. Aeons of weathering then widened the joints to form the extraordinary granite landforms of Zimbabwe's Matopo Hills.

Here, black eagles, guardians of the ancestral spirits of the place, soar high above their last stronghold in Africa.

The 'chaotic grandeur' of these ancient hills so awed diamond magnate Cecil Rhodes that he chose them as his final resting place. Rhodes gave his name to Rhodesia, the vast tract of Africa administered by the company he set up. What was Rhodesia is now the republics of Zambia and Zimbabwe.

GRANITE TOMB

On April 10, 1902, deep in the heart of the Matopo Hills, 12 black oxen drew the gun carriage containing Rhodes's coffin up the slope of a great granite dome, which he had called View of the World, but which was known to the Matabele people as Malindidzimu, 'Place of the Ancient Spirits'. There, in a tomb hewn out of solid granite and covered with a 3-ton granite seal, he was interred overlooking a panorama of fertile plains and distant hills. As his casket was lowered in place, the royal salute of the Matabele warriors standing at his graveside reverberated through the surrounding hills: 'Bayete! Bayete! Bayete!'

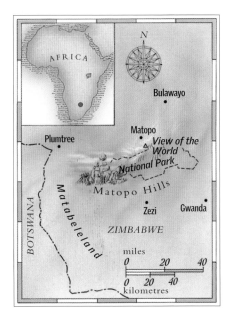

Just 9 miles (15km) away from the grave the tomb of Mzilikazi, the first paramount chief of Zimbabwe's Matabele tribe, lies in a cleft between the rocks. In the mid 19th century, Mzilikazi – in a moment of levity – named these hills *ama Tobo*, meaning 'bald heads',

because they reminded him of his senior advisers.

ART GALLERIES

The mystical atmosphere of the Matopos influenced the San (or Bushmen) people who occupied caves in the hills between 20,000 and 2000 years ago. Rock walls and caves are now natural galleries of primitive art. In the late Stone Age, the San used clays mixed with animal fat and the latex of the euphorbia plant to paint animals, landscapes, spiritual forms and geometric puzzles on their granite canvases. In reds, browns and yellows, they show hunters with bows and arrows, rhinos, elephants, impalas, lions and zebras. One painting depicts the veined wings of a flying termite.

The Matopos National Park, just south of Bulawayo, was Cecil Rhodes's gift to the people of the town. He granted it to them in order that they could 'enjoy the glory' of the Matopos 'from Saturday to Monday'.

ROCKY RESTING PLACE *Balancing rocks tower precariously above the Matopo Hills woodland. Cecil Rhodes poses third from the left at View of the World (inset) in 1897.*

Victoria Falls

'THE SMOKE THAT THUNDERS' – THE WIDEST SHEET OF FALLING WATER IN THE WORLD VANISHES IN A ROARING WHITE CLOUD

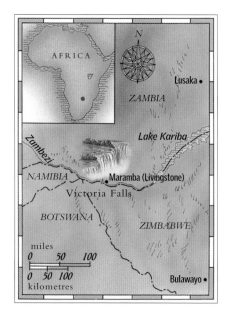

Approached from the north, the Victoria Falls announce themselves as a cloud of vapour hurled, grumbling loudly at its own immensity, into the African sky. A local tribe gave the falls the name *Mosi-oa-Tunya* – 'the smoke that thunders'.

Soaring 1600ft (500m) high, the misty plumes – which are visible from about 25 miles (40km) away – signal an unwary river's magnificent catastrophe. For as it moves towards them, the great Zambezi River is serene and mature, with only a scattering of islands to trouble its somnolent flow.

Nothing in the surrounding landscape – undulating, tree-scattered grassland on the Zambia–Zimbabwe border – or in the river's stately progress hints at the drama to come. Peaceful and 1 mile (1.6km) wide here in mid-course, the Zambezi abruptly plunges over a rock edge and changes its character completely. Riven from bank to bank,

the water drops in long sheets that seethe and roar in unimaginable fury as they cascade into a narrow, rocky, steep-sided chasm that reduces the river's width to a mere 65yds (60m). The spectacle is truly astonishing. Although the volume of water varies according to the season, rains can cause the swollen river to tip 540,000 tons (550 million litres) a minute over the mile-wide rock rim – the world's widest sheet of falling water.

At Danger Point, a cliff ledge on the opposite side of the chasm, the downpour causes such an uprush of spray-soaked air that it can carry visitors' handkerchiefs skyward with the famous plumes of mist.

Brilliant rainbows are created as the sun's rays are refracted through drops of water in the air. Upthrusting rocks and islands divide the great front of falling water into three main sections, and one

of them, the Rainbow Falls, takes its name from this effect (the other two are the Main Falls and the Eastern Cataract). And on a bright, moonlit night, the veil of vapour creates an unusual lunar rainbow.

Along the cliffs facing the falls there is luxurious woodland that is green all year round, in spite of the bleaching effect of the dry season on the surrounding grassland. This woodland, known as the Rain Forest, owes its verdancy to the moist microclimate created by spray from the cascade.

Downstream the grandeur continues as the entire volume of the river plunges into the narrow gorge and hurtles in all its wild glory towards a swirling pool called the Boiling Pot. Beyond, it continues through zigzag gorges for more than 40 miles (64km).

A SACRED PLACE

Few places on Earth are so awesome. The Kololo people who once lived above the falls – those who named them 'the smoke that thunders' – had such a dread of the torrent that they never went anywhere near it. The neighbouring Tonga tribe regarded the falls as sacred and the rainbows as God's presence. They held religious ceremonies at the Eastern Cataract, where they sacrificed black bulls.

David Livingstone, the Scottish missionary-doctor who in 1855 was the first European to set eyes on the falls, named them after his sovereign, Queen Victoria. A great explorer, he was navigating the 1700 mile- (2700km) long Zambezi as an artery which, he hoped, might act as 'God's Highway' to open up central Africa. Travelling downriver in a canoe, he reached the falls on November 16, having seen the vapour columns well beforehand. He landed on a small island at the lip of the cascade, and noticed how, up ahead, the whole body of water seemed to simply vanish. Livingstone wrote: '... it seemed to lose itself in the earth, the opposite lip of the fissure into which it disappeared being only eighty feet distant'.

He went on: '... I did not comprehend it till, creeping in awe to the verge, I peered down into a great rent which had been made from bank to bank, and saw that a stream a thousand yards broad

AFRICAN WONDER
Dr David Livingstone's statue (right) looks across the breathtaking Victoria Falls (above), which he first saw in 1855 and sketched (inset) in his notebook.

leaped down a hundred feet, and then became suddenly compressed into a space of fifteen or twenty yards. The entire falls are simply a crack made in a hard basaltic rock from the right to the left bank, and then prolonged from the left bank away through thirty or forty miles of hills.' Later he pointed out that he had underestimated the measurements. These falls were, in Livingstone's view, 'the most wonderful sight I had witnessed in Africa'. He wrote: '... one sees nothing but a dense white cloud ... The snow-white sheet seemed like myriads of small comets rushing in one direction, each of which left behind its nucleus rays of foam.'

> ## 'THE MOST WONDERFUL SIGHT I HAD WITNESSED IN AFRICA'
> ### Dr David Livingstone

Next day Livingstone returned to the island from which he had first viewed the cascade (now known as Kazeruka, or Livingstone Island), and planted peach and apricot stones and some coffee beans. He also carved the date and his initials on a tree (said to have been a baobab) – the only occasion in Africa on which he succumbed to such vanity, he later admitted.

On his second trip to the falls in August 1860, the explorer estimated the depth of the chasm. This was done by lowering a line weighted with a few bullets and with a length of white cotton cloth attached. 'One of us lay with his head over a projecting crag and watched the descending calico till, after his companions had paid out 310 feet, the weight rested upon a sloping projection, probably 50 feet from the water below, the actual bottom being still farther down. The white cloth now appeared the size of a crown piece.'

The depth was, he now estimated, about 354ft (108m) – which is roughly twice that of Niagara Falls.

HOW THE VICTORIA FALLS WERE CREATED

More is known today than in Livingstone's time about how the falls were created. Zambia's central plateau is a great bed of basalt lava 1000ft (300m) thick, spilled by volcanic action 200 million years ago – long before the Zambezi River existed. As the molten rock cooled, it hardened and cracked in a latticework of fissures. These cracks filled with softer material to form a more or less level sheet.

But about half a million years ago, when the Zambezi started to flow down across the plateau, it met one of the cracks. The water began to scour out the soft filling of the crack, creating a trench. The river flooded in, churning and thundering amid clouds of spray, until it found an escape at its lower edge – a place where it could plunge down over a low ledge and into a gorge. And so the first waterfall made its appearance.

The process did not end there, however. The incessant downpour at the lip of the waterfall began to erode the rock edge at its weakest point. Tumultuous flows of water ate away ever more of the fault, cutting the riverbed upstream to form a new gorge running back at a diagonal to the original.

Then, slanting back yet farther, the river found another east–west crack and gouged out its soft filling. Working its way back up the latticework of cracks, the river left a network of zigzag gorges downstream of the falls.

THE EIGHTH FALLS

Today, seven such gorges can be seen downriver, and each one of them is the ghost of a now-vanished waterfall. The eighth gorge is that of the present Victoria Falls, but even this is being eroded. Over the length of the gorges, the pace of erosion has been about 1 mile (1.6km) every 10,000 years. The likely site of the ninth falls is the Devil's Cataract at the western end.

Much has changed since the time when Livingstone cut his initials above the cataracts. Settlers from Europe founded the township of Livingstone, now Maramba, 7 miles (11km) to the north-east of the waterfall. It is now a sizable tourist centre, with a population of 72,000 and a museum devoted to the life and travels of the Scottish explorer.

A statue of Livingstone stands at the waterfall itself, and the gorge is spanned at the Boiling Pot by a bridge completed in 1905 to carry the railway from Bulawayo. In 1938 a power station was built downstream, and a later addition was the Knife Edge footbridge, built in 1969. It runs between the mainland and a dramatic promontory to offer splendid views for sightseers.

The dry season from August to December provides classic, bank-to-bank panoramas of the Victoria Falls, but the water level then can be very low. The flood season (March–May) is the time for sheer drama. The Zambezi then is in full frenzied spate and falls in unbridled power at as much as 15 times its volume in the dry season.

IN RETREAT

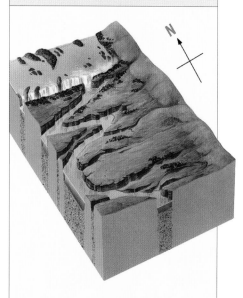

The Victoria Falls are forever on the retreat. The present falls are the eighth to have appeared on the river's zigzag course during the past half million years. Each waterfall appears at a fault in the lava bed of the river, which is criss-crossed with cracks. The river scours out the soft filling from a fault, and tumbles into the void it has created for itself. Immediately, it begins the task of scouring out one of the weaker cracks, cutting back a gorge until it reaches another crosswise fault.

The weakest spot of the present falls is the Devil's Cataract, at the western end. It has already been cut down to a level about 100ft (30m) below the main fall line, and will deepen until the whole Zambezi is enticed into its fracture. This is the likely ninth site of the retreating falls.

Mont-aux-Sources

MAJESTIC CLIFFS HUNG WITH CASCADES OF WATER MARK THE EDGE OF A HIGH PLATEAU IN SOUTH AFRICA'S DRAKENSBERG RANGE

At the northern end of South Africa's Drakensberg range, a curving wall of sheer cliffs soars skywards above grass-covered plains. Known as the Amphitheatre, the towering crescent forms the precipitous edge of Mont-aux-Sources, a boggy and misty plateau overlooked by a summit more than 10,500ft (3200m) high.

Crystal-clear springs bubble up on Mont-aux-Sources. The Tugela River starts here, darting across a gentle incline and then leaping wildly over the Amphitheatre's edge in a series of magnificent falls and cascades. Its total drop of 3110ft (948m) makes it the world's second-highest waterfall.

It was the springs that led two French missionaries to name the mountain Mont-aux-Sources – 'mountain of springs'. To the Sotho people, it is

MOUNTAIN RAMPARTS *The finger of rock between Eastern Buttress (left) and Inner Tower is the Devil's Tooth – a formidable challenge to climbers.*

Phofung – the place of the eland, an antelope that roams the area. The missionaries, who explored the plateau in 1836, noticed that it is the source of major rivers, some flowing to the Atlantic and others to the Indian Ocean. As they approached the mountain, their guides killed an eland which, they wrote,

UNDER ATTACK *Spears fly through the air (above) as Voortrekker womenfolk – a tough breed – load guns for the men to fire from their defensive laager of wagons.*

was 'hastily broiled and devoured' by the hungry and travel-weary party.

Two great outcrops of rock stand at the plateau's edge. The fang-shaped Sentinel marks one end of the Amphitheatre's 2$\frac{1}{2}$ mile (4km) wall. At the other end is the Eastern Buttress, an imposing pedestal of rock that stands dark and serene above the emerald valleys below. Forbidding at night, the Amphitheatre's mood switches suddenly as the sun rises and its lofty ramparts are charged with gold.

To those who have scaled Mont-aux-Sources it seems an enchanting, though lonely, place. The summit gives extraor-dinary views of other great peaks along the precipitous eastern edge of the Drakensberg.

The Drakensberg, or dragons' mountain, takes its name from a Bushman tale of fire-breathing dragons that once lived there. The mountain range is the result of volcanic eruptions 150 million years ago. Molten lava poured out of cracks in the Earth's crust, cooled, and was overlaid by further outpourings of lava. When the eruptions ended, a blanket of solidified lava 5000ft (1500m) thick in places lay over much of southern Africa. Water and wind have since carved valleys and gorges, and created the towers and buttresses that

stand out against the skyline.

From time to time a booming bark rolls across the Drakensberg's ravines and gorges, for they are the home of the human-like chacma baboons. Their waa-hoo call is a warning that alerts the rest of the troop of 15 to 100 animals to danger. The baboons react at once. With the females and young in the lead they scurry for high ground, letting off a fusillade of threat-ening barks. Yet faced by a leopard, their chief enemy, they may lash out, throwing a barrage of stones and advancing on the marauder with shrieks until it retreats.

A group of Boer Voortrekkers struggled down the edge of the Drakensberg near to Mont-aux-Sources in 1837. Descendants of Dutch settlers, the Voortrekkers – 'forward journeyers' – were dissatisfied with British rule in

'PEOPLE WEEPING BY THE PLUNDERED WAGONS, PAINTED WITH BLOOD'

PART OF THE GROUP *Chacma baboons live in well-organised troops, headed by an older male. They feed on grass, insects, roots and eggs.*

A DIFFICULT DRIVE *The Voortrekkers' ox-drawn wagons were built to cope with steep slopes, narrow rocky chasms and rivers. If necessary, they could be dismantled and floated across water.*

Cape Colony, and wanted to find empty land where they could set up an Afrikaner state with their own religion, language and ways.

Between 1836 and 1838 about 10,000 Voortrekkers left their farms and headed northwards in covered wagons about 15ft (4.5m) long. A storage box at the front served as a driving seat and held, amongst other things, the family Bible. The group heading for Natal faced the steep descent from the Drakensberg plateau. To slow the wagons on the way down, the rear wheels were replaced with trees. The drivers then walked behind, taking some of the wagons' weight by hauling back on leather straps.

Only a few months later, an attack by Zulus on scattered wagons left 500 of the Natal Voortrekkers and their servants dead; one witness wrote of 'people weeping by the plundered wagons, painted with blood'. After this attack the Voortrekkers formed their wagons into laagers – circles of wagons chained together end to end to make a defensive wall, with the livestock herded inside. More battles with the Zulus followed, before the Voortrekkers settled down to farm their new land, with the cliffs and peaks of the Drakensberg as a dramatic backdrop.

Table Mountain

THE FLAT-TOPPED SUMMIT AT THE TOE OF AFRICA IS ONE OF THE WORLD'S MOST UNFORGETTABLE AND BEST-KNOWN LANDMARKS

In Africa's south-west corner ramparts of sandstone rise out of the sea. Visible from more than 125 miles (200km) away, they have served as a spectacular and comforting beacon for seamen ever since the Portuguese explorer Bartholomew Dias became the first European navigator to see them in 1488. Now they are one of the world's most unforgettable landmarks – South Africa's Table Mountain.

The flat-topped monolith, its summit more than 2 miles (3km) long, stands regally above Cape Town. From the top,

LANDMARK *At sunset, the flat top of Table Mountain is clearly visible across the waters of Table Bay. Devil's Peak rises to its left, Lion's Head to the right.*

beyond the city spread out below, you can look west across the Atlantic Ocean, south to the Cape of Good Hope and then turn north to see Africa rolling away into the interminable distance.

A 'CLOTH' FOR THE TABLE

In summer a mantle of white cloud, fanned by the south-east wind, can billow across the top of the mountain and slip below its northern face to create an extraordinary 'tablecloth' of white across its entire surface.

Table Mountain is a huge block of sandstone, originally laid on a shallow seabed between 400 and 500 million years ago. Geological upheavals have since lifted it so that the summit is 3560ft (1086m) above sea level. Its

northern face rises as a sheer precipice between distinctive peaks – Devil's Peak on the eastern side, and Lion's Head on the north-west.

Below the summit, Table Mountain's green slopes fall away in a brilliant panorama of wild flowers. At least 400 footpaths – and a cable car that carries half a million people each year – now give access to the mountain, once the domain of lions and leopards.

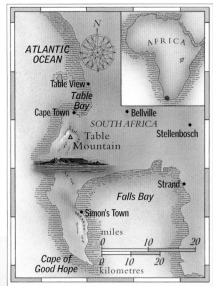

Cango Caves

AN ENCHANTED
FAIRYLAND OF
LIMESTONE WAS FORMED
IN TOTAL DARKNESS BY
THE NEVER ENDING DRIP,
DRIP OF WATER

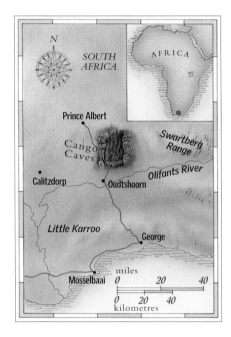

BROUGHT TO LIGHT *Cango Caves have been illuminated by man to reveal the beautiful and bizarre limestone formations buried in darkness beneath rugged mountains for millennia.*

One of Nature's most spectacular creations lies beneath South Africa's Swartberg Range: a cavernous world of limestone formations, lakes, deep pits and interconnecting tunnels. This fairyland of glittering crystal shapes forms one of the world's most varied underground cave sequences – Cango Caves.

In the caverns, 'organ pipes' of stalagmites rear up to ceilings of fluted stalactites. Strange formations cast twisted shadows on walls tinged orange and red by iron oxides. Delicate twisting rods grow in dense clusters, and striped 'curtains' hang in soft folds.

The bizarre limestone formations of the Cango Caves were built up, millimetre by millimetre, over more than 150,000 years, by the dripping of water through fissures filled with calcite – a crystallised form of chalk.

The wandering route through the caves leads through chamber after chamber with names such as Throne Room, Crystal Forest and Rainbow Room that attempt to describe their most distinctive formations. The Bridal Chamber has a collection of stalagmites that resemble a four-poster bed.

CLEOPATRA'S NEEDLE

Nature's work was revealed in 1780 when a cattle herdsman stumbled into the entrance of the caves. The man's employer, a farmer named Van Zyl, accompanied by eight slaves, entered the caves with flickering torches to discover a great chamber 320ft (100m) long and 50ft (15m) high. Within it a stalagmite, now known as Cleopatra's Needle, soared 30ft (9m) into the air.

In the 1950s, experts started to investigate draughts that signalled the existence of further caves beyond an apparent dead end. In 1972 two professional cave guides broke through a small crevice to discover more wonders. The

GLOWING WHITE *A stalagmite like a white-hot metal rod lacks the iron oxide that tinges the surrounding formations.*

journey of discovery did not end there, and yet more chambers have been found, one of which is more than 980ft (300m) long. The most recently discovered caves have taken explorers 800 metres underground.

Blyde River Canyon

A DRAMATIC RAVINE WHERE PROSPECTORS ONCE FOSSICKED FOR GOLD IS ONE OF AFRICA'S MOST HAUNTING LANDSCAPES

The granite domes of the Drakensberg range of mountains in South Africa's Transvaal rise above the twisting valleys of the Blyde River Canyon, their summits separated by terrifying ravines.

Below, rivers and streams run through a tranquil landscape, bypassing old prospectors' posts, forgotten forestry stations and vertical cascades of lichen–covered rock. The river sounds mingle with the calls of rare birds and the barks of baboons beneath cliffs dyed red, yellow and orange by minerals.

This extraordinary canyon, which is part of the dividing line between the great plateau of southern Africa and the Lowveld to the east, is one of the most

JOURNEY'S END *Placid now behind the wall of the Blydepoort dam, the waters of the Blyde River have carved a vast canyon through the Drakensberg range.*

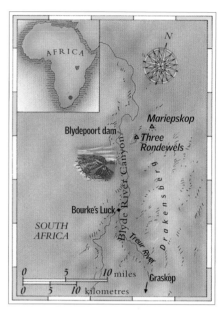

hauntingly beautiful landscapes in all of Africa. Nearly 3300ft (1000m) high, the escarpment plummets sheer to the floor of the Blyde River Canyon.

High on the escarpment stand the triplet peaks of the Three Rondawels, named for their resemblance to the circular thatched huts traditional to some African communities.

STONE AGE HUNTERS

A hundred thousand years ago, Stone Age hunters roamed these valleys and verdant hillsides, long before the arrival of the Bushmen (or San people) who have left rock paintings on the canyon's walls. Another, more macabre, legacy in the valley are the bones of Swazi warriors, killed in the tribal wars against the Pedi and Pulana in 1864. The Swazis suffered heavy casualties as spears rained down on them from the summit of Mariepskop, which their enemies chose as a natural fortress.

The Drakensberg escarpment offers astonishing views over the Lowveld and one of Africa's most famous game reserves – the Kruger National Park.

Wildlife roams the craggy mountains and valleys of the reserve. Baboons and monkeys keep to the shelter of the forests, while antelopes – kudu and klipspringers – hold the high ground.

Predators include leopards, and hippos and otters live in the dams and streams.

It was here in 1840 that a party of Boer pioneers left their women and children behind while they explored eastwards to the port of Lourenço Marques (now Maputo). When they failed to return on the promised date, the women assumed the men had died and named the stream on which they had camped Treur, meaning 'sorrow'. Shortly afterwards at another river, the two parties were reunited. They called the river Blyde, meaning 'joy'.

The Blyde rises on the escarpment, near the small village of Pilgrim's Rest, where prospectors scrambled for gold more than a century ago. Today, the prospectors are gone, but the water of the Blyde hurtles on, dropping to the floor of the canyon in a series of stunning rapids and cascades.

Through the ages the Blyde has brought down thousands of tons of waterborne particles which have eroded its spectacular path for 15 miles (24km) through the canyon.

GUARDIANS *The Three Rondawels loom above the Blyde River Canyon, proud and colourful sentinels in one of Africa's most scenic wonderlands.*

THE WINNING LOGIC OF TOM BOURKE

Near the start of the huge Blyde River Canyon, the waters of the Treur River accelerate down a small cataract and then flow, almost at a right angle, into the Blyde.

The sudden change of direction sets up a swirling current that has sculpted the feature known as Bourke's Luck potholes. Following the motion of the current, waterborne stones, tumbled about over many millennia, have scoured the soft sandstone to form bowl-shaped depressions up to 20ft (6m) deep.

Tom Bourke was the farmer on whose land the potholes stood. He reasoned that,

if prospectors were finding gold upstream, he might find nuggets deposited at the bottom of his 'potholes'. Bourke's logic proved to be correct, and this strange feature became known as Bourke's Luck.

LUCKY POTHOLES *Swirling water at the meeting point of the Treur and Blyde Rivers has worn away the rock to create Bourke's Luck potholes.*

Madagascar's Tsingy Lands

WAFER-THIN SPIRES, LIKE LIMESTONE RAZORS, CREATE REFUGES FOR UNIQUE WILD CREATURES ON ONE OF THE WORLD'S BIGGEST ISLANDS

Imagine a miniature lost world, at the top of a limestone cliff more than 600ft (180m) high. A world of razor-sharp rock spires up to 100ft (30m) tall, where the toughest boots are torn to shreds in minutes and a single false step can skin a limb or sever an artery. A world where crocodiles live deep in underground caves, where wide-eyed lemurs peer like shy ghosts from the trees, where tiny bees attack in a viciously stinging swarm if a single member of their hive is crushed.

This is the Ankarana Plateau at the northern tip of Madagascar, and it is perhaps the most extraordinary region of the whole extraordinary island. Madagascar itself lies 375 miles (600km) off the East African coast. Measuring 1000 miles (1600km) north to south and covering 230,000sq miles (600,000km²), it is the world's fourth largest island after Greenland, New Guinea and Borneo. Known as the 'Great Red Island' from the colour of its soil – now washing into the sea at a terrifying rate due to man-made erosion – it has evolved its own plants and animals.

Its unique ecosystem began about 120 million years ago, when the continents began to split apart. The map of the original supercontinent of Gondwanaland shows Madagascar sandwiched neatly between the

southern tip of India, the east coast of Africa and the northern coast of Antarctica.

In the age of the giant reptiles, dinosaurs could still plod across from Africa on dry land, and for millions of years after the split began plants and animals could float across the gap on rafts of vegetation to colonise Madagascar. But around 40 million years ago the gap became too great, and this evolutionary traffic came to an end – until about AD 500, when the first humans came on the scene, arriving by boat from Indonesia, rather than from neighbouring East Africa

PINNACLES, CAVES AND UNDERGROUND RIVERS

The Ankarana Plateau consists of limestone scenery of the type known as *karst*. Millennia of heavy rainstorms, averaging 70in (1800mm) a year, have dissolved the rock – which is soft and chalky in its upper part and hard and crystalline at its base – into spires, pinnacles and ridges, often honed to wafer thinness. The limestone is cut by deep forested canyons, where baobabs, figs and palm trees flourish, forming a green canopy 80ft (25m) overhead. More than 450 miles (720km) to the south, this landscape is repeated in the Bemaraha National Reserve in western Madagascar.

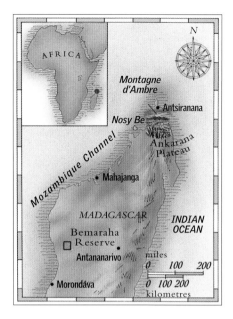

NEEDLE LANDSCAPE *Treacherous limestone needles, sheltering rare animals and birds, make up the unique* tsingy *landscape (right) of Madagascar.*

Seeping through the Ankarana rock, the rainwater has hollowed out deep caves, where lime deposits have formed spectacular stalagmites and stalactites. Streams swallowed by fissures in the limestone reappear far underground as rivers flowing through tunnels and caverns, like the vast Grotte d'Andrafiabe, where 7 miles (11km) of passages have so far been explored. The roofs of some of the larger caves have collapsed, and their floors have been colonised by plants and animals to form isolated pockets of virgin forest.

The fearsome rocks at the centre of the plateau are known locally as *tsingy*, from the sound they make when they are struck, which is like the dull clanging of a cracked bell. The Malagasy (the people of Madagascar) say there is not enough level ground in the *tsingy* for a single foot to be placed flat. Brave naturalists sometimes struggle through the outer fringes of the labyrinth of rock spikes before getting hopelessly confused and beating a retreat. The few people who have tried to penetrate it say that the *tsingy* is best seen from an aircraft, at a safe distance.

Most of Madagascar's wildlife is threatened by the human population's constant need for more land, but the fortress-like character of the Ankarana

VERSATILE SPINES *A streaked tenrec, found only in Madagascar, uses its snout to find worms. Sharp spines give it protection as well as help it to communicate – it vibrates them to produce sound.*

Plateau and the Bemaraha Reserve has so far managed to safeguard the rare creatures that live there. Several species of lemur – Madagascar's most typical indigenous mammal – live in trees which grow in crevices and sinkholes between the knife-edged rocks.

Lemurs are lower primates, distantly related to monkeys, apes and humans. Some, like the tiny and rare Coquerel's dwarf lemur, forage on their own at night; others, like the larger sifaka roam in large groups and feed in broad daylight, leaping from branch to branch and clinging on with amazingly human-looking hands.

Other mammals that are found in the Ankarana include the ring-tailed mongoose and the strange cat-like fossa. It is Madagascar's largest predator and has been described as being 'built like a mountain lion cut off at the knees'. It lives mainly on sifakas.

Deep below the Ankarana Plateau, the Earth's only cave-dwelling crocodiles take refuge in underground rivers for the duration of the six-month dry season, which lasts from May to October. Large specimens can grow almost 20ft (6m) long, and are capable of seizing and devouring a human being.

Fortunately for anyone venturing into the caves, crocodiles need to bask in the sun before they become active, and the water temperature in the underground rivers is low enough – below 26°C (79°F) – to keep them in a state of near lethargy.

Smaller than the crocodiles but a good deal more dangerous are the leather-tough eels which live in the underground rivers. At least 4ft (1.2m) long, aggressive and armed with ferocious teeth, they are said to attack swimmers, or even inflatable boats, without provocation.

While the remote and inhospitable nature of the Ankarana and Bemaraha reserves has so far managed to preserve their wildlife, this is not true of the rest of the country.

At risk is a treasure house of species unparalleled anywhere else in the world. Among the mammals, true lemurs are found nowhere else,

and most of Madagascar's 235 known species of reptile are native to the country.

There is similar variety among the birds. Madagascar has more than 250 bird species, of which more than 100 are unique to the island. Their numbers have been affected mainly by the cutting down of the rainforest; but a contributory factor is the shooting of birds for sport by foreign tourists.

What can easily happen to a bird species was shown by the sad story of the flightless *Aepyornis* or 'elephant bird', the world's largest known bird, one and a half times the size of an ostrich. Weighing about 1000lb (450kg), and laying eggs six times as large as an ostrich egg, this bird was eventually hunted to extinction. It was last recorded in 1666.

Chameleons are also under threat, and half the world's species are native to Madagascar. Though they are completely harmless, the Malagasy are afraid of them, believing that they embody human spirits not yet at rest, while their independently rotating eyes allow them to keep one eye on the past and one on the future.

However, there are hopeful signs. Here and there, projects aimed at saving endangered species have been started – ornithologists, for example, are studying threatened populations of fish eagles and serpent eagles.

A few miles north of the Ankarana, in the Montagne d'Ambre National Park, farmers are being encouraged to manage their land for its long-term good, by planting indigenous trees rather than cutting down the rainforest to make charcoal, and by using efficient irrigation systems. The promotion of green tourism aims to ensure that unique sites such as the Ankarana Plateau act as treasure houses of rare plants and animals in future centuries.

EARTH'S ONLY CAVE-DWELLING CROCODILES TAKE REFUGE IN UNDERGROUND RIVERS

RAZOR PINNACLES *The razor-sharp limestone* tsingy *gets its name from the metallic sound it makes when struck.*

AGILE BEAUTIES

Named after the *lemures,* the Roman spirits of the dead, lemurs come in all sizes from that of a mouse to a cat – apart from the far larger indri, which is the size of a small child. They were described by a traveller in the 1920s as 'the daintiest little animals extant. Neither cat nor monkey, they've been dowered by Nature with the privileges of both – beauty with agility'.

The playful ring-tailed lemur, often tame enough to take food from the hand, has become the mascot of Madagascar. Another species, the greater bamboo lemur, was long thought to be extinct; but in 1986 naturalists discovered surviving specimens – a solitary plus in Madagascar's sad catalogue of extinctions.

A close relative of the lemur, the bushy-tailed aye-aye, lives mainly in the rainforests of the island's east coast but is also found in the Ankarana. This shy nocturnal animal, which is about 16in (400mm) long, feeds on fruit, seeds, insects and wood-boring grubs. Its acute hearing enables it to hear beetle grubs tunnelling inside rotten wood. The aye-aye uses its exceptionally long, thin third digit to winkle them out.

TSINGY CREATURE *A crowned lemur, with a tail much longer than its body, is one of the rare creatures that shelter in the* tsingy *regions.*

Europe

Vatnajökull

ICELAND'S MIGHTY ICE SHEET PULSES TO THE THROBBING HEARTBEAT OF A VIOLENT VOLCANO BURNING BENEATH IT

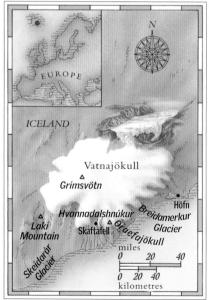

On Vatnajökull, Iceland's massive ice sheet, there is nearly as much ice as on all Europe's other glaciers put together. It covers an area almost half the size of Wales or New Jersey, and pushes out a dozen major glaciers from its smooth cap.

When viewed from the coastal road, Vatnajökull seems a lifeless wilderness.

From the desert of black gravel, ash and sand at its feet, the ice rises through mountains to form a sweeping white plain over ½ mile (800m) thick that forbids all life. But life – of a fiery, geological sort – certainly exists here. The icy wasteland is continually growing, contracting, pulsing, to a slow and sometimes violent volcanic heartbeat.

Vatnajökull's restlessness is typical of the landscape of Iceland, an island almost the size of England but with a population no larger than that of a medium-sized town, scattered mainly along its narrow coastal strip. Geologically new and still forming, Iceland stands on basalt rock 4 miles (6.4km) thick that has, over the last 20 million years, been poured out from a 'hot spot' on the Mid Atlantic Ridge,

GRIMY EDGE *The side of Fjallsjökull, one of Vatnajökull's southern outlet glaciers, is darkened by debris that it has scraped from the volcanic uplands.*

MELTING FLOES *At the broad snout of Breidamerkur Glacier, ice breaks off into the meltwater lagoon. When the floes melt, they join glacial waters flowing nearly 1 mile (1.6km) to the ocean.*

nature is semi-liquid and flows without melting, like pitch.' Ice grinds down into the warmer valleys at the rate of about ½ mile (800m) a year, cracking open to form crevasses as it tumbles over uneven bedrock. When, at the lower levels, the ice reaches melting point and peters out, it dumps a chaos of rubble – rocks, sand and gravel scraped from the mountains.

According to an Icelandic saying, 'The glacier delivers back what it takes'. In 1927, John Palsson, a postman, fell into a crevasse with four horses while crossing a snow bridge on the Breidamerkur glacier. Seven months later, all the bodies were found on the surface – the circular movement of the ice at the glacier's snout, with the top ice carried under and the bottom ice rising, had apparently brought them to the top.

VOLCANIC DESTRUCTION
Great eruptions are part of Iceland's past and present. The most awe-inspiring of all – Earth's largest lava flow in modern times – occurred in 1783. Laki, the mountain at Vatnajökull's south-western edge, was riven almost across its summit during the eruption, in which a 15 mile (24km) chain of 100 separate craters burst open. Lava was spewed over more than 200sq miles (520km²) of land. The

HIDDEN HEAT *A deep blue meltwater lake reveals the presence below the volcano, Grimsvötn, which rumbles underneath the massive ice cap.*

which is a deep cleft created as Europe and North America slowly pull apart under the influence of continental drift.

Iceland's volcanic rock surface was gouged by glaciers more than 1 mile (1.6km) thick during the 2 million years of the last Ice Age, which ended about 10,000 years ago. The centre of the country is a wilderness of volcanic mountains, craters and lava. One-tenth of the land is covered with lava that has erupted from its 200 volcanoes – one of the lava fields extends for more than 1000sq miles (2600km²).

The first record of Iceland may have been made some 1500 years ago,

by St Brendan (about AD 484–578), Abbot of Clonfert in County Galway, Ireland. He reputedly voyaged to America about 300 years before the Vikings settled Iceland (traditionally in AD 874). At one time the account of his voyage was considered a fantasy. Now most scholars accept that it may have occurred.

When the Vikings arrived, the land was favourable for crop growing. But from about the 14th century, Iceland's climate became more severe, glaciers advanced and sea ice greatly increased. The climate improved in the late 19th century, but ice still covers one-tenth of the land, and crop growing is restricted.

Icelanders have always understood the shifting nature of the ice. In the words of an 18th-century scientist, Sveinn Palsson: 'The ice by its very flow continued for some three months, blanketing the island in a blue haze that contaminated the grass and led to the death of three-quarters of the livestock. As a result of this 'Haze Famine', nearly 10,000 people starved to death.

In the early hours of January 23, 1973, the volcano Helgafell on Heimaey – one of the 15 islands of Vestmannaeyjar (Westman Islands) – which had been dormant for about 5000 years and was considered extinct, awoke from its long sleep. Near the edge of the town, the ground split open, forming a curtain of fire 1 mile (1.6km) long. Luckily, the local fishing fleet had been kept in port by a storm, and by midday 5000 islanders had been carried to safety.

EXTENDED COASTLINE

Lava oozed into the edge of town, pushing over houses and setting them on fire. By April, despite a massive operation to cool the advancing lava with jets of seawater, the eastern part of the town had been buried under lava and dust. The eruption ended after several weeks, without wreaking total havoc. It gave Heimaey an extension to its eastern coast, including a new protective wall to the harbour approaches.

Volcanic fire and glacial ice combined underlie Vatnajökull's shifting moods. The effects are clear at the core of the ice cap, which, seen from an aeroplane ride, sometimes reveals an astonishing sight: a deep-blue lake measuring 2 miles (3km) across, melted from the ice by the volcano Grimsvötn, which grumbles below the ice cap.

ICE AND FIRE

- The ice on parts of Vatnajökull is 3609ft (1100m) thick – more than twice as high as the Empire State Building in New York, USA.
- At the bottom, it is 1000 years old.
- The glaciers can advance by as much as 5 miles (8km) in one surge.
- At least 150 volcanoes have been active in Iceland since the Ice Age – one erupting about every five years.
- Since the year 1500, a third of all the lava flows occurring on Earth have been in Iceland.

Usually the lake is covered by a sheet of ice, but even while invisible it remains as a sump of meltwater.

The ice on one side of the lake acts as a giant stopper and prevents water from flooding down a valley. However, the lake water rises some 40ft (12m) a year, and every 5–10 years there is enough to force a way under the ice dam in a torrent called a 'glacial burst'. The lake level drops by up to 700ft (215m) as the floodwater flows down to the plain below, spreading volcanic mud.

JOURNEY'S END *At its southern edge, the great ice sheet Vatnajökull sends out a fleet of newly born icebergs into the icy blue chill of a meltwater lake.*

Grimsvötn is an extension of the Laki fault to the south-west. It is part of a huge, hidden region of geothermal activity that pumps out enough heat to warm houses and generate electricity for the domestic needs of a city the size of London. Occasionally, Grimsvötn does something more than pump out heat. In November 2004, seismographs picked up tremors – the volcano had erupted through its mantle of ice and water, sending up a cloud some 7.5 miles (12km) above the glacier, causing air traffic to be diverted. It melted a hole clean through the ice, creating a crater filled with slush and ice floes. After a few days, the eruption died and the ice returned.

On Vatnajökull's southern edge, the outlet glacier, Skeidarárjökull, melts into a river which snakes out over a gravelly wasteland. To one side of the glacier lies a meltwater lake. Eventually, the lake water rises high enough for the whole glacier, like a giant sluice gate, to float clear of its base. The water sweeps out underneath in a glacier burst, scouring the plain, and scattering it anew with debris. To the east of the glacier lies the snout of Breidamerkur Glacier, marked by snaking strips of rock and clay scraped from upland valleys. This glacier ends in a lagoon, and occasionally, with a roar of water, huge grimy slabs of ice break away to float in the lagoon as icebergs.

Between these two glaciers lies a small ice cap, Oraefajökull, covering a volcano of the same name from which many glaciers descend. Oraefajökull volcano, Europe's third highest, has exploded twice in recorded history – in the 14th century and the 18th century with devastating effects.

Below the glacier, the extraordinary area of barrens is known simply as Oraefi, 'wilderness'. It was once said that not even a mouse could cross these southern wastelands. Now the coastal road brings visitors to a once-isolated oasis of green nestling in the lee of Oraefajökull. This area, Skaftafell, has escaped the destructive power of glacier bursts. A lush area that was once

farmland, it is now a national park with a varied landscape of grassy hills and woods of birch, rowan and willow.

At one spot, an 80ft (25m) waterfall, Svartifoss, pours over two layers of volcanic basalt pillars, stacked vertically like organ pipes. A ravine leads up to a vantage point. Here – in summer at least – travellers can safely view the vast, treacherous landscape, from the icy fastness of Oraefajökull, over the badlands and snaking rivers to the sea.

ON THE GLACIER

At close quarters, Vatnajökull seems to surge with life. New snow, sun, wind and frost remake the surface, stippling and rippling it in a variety of textures. Dawns and sunsets bathe the ice cap in fire. Deep within the shifting ice, meltwaters create glassy caves where daylight filters down in a medley of blues.

Glacial rivers by the hundred snake out from beneath the fractured snouts of ice, grimy with volcanic debris scraped from the highlands. The sound of rushing water or the thunder of falling ice can often be heard.

Those equipped to explore the glacier's surface sometimes feel they are stepping on the skin of a giant animal – at any moment it may react with a fatal shiver.

EARLY VISITOR *This old German manuscript shows a wild man, probably representing an Icelandic volcano, about to hurl a flaming rock at St Brendan.*

Geysir and Strokkur

A TOWERING JET OF BOILING WATER, DRIVEN BY VOLCANIC HEAT, HAS GIVEN ITS NAME TO ALL THE WORLD'S HOT SPRINGS

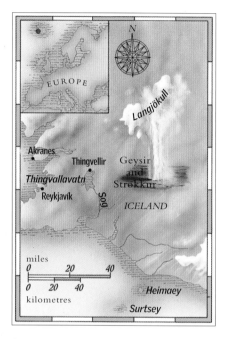

Water seething and exploding in a boiling basin, followed by a jet of chalk-white spray shooting up to the height of a five-storey house – a magnificent sight that continues for seven or eight minutes before subsiding. Then, suddenly, a column of boiling water again shoots rocket-like into the air, this time 100ft (30m) or more, and is carried by the wind in a great fan. The eruption continues, the fountain working itself higher and higher – even to 200ft (60m). Finally there comes a column of scalding steam, pouring out with a mighty roar, and all is quiet again.

This was Geysir hot spring in action in the 1930s, when it was Iceland's prime attraction – the original 'geyser', or 'gusher'. Now visitors are more likely to see a performance by its smaller neighbour, Strokkur, which boils over every ten minutes or so, blasting out a 70ft (22m) column of boiling water.

Geysir and Strokkur lie in a wooded valley, an area of some 50 hot springs that can be heard boiling underground with a far-off grumbling sound.

The geyser area was first mentioned in 1294, when an earthquake destroyed several hot-water springs and created two others, probably Geysir and Strokkur. Geysir became a tourist attraction almost as soon as it was named in 1647. At that time it erupted daily. Around 1800, Geysir was spouting several times a day, and once erupted 14 times in 24 hours. In 1907, however, it became dormant for almost 30 years. In 1935 eruptions were induced artificially by draining off some water and thus lowering the pressure below. Now it explodes only rarely, but its blasts are still as spectacular as ever.

A COLUMN OF BOILING WATER SHOOTS INTO THE AIR LIKE A ROCKET

As well as Geysir and Strokkur, there are some 3000 hot springs, steam vents, mudbaths and geysers in Iceland. They include the boiling, sulphurous mud pits at Namaskard in the north, where visitors have to watch where they tread to avoid getting burnt feet. In the Middle Ages, volcanoes were considered to be the Gates of Hell but in modern Iceland the natural hot water from volcanic heat is harnessed for heating houses.

A dramatic display of the area's unceasing turbulence occurred on November 14, 1963, when a cloud 12,000ft (3600m) high billowed from the sea off Iceland's south coast. Not a spouting geyser, but the birth of a new island – Surtsey. Another Iceland in miniature, it was built from the debris of a volcanic eruption under the sea.

FIERY BIRTH *Smoke rises from the sea as the island of Surtsey (left), named after the Norse fire-god Surt, is built up from the clinker of an erupting volcano.*

UNLEASHED ENERGY *Steam and spray heave sky high from a churning pool as the geyser Strokkur (right) spurts forth.*

Giant's Causeway

WHEN NATURE BECAME A MATHEMATICIAN, IRELAND'S COAST PRODUCED THE UNCANNY SIGHT OF A SYMMETRY IN STONE

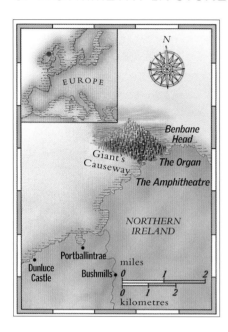

Nature's symmetry is something we take for granted in flowers, insects and in the face of a tiger, for example. In geology, however, it is rarer and its occurrence is something to marvel at. In the Giant's Causeway, Nature has spectacularly revealed her mathematical genius, producing tens of thousands of multisided columns of rock packed together like a giant-sized handful of hexagonal pencils.

From a distance, this looks like just another part of County Antrim's enchanting coast, but suddenly the eye is caught by a strangely chequered promontory. It leads out from the base of the cliffs and descends gently into the sea like a huge, crudely fashioned slipway. For a moment it causes the mind to reel. It looks for all the world like the kind of landscape that is produced by computer graphics for a video game. Yet this extraordinary geological freak has an ancestry dating back some 60 million years.

The continents of North America and Europe, which had been joined together, began to split apart. The Atlantic Ocean opened up between them, and gradually spread out from a central volcanic rift on the ocean floor. Iceland, with its numerous active volcanoes, stands on the rift today. Lava areas in Ireland and Scotland were produced on the rift as the continents began their slow journey.

40,000 BASALT COLUMNS

As the lava poured forth in County Antrim it formed the largest lava plateau in Europe. The basalt content of some of the lava was unusually consistent. As it solidified, it contracted, but the forces of contraction were so evenly distributed that it cracked with geometric precision. The same process can be seen when the thick layer of mud in the bottom of a puddle dries in the sun.

On the Giant's Causeway the basalt columns average 18in (460mm) across and vary from about 3ft to 6ft (1m to 2m) high. The Causeway is about 200yds (180m) across at its widest, extends 170yds (150m) into the sea and consists of some 40,000 columns.

Over the millennia, erosion by glaciers in the Ice Age and relentless battering by the Atlantic have shaped the Giant's Causeway into the form we see today. Each column of basalt actually consists of a series of segments about 14in (360mm) long which have been welded together, but which separate under stress. Now and then exposed sections are sheared off by the waves at the fault line between segments. This has given the Causeway its stepped effect.

The Giant's Causeway is the most famous of the basalt features in this

A GIANT'S HANDIWORK? *Sea mists eddy around this bizarre staircase. Said to be the work of an Irish giant, it is formed by the neatly squared-off tops of closely packed hexagonal columns.*

'WOODEN WINGS' *A fulmar colony lives along the cliffs above the Giant's Causeway. They are known as 'wooden wings' for their stiff pose when gliding.*

piece of coastline, but there are many others in the cliffs behind the Causeway and in neighbouring bays. Over the years they have gained descriptive titles. The Organ is a group of towering columns embedded in the cliff face of the next bay, Port Noffer. The Amphitheatre is a bay surrounded by extraordinary clusters of columns. Other notable shapes include the Giant's Pot Lid, the Wishing Chair, the King and his Nobles, and the Coffin.

A GIANT'S LABOUR OF LOVE

Similar basalt columns can also be seen on the island of Staffa, which lies off the west coast of Scotland some 75 miles (120km) to the north, notably in Fingal's Cave. The Giant's Causeway effectively gives the impression of leading under the sea from Ireland to Staffa, and this is the origin of the legend that has given rise to its name.

The giant in question is the great hero of Irish folk legend called Finn MacCool (or Fionn MacCumhail), the leader of the warrior band called the Fianna. Tales about Finn MacCool speak with gusto of his huge appetite, of his dauntless bravery and of his prodigious feats of hunting. Among the several reasons offered for Finn MacCool's construction of the causeway is the story that it was a huge act of devotion. He hammered in pillar after pillar to create a dry walkway by which his lady-love of the moment, a female giant who lived on Staffa, could visit him in Ireland without getting wet feet.

GIRONA'S TREASURES

When the novelist William Makepeace Thackeray visited the Giant's Causeway in 1842, he was told that a wreck from the Spanish Armada lay off the bay known as Port na Spaniagh. He dismissed the story as 'a parcel of legends'. But in 1967 the legend was shown to be fact when the Belgian marine archaeologist Robert Sténuit discovered a large collection of artefacts and treasures scattered across the seabed here. They proved that this was where the Armada's biggest ship, the galleass *Girona*, had sunk in 1588.

The Armada had consisted of 131 ships carrying 30,000 men when it set sail from Spain in 1588 to invade England. After dramatic losses inflicted upon it by the English fleet, the Armada set sail for home, taking the perilous route round the north of Scotland. It was beset by foul weather and only half the original fleet got back to Spain. Some 20 ships were wrecked off the coast of Ireland.

RUBY PENDANT *Just one of the Girona's treasures is a gold pendant set with rubies in the form of a salamander.*

DUCAT *A gold ducat with the head of Charles V, the Holy Roman Emperor, was among the coins and buttons found by a team of archaeologists in 1968.*

The *Girona* had a particularly gruelling journey. As she approached the Giant's Causeway, she had on board not the 550 people she was designed to carry but 1300, including crews from two wrecked ships. On October 26, 1588, the *Girona* struck a rock close to the Causeway, and sank. There were only five survivors.

TREASURE SHIP *The Girona was a galleass, a ship that combined the fighting strength of a galleon and the speed of an oar-driven galley.*

Much of the wreck's treasure fell into the hands of 'Sorley Boy' MacDonnell who had taken Dunluce Castle, 4 miles (6km) to the west, from the English four years earlier. The rest lay on the seabed for nearly 400 years, until it was brought to the surface by Sténuit's team in 1968 and 1969. By that time, nothing was left of the ship itself, but the surviving artefacts give a fascinating insight into life on board a ship of the Spanish Armada. They can now be seen at the Ulster Museum in Belfast.

The Cliffs of Moher

IMPASSIVE SENTINELS GUARD THE WEST COAST
OF IRELAND AGAINST THE MERCILESS ASSAULTS
OF THE ATLANTIC OCEAN

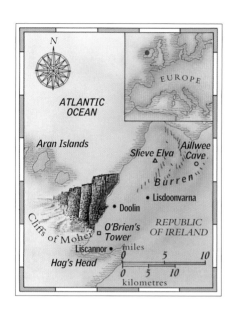

A soft mantle of green fields and hills and shallow lakes and streams cloaks most of Ireland. But here and there Nature has made a dramatic flourish, perhaps as a reminder of her awesome power. The Cliffs of Moher are one of her boldest gestures in Ireland's otherwise gentle landscape. Looming out of the Atlantic in a jagged concertina of sheer rock, these dark cliffs stretch for 5 miles (8km) along the County Clare coast.

There is nothing gentle about the Cliffs of Moher – no sandy bays at their feet, no grassy slopes on their flanks, no delicate flowers on their headlands. They rise sheer from the sea to a lofty 670ft (200m), and although the ocean batters at their base with an artillery of wind and wave, they seem capable of withstanding attack for ages to come.

Daunting indeed is the Atlantic at this point. Each foam-capped wave piles over the backwash of the one before and explodes against the cliffs in a turmoil of dark blue and grey. And on all but the calmest days, man or beast venturing near the precipitous edge of the cliffs is drenched in salty spray whipped up by the westerly winds.

SILENT ON THE WIND

Standing on the clifftop is an eerie experience. The thump and roar of the waves in the churning cauldron below is barely audible above the wailing whine of the wind, and the screaming seagulls wheeling below the cliff face appear to be mute. Only when they soar upwards on a sudden gust can their piercing cries be heard.

On a stormy day, nowhere in the British Isles can be more inhospitable yet more exhilarating. At the base of the cliffs, a thick fringe of coffee-coloured

foam hurls rock fragments high, and the cliff face takes on the blackness of the rain clouds overhead. Slabs of white-flecked gunmetal-grey sea complete the leaden, monochrome effect.

Although they seem invulnerable, the cliffs are slowly crumbling. Sections occasionally plummet into the sea, sheared off by the combined action of the rain, which loosens the clifftop soil,

SEA-GIRT BULWARK *A superb natural defence on the Country Clare coast, the Cliffs of Moher rise sheer from the ocean. Warmed by the sun, they present a dreamy diorama of yellow and browns.*

and wind-borne salt, which eats into the rock face. It was in the sea that the cliffs began their story. Their limestone base (myriad skeletons of minute sea creatures) was laid down over 300 million years ago. Century by century, the sea deposited more overlays of different coloured sandstones and shale; all was eventually pushed above the surface by continental movements.

SHAPED BY THE GODS

Only a little imagination is needed to visualise the early Irish gods playing an active part in the shaping of these cliffs. As Dublin writer James Plunkett wrote in *The Gems She Wore*: 'In misty weather they look ... like the nightmare of some deranged god; in fine weather, particularly at sunset, they belong to mythology and the underworld.' But it is not the grandeur of the cliffs alone that has inspired writers. There are pointers to a time when ancient Irish heroes, real or legendary, must have stalked the clifftops. The name Moher, for instance, refers to the ancient promontory fort of Mothair, built by settlers on the headland at Hag's Head in pre-Christian times. Unfortunately, the ruins of the fort were demolished during the Napoleonic Wars to make way for a signals tower.

Part of the cliff face nearby is said to resemble a seated woman looking out to sea. To local people she is the old hag, Mal, now turned to stone. But Mal once pursued the Ulster hero Cuchulainn along Loop Head, farther down the coast. There, it is told, she misjudged her leap, fell into the sea, and drowned. The northernmost part of the cliffs is known as Aill na Searrach (Cliff of the Colts). The colts in question were apparently of fairy origin, and for some unrecorded reason they also leapt over the cliff at this spot.

Today's visitors can approach the Cliffs of Moher from either end and easily walk the clifftop path, which is mostly well back from the cliff edge, within a day. A flattened mat of short grass on top of a layer of dark shale offers an easy footing.

From Hag's Head in the south, where the cliffs are 400ft (120m) high, they gradually rise to their highest point in the north. O'Brien's Tower conveniently marks the spot.

A GREY SWEEP OF LIMESTONE

Stone dominates this lonely place to the north-east of the Cliffs of Moher. Known as the Burren, it is a 100sq mile (260km²) tract of giant limestone terraces that climb in a series of folds to the shale-capped peak of Slieve Elva, 1134ft (345m). It was ice that scoured the terraces into their contorted shapes some 15,000 years ago, making them one of Europe's youngest landscapes.

From a distance, the Burren looks deserving of the description ascribed to Edmund Ludlow, one of Oliver Cromwell's generals: '... yielding neither water enough to drown a man, nor a tree to hang him, nor soil enough to bury him.' But there is some pastureland and pine forest, and here and there on the stony terraces hazel and juniper bushes have taken root.

And within the sweeping greyness of the stone, a latticework of fissures and crevices supports a thousand different species of plant, miraculously anchored in tiny pockets of soil. They transform the terraces into a paradise for plant lovers, for the mild, damp climate coupled with the rocky shelter produce exceptional conditions that allow Mediterranean and alpine plants to flourish side by side. In early summer the rock face is alive with jewel-like colours from plants such as bloody cranesbill, mountain avens and spring gentian.

Rainwater is not swept off the rock surface but filters down through the fissures and crevices, eating into the rock to create channels and caves, and sometimes the water wells up to form fleeting lakes called turloughs. Expert potholers have explored miles of twisting tunnels leading deep into the side of Slieve Elva. One cave, Aillwee, open to all, has 1100yds (1000m) of passageways to caverns that are bristling with stalactites and stalagmites.

Remains of stone tombs and forts, monastic settlements, and castles, confirm that people have dwelt on these unique rock gardens for thousands of years. Indeed, some scientists attribute the bareness of the rocks to erosion brought about by the felling of forests in prehistoric times.

BURREN TERRACE *Massive boulders dumped during the last Ice Age (right) give an alien aspect to the sculptured limestone slabs. Mountain avens (left) thrive in the crevices.*

Northwards along the cliff there are ledges fit only for wild goats, which occasionally venture a little way down. Then the land slopes down to a sandy bay at the fishing village of Doolin.

The most spectacular approach is from the northern end, where a well-worn, channelled track lined with huge limestone flagstones leads to O'Brien's Tower. Local landowner Sir Cornelius O'Brien MP had the tower built in 1835 as an observation point and tea house. After the exertions of their

climb, the 19th-century tourists could enjoy refreshments at a round table in the tower while a piper entertained them.

It is easy to see why O'Brien chose this spot for his tower. The views are unparalleled. To the north, the man-sized boulders strewn about the shingle beach below look the size of pebbles, and beyond the reddish banding of the northernmost cliffs rise the distant conical peaks of Connemara's Twelve Pins. To the south stands the lonely

lighthouse at Loop Head, which marks the western tip of County Clare, and in the background is the shadowy sweep of the Kerry mountains.

Reserve the westward view until last. Look down at the craggy stack below the tower, once part of the cliff itself but now worn away after aeons of assault by the elements to just this finger of rock. It is actually 200ft (60m) high, but appears dwarfed from the clifftop view-point. With the tower's binoculars trained on the nearby cliff

face, the streak of white visible halfway up is not, as might be imagined, a layer of fossilised rock. It is a line of seabirds – kittiwakes, guillemots, razorbills – confidently nesting or resting on ledges so narrow they hardly deserve the name. More difficult to distinguish against the dark rock are the black ravens and choughs that tumble and roll on the rising air with amazing acrobatic ease.

Finally, let your eyes scan the vast expanse of the Atlantic stretching to

the horizon and beyond, with only the three whale-like humps of the Aran Islands breaking the endless heave of the waves. On a fine day their silver-grey rocks glisten alluringly in the sunlight, but when the weather turns stormy they appear black and threatening, as if they might suddenly decide to cross the intervening South Sound and lay siege to the mainland. But there is little to fear with the Cliffs of Moher standing bastille-like in defence of the coast.

Benbulbin

A FLAT-TOPPED
MOUNTAIN RISING
ABOVE LOWLANDS
IN WESTERN IRELAND
HAS LINKS WITH A
POET AND A GIANT

The massive bulk of Benbulbin sits like the upturned hull of a ship amid Sligo's stonewalled pastures. Near the mountain top, the steep slopes give way abruptly to cliffs – sculpted by the weather to resemble a concertina – that rim a flat summit 1000ft (300m) above the plain.

Benbulbin looms large in Irish myths too. It was on the mountain's slopes, legend relates, that the Celtic warrior Diarmuid met his end. He had eloped with Grainne, the fiancée of the giant Finn MacCool who built the Giant's Causeway, and the unforgiving Finn tricked Diarmuid into a fatal fight with an enchanted boar. It was here, too, that the 6th-century St Colmcille (Columba) led 3000 men into battle. And it was to the protection of Benbulbin that the Irish poet W.B. Yeats turned when he chose it as his burial site; shortly before his death in 1939, he wrote:

Under bare Ben Bulben's head
In Drumcliff churchyard Yeats is laid.

BATTLE SITE *St Colmcille, it is said, led an army onto Benbulbin's slopes – to settle his right to copy a psalter lent to him by St Finian of Movilla.*

Wast Water

RUGGED PEAKS AND SCREES RING ENGLAND'S DEEPEST LAKE, GIVING IT A SOMBRE, EVEN HAUNTING, ATMOSPHERE

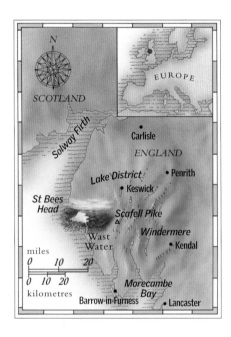

The woods and gentle contours of the road towards Wast Water give little hint of the splendour to come – a view unequalled in the whole of England's Lake District. Ahead lies a sheet of slate-grey water, hemmed in by craggy mountains. A wall of perilous-looking scree more than 1800ft (550m) high plunges steeply into the lake's depths. No pleasure boats cruise on this lake, and there are no pretty gardens softening the far shoreline – simply stern magnificence.

At the head of the 3 mile (5km) long lake, a scattering of stone-walled sheep pastures radiates from the tiny village of Wasdale Head and gives the impression of a tamed landscape. But above and beyond the fields stand Great Gable in all its grandeur, and the knife-edged ridges and crags of lofty Scafell Pike – at 3210ft (978m) England's highest peak.

Wasdale Head has been a much-loved base for rock climbers ever since adventurous Victorian climbers first described the challenges of the crags. Among these pioneers was Walter Haskett Smith, the 'father of British rock climbing', who recorded his climbs in the Visitors' Book at his lodgings. Many climbers have stayed in the village inn. In the 1870s it was owned by William Ritson, a local character whose reputation for telling epic stories spread far beyond Wasdale Head.

The tiny village church, one of the smallest in England, has only three windows, one of which carries the apt words of a psalm, 'I will lift up mine eyes unto the hills'. Buried in the graveyard are several climbers who lost their lives on the mountains – sudden squalls can make conditions on the steep slopes treacherous, even for the most experienced climbers. Rain clouds shed their load more vigorously in these mountains than anywhere else in Britain, bringing a drenching 120in (3000mm) of rain each year.

ICY ORIGINS

It was the scouring force of glaciers that gouged Wast Water's valley out of granite mountains during the Ice Age that ended 10,000 years ago. Cold, clear water from melting ice and from becks tumbling down the fells have filled the hollow to a depth of 258ft (79m), making Wast Water England's deepest lake. So few nutrients have been washed into the lake from the surrounding hills that it is almost devoid of life, and only a small number of fish – trout, char,

minnows and sticklebacks – can survive.

When winter storms sweep along the valley, they transform the lake into a wave-tossed ocean, flinging spray high into the air and draping the dark mountain peaks in a sombre curtain of clouds. In spring a deep rumble occasionally echoes down the valley as the outer layer of the rain-drenched scree slopes avalanches down from the broken crags of Illgill Head into the cold waters of the lake.

CLIMBER'S REWARD *Seen from Great Gable's steep sides, Wast Water lies still under its wall of scree, and sweeping fells cast a shadow over Wasdale Head.*

PIONEER OF ROCK CLIMBING

When Walter Haskett Smith arrived in Wasdale Head in the summer of 1881, he had no plans to climb mountain peaks - indeed, the sport was in its infancy in Britain. Yet this Oxford student's stay at Wasdale Head marked the birth of British rock climbing. With the help of veteran mountaineer F.H. Bowring, Smith tackled the amphitheatre of crags that surrounds Wast Water with an increasing enthusiasm, which he communicated to others through his example and writings.

Over the next few years, Haskett Smith returned to Wasdale Head and made increasingly difficult climbs. Then in 1886 he put British rock climbing firmly on the map, when, wearing his usual nailed boots, he climbed Great Gable to the base of a sheer pillar known as Napes Needle. After inching his way up a crack in the rock, he then, 'feeling as small as a mouse climbing a milestone', scaled the boulder capping the pillar. 'Rather a nervy proceeding', he wrote later - modest words, considering the formidable drop below him.

Encouraged by his daring, climbers who had once confined themselves to gullies and chimneys started to enjoy the challenge of exposed rocks and pinnacles. Fifty years later, at the age of 76, Smith (left) repeated his historic climb before an audience of 300 climbers.

GOAL IN SIGHT *Many climbers have scaled Napes Needle since Haskett Smith's first ascent helped to establish rock climbing as a serious sport.*

Great Glen

AN ARROW-STRAIGHT GLEN THAT MAKES AN ISLAND OF NORTHERN SCOTLAND MARKS AN ANCIENT CRACK IN THE EARTH'S CRUST

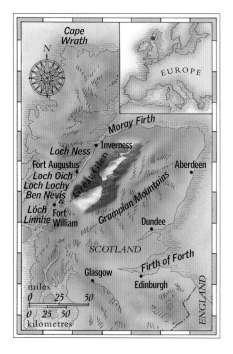

Like a gash made by some gigantic claymore, the Great Glen cuts diagonally across the Scottish Highlands from the Atlantic Ocean to the North Sea. Ribbon-shaped lochs – Ness, Oich and Lochy – fill most of the glen's 55 mile (88km) floor, and together with the canal that links them, they make Scotland north of the glen more or less an island.

Mountains rise abruptly from both sides of the lochs. Woodland on the lower slopes gives way to heather or rough grassland higher up, and on the highest summits only alpine plants such as dwarf willow can survive. Rivers in side glens cascade over waterfalls and through wooded ravines on their way down to the lochs.

The story of the glen goes back more than 350 million years to a time when colossal upheavals in the Earth's crust led to the fracture in the crust known as the Great Glen fault. Movement of rocks along the fault has not finished yet, and minor earthquakes still occur in the area. The worst on record, in 1816, sent slates falling from roofs in Inverness, at the northern end of the glen.

While the glen was being formed the rocks that lay on either side of the fault were crushed, making them easily attacked by rivers and ice. Glaciers filled the glen during the Ice Ages, and rocks caught in the slow-moving ice acted like sandpaper, gouging away the valley sides and floor. The result was the steep hillsides which contribute so much to the glen's grandeur.

CORRIDOR ACROSS SCOTLAND

From earliest times the glen was the only practicable route across this part of Scotland. The English appreciated its strategic importance in the 17th and 18th centuries and built forts to control the turbulent Highland clans – Fort William at the glen's western end, Fort Augustus at the southern end of Loch Ness, and Fort George near Inverness.

In the early 19th century, poverty and emigration were rife in the Highlands and the Caledonian Canal was built in an attempt to encourage trade and boost the economy. It connected the lochs and therefore provided ships with a trade route that avoided the long and dangerous journey round Scotland's north coast. Work on the canal began in 1804 under the

FURRED FISHER *Otters dive into the lochs' chilly waters to catch fish.*

WEATHER'S MOODS *Mist rests lightly on fields and woods (above) near the glen's western end, and the sun breaks through glowering clouds (right) to shine on the loch-filled trough. Loch Oich is in the foreground, with Loch Lochy beyond.*

direction of the engineer Thomas Telford, and it took 18 years to construct the separate lengths of waterway that link the lochs.

Wildlife in the glen is abundant and varied. Wildcats and pine martens are more common than they once were, and red squirrels, which were almost exterminated during the 19th century, now flourish in pine forests. The osprey, rarest and most magnificent of fish-eating birds, is now seen from time to time after a long absence. The lochs are a last stronghold of Scottish otters.

One aspect of the Great Glen's wild-life is the subject of intense speculation. In the 6th century St Columba is said to have confronted a monster in Loch Ness which was terrorising local villagers. Since the 1930s, when the road along the loch's western shore opened, dozens of people claim to have seen 'Nessie'. The loch's mysterious inhabitant has been described, amongst other things, as a plesiosaur preserved from 70 million years ago, a 'kelpie' or water sprite, a sea serpent, a Viking ship and oil drums. But so far Nessie has been shy of investigators, who have used hot-air balloons, searchlights, and even submarines and a sonar scan in their search for life in the loch's deep waters.

Old Man of Storr

A TAPERING PILLAR OF ROCK RISES FROM A BED OF JAGGED PINNACLES TO PIERCE THE HEBRIDEAN SKYLINE

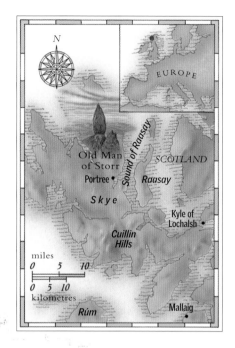

Stooping slightly in the lee of a shattered inland cliff, the Old Man of Storr stands conspicuous above the coast of Scotland's island of Skye. The 160ft (49m) basalt pillar, balanced on its stone pedestal, looks out to sea like a lonely sentinel on guard duty.

A chaotic jumble of pinnacles, broken rock and screes litters the hillside around the pillar, and is the result of massive landslips. A thick layer of basalt – the legacy of volcanic upheavals 60 million years ago – overlie earlier, more crumbly rock. Tilting and faulting of the rocks left the land very unstable, and blocks of

SEA VIEW *Flanked by splintered rocks, the Old Man of Storr dominates the view over the sea to Raasay.*

basalt have slumped towards the sea and been weathered into the rugged landscape.

The Old Man stands out so prominently that it has served as a landmark for shipping for centuries. Its sheer sides and the overhangs at its base have long presented climbers with a daunting challenge, and it was not until 1955 that the pillar was conquered.

From this rocky hillside, the sea on a still day looks mirror-calm, reflecting

a scintillating pale blue sky. But within hours the sky can blacken with glowering clouds. Then the landscape closes in, and a dense drizzle turns the rocks to glistening black.

The coastline of this part of Skye wears a long mantle of history. Fossils litter the shore below the Old Man, and finds have included the 10ft (3m) long fossilised remains of an ichthyosaurus – a dolphin-like dinosaur from some 200 million years ago. Anglo-Saxon silver coins found nearby, along with coins from the central Asian city of Samarkand, were in a hoard that may have been hidden by invading Vikings.

A FUGITIVE PASSES BY

A cave on the shore to the south of the Old Man of Storr is named after Prince Charles – the Bonnie Prince Charlie who played such a poignant part in Scottish history. In 1745 Prince Charles Edward Stuart set out to win the British throne for his father, the son of the deposed James II of England (James VII of Scotland). After defeat at the Battle of Culloden Moor in April 1746, the prince was pursued through the Highlands and islands, and passed near the Old Man on his travels across Skye. Worn down by life on the run, he left Scotland in September 1746, and remained in exile until his death in Rome in 1788.

Lake Inari

ACCORDING TO OLD LAPLAND SONGS, THIS DEEP BLUE LAKE WITH 3000 FORESTED ISLANDS IS 'AS DEEP AS IT IS LONG'

Carved out by glaciers more than 10,000 years ago, the lake is roughly 50 miles (80km) long and 500sq miles (1300km²) in extent. It looks very deep because its sides are steep, plunging straight down 318ft (97m) to the bottom. Local songs have described it as being 'as deep as it is long'.

Because the Arctic climate of the region is tempered by a warm current, the North Atlantic Drift (which extends from the Gulf Stream), the Inari summer is more like those in places 600 miles (1000km) farther south. Orange-coloured cloud-berries grow in profusion, providing Laplanders with jam and Lakka liqueur, and the lake abounds with fish – minnows, trout, whitefish, grayling, char and perch. Migrant birds such as Arctic terns join the ducks, divers and waders that regularly enjoy the lake's rich pickings. Visiting swifts feast on midsummer clouds of mosquitoes.

FEEDING TIME *Ground-nesting snowy owls breed on the Inari fells in summer, if lemmings, their main diet, are plentiful.*

Ancient Lapps left offerings to their gods on the small island of Ukko, north of Inari port. Today they might gaze in disbelief on the modern port, but would surely recognise the magical stillness that descends as the first snows whiten the islands, and ice begins to still the waters – as it will for nearly half a year.

Maps of Finnish Lapland are a surprise. For an area lying well within the Arctic Circle, they reveal a land not of ice and tundra but of innumerable lakes, rivers and streams linked by forests, bogs and swamps. And the largest, bluest area in this vivid mosaic of blues and greens is Lake Inari, its shores deeply jagged with hundreds of inlets, and its waters studded with 3000 or more tree-covered islands, some little more than rocks.

Streams cascade down the slopes of the tussocky fells lying to the south and west of the lake, and into the rivers that feed Lake Inari with clear, cold water. To the east and north, a wilderness of pine and birch forest and swamp is the home of elks, lynxes and wolverines.

ICY IMAGES *Winter begins to wrap Lake Inari in its grip (right), and the dark forested islands merge with their reflections in the bleak, blue-grey waters. The winter sun (overleaf) casts a weird pale glow above Ukko Island.*

Sognefjord

A FLAME-BLUE TONGUE OF WATER SEARS THROUGH TOWERING MOUNTAINS DEEP INTO THE HEART OF NORWAY

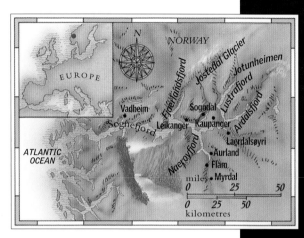

Even hardened travellers lapse into spellbound silence as ocean-going cruise liners, dwarfed by their surroundings to seem like model toys, glide into Sognefjord. The mountains rise almost vertically from the water's edge – sheer walls of strong granitic rock some 3000ft (900m) high in places. The thin ribbons of water cascading down them are meltwater from the snows overhead. Pine trees cling to the less precipitous slopes, wherever their roots can find purchase in rock fissures and the banks of loose rubble that spill down.

TRANQUIL WATERS

In sudden, incongruous contrast, tiny farms can be seen nestling here and there on the narrow, fertile ledges bordering the fjord. Farm buildings with whitewashed clapboard walls and red or grey painted corrugated-iron roofs lie amid quilts of neatly ordered fields – their trimness underlining the outlandish splendour of their surroundings. With little tide to speak of, Sognefjord has a lake-like tranquillity. Its curving route shelters it from the violence of the Atlantic, and sometimes only the tang of salt on the fresh, pure air signals that this is indeed a fjord – an arm of the sea.

Sognefjord is just one among some 200 major fjords that make the west coast of Norway look like the leading edge of a wind-torn flag. Just over 3 miles (5km) across at its widest point, the fjord is the longest and deepest in Norway, extending inland for 115 miles (184km). With water about 4000ft (1200m) deep, the valley, measured above and below water, is 7000ft (2100m) deep – nearly 2000ft (600m) deeper than the USA's Grand Canyon.

Glaciers shaped this fjord landscape. The granite mountains are perhaps 2000 million years old. Rivers flowing through their folds around 50 million years ago probably began to carve out valleys, and when the ice cap rolled in during a succession of Ice Ages, glaciers spilled down the same paths, grinding away the valley floors. As the glaciers withdrew when the last Ice Age ended about 10,000 years ago, sea water moved in to drown the valleys.

Valleys ground out by glaciers tend to be U-shaped, with steep walls, and are usually deeper in the middle of their path than at the mouth. This is so in Sognefjord; the water drops from 560ft (170m) deep at the mouth to more than seven times deeper about 30 miles (50km) inland, near Vadheim.

The last remnant of the Norwegian ice cap is at the Jostedal Glacier,

much of the day, and on cloudy days fog rolling in from the sea brings an enveloping chill. And sea mists and drizzle turn pastures into quagmires haunted by the ghostly silhouettes of disconsolate sheep, goats and cattle.

The rugged landscape has always made overland journeys across the region difficult at the best of times, and before modern roads were built in this century, boats were the main transport.

The Viking spirit was forged in such conditions, and the people of these valleys still have a reputation for being independent of mind.

Today, farmers and townsfolk can add to their incomes by catering for the thousands of summer visitors who come to enjoy the breathtaking grandeur of the landscape, culminating in the alpine splendours of Jotunheimen National Park where the Vettis Falls tumble 900ft (275m) into Ardalsfjord, the easternmost branch of Sognefjord.

VIKING HELMET

Viking longships once sheltered in Sognefjord. Viking raiders from Norway, Denmark and Sweden terrorised Europe's coasts during the 9th–11th centuries. The Vikings did not, as is often believed, wear horned helmets. Their helmets were similar in style to the one shown above, but not normally as ornate. This 7th-century Vendel helmet is in the Museum of National Antiquities in Stockholm, Sweden.

which straddles the mountains north-east of Sognefjord. Jostedal drains into Fjaerlandsfjord, which branches off Sognefjord, and also into Gaupnefjord off Lustrafjord. Mainland Europe's largest glacier, it is up to 1968ft (600m) thick and covers 188sq miles (487km²).

COOLING EFFECT

Glacier water helps to keep the water temperature of Sognefjord bracing, even in summer. Norway is in the same latitudes as Alaska and eastern Siberia, and the fjord is only 500 miles (800km) south of the Arctic Circle. But the North Atlantic Drift extends from the Gulf Stream to bring some warmth from the Caribbean to the shoreline, making the

BLUE RHAPSODY *Sognefjord winds its way majestically between blue-shadowed cliffs of sheer granite, with the blue of the sky reflected in its deep blue water.*

climate temperate enough for apple growing around Leikanger.

Small towns such as Sogndal and Laerdalsøyri have grown up on the few areas of flat land at the water's edge created by the deltas of incoming rivers. Aurland has even become an industrial centre, the site of a large hydroelectric power station and an aluminium smelting plant. Yet this is not an easy landscape to live in. On sunny days the steep valley walls cast long shadows for

Pico de Teide

TOWERING ABOVE THE ISLAND OF TENERIFE, THE IMPRESSIVE VOLCANIC MOUNTAIN CASTS THE LONGEST SHADOW IN THE WORLD

Viewed from the sea, Pico de Teide is clothed in striking colours. The white of its snow-capped peak gives way to the deep purple of its volcanic sides, and below this the rich green of its trees and farmlands is fringed with the dark blue of the ocean.

Guide books often describe Tenerife, which is the largest of the Canary Islands and about half the size of the Netherlands, as a mountainous and

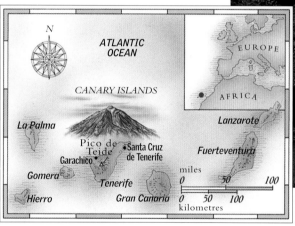

PEAK OF HELL *Contorted rocks are scattered over the floor of an older volcanic crater surrounding the snow-capped volcano Pico de Teide.*

triangular-shaped island crowned by the peak of Teide. But in fact the whole of the island is really an extension of this imposing mountain. Below its 12,198ft (3718m) summit, the highest in Spanish territory, the pine-covered slopes of its volcanic foothills reach down to the valleys of the north and the beaches of the south.

Pico de Teide is more than a glorious backdrop to Tenerife's resorts – it is the pinnacle of an extraordinary landscape formed by a series of violent volcanic eruptions. The cone-shaped peak sits in the crater of an older volcano 6500ft (2000m) above sea level – a vast natural amphitheatre of sand and pumice. The old crater, rimmed by a 46 mile (74km)

long wall, is a battlefield of tortured rocks – orange, purple, crimson, grey, ochre – torn out of the depths of the mountains. It is riven with channels and ravines (*cañadas*) gouged out by molten lava. The whole area is now the National Park of Las Cañadas del Teide.

The peak itself is battle-scarred, too. Its sheer and craggy sides show deep, dark gashes where lava has poured down from a small crater at the top. Sulphurous gases still steam out of this hole, 100ft (30m) deep, and the mountain has continued to spew out lava for centuries. In 1705 it buried much of the harbour town of Garachico. During the most recent eruption in 1909, a 3 mile (5km) long

SKY DIVER
Peregrine falcons hunt along the rocky cliffs of the Cañadas del Teide park. They plummet on small birds in a 100mph (160km/h) 'stoop', but prey is scarce.

sky as the rising sun spotlights its eastern slopes, while the rest of the island far below is drowned in a rose-tinged sea of clouds. Perhaps Teide's most startling aspect is the shadow it casts early on a clear, sunny morning – a giant pyramid darkening the water for some 124 miles (200km) out to sea, the world's longest shadow. At sunset, the dark cone is a triangle framed in crimson, the peak once more a fiery god.

But Pico de Teide also plays a vital role in Tenerife's ecology. Plants flourish in the shade and shelter of its slopes, even on the dry laval plains of the crater, where bees buzz among the scented pink and white brooms, and violets and daisies nestle beneath.

On the slopes below the park, pine trees capture moisture from low clouds on their leaves, and it drips down to the porous rock. Lower still, farmers channel this precious water to irrigate their *fincas* (walled plots) where, shielded from the north-east trade winds, vines, tomatoes, bananas and potatoes ripen in the sun. On the valley floor to the north, ancient dragon trees, orange and almond trees, laurels, myrtles, roses, mimosa and bougainvillea all thrive in a climate often described as perpetual spring.

Because of Teide's vast presence, the water on the leeward side – the island's southern and eastern shores – remains relatively calm. This allows a build-up of nutrients, so these waters have become a resting and feeding area for whales and dolphins, particularly pilot whales, now a tourist attraction.

Victorian tourists drawn to the island found crossing the crater extremely hazardous. In the words of Olivia Stone, an English travel writer who braved the 'lumps of lava' in 1883: 'There is not a square inch of smooth surface; it is one mass of tiny pinnacles; so boots and gloves are almost cut to pieces.' The peak itself was even harder going: 'We ... plunged vigorously and wildly up the loose and uncertain soil for a few yards, and then sank panting on its side until ready for a fresh start.' All this was done by moonlight, because Mrs Stone and her husband wanted to reach the top in time to watch the dawn break.

Visitors today have an easier time. The Pico de Teide can be approached by road from all sides of the island, and the park has a network of walkways leading to places such as the Cuevo del Hielo, an icy cavern at 10,990ft (3350m), where the snow never melts. There is also a cable car that whisks tourists to La Rambleta, only a half-hour climb from the summit.

There you can gaze into the steaming, whitened crater, then look beyond to the other islands. Those who arrive at dawn can experience fully what Olivia Stone called 'one of Nature's sublimest efforts' – sunrise on Pico de Teide.

'ONE OF NATURE'S SUBLIMEST EFFORTS' – THE SUN RISING ON PICO DE TEIDE

lava stream flowed down the north-west slopes. In winter, snow and ice fill the ravines, harsh winds buffet the loose covering of shale, and temperatures drop below freezing.

The original inhabitants of Tenerife, a fair-haired people known as the Guanches, christened it Peak of Hell translated as Pico de Teide by their 15th-century Spanish conquerors. The Guanches feared the peak as the residence of their God of Hell, Guayota. Other visitors have likened it to a benign padre who keeps an eternal watch on his seven daughters – Tenerife and the other main islands of the Canaries – La Palma, Hierro, Gomera, Gran Canaria, Fuerteventura and Lanzarote.

At dawn, Teide enters the realms of enchantment – dark against a lightening

SHADOW MOUNTAIN *Sunrise gilds the rocks of Las Cañadas del Teide park, casting a huge shadow of the triangular peak of the volcano over land and sea.*

PATTERNS OF TOIL AND HUSBANDRY

The land bears the marks of the close bond between human life and fertile soil

Modern human existence would be unthinkable without the work of countless generations of farmers. Settled farming and an assured food supply were the foundation blocks of the first civilisations: food surpluses led to trade, to wealth, to cities and leisure, and then matters beyond the demands of survival could be contemplated. But the relationship between land and agriculture is a delicate one, and the forces of Nature – unpredictable allies of Man at the best of times – are quick to punish those who fail to show suitable respect or understanding.

DUST BOWL
Drought and wind stripped the soil from farm land in the USA in the 1930s, producing the Dust Bowl.

BANDS OF TULIPS
Grown commercially in Holland for centuries, tulips (above) are now flown around the world.

STAR-SHAPED FARMING
Pea plants and wheat (above) grow the black soil of Washington State, USA, where striking field patterns follow the land contours.

FERTILE CIRCLE
Modern technology brings life to the arid lands of Egypt (left). This irrigation system waters crops through a vast arm rotating on wheeled supports.

FRAGRANT ROWS
Ordered ranks of lavender (left) fill French fields with radiant colour and heady fragrance. Essential oils are extracted from the plants to make perfume.

GREEN VALLEY
A river valley in Peru (right) demonstrates the essential role of water. Fertile fields line the valley floor, but the land beyond the reach of irrigation is barren.

WATER MACHINE
On the plains of China, ingenious implements (above) are used to move water.

RICE TERRACES
Intricate bands of flooded rice paddies (above) hug the contours of hills in Guangxi Province, southern China.

Ordesa

CHAMOIS AND WILD GOATS ROAM NARROW ROCK LEDGES ABOVE WOODED RIVER VALLEYS IN THE HEART OF THE PYRENEES

Beech, larch and towering conifers overhang the River Arazas as it hurries down steps and waterfalls through Ordesa Canyon. Above this looms a monumental backdrop of uncompromising ruggedness – walls of fluted limestone rising sheer from the valley for heights of more than 2000ft (600m). Ordesa Canyon stretches for about 10 miles (16km) through the Arazas valley. Upriver, the woodland gives way to boulder-strewn pastures, where the breeze ruffles grass dotted in summertime with edelweiss, gentians, anemones and orchids.

The Arazas valley is one of four river valleys in the Ordesa and Monte Perdido National Park, which covers 60sq miles (156km²) in the heart of the Pyrenees – the wild and dramatic mountain chain on the borders of Spain and France. Monte Perdido, 11,007ft (3355m), is the third highest Pyrenean peak and Europe's highest limestone mountain. All four valleys – the Arazas,

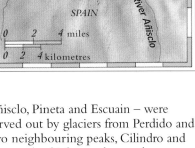

Añisclo, Pineta and Escuain – were carved out by glaciers from Perdido and two neighbouring peaks, Cilindro and Ramond, which together are known as the Three Sisters. At the head of the

GOLDEN GLOW *Like a mass of raw gold burnished by the rays of the sinking sun, massive limestone cliffs tower above the River Arazas valley in the Pyrenees.*

Arazas valley is the spectacular Circo de Soaso, with the Cascada de Cola de Caballo (Horse's Tail Waterfall) spilling down its walls. Circo de Soaso is a huge natural amphitheatre – a cirque ground out by a glacier on the slopes of Perdido more than 15,000 years ago. It is the high point of a popular seven-hour trek. More challenging trails lead up the valley walls into even wilder places, and trekkers can negotiate the more precipitous parts by means of *clavijas* – iron pegs driven into the rock.

Aeons of weathering have etched out the narrow limestone ledges known as *fajas* that line the crests of some cliffs. The Faja de las Flores stretches for nearly 2 miles (3km) at a dizzying height of 7875ft (2400m) alongside the Arazas. Those who venture onto the *fajas* can enjoy an exhilarating panorama of the valleys, which trail like green streamers through the bleached, rocky landscape of the park.

WILDLIFE REFUGE

Many nimble chamois, known here as izards, can be seen on the *fajas*, sometimes together with darker-hued and much rarer ibex (mountain goats), the males with 3ft (1m) long backward-curving horns. Ordesa is the last refuge of the

Pyrenean ibex, which is on the verge of extinction. It is also a refuge for colonies of marmots, which burrow into the stony soil, and for foxes, otters, wild boar and brown bears.

Unusual rock climbers are the sparrow-sized wallcreepers, which busily hunt spiders and insects on the sheer valley walls. Their drab grey plumage makes the birds easy to miss as they creep up the rock face, but they can be spotted by the flashing of bright scarlet wing feathers as they use their wings as climbing aids.

Golden eagles may be seen soaring above the crags, occasionally joined by the larger and rarer bearded vulture, or lammergeier, with a wingspan of 8ft (2.5m) or more.

Coto Doñana

AN ENDLESS SILENT
MARSH IN SOUTHERN
SPAIN, AND THE FOREST
AROUND IT, ABOUNDS
WITH VARIED WILDLIFE

Marshes criss-crossed by countless river channels, scrubland dense with rockroses, and sand dunes of glistening white lie side by side in a remarkably varied tract of wilderness in southern Spain. Together with pine woods, lakes and cork oak groves they make up the Coto Doñana National Park, an area of more than 190sq miles (500km²) at the mouth of the Guadalquivir River.

Coto Doñana is one of Europe's most important wildlife havens. It is the home of rare and endangered species such as the Spanish imperial eagle and the lynx, and the temporary home of many migratory birds, especially wildfowl from Scandinavia and Russia.

PINE WOOD *Dukes and kings once hunted among Coto Doñana's stone pines. Now birds nest in peace amid their broad, bushy, umbrella-like crowns.*

Doñana begins where the Atlantic Ocean laps a beach of golden sands. Behind the beach rise dunes of soft white sand, pitted with depressions called *corrales* that fill with water in spring. They look for all the world like Saharan oases, except that pine trees have taken the place of waving palms.

Beyond the dunes is Coto Doñana proper – woods, lakes and scrubland that was once the hunting ground of the dukes of Medina Sidonia and of Spanish kings. The name Doñana comes from Doña Ana, the wife of the seventh duke. This duke made a notable, though reluctant, contribution to history as the commander of the Spanish Armada, a task he had tried to avoid by telling his king that he suffered from seasickness.

The painter Francisco Goya also visited Doñana as the guest of his patron, and perhaps lover, the Duchess of Alba, who owned the estate at the end of the 18th century. The duchess was the subject of two of Goya's finest portraits, and may also have been the model for his painting *The Naked Maja*.

In Doñana's stone-pine woodlands, imperial eagles nest in the trees' strong branches. Each pair of imperial eagles needs its own hunting territory of about 19sq miles (50km²). There is an old story that it fills other birds with such terror that they commit suicide – a flamingo seeing an eagle approaching becomes so panic-stricken that it folds its wings and plunges to its death.

Among the pine woods are lakes of several colours. Charco del Toro has black water, and the waters of Santa Olalla are emerald green. Shellfish that live there are food for the lordly flamingos, and contain a substance that gives the birds' plumage its pink colour.

HUNTER *King of predators, the lynx tackles not only rabbits and small mammals, but also deer and birds in flight.*

SAHARAN SCENE *White sands corrugated by Atlantic winds stretch between the oasis-like corrales – the shallow hollows in Doñana's dunes where pine trees grow.*

In Coto Doñana's scrubland, a carpet of yellow-flowered rockroses gives way in places to dense jungles of heather and brambles. Colonies of spoonbills, herons and storks nest in groves of cork oaks, and lynxes take refuge in the hollow boles of the older trees.

Beyond the woods and scrubland lie Las Marismas, 'the marshes', a seemingly endless swamp where birds congregate in vast numbers. The entire area is flooded from autumn to early summer, forming one of Europe's largest lakes. The marsh is a stopover for more than 200 species of bird which pass over the nearby Strait of Gibraltar while migrating between Africa and northern Europe. This narrow stretch of water is particularly useful to heavy birds such as storks. Their soaring flight needs the rising currents of warm air that occur on land.

Then, under the fierce summer sun, the wetlands dry out until large tracts become concrete-hard mud. Migrant birds move on, and vultures feed on animals that have died of thirst.

The wildlife of Coto Doñana is under threat. The waters of the marsh are being siphoned off for irrigation and industry, and they could dry up. Migrant birds filling the sky over endless marshes may well become a thing of the past.

QUEENS OF THE SKY *(overleaf) On slow-beating wings, a flock of flamingos passes over Coto Doñana's marshlands.*

The Spanish Badlands

IN THE ROCKY, DESERT LANDSCAPE OF SOUTHERN SPAIN, PRICKLY PEAR SURVIVES WHERE OAKS AND CEDARS ONCE FLOURISHED

Only half an hour's drive from the nightclubs and beaches of the Mediterranean town of Almeria lies a desolate landscape of bare, wild hills fissured by massive clefts and ravines. These are the Spanish Badlands – so called by visitors because they resemble the Badlands of the North American West.

Few travellers linger here, but behind the small towns of Tabernas and Nijar, rough tracks lead into the Badlands – the ravaged uplands and arid gullies of Almeria province. One of Spain's most mountainous provinces, it is bordered on the west by the mighty Sierra Nevada and encompasses the smaller ranges of Sierra de los Filabres and Sierra Alhamilla. It is also the driest part of Spain, with the deserts of Campo de Tabernas and Campo de Nijar lying on either side of the 4215ft (1285m) spine of the Alhamillas.

Rainfall here is irregular because the Sierra Nevada in the west traps clouds coming in from the Atlantic. The Almeria deserts have only 20 or so rainy days a year – the annual rainfall is about 4½in (110mm). When the rain does come, it is usually a sudden downpour that fills rock gullies in minutes. Flash floods follow, gouging away roads, uprooting telegraph poles and cutting off remoter villages for days or weeks.

ROUGH COUNTRY *A forbidding land of barren hills and steep gullies, the Spanish Badlands have been the location for filming dozens of Westerns.*

The Spanish Badlands are one of the Mediterranean's most extreme examples of soil erosion. The sudden winter rains tear away the topsoil, and rock falls and landslips gouge out crevasses in the loose clay and shale. Man has also played a part by felling trees and allowing livestock to overgraze the fragile hills. The end result is gully erosion – networks of steep-sided channels known as *ramblas* in Spanish. Still further damage is done by rainwater collecting under the ground and forming pipes that collapse after a time, beginning the process of erosion all over again as new gullies start to form. Eventually the land becomes completely useless for agriculture.

Yet just 3000 years ago this desert was pleasantly wooded. All along the Mediterranean, from Portugal to Turkey, there were evergreen oaks with cypress and cedar growing on sandy soils, and conifers reaching up the hillsides. Herds of deer roamed wild, and even the long-vanished Mediterranean lion was found here.

Until about 1000 BC, human activities had little impact on the land. But as settlements grew, large areas of the woodland were cleared for crop-growing, firewood and building materials, and herds of goats devoured the saplings and prevented tree regeneration. Deprived of its original cover, the topsoil was washed away by rain, and the scars of erosion started to show.

As the landscape changed, *maquis*, or scrub, plants took over – the thorny bushes, stunted oaks, myrtles and low shrubs that still cover many parts. Where erosion was very bad, *maquis* gave way to semi-desert and then to rocky wastes such as the Badlands.

With summer temperatures as high as 43°C (110°F), conditions for Badland plants and animals are extremely harsh. Even so, yellow broom and pink oleander grow in the Campo de Tabernas, where gully beds are left damp after the occasional winter rains, and drought-loving prickly pear and palmetto grow in the Campo de Nijar.

One of the province's most popular tourist sites is 'Mini-Hollywood' – just off the main road outside Tabernas. Since it was built for Clint Eastwood's film *A Fistful of Dollars* in 1964, more than 100 'spaghetti' Westerns have been shot in its faded saloons and dusty streets. TV commercials or gunfights staged for tourists are still sometimes played out against the dramatic backdrop of the Badland gullies and cliffs.

THE BARRENNESS OF THE BADLANDS HAS BEEN A BOON TO FILM-MAKERS

Verdon Gorge

THE LARGEST CHASM IN EUROPE SLICES THROUGH THE SUN-BLEACHED LIMESTONE COUNTRYSIDE OF PROVENCE

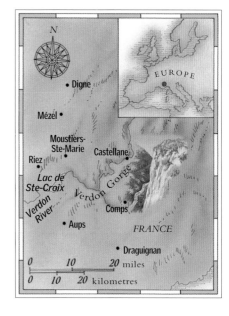

Walls of rock twice as high as the Eiffel Tower hem in the Verdon River as it winds thin and snake-like along the bottom of its precipitous gorge in southern France. The gorge is some 12 miles (20km) long and up to 2300ft (700m) deep – making it the largest chasm in Europe. At its broadest it is more than a mile (1.6km) wide at the top, yet at the bottom the rock walls

DEEP RIVER *Far below, the Verdon River glistens as it snakes its way along its forested course. Sometimes the water glows a shimmering green.*

are sometimes no farther apart than the walls of an average living room.

The Verdon is fed by melting snow from the Alps, and the gorge was formed as the swiftly flowing water gradually etched an ever deeper channel in the limestone plateau of Haute Provence. Rain falling on the plateau sinks underground, so there are no streams to erode and flatten the rock wall along the gorge. In spring, the country around is pink with almond blossom; in summer it glows deep mauve from the fields of lavender, grown for the Grasse perfume factories.

No one had made a complete descent of the Verdon Gorge until 1905 when Edouard Martel, pioneer of cave exploration in France, led an expedition through it. The journey took three-and-a-half days, and all but one of the party's collapsible canvas boats foundered on the rocks. The gorge seemed to Martel to be 'the most awe-inspiring sight in the whole of France' – but impossible for tourists to visit.

Fortunately, he was wrong. Today, two tourist roads skirt the edges of the gorge, complete with viewing points from which visitors can look dizzily down at the curious rock shapes and the sparkling waters far below.

FRENCH LAVENDER *In late spring and summer, the evergreen lavender plants put out fragrant flowers of deep mauve.*

Mer de Glace

A RESTLESS SEA OF ICE GRINDS DOWN AN ALPINE VALLEY BELOW THE SUMMIT OF MONT BLANC, THE HIGHEST PEAK IN THE ALPS

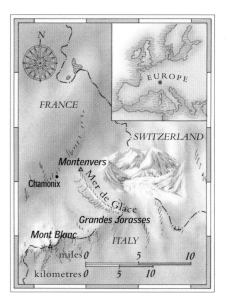

Imagine a huge, wind-whipped river roaring down a rugged, winding Alpine valley, huge waves rearing, deep troughs appearing. Suppose that, in an instant, it was frozen into a solid mass at the height of its violent movement. Then, in your mind's eye, you would see the Mer de Glace – the largest glacier of the Mont Blanc range, its jagged peaks and icy depths a source of dreadful fascination and sublime inspiration over the past 250 years.

This glacier and one of its earliest-known English admirers, William Windham, began the fashion for mountaineering in Europe. Windham came from Felbrigg in Norfolk, and was one of a colony of English people living in Geneva, Switzerland, during the 1740s. He first saw the Mer de Glace in 1741.

Windham made the arduous journey from Geneva to the Chamonix Valley in France with a party of other young Englishmen and their tutors. They camped in the Chamonix' meadows before setting out for Mont Blanc. The young men risked broken limbs, snow-blindness and frostbite.

But the sublime beauty of the area and the sharp contrast between Mont Blanc's white, soaring peak and the awe-inspiring ruggedness of the Mer de Glace winding down its slopes justified

SEA OF ICE *The Mer de Glace thrusts through an Alpine valley in the Mont Blanc massif. In the background stands Grandes Jorasses, at 13,806ft (4208m).*

the enormous effort and discomfort.

After climbing for four-and-a-half hours to the spot where the Hotel Montenvers now stands, they stepped onto the glacier and into history, for Windham's description gave rise to the glacier's popular name – Mer de Glace (Sea of Ice). 'The Descriptions which Travellers give of the Seas of Greenland seem to come nearest to it,' he wrote.

Today, visitors can enjoy the rugged grandeur of the glacier with far less effort and in greater comfort. From Chamonix a rack-and-pinion railway clanks its way up through spruce and pine forests to the hotel complex on the very edge of the Mer de Glace.

ADVANCE AND RETREAT

A glacier moves imperceptibly but constantly – as is dramatically shown when it ejects at its snout the remains of a victim who fell into a crevasse many years before and much farther back.

The ice that is lost by melting when the glacier reaches the lower levels is generally replaced by the snow that accumulates at higher levels. But measurements taken over the last century have revealed that some glaciers are maintaining their lengths and others are either increasing or diminishing. The Mer de Glace, now about 4.4 miles (7km) long, is shorter and thinner than it was in the 1820s, during the cooler temperatures of the Little Ice Age. It was probably at its longest in the mid 17th century. The retreat of the ice

> JAGGED PEAKS AND ICY DEPTHS ... A SOURCE OF DREADFUL FASCINATION

is evident from the isolated mountain huts that stand on steep slopes or are reached by ladders – once they were easily accessible from the icy surface.

The writings of Windham and others of his party aroused the curiosity of other adventurers. At that time, few mountain peaks had been climbed. It was a dangerous

undertaking, for often men venturing into the mountains failed to return. But in 1760 Horace Bénédict de Saussure, a Professor of Natural Philosophy in Geneva, was so moved by the sight of Mont Blanc towering above the Mer de Glace that he offered a cash prize to the first man to reach the 15,770ft (4807m) summit of the highest mountain in the Alps.

But 26 years passed before the prize was won. Dr Michel Gabriel Paccard, a doctor in Chamonix, and Jacques Balmat, a guide and crystal hunter, together reached Mont Blanc's summit on August 8, 1786, after a 14-hour climb. Saussure awarded the prize to Jacques Balmat because he thought that Dr Paccard, who was a 'gentleman amateur', would not accept it.

The drama and magnificence of Mont Blanc and the Mer de Glace attracted many writers, among them Lord Byron, Percy Bysshe Shelley and Mary Shelley. Their reactions to the wild beauty of the area appear in their writings, perhaps most famously in Mary Shelley's story of Frankenstein – the first science-fiction novel.

REFUGE OF A MONSTER

Deeply affected by the frozen violence of the Mer de Glace, Mary Shelley chose it as the dramatic setting for Dr Frankenstein's meeting with his monster in her novel *Frankenstein*. 'Dreary glaciers are my refuge,' the unhappy monster tells him, 'these bleak skies ... are kinder to me than your fellow beings.' The doctor, when he created the monster, had intended it to be beautiful, and had fled in horror when the hideous creature came to life and sought him as he lay in bed. Their next meeting was some two years later, after murder and tragedy.

The story came to 19-year-old Mary Shelley in a dream, after an evening with the poets Percy Bysshe Shelley and Lord Byron. It was published anonymously in 1818 and was a best-seller.

MONSTER AND MAKER *Dr Victor Frankenstein recoils in horror at the approach of the monster he has made.*

DEFYING GRAVITY
Agile Alpine chamois leap with ease among craggy outcrops and narrow ledges. Even hours-old kids leap with their mothers.

Eisriesenwelt

CAVES RESPLENDENT
WITH GLISTENING ICE
MAKE UP A FROZEN
WONDERLAND HIGH IN
THE AUSTRIAN ALPS

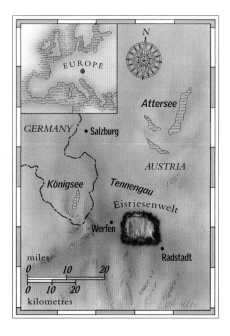

SHEER WONDER *Deep in the Eisriesenwelt a solid mass of ice (above) 'pours' over a ledge. The ice sculpture (right) is the result of water dripping from the cave roof onto an ice wall.*

Frozen cascades hung with giant icicles stand in immobilised majesty deep in an Alpine mountainside. Eisriesenwelt – the World of the Ice Giants – is thought to be the largest ice cave system in Europe, and its maze of galleries and cathedral-like halls extends more than 26 miles (42km) into the Tennen massif, south of the Austrian city of Salzburg.

The caves' gaping entrance leads to a 100ft (30m) high wall of ice, at the top of which is a labyrinth of caverns and passageways. Here the soft yellow beams of lamps and the glare of the guide's flares pick out curtains and statuesque columns of ice, and illuminate the hoar frost that glitters on the cave walls. Fairy-tale ice formations have earned names such as 'ice organ' and 'ice chapel', and deep in the mountain frozen curtains drape the 'ice door'. In places, icy draughts whistle along narrow passageways

as air moves between cave entrances higher up the mountain.

The 'ice giants' are the result of water seeping into limestone caves that formed well over 2 million years ago. At this altitude Eisriesenwelt lies more than 5000ft (1500m) above sea level – the winter temperature inside the caves is very low. Spring meltwater and rain that seeps and drips into the caves freezes instantly into spectacular ice formations, instead of forming the stalactites and stalagmites usually found in limestone caves.

ICE GIANTS DISCOVERED

The caves were first investigated in 1879 by the explorer Anton von Posselt-Czorich. After penetrating about 650ft (200m) into the mountain, he found the wall of ice and proceeded no further. It was more than 30 years before the caves were entered again, this time by Alexander von Mörk, an

accomplished explorer of caves who led expeditions in 1912 and 1913. He and his party cut steps into the ice wall, and beyond it discovered the awesome world that von Mörk named Eisriesenwelt.

After World War I, exploration began again – this time without von Mörk, who had been killed in action. A vast cavern was named Alexander von Mörk's Cathedral as a memorial to his work in bringing the caves to the world's attention, and an urn containing von Mörk's ashes stands in the cavern.

The Matterhorn

THIS STARK, FORBIDDING PYRAMID OF ROCK WAS
CARVED AND CHISELLED BY ICE AGE GLACIERS AND
ETCHED BY THE ELEMENTS

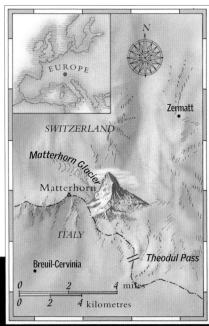

Towering in magnificent isolation above its Alpine surroundings, the Matterhorn is celebrated for its horn – a slightly bent pyramidal peak. It straddles the Swiss–Italian frontier, and in English and German is known as the Matterhorn, in Italian as Monte Cervino and in French as Mont Cervin.

The mountain, 14,688ft (4477m) high, is a spectacular remnant of rock slab thrust up by earth movements 50 million years ago when the African and European continents collided. It owes the shape of its peak to Ice Age glaciers that ground out cirques

(circular hollows) around it. Between the Matterhorn and the Italian peak of Monte Rosa, 15,203ft (4634m), lies the Theodul Pass, 10,882ft (3317m), from where Servius Galba, Julius Caesar's consul, saw the Matterhorn in AD 55. This may account for the French name Servin (eventually changed to Cervin).

It was from the Theodul Pass in 1789 that the Swiss physicist and geologist, Horace Bénédict de Saussure, who had earlier scaled Mont Blanc, contemplated climbing the Matterhorn. But he felt that: 'Its precipitous sides, which give no hold to the very snows, are such as to afford no means of access.'

An English wood engraver, Edward Whymper, was to prove him wrong. He made seven unsuccessful attempts to climb the Matterhorn from the Italian

BROODING SUMMIT *The raw, hypnotic beauty of the Matterhorn's famous peak, looming above the surrounding Alps, has challenged innumerable mountaineers.*

side between 1861 and 1863, but in 1865, at the age of 25, he decided to try from the Swiss side. Whymper asked the well-known Italian guide Jean-Antoine Carrel to go with him, but Carrel had already been engaged by the Italian Alpine Club, also preparing for an assault on the Matterhorn.

THE RACE TO THE SUMMIT

Whymper moved fast. With 18-year-old Lord Francis Douglas he enlisted the aid of Peter Taugwalder, a renowned Zermatt guide who thought that the fore-shortened view of the Matterhorn ridge from the Swiss side made it look steeper than it is. Others in the party were Taugwalder's son Peter, aged 22, Michael Croz, 35, a guide from Chamonix, the Reverend Charles Hudson, 37, and 19-year-old Robert Hadow.

The party set off from Zermatt at 5.30am on July 13. The going was good and at 11,000ft (3350m) they made camp. Next day they reached the summit at 1.40pm after a relatively straight-forward climb. From here they were able to see their Italian rivals still about 1000ft (300m) below. Realising they had been beaten, the Italians abandoned the climb. Whymper and his companions stayed for an hour at the summit.

In *Scrambles amongst the Alps*, written in 1871, Whymper described the view: 'The atmosphere was perfectly still, and free from all clouds or vapours. Mountains fifty – nay, a hundred – miles off, looked sharp and near. All their details – ridge and crag, snow and glacier – stood out with faultless definition.'

The descent was slow and tricky, and as the party began to negotiate a particularly difficult section, tragedy struck. Hadow slipped and fell against Croz, and the two men began to slide downwards, dragging Hudson and Douglas with them. The rope snapped and the four men disappeared over the precipice onto the Matterhorn Glacier 4000ft (1200m) below. Three of the bodies were recovered next day, but Lord Francis Douglas was never found.

Today, climbers can use the huts, ropes, cables and footholds provided, and about 2000 ascend the Matterhorn every year. But it remains awesome, and accidents still occur – up to 15 climbers die every year.

SURVIVOR *Edward Whymper led the 1865 climb.*

DISASTROUS DESCENT *Gustav Doré's engraving (above) shows the disaster that followed the 1865 Matterhorn conquest.*

HOW THE HORN WAS SHAPED

The Matterhorn's distinctive pyramidal peak, or horn, is the meeting point of sharp, jagged ridges known as arêtes. These ridges remained when four circular basins known as cirques (or corries or cwms), were gouged from the rock. Three faces of the pyramid – the north, east and south – are each the typical, smooth back wall of a cirque. The steep, broken west face retains little trace of its cirque ancestry.

A cirque is formed when successive snowfalls build up in a sheltered hollow on a mountain side. Year by year, unmelted snow is packed down hard by snow layers on top, and compressed into ice. Each year the surrounding rock is eroded by a combination of frost shattering it, ice plucking at it, and meltwater scouring it, and the basin is deepened. Gradually, increasing weight from above squeezes ice out sideways to overflow at the lowest point in the basin rim, and stretch away as a newborn glacier.

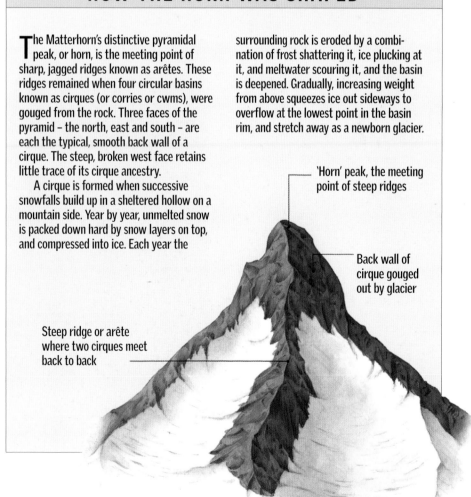

'Horn' peak, the meeting point of steep ridges

Back wall of cirque gouged out by glacier

Steep ridge or arête where two cirques meet back to back

Ritten Earth Pillars

PILLARS OF EARTH – SOME TOPPED WITH BOULDERS LIKE STONE HATS – SPROUT FROM WOODED RAVINES IN NORTHERN ITALY

At first sight the Ritten Earth Pillars of north Italy look like some kind of practical joke. On this mountainside in the South Tyrol, boulders float above the treetops, balancing precariously on jagged spires that glow with reds, ochres and violets. This *tour-de-force* of Nature is rather like a plate-balancing act at a circus – it leaves the audience in a state of bemused but delighted wonderment.

The ridged and pitted pillars taper upwards from a broad base. Some are short and stumpy, and others soar upwards and slim out into long thin necks. The tallest reach 130ft (40m) in height, and pillars of any height can support the bizarre stone 'hat'.

The stone hats, and the material that forms the earth pillars, were brought to the Ritten's slopes during the Ice Age. Rock debris of all sizes, from boulders to finely ground rocks, was caught up in glaciers that moved over the land. When the ice retreated about 10,000 years ago, this 'boulder clay' was dumped by melting ice in a thick layer on the mountain slopes.

YOUNG LADIES WEARING HATS

Earth pillars such as these occur in only a few places in the world, and all attract their own folklore and nicknames. Pillars in north Italy are called 'little men' in one place, and 'earth mushrooms' in another, and a group of pillars in the French Alps is known by the more elegant name of *demoiselles coiffées* – 'young ladies with their hats on'.

There are three groups of earth pillars on the Ritten, which rises sharply from the Eisack valley. Terraced vineyards clothe the mountain's lower slopes, and higher up are woods and meadows. The earth pillars all lie at about 3250ft (1000m) above sea level, clustered in wooded ravines that plunge down to the Eisack.

German knights settled on the Ritten in the 13th century and cleared

RAIN HAT *A colourful earth pillar, knobbly with stones, balances the boulder that shields the underlying material from rain and prevents it being washed away.*

the forested slopes for agriculture. In doing so they may have accelerated the pillars' formation, as land was laid open to the erosive power of rain (see below).

Before World War I, South Tyrol was part of Austria–Hungary. Place names have both German and Italian forms – the Ritten is known as Renon in Italian, and the town of Bozen at its foot has the Italian name Bolzano.

On a geological time-scale, earth pillars are nine-day wonders. The length of time that a pillar lasts is something of a mystery, although it is known that some will change little in decades. What is certain is that once a pillar loses its capstone, it disintegrates very rapidly. But while the weather destroys some pillars, rainfall creates new ones until there is no more boulder clay left. Not so very far into the future, the behatted earth pillars of north Italy could be a thing of the past.

VAGARY OF NATURE *Tapering earth pillars cluster on the wooded slopes of the Ritten, in north Italy. Some support the boulders that enabled them to form.*

LIFE OF A PILLAR

Rocks buried in boulder clay left by glaciers are the key to the Ritten Earth Pillars. Rainwater carves a network of deep gullies, and any large rocks between the gullies act like umbrellas and protect the boulder clay underneath from the rain's destructive force. While the rest of the boulder clay wears away, rocks and the material they cover stand increasingly high above the gully network. Eventually each rock falls and its pillar is quickly washed away.

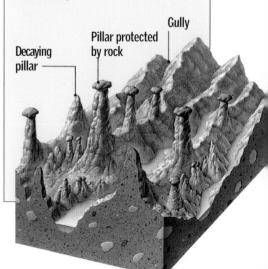

Decaying pillar

Pillar protected by rock

Gully

Elbe Valley

SOUTH OF DRESDEN LIES A FAIRY-TALE LANDSCAPE FAMED BOTH FOR ITS BEAUTY AND ITS FABULOUS 'WHITE GOLD'

Rising in the Czech Republic, the River Elbe enters Germany via a deep and shadowy gorge sliced through the Erzgebirge (Ore Mountains), then flows to the North Sea. For most of its 720 miles (1160km) the river is intensely serious. Along with associated waterways such as the Kiel canal, it is one of Europe's great commercial highways, bearing huge bargeloads of coal, steel, grain, chemicals and manufactured goods on its ample bosom.

Only occasionally does this majestic stream reveal a romantic streak, such as the phalanxes of rocky bastions that suddenly loom out of either bank about an hour's journey south of Dresden. Carved by aeons of rain and frost out of sandstone laid down some 80 million years ago, they combine in a Gothic fantasy of towers and turrets, spires and domes divided by gorges wild with the roar of rushing streams and waterfalls.

Some formations stand alone, others are crowded in a manner that suggests a block in Manhattan. One such is the Bastei, a rocky labyrinth with a viewing point from where you can see, towering over the sparkling blue waters of the Amsel lake, the weird silhouette of the Lokomotive – a mountain shaped like a steam engine. Other strange formations include the Lilienstein (the lily

stone), crowned by a ruined castle, and the higgledy-piggledy bulk of the Pfaffenstein (the priest's stone). Near the town of Rathen is the Felsenbühne, a natural theatre among the rocks where plays are performed in summer.

Historically, the area was known simply as the Meissen Highlands, a name too prosaic for its 19th-century admirers who renamed it Saxonian Switzerland. Shortly after the reunification of the country in 1990, the district was declared a national park. Before that, opportunities for military engineering had excited more attention than the scenery. Surviving witness of this is the Königstein, a breathtaking citadel high on a crag above the Elbe. Built as a stronghold of the Bohemian kings in the early Middle Ages, it was

later added to by the rulers (or Electors) of Saxony – Augustus the Strong (1670–1733) gave it a fine Baroque exterior.

The building's inaccessibility underlined both its immunity from attack and its advantages as a prison. The most melancholy of its inmates must surely have been Johann Böttger, a brilliant young apothecary from Berlin who specialised in alchemy – attempting to turn base metals into gold. Having somehow upset the Prussian authorities, he fled to Saxony in 1700 and was promptly clapped into jail and put to work by Augustus, who was as anxious as any other prince of his day for an economical supply of gold.

Although Böttger's breakthrough failed to materialise, his abilities made a marked impression. As it happened, the Elector had a passion that overrode even that for gold. An inveterate collector of Chinese porcelain, he had amassed one of the Western World's finest collections. But his dream was to produce the first European porcelain, and it was to this end that Böttger was redirected. During years of incarceration, the recipe for porcelain seemed as elusive to him as that for gold.

'WHITE GOLD'

But in 1708, after experimenting with ground feldspar and local clay, he managed to produce a dish in red porcelain. The Elector was delighted, but Böttger remained a prisoner, if an honoured one.

To rival the Chinese, white porcelain still had to be produced. In 1713, by adding quartz and substituting kaolin for local clay, Böttger succeeded. Meissen and Dresden porcelain became world famous.

Sadly, Böttger died aged 37 in 1719, blinded and poisoned by the fumes from his experiments, and a statue was erected to his memory. Perhaps, considering his original ambition, he may have drawn some consolation from the fact that his last invention became known far and wide as 'white gold'.

SAXON SWITZERLAND *Divided by gorges resembling streets overgrown by trees, the Bastei rocks (left) suggest the towers of an abandoned city. 'Barberine' (right) is a strangely eroded rock on the edge of the Pfaffenstein.*

Mount Etna

FROM ODYSSEUS TO THE US MARINES – TACKLING ETNA'S VIOLENCE HAS ALWAYS BEEN A TASK FOR HEROES

Not far from Catania, on the east coast of Sicily, lie three massive rocks, lapped by waves. Known as the Scogli dei Ciclopi, they are of volcanic origin and quite unlike other rocks along the shore. These selfsame boulders, it is said, were hurled by a monster at the ship of Odysseus (or Ulysses), the leader in the Trojan Wars of Greek mythology.

Homer, the 8th-century BC Greek poet, tells in his *Odyssey* how the hero and his companions were imprisoned on Sicily by the Cyclops, a race of man-eating giants. Their leader was Polyphemus, whose attractions were further lessened because he had only a single eye, set in the middle of his forehead. While Polyphemus slept, Odysseus and his men drove a sharpened olive beam, hardened in fire and still burning, into the giant's eye, then fled for their lives – and their ship.

Blinded and in agony though he was, the Cyclops was yet able to tear rocks out of the mountainside and fling them after his tormentors. He missed, but the rocks lie where they landed, a memento still of the monster's strength.

As for the truth of the tale, if you look a dozen miles (20km) or so inland from the rocks, etched high against the powder-blue Sicilian sky you will see the summit of the volcano, Mount Etna. Its single crater, blind and hollowed, is like the giant's eye.

VIOLENT ERUPTIONS

Not once but several times through the centuries, Etna has proved its ability to hurl boulders at least as large as the Scogli dei Ciclopi over even greater distances, and it continues to give spectacular evidence of its wrath down to our own times.

Massive eruptions were reported in 475 and 396 BC, again in either AD 812 or 1169, and in the 14th century. In 1669 Etna was rent from top to bottom, pouring out millions of tons of lava to devastate the city at its foot, Catania, and the surrounding countryside. Lesser eruptions before and since – including more than a dozen in the 20th century – have regularly destroyed farmland and buried villages.

Although reports of Etna's activities go back to mythical times, it is fairly young as volcanoes go. It emerged from the sea about a million years ago, and first erupted some half million years later. Now it is Europe's largest active

volcano, measuring roughly 100 miles (160km) round its base and covering an area almost the size of Greater London.

As with many volcanoes, Etna's height varies; at present the summit is about 10,991ft (3350m) high, but less than two decades ago it was almost 100ft (30m) shorter. The summit is also something of a movable feast, since repeated eruptions cause the tops of volcanoes to cave in, leaving saucer-shaped depressions, or calderas, while

CYCLOP'S EYE *A new vent opens on Etna's side, a little below the main crater. This may well presage an eruption.*

new summits build up close by. There were at least two Etna summits before the present one, and on the volcano's side there is a caldera of quite staggering proportions – a great hole 12 miles (20km) round, with sides dropping sheer for 3000ft (900m).

All the business of growth and renewal imparts an uneasy impression of being in the presence of a huge, if primitive, living creature. This is made all the more vivid by breathy exhalations of gases and vapours from fumaroles (steam vents) and mini-craters. In fact, Etna, like other active volcanoes, might be more accurately likened to a leaky valve covering a weak spot in the Earth's crust.

Its eruptions are thought to emerge from a lava reservoir some 18 miles (30km) long by 2½ miles (4km) deep, located below the mountain and fed by gargantuan quantities of gas-charged molten matter welling up from beneath the crust. Titanic pressures mount, seeking exits in the sides and top of the volcano, finally to emerge on the surface as fountains of fire, clouds of sulphurous gas and torrents of lava, pouring down the mountainside.

FERTILITY FROM FIRE

Not, it would be thought, an ideal setting for human habitation. Yet, as it happens, the slopes of Etna are among the most densely populated parts of Sicily. Although the volcano's lava rivers are immensely destructive of property and such things as roads and railways, they flow only occasionally and slowly, and rarely kill anyone.

The attraction is that the slopes are well watered by springs, and the volcanic ash produces some of the most fertile soils in the world. As many as five crops of vegetables a year can be raised, fruit grows in abundance and the richness of Etna wines is proverbial. Which is why, since time immemorial, the inhabitants have endlessly persisted in rebuilding their villages in the same places, and starting all over again.

For most of recorded history, those who live by the richness of Etna's soil have faced the mountain's most violent moments armed with little more than prayers for divine intervention. On one or two occasions, the Veil of St Agatha, carried in solemn procession, is credited

with having stopped the lava in its tracks, but when such things failed, the villagers accepted their fate with a philosophic shrug, and awaited the time to rebuild on the ruins.

It cannot be said that early efforts to defeat eruptions by physical means met with universal acclaim. In 1669, the inhabitants of Catania made the first recorded attempt to divert a lava flow by digging a trench above the village. But when it seemed that the diverted stream might descend upon a neighbouring village, they were forced to desist.

MODERN METHODS

Similar problems arose in recent times. In the eruption of 1991–2, when the town of Zafferana had only days to live, the government volcanologist, Professor Franco Barberi, pointed out that the greatest danger was posed not by lava spreads, which quickly solidified in the open air, but by narrow, molten streams moving swiftly down through self-dug channels and tunnels to break out on the lower slopes.

He therefore employed helicopters of the Italian Air Force and US Marines to drop huge blocks of concrete, chained together, into channels higher up the mountainside, while dynamiting the tunnels lower down. For the helicopter crews flying through gas, steam and smoke, conditions were hazardous in the extreme, but they placed the blocks accurately. These dropped down to the dynamited sections of the tunnels to block them like potatoes in a drain,

HIGH FLOWER
The Etna violet is found only on the scree slopes of the volcano.

causing the lava to spread out over the upper slopes, where it solidified, blocking further flows.

For the time being, Zafferana was saved. Or almost. Several outlying houses had already succumbed, in one of which the owner, with true Sicilian hospitality, left a bottle of wine on the table. 'For Etna,' he explained. 'It's tired, and must be thirsty.'

THE VIEW FROM THE TOP

To ascend Etna on foot – not difficult, as the slopes are gentle – is to have the natural history of the area unfurled before you. Vines and oranges and pistachios cloak the lower slopes, giving way gradually to apples and cherries. Above are wooded slopes of oak, sweet chestnut, hazel and birch, and higher still is the tumbled, weathered lava where little grows but alpines and occasional hummocks of Sicilian milk-vetch.

Here also there are pockets of permanent snow. In the old days this was shovelled over with layers of cold ash and exported in summer to Naples and Rome to be used in ice-cream manufacture – the local aristocracy regarded it as a crop more important than wine.

But towards the summit is an area totally inimical to life, a grey, shapeless waste of slag, ash and lava, punctuated by steaming fissures – an echo of the world's first beginnings. The crater's gaping maw is stained with oxides and sulphates, and its depth varies constantly with the heaving of the lava plug.

The time to see it all is just before dawn, when the crater pulsates with the red glow that has been a marker for sailors since ships first sailed the Mediterranean. Then, as the sun comes up, all of Sicily and Calabria are laid out below, with Etna's shadow pulling in towards you and, far off, a glimpse of Malta. These are lands that witnessed the beginnings of European civilisation; a comforting thought, when primeval chaos lies below one's feet.

NIGHT HEAT *As darkness falls, a lava stream glows through the fallen roof of a natural tunnel on Mount Etna. The deep colour indicates that the lava is cooling, and will solidify at the surface.*

Dolomites

SPECTACULAR LIMESTONE PEAKS IN THE NORTH OF ITALY WERE FORMED FROM CORAL REEFS THAT GREW BENEATH THE SEA

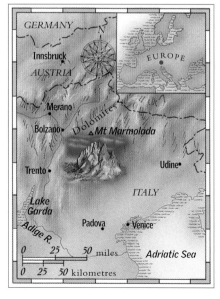

Carved by glaciers and fretted by frost, the extraordinary rock skyline of the Dolomites looks like vast battlements, needles, towers and walls. This mountain range in north-east Italy is a series of light-coloured limestone crags separated by green valleys, and rivalling each other in their spectacular shapes.

VALLEY GUARDIANS *The jagged peaks of the Sasso Lungo group stand guard over the Val Gardena, the home of many of the descendants of Roman soldiers sent to conquer the Celts.*

They started life as coral reefs submerged in shallow seas and were thrust upwards, with the rest of the Alps, some 65 million years ago.

Legend tells that these Monti Pallidi, as they were originally called, acquired their pale rock faces when gnomes, anxious to please a homesick Moon Princess who had married an Alpine Prince, draped them in a gossamer mantle woven from moonbeams.

When the French geologist Deodat de Dolomieu examined the rock in the 1780s he discovered that it contained

138

small amounts of magnesium. This distinctive limestone has since been known as dolomite in recognition of his discovery. In daylight it ranges in colour from pale grey to near-white, but at sunset the massive rock faces are often bathed in shades of orange and pink.

In winter the bare rock peaks rise dramatically from the snow-covered slopes. But with the arrival of spring a gentler scene is revealed: flower-filled meadows swathe the upper slopes, and rock crevices shelter clumps of gem-like alpines such as saxifrage, edelweiss and pasqueflowers. Lower down, song birds nest in the woods, and along the valley floors farmers busy themselves in orchards and pastures. A network of paths snakes along the lower slopes, and higher up long-distance trails crest the ridges, providing exhilarating views for experienced walkers.

At the heart of the Dolomites are the Alpe di Siusi, the Catinaccio ranges and glacier-topped Marmolada. Crowned with a 330ft (100m) pyramid of rock, Marmolada is the undisputed Queen of the Dolomites, her southern face a sheer cliff 2000ft (600m) high. The plateaus of the Alpe di Siusi are a wonderland of brightly coloured and fragrant meadows, enclosed by soaring dolomite spires. The massive walls of Catinaccio, which glow red in the rising and setting sun, rise sheer where once the rose garden of Lauren, King of the Dwarfs, is said to have flourished.

Because of the region's chequered history many places retain both Italian and Austrian names – Catinaccio is also known as Rosengarten. The Dolomites were under Roman rule for centuries, then in the 14th century became part of the Habsburg Empire. After World War I they were returned to Italy.

South of Marmolada, the bare peaks of Pale de San Martin preside over the tranquil forests of Paneveggio National Park which once furnished the Venetians with timber for their ships.

CLIMBING WITH A LADDER AND A STOUT STICK

Isolated from the other ranges but sharing the same dolomite rock are the battlemented peaks of the Brenta to the west. These rugged pinnacles were scaled in the 19th century by British pioneer climbers, among them Francis Fox Tuckett. With only a ladder and a stout stick, he carved out a new route 'amongst toppling rocks, and spires of white and brown and bronze'. At the summit, he rewarded himself with a joint of meat and a draught of red wine. Today, Brenta's crags are still among the most challenging in the Dolomites.

LIMESTONE FLOWERS Primula minima *thrives, as do orchids and gentians, on the limestone soil.*

ALPINE HAY *Meadows that carpet the rocky slopes high above the tree-line in the central Dolomites provide farmers with a welcome crop of hay.*

Samariá Gorge

ON THE GREEK ISLAND OF CRETE, HIGH ROCK WALLS ENCLOSE A DEEP CHASM WHERE OUTLAWS ONCE TOOK REFUGE

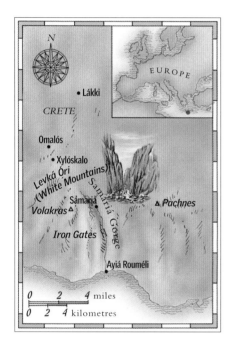

A deep ravine, sheer-sided in places, cuts a spectacular slice into towering sea cliffs and high mountains in western Crete. For 11 miles (18km) the Samariá Gorge twists and turns, widening and narrowing as it traces a serpentine course through the Levká Ori, or White Mountains, whose slopes gleam white in the summer sun and are snow-covered in winter.

Cypresses, fig trees and oleanders spring from crevices and ledges in the gorge's walls. In places, fully grown cypress trees have rooted in the wallpaper-like limestone crust that has been deposited on the walls by water seeping down the mountainsides. High above, eagles and falcons soar and choughs circle in swarms, swirling like the black embers of a forest fire.

The gorge has been cut by the River Tarraíos that flows along a fault between the Pachnes massif to the east and the Gíngilos and Volakiás mountains to the west. In winter the river is a fast-flowing torrent that races through the gorge, but in summer it dwindles to a bubbling stream.

For centuries the gorge was a refuge for bandits and outlaws, and for people trying to escape from the vendettas that existed between many of Crete's villages. In the 1940s it was an ideal hiding place for communist guerillas fighting in the Greek Civil War.

At the northern end of the gorge, nearly 4000ft (1200m) above sea level, a steep wooden staircase descends into the ravine, and takes the visitor through pine trees to the riverbed. About 5 miles (8km) into the gorge is the deserted village of Samariá, which was abandoned in 1962 when the gorge became part of a national park. Its Byzantine church of Osía María, which contains early frescoes, is thought to be the origin of the gorge's name.

Every turn of the path brings some new breathtaking vista. Giant boulders pile high one above the other, the river swirls over rocks and fills pools, and the incessant erosive force of water carves rocks into enchanting shapes.

Beyond Samariá the gorge starts to narrow, and towering cliffs that rise sheer from the riverbed start to close in. In this deep and narrow corridor the sky shrinks to a slender ribbon of blue, and the sun's rays penetrate for only a short while each day.

The gorge reaches its narrowest point at the Iron Gates, which were described by an Englishman, Robert Pashley, who travelled through the gorge on a mule in the early 19th century. 'The width of this lofty chasm,' he wrote, 'is about ten feet at the ground and widens to about thirty or at the most forty feet at the top. The length of the way along which we have to pass in the middle of the rapid stream is about sixty paces.' With walls at least 1600ft (500m) high, the Iron Gates can be an awesome place, especially when the wind howls through the narrow gap.

CLIFFS THAT RISE SHEER FROM THE RIVERBED START TO CLOSE IN

HIDDEN FROM PIRATES

Between the Iron Gates and the sea, the gorge widens out. An abandoned village lies a little way inland, invisible from the coast and therefore hidden from the eyes of marauding pirates. It was once part of Ayiá Rouméli, one of the few settlements in the high cliffs bordering this part of the island.

Ayiá Rouméli sits prettily among oleanders and olives, occupying the site of the ancient city of Tarrhia. This once-busy port, destroyed by an earthquake in AD 66, exported cypress trees to Troy and Mycenae. The people of Ayiá Rouméli sell *diktamos*, a rare plant used in herbal teas. It grows in the gorge in high and almost inaccessible places that are also the domain of the fleet-footed Agrími wild goat, known locally as the 'kri-kri'. Difficult to spot among the rocky ledges, these elusive creatures graze the patches of diktamos.

The gorge usually opens to tourists in May when the river level drops, and closes in October. The walk down the gorge takes at least five hours, and should be attempted only by experienced walkers.

ENCLOSING CLIFFS *The sides of the Samariá Gorge (left) almost touch at the Iron Gates, dwarfing a lone rider. Early morning mist (below) rises to swirl wraith-like between its wooded cliffs.*

The Middle East and Asia

Cappadocia's Cones

FANTASTIC CONICAL HILLS IN CENTRAL TURKEY HAVE BEEN MADE EVEN MORE EXTRAORDINARY BY LOCAL CAVE DWELLERS

Until well into the 20th century, the name Cappadocia meant little to most of the Western World. It was known, perhaps hazily, as a place in Asia Minor that was mentioned in the Bible – St Peter's first letter is addressed to the Cappadocians. Yet today, the part of central Turkey around Ürgüp and Göreme is known to travellers the world over for a landscape that, stunning in itself, also has an unexpected twist.

In the most weird of fairy-tale landscapes, cones and pyramids of rock rise from barren valleys. Some taper smoothly to summits as high as 160ft (50m). Others are rugged and irregular, as though carelessly fashioned or abandoned before they were finished. There are pillars and rocky outcrops, too, of every imaginable shape and size. A magical colour scheme – rich cream, pink, red, pale blue or grey – makes the atmosphere even more unreal.

To add to the landscape's outlandishness, cones and rocks here and there are capped with slabs or bobbles of darker stone. Some look like oddly shaped mushrooms, while others resemble cloaked figures wearing hats tilted at jaunty angles. In some places, cones and rocks are scattered in a

SCULPTURE PARK *A surreal jumble of rocks sprouts up from Cappadocia's Göreme Valley, their varied forms carved from the soft rock by rain and wind.*

haphazard way over the valley floors; elsewhere, cones stretch away in serried ranks. Then it is easy to understand the mythical explanation of their origins – besieged by a marauding army, the people prayed to Allah, who turned their attackers to stone.

Cappadocia's other-worldly rock sculptures stand on a plateau dominated by the extinct volcano, Erciyas Daği. This 12,848ft (3916m) mountain was the source of the cones' building material. Millions of years ago it erupted violently, hurling out ash that fell over a wide area. The ash cooled and hardened to form a thick mantle

CONES IN THE MAKING *Like ripples in sand, cliffs of tuff have been weathered to form the first stage of cones. Overlapping now, they will be separated out by further erosion.*

HOMES CUT INTO THE ROCK

The caves hollowed into Cappadocia's cones and cliffs made congenial homes. The temperature remained fairly constant throughout the year, protecting the inhabitants from the extremes of summer heat and winter cold. Some cave settlements were on a large scale; at Üçhisar as many as 1000 people might have lived in a warren of rooms cut out of a huge outcrop of rock.

The homes of many more Cappadocians were hidden from view, in vast underground cities. Deep in the earth, yet more warrens of rooms were connected by narrow tunnels, with staircases leading from one level to another.

The city of Derinkuyu, with an estimated population of 20,000, may have had as many as 20 levels – Derinkuyu means 'deep well'. Not only were there living quarters, communal kitchens, and shafts for ventilation and water, but also wine presses and cellars, stables complete with mangers, a church and even cemeteries. Oil lamps lit the rooms. When danger threatened, large stone discs could be rolled across tunnel entrances to seal off the city.

WARREN *A maze of caves, some exposed by landslips, riddles the rock at Üçhisar.*

of tuff, a white rock soft enough to be worked with a knife. Since then the tuff has been attacked by rain, snow and wind. Rainwater run-off has cut twisting valleys and ravines, and has then eaten away at their sides to leave the conical hills and other rock formations.

The volcano's eruptions produced some layers of tuff so hot that they welded as they landed – forming stronger layers of rock, which are mostly darker in colour. As gullies have been cut down through these layers, remnant caps and blocks of the strong dark tuff have survived on top of individual cones, protecting the softer tuff below and creating some of the more bizarre shapes.

HUMAN TOUCH

As if the landscape were not improbable enough, a further surprise is in store for the visitor. The conical hills, and the cliffs of the valley sides, have doors and windows cut into them.

Until well into the 20th century, people made their homes in rooms hollowed out of the cones and cliffs. The idea could have started as early as 4000 BC, with people enlarging natural caves and then tunnelling further into the soft rock. In about 2000 BC, waves of Hittites appeared from the east. It could have been then that the cave dwellers started to burrow downwards, digging underground refuges that later developed into vast subterranean cities.

Christianity spread quickly to this upland plateau, and the solitude of the valleys with their strange conical hills attracted men and women who wanted to follow the contemplative life. By the end of the 4th century small groups of monks and nuns were creating monasteries and convents in the cones and cliffs, with cells, kitchens and refectories.

UNDERGROUND REFUGES LATER DEVELOPED INTO VAST CITIES

Far more remarkable than the monks' homes, however, are the 400 or so richly decorated churches in the area. Between the 7th and 12th centuries, monks hewed out churches complete with pillars, crypts and domes. Using strongly coloured pigments, they covered the walls with frescoes whose colours are still bright. A fresco in one of the Göreme Valley churches shows St George fighting a serpent; others show scenes from the New Testament, such as the Flight into Egypt.

The conical hills and their decorated churches attract large numbers of tourists, and with them comes wear and tear on the landscape and frescoes. Landslides can carry away centuries-old frescoes, for the weathering that created the cones is a continuous process. But while existing formations are being whittled away, new ones are forming.

Dead Sea

A SALTY, SUN-BAKED WORLD FAR BELOW SEA LEVEL IS THE SETTING FOR STORIES OF LOT'S WIFE AND KING DAVID

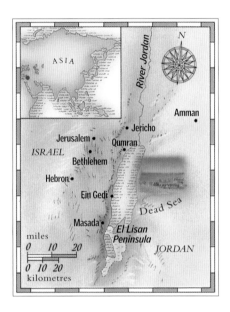

At the lowest point on Earth, there is a stretch of water whose calm blue surface is punctured by columns of salt. In places, lumps of salt float on the water like crumbling icebergs. This almost lifeless landscape is the Dead Sea, scene of the Biblical tale of Lot's wife. Disobediently looking back as the sinful cities of Sodom and Gomorrah were destroyed by fire and brimstone, she herself was turned into one of the pillars of salt. According to some archaeologists, the two cities lie submerged in the sea's southern shallows.

The Dead Sea, its surface 1299ft (396m) below sea level, lies at the bottom of the Jordan valley, in the north of the Great Rift Valley. The rift valley begins in the upper reaches of the River Jordan and continues southwards through the Dead Sea, the Red Sea and east Africa. In places, the lake is a further 1300ft (400m) or so deep, and there the lake's floor lies almost half a mile (0.8km) below sea level.

Against a backdrop of the arid Judaean Hills to the west and the plateaus of Biblical Moab and Edom to the east, the Dead Sea stretches for almost 50 miles (80km) along the valley floor and is 11 miles (18km) wide at its broadest point.

The lake is divided in two by the peninsula of El Lisan ('the tongue'). The northern portion is the larger and

POTS AND PANS *Sunrise over the Dead Sea (below) highlights the salt pans. (Overleaf) The tops of salt columns rise above the waters of the Dead Sea like crusty chimney-stacks.*

deeper of the two, and the southern portion of the lake – only 20ft (6m) deep on average – is where the white salt columns are seen.

The columns are the top layer of a thick covering of sediments that began to be laid down more than 2 million years ago. Water from the Jordan and several smaller streams quickly evaporates in summer temperatures of more than 50°C (122°F), leaving sediments of clay, sand, rock salt and gypsum on the lake floor. During especially wet winters more than 6½ million tons of water pour into the Dead Sea each day.

Were it not for the evaporation, the lake level would rise some 10ft (3m) each year. Since the early years of the 20th century the level of the lake has in fact fallen, partly because of a changing climate and partly because Jordan and Israel extract water for irrigation from the River Jordan and other streams that flow into the lake.

FEW SIGNS OF LIFE

Plants and animals are scarce. Only a few single-celled organisms are able to survive in the water, which has a salt content six times higher than that of the oceans. The constant evaporation of the lake often causes thick swathes of mist to obscure its surface. Arab settlers in the Middle Ages believed that birds would not fly across the lake because its misty vapours were poisonous. But flocks of starlings known as Tristram's Grackle bring life to the area, feeding on insects and fruit around the lake's shores. They are named after Canon H.B. Tristram, an English naturalist.

Apart from its salt, the Dead Sea is rich in other minerals, such as potash, magnesium and bromine. These minerals are said to provide those who bathe in them with natural therapy for various ailments, particularly skin diseases, arthritis and respiratory problems, while the black mud of the Dead Sea is supposed to rejuvenate the skin. Mineral extraction is as commercially viable today as it was in the 4th century AD, when bitumen was sold to the Egyptians for embalming. Since 1930 potash has been extracted, for use in agricultural fertilisers.

Rain and rivers are scarce in this region, although dry riverbeds are numerous. On the occasions when heavy rain falls, they turn into raging torrents, sweeping sediments off the rock face into the lake.

For such a small and almost lifeless lake, the Dead Sea has played a surprisingly large role in history. On the western shore, the mountain fortress of Masada (see right) gave protection and a commanding view of the lake to Herod the Great, King of Judaea, who added to the fort first built by Jonathan Maccabeus. North

THE WATER'S SALT CONTENT IS SIX TIMES HIGHER THAN THAT OF THE OCEANS

of Masada is Ein Gedi (meaning 'goats' spring') – the place where, according to the Book of Samuel, David took refuge when Saul was searching for him in a fit of anger. Ein Gedi is an oasis with springs and lush vegetation; wild ibexes and, so it is said by some, leopards live here. Farther north in hillside caves at Qumran, the Essenes – an ancient Jewish sect – hid the now famous Dead Sea Scrolls. The documents date from the mid 3rd century BC to AD 68, and some record daily monastic life within the community.

MIGHTY MASADA

The fortress of Masada (above), rebuilt by Herod the Great, nests on a craggy cliff top above the south-western shores of the Dead Sea. Pilgrims struggle up Masada's snake-like path to commemorate the Jewish rebels who, besieged there by the Romans in AD 73, took their lives rather than submit to slavery.

Christian monks built a chapel on the site, but Masada later became buried beneath layers of debris. Then, in the 1960s, archaeologists unearthed Herod's two lavish palaces, complete with bathhouse, swimming pool and vast water cisterns. They also found the living quarters of the Jewish rebels, their ritual baths and what is believed to be the world's oldest synagogue.

Pamukkale's Springs

A WHITE WONDERLAND GLISTENS ON A TURKISH HILLSIDE BELOW A RUINED CITY WHERE GREEKS AND ROMANS ONCE TOOK THE WATERS

Travelling through Asia Minor in 1765, the English classical scholar Richard Chandler first noticed Pamukkale as a vast white slope in the distance. Moving closer he 'beheld with wonder' what seemed to be 'an immense frozen cascade, the surface wavy, as of water at once fixed, or in its headlong course suddenly petrified'.

Modern visitors to western Turkey feel the same sense of wonder when they see Pamukkale's white-walled, scalloped-edged terraces rising one above another. Pools of water reflect the fluffy-textured walls, and stalactites like frozen waterfalls hang round the periphery of the whole area, the slender pillars backed by masses of scarlet oleanders. Dark, pine-clad mountains

WATER OF LIFE *Innumerable pools lie along Pamukkale's terraces. The warm, mineral-rich water has been credited with therapeutic powers for centuries.*

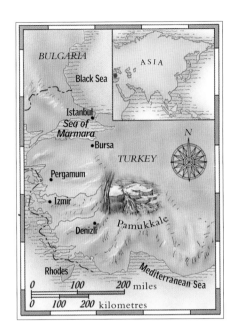

rise behind, making a dramatic setting for the white formations as they glisten in the bright sunlight.

The name Pamukkale means 'cotton castle'. Some say that the name comes from the fluffy appearance of the walls and terraces, although local legend maintains that in ancient times giants dried cotton crops on the terraces.

The walls, terraces and stalactites at Pamukkale cover an area nearly 1½ miles (2.5km) long and one-third of a mile (0.5km) wide. They are the work of hot volcanic springs that bubble up on a plateau above them. The springs' water is heavily laden with lime and other minerals that have been dissolved out of the rocks by rainwater as it seeps through the ground on its way to the springs.

Almost anything that is immersed in the spring water acquires a coating of lime, and objects dropped into the water appear to turn to stone in a matter of days. When it runs off the edge of the plateau, the spring water deposits lime on the hillside. Over many thousands of years, layer upon layer of the lime has built up to form the walls, terraces and stalactites of glistening white.

For thousands of years, the mineral-rich hot springs have had a reputation for their healing properties. They have been said to cure or ease complaints such as rheumatism, high blood pressure and heart disease.

The springs' reputation was almost certainly known in 190 BC. It was then that Eumenes II, the king of the Greek

A CAVE GAVE OFF FUMES THAT WOULD KILL A BULL INSTANTLY

DAZZLING CONFECTION *Like icing on a cake. Pamukkale's stunning white mineral deposits form high sheer walls in some places (above), and shallower terraces in others (right).*

city of Pergamum near Turkey's west coast, is thought to have founded the city of Hierapolis on the plateau where the springs rise. He named the city after Hiera, who was the wife of Pergamum's legendary founder Telephus.

In 129 BC Hierapolis became part of the Roman Empire, and found favour as a watering place with a succession of emperors, including Nero and Hadrian, who came to drink or bathe in the waters. During Nero's reign, in AD 60, the city was devastated by an earth-quake. The new city built to replace it was larger and more magnificent than before, with wide streets, a theatre, public baths and houses supplied with warm water carried in channels.

The 2nd-century baths had rooms of different temperature which the bather used in turn. He started in the cold *frigidarium*, went on to the warm *tepidarium* where he oiled his body, and then progressed to the hot and steamy *caldarium* where he scraped the oil and dirt from his skin with a blade called a strigil. Part of the baths houses a museum with a fine collection of statues, and other finds including medical instruments and jewellery.

One of the city's most interesting remains is the sanctuary of Pluto, the god of the underworld, which stands next to the temple dedicated to Apollo, the god of the sun, music, poetry and medicine. They were placed next to each other in order to cancel out each god's light and dark powers.

The dark powers of Pluto must have seemed formidable indeed, for emanating from a cave at the site were poisonous fumes that Strabo, the Greek geographer and historian, said would kill a bull instantly. The fumes were associated with evil spirits, and it was said that the eunuch priests who guarded the entrance were the only people who could enter the cave without harm. The fumes are now known to come from a hot spring, and the chamber still gives off a vapour that brings tears to the eyes.

HOMES FOR THE NEXT LIFE

Outside the city wall stands an extensive cemetery containing 1200 tombs, many of them elaborately ornamented and of grand proportions. They bear witness to the many wealthy Romans who came to the city in search of a cure – and failed to find it.

Today's tourists are the successors to wealthy Roman holidaymakers. They come to bathe in the warm pools – one of which has broken Roman columns lying on the bottom – and to marvel at the sparkling white terraces lying on the hillside below the ruined city.

NATIVE FLOWER *Bright pink oleander flowers bring dashes of contrasting colour to the periphery of the white terraces, and to the Roman city's remains.*

Kamchatka Peninsula

SMOKE, STEAM AND FIRE PREVAIL IN THIS COLD AND REMOTE LAND OF VOLCANOES AND GEYSERS AT THE EASTERN EDGE OF SIBERIA

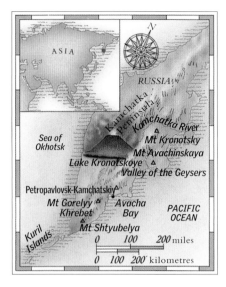

Mount Klyuchevskaya, the highest point on the Kamchatka Peninsula, is one of the greatest and most perfectly cone-shaped active volcanoes on Earth. Smoke billows constantly from its summit – which, at 15,580ft (4750m), is almost as high as Mont Blanc – and it has erupted more than 50 times in the last 300 years or so.

Yet Klyuchevskaya is just one of 150 or more volcanoes on this icy, isolated and mountainous peninsula that juts south from the far east of Siberia. Some 30 of the volcanoes are still active.

Together with the Kuril Islands – a chain of 56 volcanic islands stretching from the tip of the peninsula – they form one of the most active parts of the Ring of Fire, the volcano belt girdling

the Pacific. And together they make up 10 per cent of the world's active volcanoes. In 1907, Mount Shtyubelya hurled forth enough ash and dust to have covered the whole peninsula, which is about the size of Japan, and darkened the city of Petropavlovsk-Kamchatskiy, 60 miles (100km) away.

Earthquakes are frequent – there have been more than 150 in the last 200 years. One in November 1952 was the second strongest on record, measuring 8.4 on the Richter scale.

The hundreds of bubbling hot springs are used for heating the city and the hothouses that provide fresh vegetables – and enough potatoes for export. The Valley of the Geysers, near the active volcano of Kronotsky, is alive

with the hissing, rumbling and steaming of 25 geysers, and the minerals they deposit paint the rocks around them red, pink, violet and brown. Veikon, the largest, spouts boiling water and steam

SMOKING VOLCANO *Mount Gorelyy Khrebet, constantly active, is one of a line of volcanoes that form a backdrop to the city of Petropavlovsk-Kamchatskiy.*

some 160ft (49m) into the air for four minutes every three hours or so.

The Valley of the Geysers lies within the beautiful Kronotsky Nature Reserve, which covers nearly 4000sq miles (10,300km²). Lake Kronotskoye, below Kronotsky's western slopes, is Kamchatka's largest lake. Like the rest of the peninsula, the reserve has a coastal strip of marshy tundra, where mosses and lichens prevail. As the land rises to the mountains inland, scrub and forests, mainly birch, take over.

The biggest brown bears in Eurasia roam here, as do reindeer, Siberian bighorn sheep, blue foxes, silver foxes, sables, mink, black-capped marmots and Arctic ground squirrels. Seals and sea birds feast on fish along the coast. Fur and fish, especially sable and salmon, provide the inhabitants of Kamchatka with their main livelihood.

Petropavlovsk-Kamchatskiy, a city of about 240,000 people, is a major fisheries port with a fleet of factory ships. Kamchatka's climate is severe, with long, cold and snowy winters and short, cool, wet summers. But water

FIERY FOUNTAIN *Hot gases shoot towards the sky, clouds of acrid smoke billow into the air and red-hot lava begins to flow as Mount Avachinskaya, one of the 30 or so active volcanoes on the peninsula, puts on a spectacular display.*

from the hot springs keeps stretches of the River Kamchatka free of ice, even in winter.

Its harsh weather and its remoteness gave Kamchatka a grim reputation in old Russia. Naughty children or dunces were sent to the back of the classroom. Those relegated to the back benches were known as 'kamchatkas' – the schoolroom equivalent of Siberia, the place of exile for criminals. Yet no criminals were ever sent to Kamchatka; no-one would live there to guard them.

The original Kamchatkan inhabitants, the Koryaks and the Chukchis, were very nearly wiped out by the Tsar's Cossacks in the 18th century.

Some of their descendants still live on the peninsula, which, with modern transport and trade, is not as remote as it used to be. But this harsh, wild and beautiful land is still one of the last frontiers – romantic, mysterious and largely unexplored.

ONE OF THE MOST ACTIVE PARTS OF THE RING OF FIRE ROUND THE PACIFIC

SEETHING SPRING *Bubbling, sulphurous hot springs vary in colour according to the chemicals in the clay.*

155

Siberian Tundra

SUMMER IS BRIEF BUT BLOOMING IN THE COLD, TREELESS PLAIN THAT BORDERS THE ARCTIC ICE CAP AT THE TOP OF THE WORLD

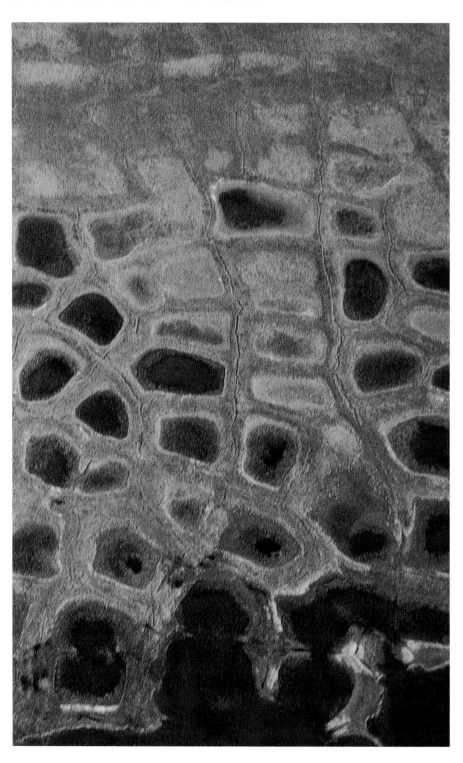

A mossy carpet covers much of the Siberian tundra – a vast plain dotted with lakes and bogs. The tundra stretches for some 2000 miles (3200km) across northern Siberia along the fringes of Arctic ice, its scenery typically that of the Taymyr Peninsula, which is the northernmost part of the Eurasian mainland.

The writers and zoologists Gerald and Lee Durrell, visiting the Taymyr Peninsula one summer in the 1980s, wrote of 'a thick rug of moss and herbs laid over a floor of frozen earth. There were fuzzy little daisy-like flowers and others madonna-blue, like miniature forget-me-nots shining up at you. Everywhere there were ankle-high forests of dwarf willow, with pink flowers like muffs growing sturdily in the emerald-green layer of moss.'

For up to three months of the year there is constant daylight, but the sunlight is low-angled and midsummer temperatures are mostly around 5°C (40°F). In winter, for a period not quite as long as that of the 24-hour daylight, there is no sunrise – just perpetual moonlight and sometimes the spectacular northern lights. Winter temperatures can plummet to –44°C (–47°F). This gives plants little time in

POLYGONAL TUNDRA *From the air, the typical tundra landscape of the Taymyr Peninsula – a pattern of small lakes and ridges – is clearly seen.*

which to flower and seed. Most are perennials and are tiny and low-growing to protect them from the ever-present cold winds.

Permafrost, or permanently frozen subsoil, extends across much of the tundra. At its deepest it goes down about 4500ft (1370m). In winter all the soil is frozen solid, but in summer the top layer melts to give a thin, boggy surface layer in which plants can root and grow. In the northernmost parts this amounts to the top 6–12in (150–300mm), but farther south it is progressively deeper, down to about 10ft (3m), allowing taller vegetation such as birch and larch scrub to flourish.

Large areas of the Taymyr Peninsula are spotted or polygonal tundra – an extraordinary landscape of boggy pools and small lakes separated by ridges into a honeycomb of irregular shapes. This formation results from the continual cycle of freezing and thawing, which causes the ground to crack. Ice wedges that gradually form in the cracks force the ridge material to the surface, and the thawed soil and meltwater moves down the slopes.

OLD INHABITANTS

Bones or the curling tusks of long-dead woolly mammoths can sometimes be found lying on the tundra and, for centuries, Siberians made money by digging tusks out of the permafrost and selling them to ivory traders.

SIBERIAN SUMMER *In the short tundra summer, the sun shines weakly for 24 hours a day, lighting up the mossy landscape crisscrossed by lakes, pools and rivers.*

Elephant-like woolly mammoths – up to about 13ft (4m) at the shoulder and with tusks as long as 15ft (4.5m) – once roamed northern Eurasia and North America. They became extinct around 12,000 years ago, but remains, including whole animals, have been found preserved in the permafrost – most in Siberia. The word mammoth comes from a Siberian Tatar word for earth. The first almost complete carcass was found in the Lena Peninsula in 1799 by an ivory hunter. The animal became fully exposed in 1803 and was studied by scientists.

The Byrranga Plateau, some 5000ft (1500m) high, forms the spine of the Taymyr Peninsula. Near its southern edge is Lake Taymyr, the Arctic's largest lake – slightly larger than the island of Majorca but only about 10ft (3m) deep. It fills during the spring floods, empties about three-quarters of its water into the rivers in summer, and freezes solid in winter. A nature reserve on the lake shore is the haunt of musk oxen and reindeer, which graze on the spongy mosses and lichens, and of lemmings that tunnel through them. Lemmings are the chief food of arctic foxes and snowy owls. Wolves live here too, and prey on reindeer and musk oxen.

Many animals, such as reindeer, go south to warmer parts in winter. This is true of most birds – the lakes and islets make ideal summer nesting grounds for water birds such as the colourful red-breasted goose, but by the end of August they have all flown south. In Western Siberia, where the marshy lowlands extend across the River Ob to the Urals, rare Siberian cranes, with wings spanning up to 8ft (2.4m), spend summer in the Ob's lower reaches.

COLOUR WASH *(overleaf) In high summer and autumn, the tundra is aglow with yellow, orange and red from flowers, berries and autumn leaves.*

SHOW-OFF *A rare Siberian crane, with wings outstretched, courts a partner.*

Lake Baikal

A MOUNTAIN-RINGED LAKE IN SOUTHERN SIBERIA, THE DEEPEST ON EARTH, CONTAINS ONE-FIFTH OF THE WORLD'S FRESH WATER

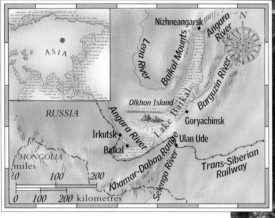

SIBERIAN GRANDEUR *In the depths of winter, Lake Baikal is locked in thick, fissured ice – a giant skating rink that will support the weight of a convoy of trucks.*

At a forest viewpoint beside Baikal, with a glorious view of the lake, there are ribbons or strips of cloth tied to branches. Travellers who tie them there make a wish to return to Baikal one day. Certainly the deep blue lake has a magnetic attraction, and to Russians from far and wide it is the Sacred Sea, the greatest natural wonder of their vast land – a symbol of Russia on a par with Britain's white cliffs of Dover or the USA's Grand Canyon.

Baikal is thought to mean 'much water' in the language of the Kurykan people, who lived in the region about 1300 years ago. It is around 5380ft (1640m) deep and holds one-fifth of the world's fresh water – 5,500 cubic miles (23,000km³), as much as all North America's Great Lakes put together.

AN AGE-OLD LAKE

Baikal is the world's deepest lake, yet in area it is only the ninth largest – a crescent shape 394 miles (635km) long with a 1245 mile (2000km) shoreline, and on average 30 miles (48km) wide. One of the world's oldest lakes, it formed 15–25 million years ago after a huge trench opened up along a fault in

the Earth's crust where Asia is slowly pulling apart. Originally the trench was 5 miles (8km) or more deep, but has silted with time; the remains of tiny life forms in the silt indicate its age. Hot water springs in the lake bed, and frequent minor earth tremors, show continuing activity along the fault line.

Although 336 rivers flow into Baikal, only one flows out – the Angara. People living in the 40 or so small towns round

the shore were once happy to drink water from the lake, because – thanks mainly to minute algae-eating shrimps – it was outstandingly pure. Now it suffers from industrial pollution. But it is mostly clear. In May, just after the ice has melted, you can see down some 130ft (40m) – even half that depth would be exceptional in other lakes.

The surrounding Siberian landscape freezes over well before Baikal. From

October, winter cloaks the mountain crags in brilliant slabs of white, and freezes the forests of larch, spruce and Siberian cedar into spangled silhouettes. Not until January does most of the lake have a covering of ice – more than 5ft (1.5m) thick in places. People drive out in cars and lorries to fish through holes in the ice. Where ice has formed in absolute calm, it is as transparent as a pane of glass, and you can see fish swimming below.

Mostly, however, it is a jagged patchwork of floes. Fissures in the ice erupt regularly, with loud bangs like cannon fire. Some ice lasts until June, but by August the water in many places is warm enough to swim in with comfort.

The lake can be treacherous at any time of year. Dense summer fogs may bring lake traffic to an eerie standstill. Even on tranquil days, a sudden squall may whip the water into a frenzy. Among the Buryats, the Mongol people of the region, the lake is traditionally the domain of angry gods, chief among whom is Burkhan, who lives on the lake's only large island, Olkhon. Of Lake Baikal's 1800 animal species, more than half are found nowhere else. They include the translucent golomyanka, a fish that gives birth to live young, and the silver-grey Baikal seal (or nerpa).

Heavenly Mountains

DESERTS AND STEPPES SURROUND THE SNOW-CAPPED TIEN SHAN MOUNTAINS OF CENTRAL ASIA, ABUNDANT WITH WILD FLOWERS

Pansies of every shade – from white, yellow and blue to deep purple – met the eye of an English traveller, Charles Howard-Bury, after he had ridden up through forest to the alpine meadows of the Tien Shan Mountains in June 1913. 'So close together did they grow,' he wrote, 'that every step we took crushed some of them.' Never

anywhere else, he commented, had he seen such luxuriant flora – every flower that is grown in English gardens seemed to be represented.

Rising from arid desert to snowy peaks and glacier-covered crests, the mountains stretch for 1800 miles (2900km) across central Asia. Maybe the dramatic beauty of their steep slopes,

HEAVENLY SNOWS *When all but the highest snowfields of the Tien Shan Mountains melt in spring, the meltwater brings life to the deserts and steppes below.*

deep gorges, rushing streams, alpine meadows and glittering snowfields made the Chinese call them the Tien Shan, meaning Heavenly Mountains. A Russian, Peter Semonyov, was the first European to explore them in 1856, with an escort of Cossacks. From Alma-Ata they climbed to Lake Issyk-Kul – the sky blue 'hot lake', so called because it never freezes. It is the world's largest mountain lake, four times the size of Greater London.

It is said that Tamerlane, the 14th-century Turkic leader, bade his men each to take a stone from the lake shore and pile it by the Santash Pass (the Pass of the Counted Stones) when they crossed the mountains, probably to attack the Chinese. On the return, each man took a stone from the pile; by the number remaining Tamerlane knew how many men were lost. Semonyov crossed the Santash Pass to behold the highest Tien Shan peaks – Pik Pobedy, 24,406ft (7439m) and Hantengri Feng, 22,949ft (6995m), on the Chinese border. Among the plant life are wild fruit trees, roses, tulips and wild onions. Ibex and mountain sheep and goats graze around the snow line, and rare snow leopards haunt the forests, where wolves, wild boar and bears also roam.

SCARLET KING *The many kids of tulip that carpet the Tien Shan in spring include the rare and beautiful Greig's tulip, with flowers 3in (75mm) long.*

163

Band-e Amir Lakes

NATURAL LIMESTONE DAMS CUT ACROSS A RIVER TO FORM A CHAIN OF GLASSY LAKES HIGH IN THE HINDU KUSH MOUNTAINS

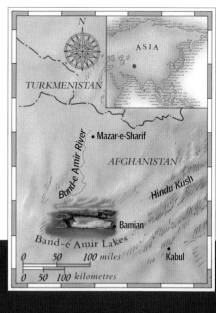

Hidden among the sunbaked western foothills of the Hindu Kush, where rain is rare and water is scarce, is a ribbon of cool, gleaming lakes. They lie along the Band-e Amir River at an altitude of just under 10,000ft (3000m), and can be reached only along 50 miles (80km) of mountain track from the Afghan town of Bamian. Those who venture this way come upon a scene of startling beauty.

Walled in by purple-tinged cliffs of limestone and clay, the lakes are scattered

along a 7 mile (11km) stretch of river. From each lake the river trickles over a natural rock dam, where it forms a meandering latticework of streams and marshy flats with willows, mosses, grass and water plants reaching down to the next lake shore.

The lakes vary in colour from milky white to blue-green, deep blue and dark green, depending on the water's depth, the light intensity and the numbers and

AFGHAN JEWELS *Natural rock dams contain the Band-e Amir River in a chain of lakes amid arid mountains.*

types of algae (minute plants) living in the water. They range in length from just 300ft (90m) to more than 4 miles (6km).

At the height of summer, midday temperatures here soar to 36°C (97°F), and people and animals – such as hyenas – seek shade. But the lakes, topped up each spring with meltwater from mountain snows, still have an icy chill. It is mainly in summer that the natural dams between the lakes, some taller than a two-storey house, develop stalactites formed from the minerals of the surrounding rocks.

These minerals, chiefly calcium carbonate, are entirely responsible for the existence of the lakes. When the snow melts, it percolates through the limestone and marl and dissolves some of their mineral content, which is then carried into the river.

SPARKLING ROCK BUILT UP BY FLOWING WATER

When the calcium carbonate solution comes into contact with water plants, chemical reactions cause some of it to be deposited as layers of residue on the lake bed and rim. Over time this crystalises and solidifies to form a porous rock known as travertine. It is the travertine coating that sparkles in

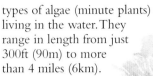

STRIPED SURVIVOR *Its layer of woolly underfur keeps the striped hyena of the Band-e Amir Valley warm in winter.*

the sunlight at the water's edge, and its reflections from the lake beds contribute to the variations in water colour.

And it is the build-up of travertine over the centuries that has dammed the river to form the chain of lakes. But Afghan folklore offers a different explanation. It tells how Ali, son-in-law of the Prophet Mohammed, was furious with a local tyrant who tried to hold him prisoner in the Band-e Amir Valley. In his rage he caused a landslide that blocked the river and created the lake now called Band-e Haibat (Dam of Wrath). There is an element of reality in the tale, for some of the travertine dams overlie debris from ancient landslides.

COLOUR VARIATION *Lakes are often coloured varying shades of green and blue (above), according to differences in their depth and the amount of minute water life.*

Indus Valley

FROM AN ICY SPRING ON THE ROOF OF THE WORLD, THE INDUS RIVER ARCS ACROSS PAKISTAN TO SCORCHING COASTAL PLAINS

Although the Indus River takes its name from the Sanskrit word *sindhu*, meaning 'defender', it was known in ancient Hindu legend as the Lion River, said to issue from a lion's mouth. Not until 1907 was the mouth of the lion discovered – by a Swedish explorer named Sven Hedin. He traced the river back to a small spring at 17,000ft (5200m) on a Tibetan mountainside in the Kailas Range, one of the most rugged parts of the Himalayas.

Hemmed in on each side by the towering, snow-capped Himalayan peaks and the Karakoram Range, the Indus cuts across the roof of the world through harsh, barren gorges, dropping 12,000ft (3660m) in 350 miles (560km).

THE BEND OF THE RIVER

Beneath the desolate, precipitous slopes of Nanga Parbat (the Naked Mountain), which rises to 26,660ft (8126m), the river makes a sharp turn and continues through gorges more than 15,000ft (4600m) deep – some so overshadowed that the sun can scarcely reach down into them.

At Kalabagh, at the southern end of the 1 mile (1.6km) wide Attock Gorge, the Indus finally breaks out of the mountains, and widens to about 10 miles (16km) as it spreads onto the plains of the Punjab. Here, joined by five major tributaries and with innumerable canals, it provides the plains of the Punjab and Sindh with the world's largest irrigation system.

During summer, temperatures here can reach 50°C (122°F). Summer is the

MOUNTAIN FASTNESS *Near Skardu on the upper Indus, the river gorge widens for 20 miles (32km) to form a sandy basin enclosed by high purple mountains.*

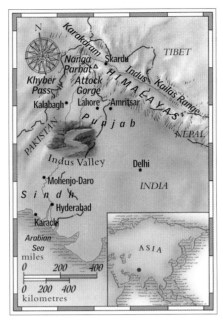

time when melting snow and monsoon rains bring three months of flooding. The floods may create havoc, breaking down flood barriers and forming a large inland sea. In September 1992, the worst floods for some 50 years drowned more than 2000 people and ruined about 4 million acres (1,620,000 hectares) of crops.

The plains of Sind have been rich farmland for more than 4000 years. In 1922 excavations uncovered the city of Mohenjo-Daro beside the river. It was part of the Indus Valley civilisation that flourished for some 1000 years at about the same time as the Egyptian and Mesopotamian civilisations, and is known to have traded with China and the Middle East. The citizens lived in brick-built houses – some with drains, baths and lavatories – and made pots of copper and bronze. Transport was by elephant (the first known to be domesticated) or bullock cart.

Alexander the Great sailed down the Indus in 327–326 BC. His army crossed the Khyber Pass and built a bridge across the Attock Gorge. From there it took them nine months to travel some 700 miles (1120km) to the sea.

As the Indus reaches the Arabian Sea at the end of its 1740 mile (2800km) course, it spreads sluggishly to a marshy delta almost the size of Corsica. Approaching the coast, tamarisk trees lining streams give way to mangroves on the many islands. And for about 10 miles (16km) from shore, the sea's reddish hue comes from the millions of tons of silt the river deposits daily.

MIGHTY BUT MILD

Despite its fearsome appearance, the gharial (or gavial) - a crocodile found in the Indus River - lives mainly on fish. Gharials are among the largest members of the crocodile family, and have hardly changed in 200 million years. A male can weigh 30 stone (200kg) and be 21ft (6.4m) long from its panhandle snout to its thick, scaly tail.

The gharial is found in clear, fast-flowing water. To catch fish, it snaps with its long, slender jaws (which are easier to clap together underwater than are broad jaws) and seizes small fish with its sharp teeth. Like many other crocodiles, gharials were hunted for their skins; this, along with habitat loss, brought them almost to extinction. Now they are an endangered species.

LIGHT BITE *A gharial catches a fish with a quick snap of its long and slender jaws.*

Kopet Dag

BARREN PEAKS STAND
GUARD OVER A DESERT
THAT IS ONE OF THE
WORLD'S LARGEST AND
MOST INHOSPITABLE

Bare and mercilessly arid, the Kopet Dag mountains form an impenetrable barrier that divides the former Soviet state of Turkmenistan from its southern neighbour Iran.

The weathered peaks resemble sentinels that have stood guard over the Turkmenistan capital, Ashkhabad, and its vast desert hinterland since the beginning of time. But Kopet Dag, by geological standards, is young, and violent earthquakes shake the region, indicating that the Earth's crust is still heaving upwards.

From the base of the Kopet Dag range, the desert of Karakum, one of the hottest and biggest in the world, stretches far away beyond the northern horizon. Dust fills the moistureless air, covering the land in an eerie canopy which almost obscures a sea of crescent-shaped sand dunes.

MOON MOUNTAINS *Local people call these pale foothills of Kopet Dag 'moon mountains'. The dry climate and thin soil keep them almost devoid of plants.*

KOPET DAG

Kali Gandaki

A RIVER RISING IN LITTLE-KNOWN COUNTRY HAS CARVED EARTH'S DEEPEST VALLEY BETWEEN THE HIGHEST PEAKS OF THE HIMALAYAS

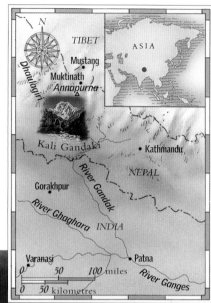

When men first walked upon the Earth, the Himalayas bore only a passing likeness to the mighty bastion that we know today. This is not because mankind is so ancient, but because the Himalayas, geologically speaking, are so very young. Far older than the Himalayas, however, is the Kali Gandaki River that flows between towering mountains in the Himalayan kingdom of Nepal.

Some 50 million years ago the Kali Gandaki drained down from the Tibetan plains and then wound through

gentle hills. Since then, and especially in the last few million years, the land has been pushed up to form the mightiest of mountain ranges, the product of a collision between two plates of the Earth's crust.

DEEPER AND DEEPER

While the mountains rose upwards, the Kali Gandaki maintained its ancient course. The river's downward cutting kept pace with the mountains' uplift, and its valley grew ever deeper as great mountain walls rose about it.

And what walls they are. Where it passes between Annapurna Himal and Dhaulagiri Himal, both soaring to over 26,000ft (8000m), the river lies in the deepest valley on Earth. Its waters, 14,400ft (4400m) below the mountain summits that tower above on either side, are black with mud after the rains, as black as Kali, the Hindu destroyer-goddess who gave the river her name.

The north–south cut that the Kali Gandaki made through the Himalayas has for millennia been one of the great thoroughfares of Asia. Deeply worn paths scramble high above the river's staircase rapids, varying the pace occasionally with a dizzily swaying suspension bridge. Following this route between India and Tibet down the ages came an endless cavalcade of holy men and pilgrims, merchants and soldiers, and ordinary folk. Most importantly, it was the way of the horse and mule caravans that traded Tibetan salt for Nepalese grain.

On its course through the Himalayan massif, the valley's climate changes dramatically. The northern end, in the rain shadow of the mountains, is more or less a cold desert, supporting only thin scrub. Just two days' march to the south, however, brings you to an astonishing contrast of semitropical monsoon forest, with bananas and oranges, while in between the deepest part of the gorge holds villages of stone houses among terraced fields of barley.

As befits a great and ancient highway, many different peoples have settled in the valley. Dominant among them are the Thakali, whose stone houses have enclosed courtyards to ward off the winter winds. They traditionally divided their time between farming and salt trading, but recently, since the valley has become popular with Western mountaineers and trekkers, many have

HIGH PEAKS DRIFTER *The Himalayan griffon may soar effortlessly for hours on rising air currents, while seeking out carrion in the valleys below.*

taken up innkeeping as well. Not that this is a novel occupation along the Kali Gandaki, for near its northern end is Muktinath, a place of Hindu pilgrimage for many centuries. Equally revered by Buddhists, Muktinath temple is built over a 'miraculous' burning spring, where flames of natural gas dance over spring water which flows from the same fissure in the limestone rock.

Appropriately for a river surrounded by wonders, the Kali Gandaki rises in the poetically named Land of Lo – the ancient kingdom of Mustang. Situated just inside Nepal, on its border with Tibet, the area is virtually cut off from the rest of the world by deserts and mountains. Isolation and necessity have enforced unusual social patterns – women take several husbands, which contributes to sexual equality and ensures that children are very unlikely to be orphaned. In these harsh mountains there is no land to spare for burials, nor fuel for funeral pyres, so the dead are reverently laid on the mountainside, under the immense airy skies and with towering peaks for monuments, to await the vultures.

FOR MILLENNIA IT HAS BEEN ONE OF ASIA'S GREAT THOROUGHFARES

SILVER RIBBON *The shining thread of the Kali Gandaki flows far below the ethereal peak of Dhaulagiri, on the right of the picture, and the slopes of the Annapurna range on the left.*

Mt Everest

EARTH'S HIGHEST
MOUNTAIN ROSE FROM
THE SEA INTO THE
CLOUDS, CREATING A
TEMPTING TARGET FOR
ADVENTURERS

Fossilised fish remains have been found high on the frozen slopes of Mount Everest – proof that once, millions of years ago, the world's highest mountain lay at the bottom of the sea. How Everest came to travel halfway across the world and then rise up to reach two-thirds of the way through the Earth's atmosphere is just one of the fascinating stories that add to the romance of this magnificent mountain. About 200 million years ago the Indian subcontinent broke away from a vast southern super-continent called Gondwanaland. It drifted north-east across the sea, and collided with the Asian landmass. Just as two cars in a head-on collision crumple, compact and then rise towards each other, so these immense landmasses buckled, folded and rose up to form the world's loftiest mountains, one of which is the 29,028ft (8848m) Mount Everest.

The Tibetan names for the mountain translate variously as 'Goddess of the Mountain Snows', 'Goddess Mother of the World' and 'Mountain So High That No Bird Can Fly Over It'. It was first measured in 1852 and was called Peak XV until 1865, when it was named Mount Everest, after the British Surveyor General of India, Sir George Everest. He was a tireless, meticulous military engineer, instrumental in achieving the first accurate mapping of India and the Himalayas.

This had been no easy task. Both Nepal and Tibet were reluctant to admit foreigners, and all observations had to be made from a distance, some from as far as 100 miles (160km) away. This gave rise to inaccuracy on a grand scale. So it was with great secrecy that Sir George Everest recruited Himalayan traders (later known as Pundits – a Hindi word meaning 'learned experts') to infiltrate the area and, painstakingly and

HIGH COLOUR *Sunset serenity on Mount Everest can change to nights and days of swirling mists, blizzards and sudden rock falls.*

discreetly, gather enough information to allow accurate maps to be made.

After 1920, the Tibetans allowed a number of British expeditions to visit Mount Everest. The most famous of them, in 1924, included George Leigh

Mallory, a schoolteacher and experienced mountaineer who, when asked why he was so determined to climb the mountain, gave the laconic and much-quoted reply, 'Because it's there'.

Mallory and Andrew Irvine, a 22-

year-old mountaineer on his first Himalayan expedition, were last seen about 800ft (244m) from the top on June 8, before swirling cloud and mist hid them from sight. They were never seen alive again. Nine years later an ice

REACHING NEW HEIGHTS

GOING UP *The highest ever hot-air balloon launch took place on October 21, 1991, beside Lake Gokyo (above) – 15,800ft (4816m) above sea level in the Himalayas.*

HIGH DRAMA *Star Flyer I passes above Everest, an event recorded by a camera mounted outside the basket.*

Perched on a platform mounted outside the basket of a hot air balloon, British cameraman Leo Dickinson set out to film the first ever flight of a hot air balloon across the summit of Everest. Unfortunately the balloons – Star Flyer I and II – failed to take off together, and a separation of 10 miles (16km) made filming between balloons impossible.

This was the first disaster to strike the adventurous Star Over Everest project.

Star Flyer I made a rapid ascent and cleared the top of Everest. Then, over Tibet, it began to run short of fuel and dropped quickly. The wind swept it into a moraine at a glacier's foot, and up a hill. It hit a boulder, and the crew (who both survived) fell from the basket. Star Flyer II's burners failed 2000ft (600m) below the summit, giving its crew just four minutes to clear the summit. It was a close shave – but they succeeded.

axe belonging to one of them was found, well below the position of their last sighting. Whether they reached the top and died on their way down, or perished before reaching it, will never be known. In 1999 Mallory's remains were found, but there was no trace of Irvine, or their camera.

Sherpa guides and porters were essential on climbs. Sherpa, a Tibetan word meaning 'men of the East', is not the name for anybody who carries loads in the Himalayas, but refers to the sturdy people who live in the high valleys south of Everest. Their good-humoured tolerance of eccentric foreigners and reverence for the mountains themselves meant they were loyal to the point of self-sacrifice.

In the early 1950s the Nepalese government admitted foreign climbers, which opened up a totally different approach route. In 1953, the British mountaineer Colonel John Hunt led an expedition which included a 33-year-old New Zealand beekeeper, Edmund Hillary. After several unsuccessful attempts by other team members, Hillary and Sherpa Tenzing Norgay set out from the base camp on the South Col of the mountain at dawn on May 29. Five hours later they reached the summit. Everest was conquered!

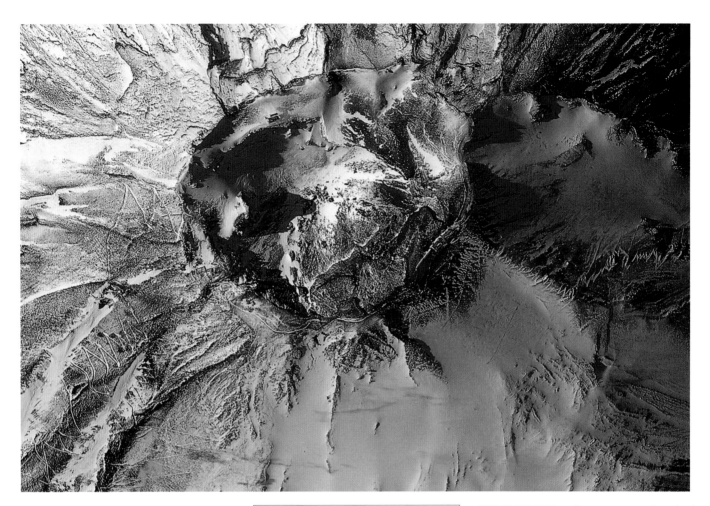

Mount Fuji

THE ELEGANT CONE THAT FORMS JAPAN'S HIGHEST MOUNTAIN HAS LONG INSPIRED RESPECT AND DEVOTION

Mount Fuji is as much a symbol of Japan as the rising sun. Its huge cone, cloaked in snow for most of the year, rises lonely and graceful from low plains behind Honshu's Pacific coast. Countless artists and photographers have made its distinctive profile familiar the world over, and poets have tried to capture its splendour in words. Yet for those who visit it, the mountain evokes a feeling of awe and wonder for which no amount of words and pictures can prepare them.

Mount Fuji's appeal lies in more than its massive, isolated elegance. It comes also from the way in which the mountain is constantly changing – its lights and moods vary, the hem of its uneven mantle of snow rises and falls, and clouds often move in to obscure its

CHILLY SUMMIT *Walkers in vast numbers climb the zigzagging paths to Mount Fuji's summit – a volcanic crater covered in snow for most of the year.*

summit, to the disappointment of those whose visit is brief. And although writers galore have proclaimed the geometrical perfection of Mount Fuji's cone, another part of the mountain's appeal lies in its slight departures from perfect symmetry. There is just a slight difference in the way its sides sweep upward, and they meet at a wrinkled horizontal line, not at a point.

The rough-edged summit is in fact the rim of a crater, for the 12,389ft (3776m) Mount Fuji is a volcano – and not an extinct one. Successive out-pourings of lava and ash have built up this massive mountain whose base measures 78 miles (125km) around. An eruption was first recorded in AD 800, and several others occurred between then and the most recent outburst, in 1707, when black ash fell in the streets of Tokyo, some 60 miles (96km) away.

The Japanese refer to the mountain as Fuji-san, giving it the respectful title due an honoured person. Japan's indigenous Ainu people held the mountain sacred, and its name may be derived from *fuchi*, an Ainu word meaning 'fire'. It has also been sacred to followers of Shinto, the Japanese religion in which nature spirits and ancestors are venerated, and to Buddhists. Fuji-ko (Society of Fuji) is a religious sect dedicated to the mountain; it was founded in 1558 and has many followers today.

Buddhist artists have often portrayed the scene at Lake Kawaguchi, where Mount Fuji is mirrored in the still waters. The lake is one of five lying in an area rich in forests, streams and waterfalls where, despite the trappings of tourism, Fuji can be seen at its most imposing. Together with the nearby coastline, the mountain, lakes and forests form a national park that is visited each year by a staggering 80 million people – equivalent to two-thirds of Japan's population.

THE HEM OF FUJI'S UNEVEN MANTLE OF SNOW RISES AND FALLS

Of this vast influx of visitors, at least 250,000 climb up Mount Fuji's slopes. The mountain has been a place of pilgrimage, for men at least, for centuries – women were not allowed to climb it until 1868. Each pilgrim carried a stone, as a symbolic way of lightening the burden of sin the world below.

Most of today's visitors come in July and August, when the summit is almost clear of snow, and they follow one of six well-trodden routes to the top. Among the mountain walkers are a few white-clad Fuji-ko pilgrims. Walkers and pilgrims make their way up from pine and larch forests where cherry trees and azaleas bloom in spring, to windswept upper slopes where only the hardiest of low shrubs can maintain a foothold. The climb is strenuous, the weather can change abruptly, and it becomes steadily colder towards the top, where even in August the temperature may be only around 6°C (43°F).

On the final leg of the ascent, the paths climb up boulder-strewn slopes to Fuji's summit – the crater rim. Eight peaks – the 'eight petals of Fuji' – rise

SLIPPERY SLOPE *Climbers can speed their descent from Fuji's summit by sliding down fine volcanic ash (left).*

from the roughly circular rim, giving the summit its scalloped appearance. The 750yd (700m) wide crater, known as Nai-in (the Sanctuary), is venerated, too.

Many visitors make the long climb at night, and reach the summit in time to watch the sunrise. At the end of the cold summer night, the hidden sun briefly casts glorious splashes of purple, copper and red over the sky before starting its passage over the horizon. As the light strengthens there are unforgettable views over lakes and forests to the coastline, likened by one writer to 'a meandering smear brushed in with purple ink'. Behind, meanwhile, the triangular shadow of Japan's sacred mountain creeps across the land.

ROSE TINTED *The rising sun spotlights snow on Mount Fuji, whose classic lines have made it an ideal of natural beauty.*

MOUNT FUJI IN ART

Mount Fuji has appeared in paintings since the Middle Ages, when Zen Buddhist monks sought harmonious landscapes as an aid to contemplation. Later it was a favourite subject with the wood block artists Harunobu (1725–70) and Hokusai (1760–1849).

Harunobu's scenes of graceful figures sometimes have Fuji in the background; Hokusai's landscape prints drew attention to Fuji as a symbol of purity and beauty.

BACKDROP *Mount Fuji appears in Harunobu's* Salt Maidens *(left) and in this detail of Hokusai's* Great Wave at Kanagawa.

Yangtze Gorges

THE WORLD'S THIRD-LONGEST RIVER WHIRLS THROUGH THREE SCENIC MOUNTAIN GORGES IN THE HEART OF CHINA

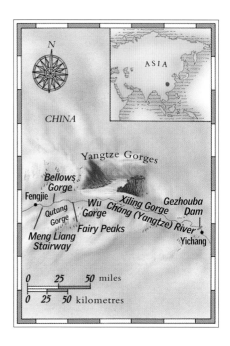

D u Fu, a Chinese poet of the 7th century Tang Dynasty, described the entrance to Qutang Gorge as the gateway where all the waters of Sichuan province battled to gain access. The water boils and swells as the Yangtze River enters the narrow mouth – less than 330ft (100m) wide – between sheer limestone cliffs twice the height of the Eiffel Tower.

After heavy rain, the river here has been known to flow at 20mph (32km/h) and the water to rise by 170ft (50m). Isabella Bird, a British traveller who was returning downriver in 1897, wrote: 'We went down like a flash – down smooth hills of water, where rapids had been obliterated; down leaping races, where they had been created; past hideous whirlpools, where

EASTERN MYSTERY *Mist-shrouded mountains rise in splendour high above the narrow Xiling Gorge, which is the easternmost of the three Yangtze Gorges.*

to have been sucked in would have been destruction.'

Qutang Gorge, 5 miles (8km) long, is the shortest of the three Yangtze Gorges. They stretch for about 120 miles (190km) between Fengjie to Yichang – about midway along the river's 3915 mile (6300km) course from

Tibet to the sea. In Chinese the river, the world's third longest, is known as Chang Jiang ('Long River'); the name Yangtze refers only to the estuary near Shanghai, but Europeans have applied the name to the whole river.

The three gorges were carved by the river's powerful action as it cut its way through the mountain rim of China's great Sichuan (or Red) Basin. Some of the flanking cliffs form strange shapes that figure in Chinese legends, and bear names such as 'Wise Grandmother's

green hillsides have cultivated terraces, where grain and fruit such as apples, peaches, apricots, persimmons and Chinese chestnuts are grown. Isabella Bird described similar cultivation in Xiling Gorge, the third gorge, which winds for 47 miles (75km). She told of carefully tended patches, some no larger than a bath towel, to which the cultivators descended on ropes. Today there are still some farmhouses perched dramatically on rocky spurs amid groves of golden and green bamboo, and of mauve primulas blooming among profusions of maidenhair fern.

DANGERS REMOVED

Xiling Gorge was once the most dangerous gorge of all, with narrow passages, reefs, rapids and whirlpools. In the 1950s, huge rocks jutting up from the middle of the river were blown up to make the river safer for boats. One such rock was the Goose Tail described by Isabella Bird, which was 130ft (40m) above the water on her upstream journey but only just visible on the return four months later.

Modern travellers go through the gorges aboard diesel-powered ferries, but old-time travellers had cramped journeys in junks powered by sail and oars. When travelling upriver, junks had to be rope-hauled by sweating men known as trackers, each tied into a shoulder harness and struggling to find a meagre footing on the muddy banks. Isabella Bird described the scene: 'The wild rush of the cataract; the great junks hauled up the channel on the north side by 400 men each, hanging trembling in the surges, or, as in one case, from a tow-rope breaking, spinning down the cataract at tremendous speed into frightful perils.' The French missionary, Pere David, narrowly escaped death in the boiling Xintan Rapids in Xiling Gorge in the 1860s – the boat in which he was being hauled upriver almost collided with one hurtling down.

The massive Gezhouba Dam now controls the river just below the Xiling Gorge, taming the flow before it spreads wide on its way to Shanghai. Soon the much higher Sanxia (Three Gorges) Dam will occupy the site. Planned amid much controversy, this will change the Yangtze into a placid reservoir all through the gorges.

Spring' and 'Rhinoceros Looking at the Moon'. On each side of the mouth of Qutang Gorge, there are 1000-year-old iron pillars embedded in the rock from which chains were slung across the river – first as a defence barrier, later as a toll bar for collecting fees from boats.

CLIFF STAIRWAY

The Meng Liang Stairway, a series of small holes forming a Z shape, is visible on the side of Bai Yan Shan (White Salt Mountain). The holes were once used to slot in rungs for a cliff ladder, perhaps for collecting rare medicinal herbs. Opposite is a steep section of cliff called Bellows Gorge because of its shape. Warriors were once buried in caves near the top; some ancient coffins are still lodged in crevices.

Scenic Wu Gorge, 25 miles (40km) long, is dominated by the twelve Fairy Peaks. Legend says they were once the daughters of the Goddess of the West, sent by the Queen of Heaven to help create the gorges. Some of the steep

Yellow Mountain

VISITING THE YELLOW MOUNTAIN IS LIKE STEPPING INTO A CHINESE PAINTING OF PRECIPITOUS CRAGS AND GNARLED TREES

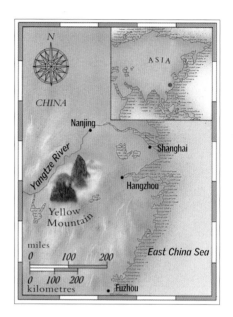

towering pinnacles in the hard rock.

Chinese poets and painters identified four 'ultimate beauties' in the Yellow Mountain. The rocks and the mountain peaks are one. Second are the statuesque pines, some over 1000 years old, and third, the hot, restorative springs that flow at a constant 42°C (108°F) all year. The fourth ultimate beauty is the sea of clouds.

Cloud is an essential feature of the landscape, bringing an average of 94in (2400mm) of rain and snow each year. Banks of fog and drizzle swirl around the peaks, veiling them and revealing them in a ceaseless dance. The hundreds of thousands of visitors who flock to the Yellow Mountain every summer

TRUE LIKENESS *On a silk scroll (below), tiny figures make their way between towering crags in a landscape not dissimilar to the Yellow Mountain.*

C hina's Yellow Mountain might be a landscape from the world of make-believe. Vertical walls of rock rise from soft folds of mist and cloud. Here and there, spindly pines lean out from unlikely toeholds in ledges and clefts, defying gravity like circus acrobats. The impression is of a Chinese painting made real – the artists had invented nothing.

The Yellow Mountain (Huang Shan) lies to the south of the Yangtze River where it makes its final huge sweep through lowlands to the sea. It is a mountain in the Chinese sense of the word – not just one peak but a cluster of 72 of them. The tallest three rise over 5900ft (1800m); they are Lianhua Feng, 'Lotus Flower Peak'; Guangming Ding, 'Summit of Brightness'; and Tiandu Feng, 'Heavenly Capital Peak'.

GRANITE PINNACLES

All the peaks are hewn from granite that crystallised from molten rock far underground before being exposed at the surface. The granite's few fractures have been attacked by the weather, and erosion has left massive rock faces and

WINTER GUISE *Above the clouds, snow dusts pine trees that sprout from the Yellow Mountain's angular pillars of rock.*

come prepared with raincoats, and with padded jackets to keep out the chill, for even in summer the temperature on high ground is no higher than 8°C (46°F).

The ambition of China's 1000 million people, it is said, is to visit the Yellow Mountain at least once in their lives. Carefully marked paths take walkers past the shrines, waterfalls and pools, the unusual rock

formations, and the most revered pine trees. Some of these paths are not for the faint-hearted. To reach the Heavenly Capital Peak, visitors have to climb 1300 steps and cross the Carp's Backbone, a ridge less than 3ft (1m) wide with only a chain to hold on to.

There are five sacred mountains in China, but the Yellow Mountain is not one of them. Nonetheless, its beauty has been revered

for centuries. Xu Xiake, a traveller of medieval China, gave it the ultimate accolade when he wrote: 'Having returned from the five sacred mountains, one does not want to look at ordinary mountains; having returned from the Yellow Mountain, one does not want to look at the five sacred mountains.'

MORNING BLUSH *(overleaf) The rising sun bathes the Yellow Mountain's peaks and sea of clouds with light.*

A CHINESE PAINTING MADE REAL – THE ARTISTS INVENTED NOTHING

Guilin Hills

CLUSTERS OF STEEP, NARROW HILLS IN SOUTHERN CHINA LOOK LIKE THE MODEL FOR A TYPICAL CHINESE PAINTING

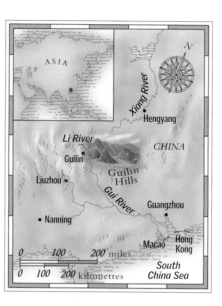

Cinnamon scents the air in the Chinese town of Guilin from August to October, when the cassia trees are in bloom. These yellow-flowered tropical trees grow there in profusion, and give the town its name – Chinese for 'forest of cassia'. But Guilin, and the countryside nearby, is most renowned for its dream-like landscape of strange limestone hills, which make it one of the most stunningly beautiful places in China – the inspiration for Chinese poets and painters of the past.

These limestone towers rise abruptly for a 75 mile (120km) stretch along the banks of the Li River, amid a flat landscape of rice paddies. The poet Han Yu (768–834) described the river as a turquoise belt and the hills as jade hair ornaments. Stunted trees draped with slender vines cling precariously to the steep hillsides, which are often shrouded in mist. Bamboo boats on the river carry fishermen and the cormorants that they use to make their catch.

Because of their weird shapes, the hills have been given descriptive names such as Five Tigers Catching a Goat and Climbing Tortoise. Camel Hill looks so much like a seated camel that it could have been sculpted from the rock. But from some angles it also resembles a wine ewer, so it is also known as Ewer Hill. At its foot there is a spot known as the Grave of Lei the Drinker, said to be that of Lei Mingchun of the Ming dynasty (1368-1644) who, after the collapse of the Ming, used to climb the hill to drown his sorrows. The tallest hill is Piled Festoon Hill, 400ft (120m) high.

According to legend, Elephant Trunk Hill, which stands beside the Li River, was once the elephant on which the King of Heaven toured southern China. The elephant became ill, and a Guilin farmer restored it to health. The grateful elephant helped him in his fields, and the King of Heaven was so angry that he turned the animal to stone. At the base of the hill the elephant's 'trunk' dips into the water forming an archway called Moon in the Water Arch, because it reflects in the water like a full moon.

WEATHERED LIMESTONE

The truth about the Guilin Hills, however, is far less romantic. About 300 million years ago the region was covered by an ocean, but movements in the Earth's crust pushed the ocean floor above sea level. Thick layers of limestone were exposed to the wind and waves, and only the most resistant parts survived as the mounds of rock formations known as tower karst.

Seven Star Park on the outskirts of Guilin is named after Seven Star Hill, which has seven peaks arranged like the Great Bear constellation, and there is also a Seven Star Cave. The park's Flower Bridge, built in 1540, has arches that form a complete circle with their reflection in the water. From the top of the bridge there are marvellous views of the surrounding landscape.

CHINESE CHARM *Set against an azure sky, the steep Guilin Hills rise abruptly from the peaceful landscape, and are reflected in the mirror-calm Li River.*

FANTASTIC UNDERWORLD

Beneath the Guilin Hills lies a vast network of limestone caverns such as Gaoyan, or High Cave (below), which passes through a conical hill. In many caves, an amazing array of stalagmites and stalactites create an underworld as dramatic as the scenery above.

One of the most magnificent caves is the Reed Flute Cave, so called because the entrance was once hidden by clumps of reeds that were used by the locals to fashion musical instruments. The cave is over 275yds (250m) long and 130yds (120m) across, and its rock formations include one known as the Old Scholar. Legend says that he was once a poet who sat down to describe the beauties of the cave. Unable to find words vivid enough to finish his poem, he turned to stone.

Thousands of tourists visit the most spectacular of Guilin's caves every year. During World War II, however, the caves served a different purpose – the people of Guilin used them as air-raid shelters when the town was bombed by the Japanese.

SOARING SPLENDOUR *Astounding stalagmites around 100ft (30m) high (left) can be seen in Guilin's caves.*

Taklimakan Desert

ONE OF THE WORLD'S LARGEST SANDY WASTES WAS SKIRTED BY SILK ROAD TRAVELLERS BETWEEN CHINA AND THE MEDITERRANEAN

DESOLATION *The barren, sandy wastes of the Taklimakan Desert cover an area about the size of New Zealand.*

Wind-blown sand shrouds the Taklimakan Desert in western China for most of the year. Sand dunes rise as high as 1000ft (300m), and when winds reach hurricane force, they blow up walls of sand three times as high. The name Taklimakan is from the Turkic for 'Go in and you won't come out'.

To travellers on the ancient Silk Route from China to the Levant (East Mediterranean), the oases of Turpan (Turfan) and Kashi (Kashgar) must have been welcome indeed. Yet Turpan, on the eastern fringe of the Taklimakan Desert, seems an unlikely spot for an oasis. It lies within a great saucer of arid rock – the Turpan Depression, which, at 505ft (154m) below sea level, is one of the world's lowest and hottest places. It seldom rains, and temperatures can be around 40°C (104°F) for weeks on end.

Yet melons and grapes grown here have refreshed travellers for centuries. Turpan's water supply comes from the Heavenly Mountains (Tien Shan) to the north and is carried to the town by an ingenious system of wells and underground channels, known as *karez*, that was invented by the ancient Persians.

SILK ROUTE CITY

Until sea routes took over in the 15th century, goods were carried by camel caravans between the Mediterranean and China along the 4000 mile (6400km) Silk Route.

Mud-brick ruins 10 miles (16km) west of Turpan are all that remains of Jiaohe (below), founded in 200 BC. It was part of a kingdom with Indian and Persian elements and became a key town on the route, as did Gaochang, whose ruins lie east of Turpan.

ACCEPTING A CHALLENGE FROM NATURE

For some adventurers, no landscape is too difficult or too threatening to tackle

Most people are content to view Nature's more extreme spectacles, such as burning fields of lava or pinnacles of frozen rock, from a distance. Others feel compelled to savour them at first hand, to take up the challenges they present. What draws these people to perform feats of such astounding daring that one false step can result in death? Perhaps it is the thrill of combining strength and stamina with mental agility, or the desire to be overwhelmed by Nature's grandeur or, in the words of a Swiss mountain lover, to play a game 'in which the player tastes most keenly the joy of being alive'.

LIFE IN HER HANDS
French rock climber Catherine Destivelle (above) dangles from the edge of a flat-topped cone of rock above a yawning gorge in Canyonlands, Utah.

MOUNTAIN DAWN
Mountaineer Chris Bonington photographed dawn breaking on Mount Cook, New Zealand, which he scaled with fellow 'Everesters' in 1976.

FROZEN CASCADE
An Alaskan rock climber, Roman Dial, seeks out frozen waterfalls as a test of skill and nerves.

FIRE WALKER
German scientist Katia Krafft (below), who with her husband spent 20 years studying volcanoes, walks in protective clothing by a lava flow on Hawaii's Mauna Loa.

EARLY MOUNTAINEERS
An 1840 print of Mont Blanc (above) shows the popularity of mountaineering in the 19th century, and the simplicity of the climbers' equipment.

HIGH KICK
Overhanging Rock, in Yosemite Valley (left), has tempted daredevils since 1879 when a guide threatened to throw his girlfriend off unless she married him.

ALPINE FLIGHT
Powered only by air currents, a hang-glider drifts high above the clouds over the Swiss Alps, body held prone to minimise drag.

Lunan Stone Forest

CLUSTERS OF FLUTED LIMESTONE PILLARS TOWER TOWARDS THE SKY, WITH A MAZE OF NARROW PATHWAYS WINDING AMONG THEM

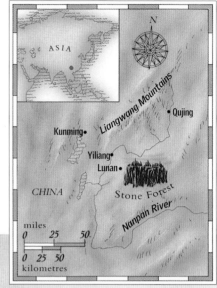

Rhododendrons and camellias grow wild in profusion in the subtropical climate of China's south-western Yunnan province. Kunming, the capital, is known as the City of Eternal Spring, and the area is a treasure house of plants and trees. But the forest that lies on a plateau 75 miles (120km) south-east of Kunming is not noted for trees – it is named for its forest of limestone pillars carved to strange shapes by time and the elements.

Lunan Stone Forest, which covers an area of about 2sq miles (5km²), has countless stone pillars that range from about human height to a soaring 100ft (30m). Some look like clumps of bamboo, some like gigantic swords, others like birds and beasts, huge mushrooms and pagodas. Describing them has stimulated the imagination of generations, as some of the allotted names reveal – 'Phoenix Preening its Feathers', 'Layered Waterfall',

A LABYRINTH OF SHELTERED PLACES FOR LOVERS' MEETINGS

'Lion Arbour' and 'Lotus Blossom Peak'.

Some of the pillars are clustered together in their hundreds, others stand in relative isolation. In the dark recesses between the pillars there are pools and grottoes and twisting passageways matted with vegetation.

Man-made footpaths thread their way between vertical rock walls and, with endless junctions dictated by the whims of the rock pattern, the paths form a maze that

outdoes any human creation. In places there are bridges, both man-made and natural, and pavilions that give the feel of a forest garden.

Many of the rocks are coated with lichen and moss, and despite the scarcity of soil and the limited daylight in the denser parts of the forest, some creepers manage to thrive, clinging to the rock

LUNAN WILDERNESS *Limestone pinnacles, weathered to angular shapes, stand shoulder to shoulder in a strange Stone Forest in south-west China.*

face, their red and pink flowers adding a splash of colour to the scene.

Millions of years ago this fantastic forest was a solid bed of limestone. Earth movements lifted the rock bed to form a gently sloping plateau and also broke up the limestone with a criss-cross of vertical fractures. Rainwater and soil water, charged with carbon dioxide from the plentiful vegetation, becomes a weak acid that is very effective at dissolving limestone, and the initial fractures were soon enlarged to wide fissures. In the heart of the Stone Forest, much of the original bed of limestone is now gone, dissolved away by the acid, and the rest stands as the sharp, fluted rock pinnacles.

TIGER DANCE

Paddy fields border the forest fringes, and local farmers use water buffaloes to draw the plough. The Sani people who live around the Stone Forest are a branch of the Yi – a minority people within China. In late June each year they hold a Torch Festival with singing and dancing, including a tiger dance with two men dressed as a tiger threatening women picking fruit; the beast is challenged by men with pitchforks.

One of the rocks of the Stone Forest, Ashima Rock, is named after Ashima, a beautiful Sani girl who, according to legend, was kidnapped by a wealthy landowner. Her lover, Ahai, armed with magic, set off in pursuit to rescue her. But tragedy struck – Ashima died and was turned into a rock. Now she waits for Ahai to come to her.

Folk legend also has an explanation for the creation of the Stone Forest. It is accredited to Zhang Guolao, one of the eight Chinese Immortals. The kindly sage was one day riding a donkey across the huge plain when he came upon couples courting in the open. 'Why,' he exclaimed, 'young lovers don't even have a place where they can enjoy a little privacy.' He promptly caused the nearest mountains to tumble stones in a heap around him, creating a labyrinth of sheltered places between them for lovers' meetings.

NATURAL SCULPTURE *The beauty and elegance of the Stone Forest's fluted pillars has inspired Chinese poets.*

Taroko Gorge

THE WONDERS OF A MARBLE VALLEY WERE REVEALED BY A HIGHWAY HACKED THROUGH IMPENETRABLE MOUNTAINS

Taiwan is one of the 'Little Dragons' of Asia – those small places that dragged themselves from the ashes of World War II to astonish the world with the dynamism of their economies. It evokes a picture of container ships, humming factories and seething crowds – for after all, when 20 million busy people are crammed into an island not much bigger than Belgium, there would seem to be little room for idyllic scenery.

SPACE AND BEAUTY

As it happens though, the north-east corner of Taiwan, and much of the east coast, is only sparsely inhabited, largely by the dwindling survivors of aboriginal tribes who lived there thousands of years before the Chinese came. The area is frequently visited by typhoons, and is too rugged and mountainous for intensive farming or industrialisation.

But the scenery here is gorgeous – a land of misty lakes, rushing streams and shapely mountains, of rich forests and of

THE BIG DROP *It took aeons for the Liwu River to carve out the Taroko Gorge, but only five years for men to hack a road into one of its marble cliffs.*

precipices hung with twisty-trunked trees, all in the delicate hues of a Chinese watercolour. It is easy to see why Portuguese sailors named the place Ilha Formosa – 'beautiful island'.

One reason for the isolation of the east coast was the north–south barrier formed by the Central Mountain Range. In the late 1950s, it was decided to push a road through it, connecting Taichung in the west with Taroko in the east, 121 miles (195km) away. The result was the East-West Cross Island Highway, in many places hacked out of

the sheer sides of cliffs, and everywhere an astounding feat of engineering. It is known as 'The Rainbow of Taiwan', and in the five years of its building, it cost the lives of 450 workers, most of them veterans of General Chiang Kai-shek's Kuomintang (Nationalist) Army.

Above the Taroko Gorge there is a monument to them – the Shrine of Eternal Spring, a red-roofed pavilion with a waterfall running through and spilling onto the rocks far below. A bell is rung each morning to greet the dawn, and a drumbeat salutes each sunset.

Taroko Gorge is certainly the loveliest stretch of a remarkable highway, and is, in its own right, a spectacle of world class. Sheer walls of varicoloured marble enclose the wild, tumbling waters of the Liwu River, which winds its way for 12 picturesque miles (20km) from the mountains to the sea.

FANTASTIC SCENERY

Art and Nature have cooperated to make sure of Taroko's popularity with visitors, especially honeymooners. At Tienhsiang, a hotel combines with a shrine and a many-storeyed pagoda set on a misty, wooded peak high above the river. In Swallows' Grotto, the birds soar and wheel in a hole scoured so deep by river pebbles that the sun touches the water only at noon.

For the stout-hearted, there is the Tunnel of Nine Turns – a stretch of highway with many more than nine tunnels and half-tunnels carved out of marble – that give bus passengers fearful glimpses of the ravine floor and a

LIGHT AND SHADE *Water pours from the roof of a cavern along Tunnel Hike, a favourite with Taroko's visitors.*

contrasting panorama of forest climbing the mountainside beyond. At the journey's end are the Wenshan Hot Springs, reached by a swaying suspension bridge over the Liwu River. Steps cut in the cliff lead to a marble grotto filled with hot, sulphurous water opening onto the river. Bathers can lie half in hot, and half in cold, water.

The opening of the highway revealed the full extent of the richness of Taiwan's marble deposits, and there was talk of making Taroko Gorge into one vast quarry. The conservation lobby prevailed, however, and now the gorge and its surrounding mountains, forests and sea cliffs have been declared a

A LAND OF MISTY LAKES, RUSHING STREAMS AND SHAPELY MOUNTAINS

national park. The area harbours a wide variety of wildlife – black bears, wild boars, rock monkeys, sika deer and mountain sheep, some 25 species of reptiles and a large number of birds, including the rare Mikado pheasant.

Their guarantee of living space is particularly important on such a crowded island, and it has been a boon, too, to the original inhabitants of the area. The park enables them to pursue their traditional mixture of farming and hunting, and their colourful festivals attract extra income from tourists.

Marble is quarried around Hualien, the largest town on the east coast. It has probably the only marble airport in the world, as well as pavements of marble mosaic, marble temples, and hotels with bathroom suites and tables – and even wastepaper baskets – all of solid marble. Baggage allowance permitting, you can take home marble lamps, bookends or vases as imperishable reminders of Taroko Gorge.

SUN AND SHADOW *A sunbeam briefly dances over the moss-coated rocks of the gorge's Sibaiyang Falls (right).*

Chocolate Hills

CONICAL HILLS THAT ERUPT FROM THE GROUND ON A PHILIPPINE ISLAND TURN THE COLOUR OF CHOCOLATE DURING THE DRY SEASON

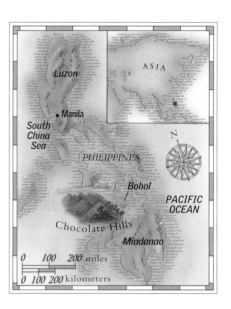

At first glance, the Chocolate Hills of the Philippine island of Bohol look artificial – the result of prodigious human effort, rather than the work of Nature. Hundreds of conical and dome-shaped hills stand in clusters one behind another, like haystacks packed into fields. Wild grasses cloak the hills, and during the February to May dry season they become so parched that the hills turn the chocolate colour that has earned them their name. Then torrential tropical rains arrive, resuscitating the grasses and turning the landscape a brilliant green.

Bohol is one of the Visayas islands that lie at the heart of the Philippines. The island – about the size of Majorca – has earned a special place in Philippine history, for it was here

in 1565 that the first formal treaty was made between the islanders and the Spanish crown. A local chief, Datu Sikatuna, entered into a treaty of friendship with Miguel López de Legazpi, the representative of Philip II of Spain from whom the country takes its name. The men sealed the treaty by drinking wine mixed with their blood, which they had dripped into the cup from cuts on their wrists. Thus the treaty is known as the 'Blood Compact'.

But to the Filipinos of today Bohol is first and foremost the land of the

GIANT'S TEARDROPS *Local legend tells that the cones and domes of the Chocolate Hills are the tears shed by a giant suffering from unrequited love.*

Chocolate Hills. There are 1268 of the steep-sided, regularly shaped mounds standing cheek by jowl on a plateau in the centre of Bohol and rising to anything from 100 to 300ft (30–100m) high.

No-one knows how these extraordinary limestone hills came into being, but it is possible that they are simply the product of millions of years of weathering by the rain. The Chocolate Hills are unusual in that there are apparently none of the cave systems that normally develop in this type of limestone areas.

The folklore of the Boholanos provides other explanations of the

THERE ARE 1268
CHOCOLATE HILLS
STANDING CHEEK
BY JOWL

Chocolate Hills' origins. In one tale, the hills were the result of a battle between two angry giants who hurled rocks at each other for days on end, but to little effect. Weary of fighting, they resolved their differences and departed the island as bosom friends – leaving the rocks exactly where they had fallen. In a further tale of tragedy, the giant Arogo was passionately in love with a mortal called Aloya, and decided to kidnap her. But she rejected the giant's advances, went into a decline and died, and the Chocolate Hills are the teardrops of the grief-stricken giant.

The Caves of Mulu

IN THE STEAMING HEART OF A MALAYSIAN
RAINFOREST, A HUGE LIMESTONE RIDGE HOUSES
THE WORLD'S LARGEST CAVERN

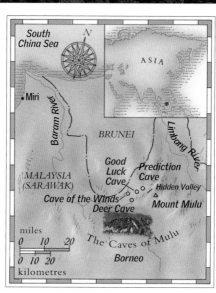

When a Malaysian geologist first recorded the huge cave openings in Mulu's limestone hills, he was searching for guano (bird dung) deposits, used commercially as fertiliser. Little could he have known that his notes would lead to the discovery of the world's largest cavern.

In 1978, after the area in Sarawak on the island of Borneo had become the Gunung Mulu National Park, a team of British cavers was asked to find out what lay inside the rain-soaked hills. They predicted that the caves would be spectacular, because the porous limestone would have been deeply eroded by aeons of tropical rain soaking into it. Access to the region, inhabited only by the nomadic Penan people, is difficult, and to reach the main ridge of

198

BORNEO GIANT *Foul-smelling Rafflesia, more than 2ft (610mm) across, are the world's largest flowers. They grow as parasites on jungle vines.*

HIDDEN WORLD *A thick canopy of trees partly hides the limestone ridge in the Malaysian jungle (left) that is riddled with caves. Many, such as the Cave of the Winds (right), contain grottoes glistening with stalagmites and stalactites.*

the hills, whose walls rise sheer from the forest, the expedition had to trek through swampy, leech-infested jungle.

The jagged ridge, about 20 miles (32km) long and 3 miles (5km) wide, lies below the shale and sandstone slopes of Gunung (or Mount) Mulu, after which the park is named.

The cavers found a passage leading into the ridge from the remote Hidden Valley, and called it Prediction Cave. Not until 1981, when exploring the Good Luck Cave, did they traverse a passageway nearly 1 mile (1.6km) long, with many cascades and an underground canal, and came upon the huge chamber now named the Sarawak Chamber. It proved to be six times bigger than Carlsbad Cavern in New

Mexico, until then the world's largest-known cavern. The Sarawak Chamber is 230ft (70m) high at its lowest parts. This is only half as high as St Peter's in Rome, but the chamber is at least twice as wide as St Peter's, and more than three times as long. On the floor there are boulders as big as houses, which at first the cavers took to be walls, making it difficult for them to assess the chamber's size by torchlight.

SARAWAK CHAMBER IS SIX TIMES BIGGER THAN THE LARGEST CAVE KNOWN BEFORE

Cavers have now mapped some 26 caves, winding for more than 125 miles (200km) beneath the mountains.

As fascinating as the caves themselves is the animal life within their mysterious depths. At dusk, clouds of bats fly out from the caves to hunt as cave swiftlets fly back in, to roost in a dark world of blind spiders, venomous centipedes, white snakes and translucent crabs.

Phangnga Bay

STRANGELY SHAPED LIMESTONE ISLANDS RISE FROM THE CLEAR, GREEN WATER OF A FOREST-FRINGED BAY IN SOUTHERN THAILAND

Shimmering heat haze veils the tree-lined shores of Phangnga Bay in southern Thailand, where the clear waters of the Andaman Sea glow green under the fierce tropical sun. About 40 limestone rocks and islands of fantastic shape are scattered in the vast bay, some jutting 900ft (275m) from the water. Most of the islands have caves and grottoes; some are pierced with tunnels.

Pekinese Rock, named for its shape, guards the mouth of the bay, and in Tham Lot caves, huge stalactites hang like swords above visiting tourists in longtail boats. Khao Kein, or 'painted mountain', has not only stalactites but also wall pictures of fish and animals, drawn in black and ochre by long-vanished primitive artists.

Ko Tapu, or Nail Island, rises from the sea like a giant nail, broadest at the top. Close by is Khoa Ping Khan, its steep, tree-draped sides and craggy heights riven in two, perhaps, by a tremor that occurred aeons ago. Its name means 'two islands leaning back to back'.

Now the uninhabited island is a major tourist attraction and has acquired a second name – James Bond Island. It was the setting for the villain's den in the 1974 James Bond film *The Man with the Golden Gun*.

NAIL ISLAND *Ko Tapu, shaped rather like a nail, is one of the weird limestone islands to be seen in Phangnga Bay.*

Krakatoa

ON THE SITE OF A
VOLCANIC ERUPTION THAT
KILLED 36,000 PEOPLE, A
NEW ISLAND HAS RISEN
OUT OF THE SEA

D ark, angry rumblings began to rise
from a startlingly pretty Indonesian
island called Krakatoa in May 1883.
Several months later they grew louder.
Passing ships reported explosions so
loud that eardrums were shattered.
Rafts of buoyant, frothy pumice began
to fill the Sunda Strait – a busy
shipping lane between the islands of
Java and Sumatra.

A thick cloud of ash spread across the
sky, blocking out the sun for several
days. Ships became clogged with fall-
out, and the hot mud and ash had to be
shovelled away in a darkness filled with
choking, sulphurous air. The sea heaved
in strange, wide troughs, and as it broke
along the shores of Java and Sumatra

CHAIN REACTION *An ash cloud rising from
Anak Krakatau is a reminder that the new
island on Krakatoa's site is also volatile.
(Overleaf) The island, born in 1927,
supports little plant life.*

it formed huge waves that surged into the coastal settlements.

Just after 10am on August 27, 1883, Krakatoa was ripped apart by one of the greatest explosions ever recorded. The boom was heard 2200 miles (3500km) away in Australia. The island collapsed in on itself and was pulverised. Some 4½ cubic miles (19km³) of volcanic material was discharged into the air. A plume of dust rose 50 miles (80km) and then orbited the Earth for years, lowering summer temperatures worldwide and creating spectacular sunsets around the globe.

A PLUME OF DUST CREATED SPECTACULAR SUNSETS AROUND THE GLOBE

More than 36,000 people died. It was not the eruption itself which was so lethal, but the giant waves – tsunamis – that reared up over 130ft (40m) high as the volcano collapsed, and flattened 163 villages along the coasts of Java and Sumatra.

The island of Krakatoa had been born from volcanic activity, but had remained dormant since an eruption in 1680. The 1883 eruption has only ever been exceeded in modern times by Mount Tambora, on another Indonesian island, Sumbawa. It erupted in 1815 and discharged around five times more volcanic matter than Krakatoa.

NEWS SPREADS IN A FLASH

Krakatoa, however, attracted more attention. It erupted in the age of mass communications, and news about it was circulated around the world by telegraph and cable within hours. Information about the explosion was meticulously gathered by scientists and provided a major inspiration to the study of the cause and behaviour of volcanoes, which in turn led to the modern theory of plate tectonics, or drifting continents.

The region stands on the front line of two tectonic plates. As the Indo-Australian plate drives beneath the Eurasian plate, it excites massive forces that shudder along the junction,

FLARE UP *Anak Krakatau erupts regularly – almost once a year – throwing thick plumes of ash and pumpkin-sized lumps of molten pumice into the atmosphere.*

occasionally erupting explosively from the many volcanoes that line its course.

The Indo-Australian plate still moves several centimetres each year. As if to underline this, a new volcano has risen up on the site of Krakatoa. When Krakatoa erupted, it collapsed beneath the surface of the sea, creating an underwater caldera – a giant volcanic crater – 4 miles (6.4km) wide.

In 1927 a plume of smoke rose out of the water from the caldera, heralding the imminent arrival of a new island. By 1928, the island of Anak Krakatau (Child of Krakatoa) had broken the surface. Fifty years later, ash and pumice

had gradually built up to give the newcomer a height of 1001ft (305m). Most of the time Anak Krakatau just hisses and steams, belching wafts of sulphurous fumes into the clear, tropical air. Scientists believe that the old volcano spent the worst of its fury in 1883, and that Anak Krakatau will never pack the same punch. But in the world of volcanoes there are no safe bets.

LIVING RELATION *Rakata (right), the surviving remnant of the original island of Krakatoa, provides a clear view of Anak Krakatau, the recent arrival.*

THE LIVING WORLD RETURNS

SPLASH OF COLOUR
*Blue-eared kingfishers
are found on Rakata.*

Immediately after the eruption of Krakatoa in 1883, the surrounding islands and coast lay covered by a thick shroud of deathly grey volcanic ash. In 1884 a scientist visited the island of Rakata – the only remnant of the original island – and found just one spider.

Watered by some 100in (2540mm) of tropical rain each year, however, Rakata soon recovered its wildlife. The seeds of grasses, ferns and trees were brought by wind or sea, or via the digestive tracts of passing birds. Corals began to rebuild the devastated reefs. Spiders crossed from land 25 miles (40km) away on strands of gossamer; snakes and monitor lizards swam the distance. Rats, land crabs, geckos, ants and termites arrived on rafts of floating vegetation. Scientists were able to study the revival of Rakata and see how the natural world recolonises devastated land.

Anak Krakatau provides a different kind of natural laboratory for study. Here, repeated layers of fresh ash have prevented nature from gaining a foothold on the island, except for its eastern end. Here there are clumps of grass, moss and wild sugar, tangles of purple convolvulus on the beaches, and stands of casuarina trees and tropical pines which provide refuge for bats.

Krakatoa's eruption virtually depopulated the western coast of Java. Left to its own devices, with no competition from humans, the wildlife recovered and thrived on the island's Ujung Kulon peninsula, 40 miles (64km) south of the volcano.

Among Ujung Kulon's stars are rare Javan rhinoceroses and leopards, as well as flying foxes (the world's largest bat), birds such as hornbills and bee-eaters, huge bird spiders, saltwater crocodiles, fiddler crabs and archer fish, which can spit a drop of water 3ft (1m) in order to catch an insect.

RARE BREED *Ujung Kulon is home
to the rare one-horned Javan rhino.*

Keli Mutu

AN INDONESIAN
ISLAND'S LAKES, TINTED
WITH CHANGING
COLOURS, ARE SAID TO
BE THE RESTING PLACE
OF SOULS

The souls of sorcerers, the people of
Flores say, live high in the mountains
of their Indonesian island home, in a
lake where the water looks black. The
lake nearby that was, until recently, a
rich green colour and is now a dark
maroon is the home of sinners' souls,
and the souls of virgins and infants rest
in a third lake coloured a vibrant green.

The three lakes lie more than 5200ft
(1600m) up, cradled in the craters of
Keli Mutu, one of Flores's many extinct
volcanoes. The island also has 14 active
volcanoes – and frequent earthquakes.

Lakes of improbable colours lying
side by side are surprising enough, until
you hear that in past years, their waters
have been many different trios of colour
– black, maroon and blue; café au lait,
red-brown and blue; pale green, bright
green and black, to name just a few.

No-one has yet discovered the reason
for the lakes' colours, let alone why they
change. They lie enigmatically in once-
fiery hollows while unknown processes
brew up the next colour change.

TRICOLOUR *Chameleon-like, Keli Mutu's
lakes change colour over the years, resulting
in lakes of new shades.*

207

Australia

Pinnacles Desert

THOUSANDS OF
LIMESTONE PILLARS
STAND IN GROUPS
IN THE SILENCE OF
SOUTH-WEST AUSTRALIA'S
'PAINTED DESERT'

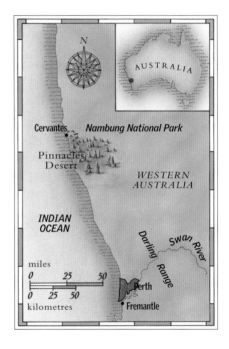

Nothing but the sighing and moaning of the wind breaks the eerie silence of the Pinnacles Desert. Any science-fiction writer seeking a setting for a spinechiller need look no further than this alien spot not far from the coast of south-west Australia. The necessary ingredients are there – a stark forest of standing stones in an area practically devoid of vegetation; not a sign of life or human activity, just the bright yellow, wind-stirred sand.

The Pinnacles Desert, one of Australia's many amazing natural landmarks, is a short drive from the nearest town, Cervantes. The road is

ENCHANTED LEGION *For thousands of years, the strange pillars of the Pinnacles Desert were buried beneath a sea of sand dunes.*

now sealed all the way, but at one time only heavy-duty vehicles could go there, because the exposed limestone outcrops shredded the tyres of ordinary cars.

The journey is well worth the effort. The first, spellbinding view of the pinnacles is of an enchanted, moon-like landscape, with sharp shadows accentuating the weird, jagged shapes. Sombre grey stones 3–16ft (1–5m) tall rise sheer from the flat sandy floor, guarding the buried secrets of tens of thousands of years. Deeper into the area the colours change, and grey gives way to gold. Some of the stones are the size of cars, some are the size of houses, others are as small and slim as pencils. Thousands of them cover an area of 1½ sq miles (4km²) of desert.

Each pinnacle is different. Their surfaces may be smooth or honeycombed, and their shapes vary. One

A STARK FOREST OF STANDING STONES ON A PLAIN OF BRIGHT YELLOW SAND

group resembles huge milk bottles waiting to be collected by a phantom milkman. Another has been named 'Spectres in Silhouette', with the central pillar seen as the figure of Death counselling a surrounding ring of ghosts. Other names are just as graphic but not as gloomy – 'Camel', 'Molars', 'Kangaroo', 'Gateway', 'Garden Wall', 'Red Indian Chief' and 'Elephant Foot'. Although the pinnacles are thousands of years old, they must have been uncovered from the sand in fairly recent times, maybe within the last 100 years.

Until Harry Turner, a Perth historian, came across them in 1956, they seem to have been unknown, apart from vague, word-of-mouth tales that early Dutch seamen had seen what they thought were the ruins of a city in the area. In the last century the Pinnacles

were never mentioned. Had they been visible, they would surely have been known to 19th-century stockmen on regular cattle drives south to Perth along the sandy coastal track. Nearby Flourbag Flat was a resting and watering place for drovers.

Explorer George Grey, who was later to become Governor of South Australia and be awarded a knighthood, must have passed close to the area in his journeys of 1837–8. He was a meticulous diarist, yet he recorded nothing about the Pinnacles.

Scientists estimate the stone pillars to be 25,000–30,000 years old, and are convinced that they must have been exposed on at least one occasion before this century, because shells and Stone Age artefacts were found stuck to the base of some pillars. The shells have been carbon dated to around 5000 years old, so the pinnacles were probably uncovered some 6000 years ago.

But later the stones must have been submerged by sand again for maybe

GOLDEN CITY *From the air the scattered Pinnacles look like a spacious stone-built city. The dark shadows accentuate the shapes.*

thousands of years, because they do not figure in Aborigine lore. Nor were they mentioned by the Dutch navigator Abraham Leeman, who was stranded in the area in 1658. Yet Leeman noted in his diary the existence of two large hills, the North Hummock and South Hummock, which lie close to the Pinnacles. Had the limestone pillars been visible, he would surely have recorded the fact.

PRESERVED IN PRINT

As the wind blows through the desert, it continually shifts the soft, loose sand to expose new aspects of the dunes and cover others. So in a few centuries more, the Pinnacles, now part of the Nambung National Park, may once again disappear from view. Should this happen, their presence has at least now been recorded in print and picture.

FROM SKELETON TO STONE

Soft-bodied sea creatures such as limpets were the original raw material from which the Pinnacles pillars were built. These creatures flourished in warm seas 700,000–120,000 years ago, and after they died their shell skeletons crumbled to form lime sand. Carried ashore by wave and wind, the sand built up layer by layer into dunes.

Eventually, encouraged by the wet winters and dry summers of a Mediterranean climate, a thick growth of vegetation developed. The dunes were stabilised by a network of roots and a build-up of humus (decaying vegetation). As acidic winter rain dribbled into the sand, some grains dissolved. When the sand dried in summer, some dissolved matter hardened into cement. Grains were glued together as limestone. Humus increased the acidity of the water leaching down, and concentrated the cementation to form a layer of harder limestone at the base of the soil layer. Plant roots pushed through cracks in this harder layer, and more limestone formed around them.

Shifting sand eventually swamped the vegetation, and the roots rotted to leave channels in the limestone. These were slowly widened by water leaching down, and some limestone weathered away, leaving only the tougher parts. These remnants are the pillars revealed when the sand was eventually blown away. Lines across many of the pillars show the build-up of sand layers and their changing slopes as the dunes receded and advanced.

WEATHERED PINNACLE
The limestone pillars were shaped below ground over the centuries by rain and plant roots.

Hamersley Range

DRAMATIC RAVINES
WITH JAGGED WALLS
ETCH DEEPLY INTO THIS
MOUNTAIN RANGE IN
WESTERN AUSTRALIA

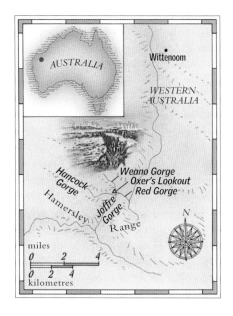

WALLS OF COLOUR *The view from Oxer's Lookout leads up the fiery chasm of Red Gorge. Iron in the rocks is responsible for the cliffs' rich colour.*

Terrifyingly steep-sided gorges slice through the barren hills and plateaus of the Hamersley Range in Western Australia. Three of the most spectacular of the 20 major gorges are the crevice-like Hancock, Joffre and Weano gorges, which converge and join the equally narrow Red Gorge.

The gorges start abruptly with insignificant seasonal streams that suddenly hurtle downwards into chasms at least 300ft (90m) deep with almost sheer walls of banded rock, to form clear, refreshing pools below.

In places the gorges are so narrow that from the bottom all that can be seen is a tunnel of dark rock. At its narrowest point, Weano Gorge is hardly a yard (1m) wide. Equally spectacular in its narrowness is Oxer's Lookout. This sliver of land separates Weano and Hancock gorges, and cliffs fall away precipitously on both sides. At the head of the 4 mile (6km) long Joffre Gorge, the vertical walls curve round to form a natural amphitheatre – the site of a waterfall after heavy rain.

PALMS IN A PARCHED LAND

The rocks of the Hamersley Range were laid down on the seabed 2500 million years ago. Layers of sediment – some rich in iron – were compressed by layers above and the whole block was then raised above sea level. It has been weathering away slowly ever since with streams cutting down through the layered rocks to form the deep gorges.

High up on the parched plateau, only low clumps of hard-leaved porcupine grass and mulga trees can withstand the fierce heat and lack of rain, and on the cliffs a few white-trunked snappy gum trees cling in the crevices.

Yet far below, the gorge floors are green with palms, eucalyptus gum trees and ferns. In the shade cast by the steep gorge walls, less water is evaporated away than in the searing heat of the plateau, so water left by the last river flow remains in pools.

Like oases in the desert, these splashes of green add even more colour to the vivid landscape.

Lake Hillier

MYSTERY SURROUNDS THE PASTEL-PINK COLOUR OF A LAKE THAT ORNAMENTS AN ISLAND HARDLY DISTURBED BY HUMAN ACTIVITY

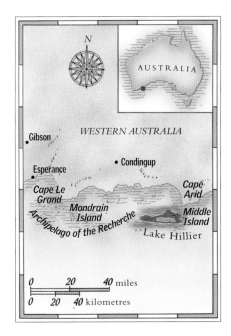

Seen from the air, the glistening pale pink surface of remote Lake Hillier looks like glacé icing on an oblong cake. The lake gives unexpected colour to a densely wooded corner of Middle Island, one of more than 100 small islands that make up the Archipelago of the Recherche that lies off Western Australia's south coast.

The shallow briny lake, about one-third of a mile (600m) across, seems to belong more to the world of Hansel and Gretel than to that of storm-tossed seas. Rimmed with white salt and encircled by dark green forests of eucalyptus and paperbark trees, the lake is separated

POOL OF COLOUR *Lake Hillier is an enigma among Australia's 'pink' lakes – the cause of its colour is unknown.*

from the ocean's deep blue waters by a narrow strip of white dunes and sand.

The reason for the lake's pink colour was investigated in 1950 by a team of scientists, who expected to find an alga such as *Dunaliella salina* in its salty water. In very saline water, this alga produces a red pigment, and is responsible for the colour of Australia's other 'pink' lakes, such as the one close to Esperance on the mainland. Samples of water from Lake Hillier, however, contained no signs of any algae, and the cause of the lake's colour remains a mystery.

The first record of Middle Island's 'pink' lake dates from 1802 when Matthew Flinders, a British navigator and hydrographer, called there on his way to Sydney. A few short-lived commercial ventures followed Flinders's

visit – between the 1820s and 1840s sealers and whalers settled on the island, and salt was extracted from the lake early in the 20th century. But salt production ended after only six years and since then the island and its 'pink' lake have been little disturbed.

Bungle Bungle Range

A MAZE OF TOWERING BEEHIVE DOMES IN WESTERN AUSTRALIA ARE AMONG THE MOST FRAGILE MOUNTAINS IN THE WORLD

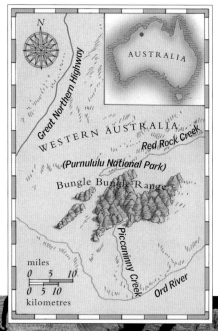

Touched by the rays of a low sun, the towers and canyons of the Bungle Bungles form a dreamland panorama that glows as if lit from within. The astonishing tiger-striped domes loom in surreal grandeur from the plains of the Ord River in Western Australia – a magical landscape resembling an undersea fantasy.

Yet the banded rock walls and fantastic swollen peaks all surge from terrain so remote that until the 1980s only a handful of travellers had set foot there. To this day, most people view the mountains from the air.

STRIPED ROCKS *Mineral seeping from the sandstone gives the Bungle Bungles their distinctive banding.*

NIGHT BIRD *The tawny frogmouth has a booming call.*

Lying in the vast Kimberley region – which is barely pinpricked with human settlement – the massif covers 175sq miles (450km²). For much of the year the heat is intense, with temperatures up to 40°C (104°F) in the shade. In the long winter dry season there is virtually no rain, and the rivers shrivel to a scattering of water holes. Then, during the wet season (November–March), the whole range explodes into green. Waterfalls cascade from glittering tiers of pools as cyclones sweep in from the Indian Ocean, shedding so much rain that the rivers flood their plains and the track to Bungle Bungle is impassable.

WEATHERED SANDSTONE

The Bungle Bungle story goes back 400 million years to a time when immense beds of layered sediment built up here, eroded from now-vanished mountains to the north. Later, streams carved out grooves and gullies in the soft rock; these deepened, linked, and were carved by wind and water to leave the isolated sandstone towers of today.

Most of the domes are on the south and east sides of the massif. The west and north sides are sheer rock walls 820ft (250m) high, fretted with fascinating canyons. Gorges and chasms are upholstered with tenacious plants such as spinifex (spiny-leaved 'porcupine grass'), acacia and fan palms, all soaring from precarious crevices to create extraordinary hanging gardens.

The vivid stripes in the rocks are formed by weathering. When freshly

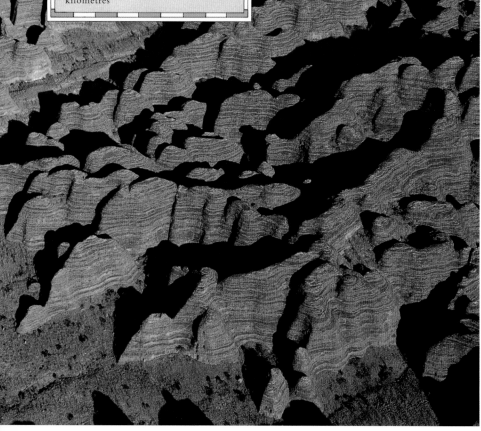

SURREAL SPLENDOUR *The beehive domes of the Bungle Bungles erupt starkly from the surrounding shrub-scattered plain.*

exposed, the sandstone is whitish, but water seeping out along the layered beds deposits a 'skin' of quartz and clay that is constantly forming and breaking off. Traces of iron give the stone its tinge of orange, and the grey or brown comes from accumulating lichens and algae, parched by the sun. The sandstone is soft, eroding to dust as fine as talcum powder.

Alexander Forrest, a Perth surveyor, led the first European party to set eyes on the great labyrinth in 1879. No-one knows why the name Bungle Bungle was given in the 1930s. The Aboriginal name is *Purnululu* (which means

TIGER-STRIPED DOMES LOOM IN SURREAL GRANDEUR FROM THE PLAINS

'sandstone'). Aborigines have lived in the Kimberleys for more than 24,000 years, and the Bungle Bungles are one of their sacred sites.

Today, Aborigines take part in managing this National Park and World Heritage Area, that is administered so as to guard the fragile stone from erosion by visitors. A few ponds shaded by rock overhangs last all year and are watering holes for animals such as wallabies and quolls (native cats). Almost as bizarre as the domes are the termite nests up to 18ft (5.5m) high on some of their flanks.

SHY HUNTER

Because of its stripes, the night-hunting brown tree snake, found in the Bungle Bungles, is also known as the night tiger. It grows to about 7ft (2m) long and preys on small animals such as lizards, poisoning them with its grooved back fangs once it has them in its jaws. The snake's venom is not deadly to humans; it does its best to avoid them and will not bite unless cornered or disturbed.

NIGHT TIGER *The brown tree snake has weak venom and preys on small animals.*

Gosses Bluff

A MYSTERIOUS CRATER
RINGED BY BARE
CRAGS IS THE GIANT
WOUND LEFT WHEN A
COMET PLUNGED INTO
THE EARTH

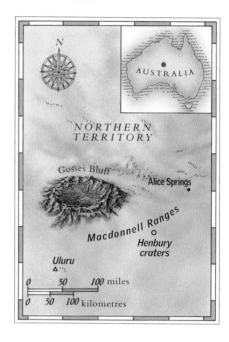

While dinosaurs forage in the green heart of Australia, a huge fireball plunges into the plain, shattering the landscape with a force hundreds of thousands of times greater than that of the nuclear bomb that destroyed the Japanese city of Hiroshima in 1945. Slowly, a huge mushroom cloud of dust and debris rises from the scene, blotting out the sun and darkening the skies of the Southern Hemisphere for months.

Such was the dramatic birth of Gosses Bluff, a massive, rock-rimmed crater gouged out by the impact of a comet 143 million years ago. The comet – a ball of frozen carbon dioxide, ice and dust one-third of a mile (600m) across – became a flaming furnace as

CALLING CARD FROM SPACE *Blasted from the ground by a colliding comet, Gosses Bluff is the core of a crater that has worn away over 130 million years.*

it hurtled to Earth. It penetrated only about half a mile (800m) into the ground, but blew up some 150sq miles (400km²) of the surrounding land, sending shock waves across the globe and flinging up gigantic rings of earth and stone like ripples in a pond.

MASSIVE THUMBPRINT

The original crater was about 12 miles (20km) in diameter. Today's crater, only 2½ miles (4km) across, is just its central core. Aeons of erosion have worn away the mass of debris that once covered it. The bluff, the crater's double-walled rim of hard sandstone crags, now rises to 590ft (180m) above the plain. This sandstone was pushed up by the explosion – layers of similar rock have been identified over 1¼ miles (2km) beneath the surface, giving some idea of the massive force involved.

Pictured by space satellite, Gosses Bluff looks like a massive thumbprint on the otherwise flat and featureless Missionary Plain 100 miles (160km) west of Alice Springs. The sandstone

ring stands out as one of the most impressive impact scars in a landscape littered with meteor craters.

A 19th-century explorer named Edmund Gosse is credited with being the first European to visit the crater in 1873. Long before this, however, the crater was known to the Aborigines and the area (now a registered sacred site) is rich in campsite remains, hunting hides and rock shelters decorated with the red hand-stencils of long-gone inhabitants.

Ernest Giles, who explored the area in 1875, described it in detail. Without the benefit of an aerial view, he was unable to appreciate the symmetry of the crater, and did not realise its significance. Unimpressed, he wrote: 'A few cypress pines are rooted in the rocky, shelving sides of the range, which is not of such elevation as it appeared at a distance. The highest points are not more than from 700 to 800 feet.'

Until recently, the origins of Gosses Bluff were a mystery, and rival theories abounded. One held that gases below the surface may have forced their way up, creating a powerful eruption of soil and water known as a 'mud volcano'. Another theory was that a meteorite could have been the cause, and that the lack of any remaining fragments was because of millions of years of weathering. But scientific research in recent times points to a different origin.

As with most similar sites, Gosses Bluff has a pattern of geological fractures radiating out from the centre. As they weather, the rocks fall apart along the fracture lines in cone-shaped patterns called 'shatter cones'. By studying their formations, scientists have verified that the crater is an impact crater, and that the colliding object had a high speed but a relatively low density – suggesting a comet's composition rather than the rock of a meteorite.

Not far from Gosses Bluff can be seen the Henbury Meteorite Craters, made by 12 fragments of a meteorite that split as it hurtled in from space 4700 years ago. The Aboriginal name, 'sun walk fire devil rock', suggests that someone saw it happen.

MARK OF A METEORITE *The saucer shape of this Henbury crater makes it comparatively well-watered. Its shrubs provide a shady retreat for wildlife.*

WOUNDED EARTH

Once Earth's whole surface was pockmarked with 'star wounds' – Impact craters from collisions with comets or meteorites from space. When the 'star' body penetrates the ground it vaporises so violently that the earth beneath it is compressed. As the force diminishes, the earth rebounds explosively upwards, forming a volcano-like crater. As time passes, the outer ridge erodes, until eventually only the central core is left.

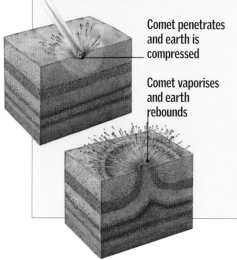

Comet penetrates and earth is compressed

Comet vaporises and earth rebounds

GOSSES BLUFF

Uluru

A MASSIVE HILL OF RED SANDSTONE STANDS IN SOLITARY SPLENDOUR AMID A PARCHED SANDY WASTELAND IN AUSTRALIA'S OUTBACK

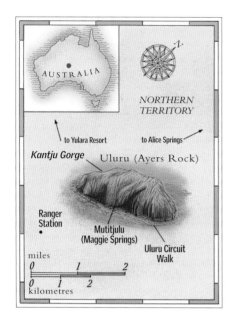

Wind-blown sands have sculpted the domed, elephantine bulk of Uluru, which rises abruptly from the flat and arid plains of the Northern Territory, almost at the very centre of Australia. To the Aborigines, the age-old red rock known as 'Uluru' has always been a sacred, mystical place. Now it has also become a national symbol.

As the sun moves across the sky, Uluru glows with ever-changing colours. See it as dawn breaks and it takes on the orange glow of sunrise. Early morning shadows give it a dark and rusty hue. Go there at noon and the rock is suffused with amber. Sunset turns it into a spectacular, crimson mass like a glowing giant coal.

Uluru is not a gigantic boulder. It is a sandstone hill that was pushed up by earth movements about 500 million years ago; most of it is submerged in the

surrounding sea of sand dunes. Only its flattened, 1142ft (348m) high tip is exposed – a formation known as an *inselberg*, or island mountain. Fine parallel grooves cover the rock surface, which is about 2 miles (3km) across. At its base, 6 miles (10km) round, there are caves and cavities weathered into strange shapes. On the north-east side, a 500ft (150m) high slab has split away, and is known as the Kangaroo's Tail.

Rainfall is mostly rare here, but can occasionally be heavy. After a rainstorm, water cascades down the rock's towering flanks, which rise sheer in

ROCK OF COLOUR *As the sun makes its daily journey across the wide sky, the light it throws onto the Earth takes Uluru through a myriad of colours from dusky pink to burning red.*

places, leaving them streaked with black. Water holes build up in rock crevices, but most rain runs off onto the plain below, sustaining plants such as blue-grey sandalwood, bloodwood (a type of eucalyptus), and groves of mulga trees (a type of acacia), as well as desert oaks and clusters of hummock grass among the surrounding sand hills. The oaks' needle-like leaves cut down water loss, and their thick cork bark keeps out the heat. On the south face, the large pool of Mutitjulu (which is also called Maggie Springs), has water in all except the very driest periods. Some other water holes persist for weeks or months, but most evaporate fairly fast in the heat.

Water snakes dwelling in the pools are believed by the Aborigines to be the pool guardians. Highly venomous king brown and western brown snakes, reaching around 6ft (1.8m) long, also inhabit the region. The frogs, lizards, marsupial moles and hopping mice living among the sand dunes offer the snakes easy prey. They are also taken by dingoes – Australian wild dogs, which scavenge camp and picnic sites.

Red kangaroos sometimes browse in the area, and the shy, smaller, rock-dwelling wallaroos spend the day in rock caves. Some 150 species of bird

> SUNSET TURNS THE ROCK INTO A CRIMSON MASS LIKE A GLOWING COAL

also manage to survive here, including the large flightless emu, the wedge-tailed eagle and the honeyeater.

For the Anangu people, Australian Aborigines who live in the area, Uluru is a place of reverence round which their lives have centred for thousands of years and is part of their code of living, the *Tjukurpa* (pronounced 'chookoorpa'). This code includes caring for the land. Since 1985 Uluru has been part of the Uluru–Kata Tjuta National Park, 500sq miles (1300km^2) in extent, owned and administered by the Anangu people. For them, the Uluru area is a focus of converging ancestral tracks, or *iwara*. Every part of the rock, every cliff, boulder and cave, has sacred significance, and some caves, chiefly at Mutitjulu and Kantju Gorge, are decorated with Aboriginal paintings in ochre, ash and charcoal.

TOURIST VENUE

Uluru was unseen by European eyes until the early 1870s, when two explorers, Ernest Giles and William C. Gosse, ventured into the area. They named the rock after Sir Henry Ayers, then premier of South Australia, and until recent times, Uluru was popularly known as Ayers Rock.

Because so many people visit the rock each year, some restrictions are in place to avoid despoiling the area. A climb to the summit takes about two hours, but is alien to Aboriginal culture and is discouraged. If temperatures above 36°C (96.8°F) are forecast, climbing is banned, as so much exertion can be dangerous. A walk round the rock takes about four hours. The shorter walking tours include the Liru Trail, with Aboriginal guides to explain their culture and point out some of their foods, such as mulga 'apples' – small wasp galls. The informative Cultural Centre can be found 1km from the rock. Visitors to Uluru are given an age-old greeting: *Pukulpa pitjama Ananguku Ngurakutu* – 'Welcome to Aboriginal land.'

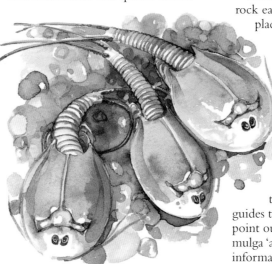

POOL LIFE *Tiny shield shrimps hatch, breed and lay their eggs in the short-lived pools that come and go on the rock.*

LANDSCAPE IN THE EYE OF THE BEHOLDER

A painter's portrayal can range from exact observation to intense evocation of mood

A landscape has many moods, constantly switching with the changing weather, the moving hour and the unfolding seasons. Armed with a palette of paint, artists have limitless scope to portray what they see – from a faithful rendition to a poetic interpretation of the mood the scene inspires. Before the invention of photography, landscape painting was the only visual way to record scenery, but it was the Romantic era, from the late 18th century, that thrust it onto centre stage. Formerly relegated to the role of backdrop, only then did landscape become widely accepted as a suitable subject in itself, and only then did its potential begin to be exploited.

NATURAL BRIDGE
The Natural Bridge of Virginia (1860) (above) by David Johnson depicts an American natural wonder. His painstaking attention to detail and virtuoso technique make the painting doubly spectacular.

ANTARCTICA
Dr E.A. (Bill) Wilson recorded the majestic beauty of Antarctica in watercolour during Captain Scott's 1901–4 expedition. (Wilson and Scott died together on the fatal expedition of 1912.)

YELLOWSTONE
In 1871, Thomas Moran accompanied a survey team to Yellowstone in the Rockies. His paintings (left) helped to persuade Congress to make Yellowstone America's first National Park.

FINGAL'S CAVE
J.M.W. Turner visited Fingal's Cave on Staffa Island in Scotland in 1831. The wind-tossed cloud at sunset made the deepest impression.

BELLE ILE
Using the rapid touch of the Impressionists' technique, Claude Monet captured the sparkle of light on a choppy sea in *The Rocks of Belle Ile* (1886), painted off Brittany.

Kata Tjuta

THE WORLD'S STRANGEST MOUNTAIN IS A CLUSTER OF RED ROCK DOMES GLOWING IN THE AUSTRALIAN DESERT

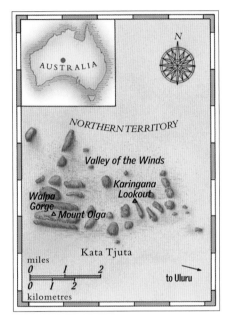

Heat haze shimmering on the vast, sandy plains of Australia's Northern Territory can make the first sight of Kata Tjuta seem like a mirage. The 36 rock domes rise sheer from the ground and form a circular cluster. Ernest Giles, an explorer who sighted them in 1872, likened them to 'enormous pink haystacks, all leaning against each other'.

From a distance it is difficult to appreciate the enormous height of the tallest dome, Mount Olga. At 1800ft (550m) it is nearly twice the height of the Eiffel Tower, and is the highest point in the Uluru–Kata Tjuta National Park. Many of the other domes are half as high again as Uluru, which lies 20 miles (32km) to the east.

Narrow ravines and chasms separate the domes, places where the sun barely reaches and the wind can whistle and howl alarmingly. The ravine at the heart of Kata Tjuta, called the Valley of the Winds, is a sheltered, red-walled, green oasis where acacias, mint bushes

and daisies grow amid spiny yellow porcupine grass. Here and there the trunks of ghost gums shine a gleaming white.

Towering above the Valley of the Winds is the Karingana Lookout, from where, in the early morning, the rich red domes are bathed in soft sunlight and the porcupine grass below glows gold like ripened grain. Kata Tjuta is an Aboriginal name meaning 'many heads'. Like Uluru, it is revered as part of the *Tjukurpa* (pronounced 'chookoorpa'), the Aborigine code of living. But unlike

Uluru, the domes are formed from a mixture of pebbles and boulders rather than solid sandstone. Dense scrub covers the ravine floors, and caves round the bases of the domes are homes for bats and animals, such as the shy wallaroo, that feed mostly in the evening or at night. Aboriginal engravings adorn the cave walls.

Rainfall amounts to only about 8in (200mm) a year, but this fills crevices to form rock pools, which can last a long time in shaded areas. They give life to an amazing number of plants, such as

MYSTERIOUS DOMES *Kata Tjuta springs surprisingly from the endless plain, like rocky red islets in a hazy sea. Sharp shadows add to the magic aura.*

the peach-like quandong, which has waxy blue-green leaves and red, fleshy fruits, which are edible.

Red, green and orange lichens pattern the rocks in some sheltered parts. Lizards and venomous whip snakes hide in rock crevices, and budgerigars breed in their hundreds, taking flight in flocks like a green

THE BIRTH OF KATA TJUTA

Aeons ago Kata Tjuta was mountain fragments dumped in a now-vanished sea. Gradually the sea pounded them into layers of pebbles and boulders that became cemented together with fine sand. About 500 million years ago, earth movements lifted this streaked rock above the sea, tilting it at an angle of about 20 degrees. Centuries of weathering along rock cracks or joints etched them to their domed shapes and ground down softer rocks into a sea of sand. This left just the giant domed tips rising above the surrounding plains. Such formations are called island mountains, or *inselbergs*.

Crack   Tilted rock layers

SACRED SITE *The soft curves and smooth surfaces of Kata Tjuta are shown to their best advantage when bathed in the warm glow of the sun.*

snowstorm. Goshawks and wedge-tailed eagles soar high above the ravines, and colourful mulga parrots nest in hollow trunks.

In Aboriginal culture certain names are sacred, and within Kata Tjuta there are areas that cannot be named due to this. One of these, a narrow cleft, has walls pockmarked with caves chiselled from the soft rock by rain and wind. On the south-east side of the mountain a dome records the story of a man attacked by dingoes; a cleft in the rock is said to denote his wound. Large domes on the western side, it is said, represent the fearsome Pungalungas, who were cannibals. A cave in Mount Olga is the den of Wanampi, a serpent that breathes raging gusts of wind through the gorges if tribal laws are infringed. Then he forms himself into a rainbow.

Ernest Giles was the first European to discover Kata Tjuta, and, like many other explorers of his time, he decided to name the newly discovered feature after royalty. He chose to call it The Olgas. It was said to have been after the Queen of Spain, at the suggestion of his patron, Baron Ferdinand von Mueller. As there has never been a Queen Olga of Spain, the story was a subject of controversy for years. It was suggested that the lady in question might be the

'ENORMOUS PINK HAYSTACKS, ALL LEANING AGAINST EACH OTHER'

Grand Duchess Olga Constantinovna of Russia, who was the grandmother of the present Duke of Edinburgh. The mystery was solved in 1981. An entry dated April 14, 1873, in the Stuttgart State Archives revealed that the queen concerned was the wife of King Karl of Wurttemberg, which is now part of Germany. Kata Tjuta was commonly known as The Olgas until recently.

THWARTED BY A QUAGMIRE

Ernest Giles opened up much of Australia's outback. He sighted Kata Tjuta in 1872, but failed to reach it because of a lake of salty mud 50 miles (80km) north. Some of his horses sank in the mud up to their thighs and were almost lost. Giles named the lake Amadeus, after the King of Spain, a science patron. Its shallow waters come and go, but sometimes rise to cover more than 300sq miles (780km^2). Giles found his way round the lake to Kata Tjuta in 1873.

More than 300,000 tourists now visit the mountain every year, especially in spring when the ravines are awash with flowers. The domes are seen at their best from a walk through Walpa Gorge, which narrows to a cleft before opening out to the Valley of the Winds. At sunset, the long shadows of trees and sand hills on the western plain darken the lower flanks of Kata Tjuta. And gradually, as the sun sinks and night envelops them, the rocks change from glowing red to deep, dusky mauve.

SPINY SURVIVOR
The thorny devil — a 6in- (150mm-) long lizard — eats black ants. Its spines deter predators (mainly snakes) and also catch dew, which trickles down its grooved skin and into its mouth.

Kakadu's Wilderness

IN TROPICAL NORTH AUSTRALIA, CROCODILES LURK IN BRACKISH RIVERS, AND SHEER INLAND CLIFFS BEAR ANCIENT ROCK PAINTINGS

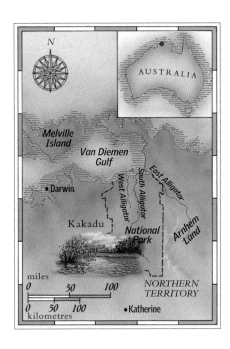

A vast and varied wilderness lies in the extreme north of Australia, the region Australians call the Top End. Kakadu National Park is twice the size of Corsica, and its landscape, as well as varying from place to place, also changes with the seasons. 'The wet' starts in early December, with dramatic rainstorms which result in large areas being flooded. In 'the dry' between May and October, almost no rain falls.

A rugged escarpment snakes for more than 300 miles (500km) along the east and south sides of the national park, marking the edge of the Arnhem Land plateau. The European explorer Ludwig Leichhardt struggled over the plateau in 1845, during an epic 16 month overland journey that had started on the east coast near Brisbane. He encountered 'sandstone blocks in

BY A BILLABONG *On Kakadu's low plains, paperbark trees grow in swamps beside a billabong's blue waters. The plains flood each year, during 'the wet'.*

fantastic figures of every shape' with 'vegetation crowding deceitfully within their fissures and gullies, and covering half of the difficulties which awaited us on our attempt to travel over it'.

Ravines cut into the cliff edge, which in places is over 1500ft (460m) high. During the wet, waterfalls thunder over the cliff. Two of the most spectacular falls are the 650ft (200m) Jim Jim, and the aptly named Twin Falls, whose two ribbons of water cascade

330ft (100m) down from the plateau.

The lowland below the escarpment is a mixture of grassland, forest and swamp, broken by quiet backwaters and crossed by rivers. Leichhardt noted the beauty of the scenery around one of Kakadu's main rivers, the East Alligator. 'We entered into a most beautiful valley,' he wrote, 'bounded on the west, east and south by abrupt hills, ranges and rocks rising abruptly out of an almost treeless plain clothed with the most luxuriant verdure.'

Kakadu is the land of the Gagudju, an Aboriginal people from whom the national park takes its name. Their ancestors came from South-east Asia at least 40,000 years ago, island-hopping and then making their way from New Guinea by land when the sea level was lower during the Ice Age.

SACRED ROCK *Sunlit Mount Brockman is one of the most sacred of Aboriginal sites. The Arnhem Land escarpment is visible on the horizon.*

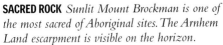

Some of Kakadu's many thousand rock paintings may be seen at Nourlangie Rock, a prominent outcrop that rises from the lowlands. Aborigines used a rock shelter here during the wet season for at least 6000 years. Near the shelter is Anbangbang gallery, where the Aborigine artist Najombolmi completed a painting in the X-ray style in 1964. The section above shows Barrkinj, wife of Namarrkon, the lightning man who creates thunder and lightning by striking the ground and clouds with stone axes. Two of the women below Barrkinj are shown with milk in their breasts.

To the Gagudju, Kakadu was created when a female ancestral being, Warramurrungundji, came out of the sea to form the landscape and to give life to the people. She was followed by other creator beings, including Ginga, a giant crocodile who made the rock country. Some of these ancestral beings, their work done, then became part of the landscape – Ginga takes the form of a rocky outcrop resembling a crocodile's back. Much of the park is owned by the Aboriginal people, who have leased their land to the Department of the Environment and Heritage.

KAKADU'S STORY IN ART

Aboriginal rock paintings spanning some 18,000 years have been found at more than 7000 sites in the park. The animals in the paintings change over the years, as the sea level rose.

The earliest paintings were made during the last Ice Age, when the sea level was lower and Kakadu lay about 186 miles (300km) inland. Then the artists painted kangaroos and emus, the Tasmanian devil – which is no longer found in northern Australia – and large animals that have no modern equivalent. The Ice Age ended about 6000 years ago, and the sea level rose. The land below the Arnhem Land cliffs was now sea and estuaries, and fish such as barramundi and mullet feature largely in the paintings. Many are shown in 'X-ray' style – with internal structures such as backbones visible.

By about 1000 years ago, freshwater swamps had formed in Kakadu behind levees that held back the sea. As well as fish, the artists of this time painted long-necked turtles, magpie geese, and women poling rafts over the swamps.

Modern Kakadu also teems with wildlife. More than 1000 different plant species grow there, and it is a bird refuge of major importance. Prominent among the bird life of Kakadu is the

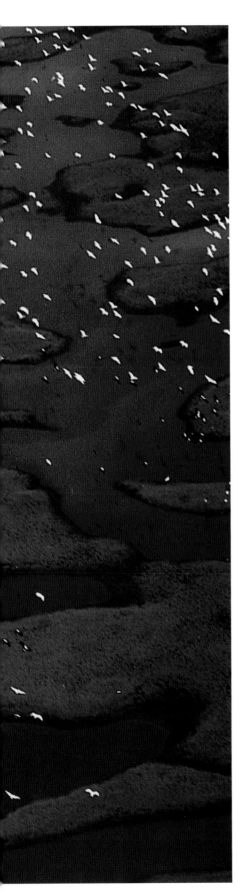

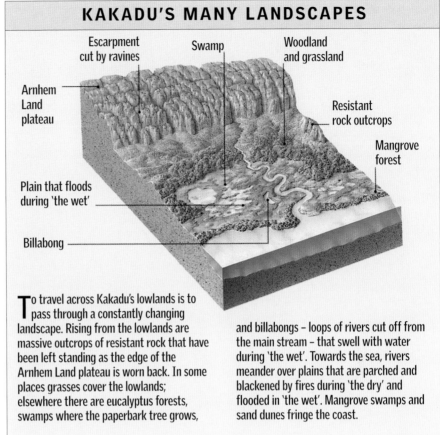

KAKADU'S MANY LANDSCAPES

Escarpment cut by ravines

Swamp

Woodland and grassland

Arnhem Land plateau

Resistant rock outcrops

Mangrove forest

Plain that floods during 'the wet'

Billabong

To travel across Kakadu's lowlands is to pass through a constantly changing landscape. Rising from the lowlands are massive outcrops of resistant rock that have been left standing as the edge of the Arnhem Land plateau is worn back. In some places grasses cover the lowlands; elsewhere there are eucalyptus forests, swamps where the paperbark tree grows,

and billabongs – loops of rivers cut off from the main stream – that swell with water during 'the wet'. Towards the sea, rivers meander over plains that are parched and blackened by fires during 'the dry' and flooded in 'the wet'. Mangrove swamps and sand dunes fringe the coast.

black-necked stork, which has become a symbol of the tropical north. This handsome bird, with its white and glossy green-black plumage, frequents the billabongs and freshwater lagoons. It shares them with a variety of birds including the blue-winged kookaburra, one of several kingfishers.

There are 75 species of reptile, one of which is the notorious saltwater crocodile which lives in brackish estuaries, rivers and billabongs. The 12–20ft (3.7–6m) long 'salties' have a reputation for attacking any creatures, including people, that come too close. In the 1960s, they were hunted almost to extinction for their skins, but since being declared a protected species in 1971 they have grown in number. The freshwater crocodile that also lives in

'SALTIES' HAVE A FEARSOME REPUTATION

INUNDATION *From December to March, monsoon rains and spring tides flood Kakadu's lowlands, creating myriad islands and creeks.*

the park is less aggressive and grows to only about 6ft (1.8m).

Another of Kakadu's reptiles is the fierce-looking but harmless frilled lizard; when alarmed, it raises the loose skin around its neck and takes on the appearance of a small dinosaur. The Gagudju believe that the lizard was given this bizarre appearance as a punishment for breaking Aboriginal law.

Water buffaloes were once common in the park. Like the 'salties' they have been hunted – at one time for their hides and horns but later as a matter of policy. Europeans introduced the animals from Indonesia in the 1820s and 30s as a substitute for their own cattle, which were not suited to the tropical climate.

In the early 1980s some 300,000 water buffaloes grazed the floodplains of the Northern Territory. The animals were considered a threat to wildlife habitats – they trampled on aquatic

LOWLAND LANDSCAPE *One of Kakadu's main rivers, the East Alligator, traces a winding path through a patchwork of greens of varying shades that is broken by pools and creeks.*

plants, and were thought to break down embankments that separated salt and freshwater habitats. In addition, the water buffaloes carried bovine tuberculosis which threatened both human health and Australia's beef cattle industry. By the end of the 1980s, nearly all the wild water buffaloes had been removed from the park or shot.

CROCODILE DUNDEE

Public interest in the once-remote Top End of Australia increased after World War II, partly because uranium was discovered there. Considerable controversy surrounded the mining of uranium, and government restrictions have kept it to a minimum.

Since the early 1980s the Kakadu National Park, which is on the World Heritage list, has become a major tourist attraction, helped by the *Crocodile Dundee* films, which were set partly in the park. Observant visitors setting out on a drive beside the West Alligator River may notice a sign bearing the down-to-earth message: 'You are entering God's Country. Keep the bloody joint clean.'

TERMITES' HIGH-RISE HOMES

Scattered over Kakadu's grasslands are mounds of all shapes and sizes, from spires soaring more than 33ft (10m) into the air to low mounds shaped like mushrooms. These earth mounds are built by colonies of termites, highly organised insects that each have a specific role, such as worker or soldier. Inside each mound's concrete-hard shell there is a maze of passageways.

The most unusual mounds are those built by the compass termites, whose homes stand 7-10ft (2-3m) high and are shaped roughly like tapering gravestones. Without exception, they are aligned the same way – the narrow sides point north and south, and the broad sides face east and west.

At one time it was thought that compass termites were able to sense magnetic north, and lined up their nests like magnetic compass needles. Now it seems that they are influenced only by the sun and build their nests so that the temperature is regulated. At midday the mounds' narrower sides face

the sun to avoid overheating. In the morning and evening, when the sun's rays are weakest, the broad sides face the sun and receive the maximum heat available. As a result, the temperature inside the mound stays at about 30°C (86°F).

REPAIR WORK *Compass termites build their tall, tapering mounds from chewed wood and soil. The workers of the colony repair holes in the walls.*

Simpson Desert

A FEARSOME WILDERNESS OF SAND AND STONE IN THE CENTRE OF AUSTRALIA CHALLENGES TRAVELLERS TO CROSS AT THEIR PERIL

DESERT OCEAN *Waves of ridged red sand ripple endlessly across Australia's Simpson Desert, one of the most parched and hostile regions on Earth.*

Ridge upon ridge of deep red sand stretches from horizon to horizon across the Simpson Desert in the dry heart of Australia. In 1845, Charles Sturt, the first European to set eyes on the scene, described how the ridges ran in parallel lines and 'succeeded each other like the waves of the sea'. Sunrise and sunset emphasise the symmetry of the dunes, for the slanting light picks out the red crests like undulating banks of burning coals, and their hollows seem like deep pools of ink.

Covering an area almost half the size of Italy, the Simpson Desert is Australia's most hostile region. Between the dunes, which reach up to 65ft (20m) high, lie clay pans and gibber plains – flats of jagged stones. The desert is the driest place on the continent, with an average of just 5in (125mm) of rain a year, and for months on end only gnarled shrubs and cane grass can eke out an existence in the baked earth. Lizards and hopping mice survive here, keeping to burrows in the heat of the day. Occasional heavy rains bring a magical transformation. Almost overnight, a carpet of living green emerges from the desert floor. Soon, bright sweeps of purple appear where succulent parakeelya plants burst into bloom, attracting insects and birds.

Charles Sturt, a government surveyor, was eager to explore the area. The migratory pattern of birds led him to believe there must be an unmapped expanse of water in the interior. It was this that he set off to find when he left Adelaide in August 1844. But a year later his party turned back defeated. After crossing an 'immense, gloomy, stone-clad plain' (now known as Sturt's Stony Desert), they were faced with thirst and starvation as they reached the eastern edge of the forbidding Simpson Desert. The scorching heat – 70°C (160°F) – of a record-breaking summer, and scurvy brought on by a diet of flour and water, had sapped their strength.

Desert explorer Dr Cecil Madigan led a scientific expedition into the desert in 1939, using camels for transport. He named the desert after Alfred Simpson, president of the South Australian Branch of the Royal Geographical Society.

STILL UNTAMED

Particles of iron oxide give the sand its red colour, but around the few watercourses it is white. The dunes were piled up by powerful winds in prehistoric times, and today are much as they were some 14,000 years ago, after the winds had dropped and rainfall had increased enough to allow shrubs and grasses to bind the sand with their roots. Travellers today can drive across the desert, but must still face sandstorms, stones, mud and searing heat.

GOLDEN TOUCH *(overleaf) Sunrise lights up the sandstone Chamber's Pillar, in the desert's northern reaches.*

235

Lake Eyre

ABOUT ONCE EVERY TEN YEARS THE BARREN SALT FLATS COME TO LIFE, AND NATURE PLAYS OUT A HIGH-SPEED DRAMA

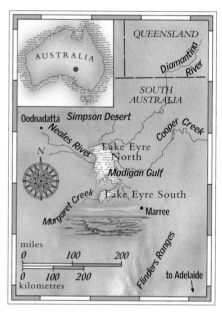

In spite of its name, Lake Eyre is barely a lake at all, but rather two huge, shallow scoops in the thirsty heartland of Australia. Its salt-caked floor is dry most of the time, and a rim of thick, encrusted minerals hangs like hoar frost round its shores. Coming upon the lake in 1858, the explorer Peter Warburton described the scene as 'terrible in its death-like stillness'.

Parched landscape stretches away on every side. To the north lie the shifting dunes of the Simpson Desert, to east and west are vast plains covered with dunes and gibbers – sharp stones that make walking difficult. To the south is a ribbon of salt lakes and dry saltpans. A glimpse of water is a tantalising prospect amid this desolation. All too often a watery vision on the horizon turns out to be a small, salty pool or a mirage

FLEETING RESERVOIR *Like a vast inland sea, Lake Eyre glimmers cool and blue beyond a bed of outlying saltpans.*

PELICAN NURSERY *Pelicans come in thousands to nest on Lake Eyre's salt-encrusted shores and islands.*

created by temperatures up to 39°C (102°F). But once in a while, a traveller may come upon the welcome sight of a vast freshwater lake.

Lying at Australia's lowest point, with its bottom 50ft (15m) below sea level, Lake Eyre receives water from a region larger than France, Spain and Portugal put together. Its two parts, Lake Eyre North and the much smaller Lake Eyre South, together cover an area of about 3700sq miles (9600km²). They are linked by the 9 mile (15km) long Godyer Channel. When it rains, water runs off the distant mountains and pours into the dry river courses. Much of the water evaporates or seeps into the sand, but if the rains have been heavy enough some may eventually reach Lake Eyre, 600 miles (1000km) downstream. Only in years of very

PELICANS AT LAKE EYRE

Why Australian pelicans took to breeding at the hottest and driest place in Australia, and how they know when to go there, is a mystery. But when the rivers flow and fill Lake Eyre, a pelican nesting colony appears around it, the birds having flown vast distances across hot, searing desert to get there. They need water for about three months in order to rear chicks.

The nests are little more than scrapes in the sand. Both parents sit on the two or three eggs for about three weeks. The chicks hatch naked and decidedly ugly, but tough. If threatened, they gather in a crèche and tumble along like a rugby scrum.

Their parents are well able to defend them – one pelican has been seen to kill an intruding swan.

Both parents feed the chicks with shrimps, tadpoles and fish, caught in their enormous beaks and pouches. Sometimes pelicans will fish in a group, forming a tight circle or horseshoe and trapping their prey within it.

FEEDING TIME *Once pelican chicks are about a week old, they take regurgitated fish from a parent's beak.*

heavy flooding does water flow along the Godyer Channel.

When the water reaches it, Lake Eyre explodes with teeming life. As if from nowhere, plants such as the vivid red Sturt's desert pea spring up. They flower rapidly in the race to complete their life cycle and produce seeds before the moisture disappears. The water revives algae (minute plants) and shrimp eggs lying dormant in the mud. Soon the lake is a seething soup of living creatures. It is not long before the birds arrive – ducks, avocets, cormorants, gulls – some having flown halfway across Australia. They feed on shrimps and on fish swept in with the rivers. Along the lake shores, pelicans and banded stilts set up noisy breeding colonies, sometimes numbering tens of thousands of nests.

ROUGH GOING *The stony gibber plains (left) to the west of Lake Eyre deter even the hardiest of travellers.*

MAGIC TOUCH *As the lake fills with water, its barren shores (below) burst into bloom with poached-egg daisies and wild hops.*

WHEN THE WATER REACHES IT, LAKE EYRE EXPLODES WITH TEEMING LIFE

When the water flow stops, the lake rapidly evaporates in the intense heat, and gets increasingly salty. Timing is now critical. Nestlings must grow and learn to fly before the lake dries up, for as food and water become scarce the birds leave, and unfledged chicks are abandoned. The fresh-water fish have no means of escape, and suffocate in the salty water. The lake eventually reverts to a hard salt crust over damp mud, and the land is again an inhospitable wilderness, awaiting a new season of rains to bring it to life.

The hot sun can bake the mud to a solid clay pavement. It was on the hard flats of Madigan Gulf, on Lake Eyre North, that Donald Campbell broke the world land speed record in 1964, reaching a speed of 403mph (644km/h) in Bluebird, his turbine-driven car.

THE BAFFLING LAKE

Speculation about lakes, or even a vast inland sea, in central Australia was popular among European pioneers. Many wondered where the rivers went that flowed towards the interior. Most of the coast had been mapped by the 1830s, but much of the hinterland was known only to Aborigines.

Edward Eyre set out from Adelaide in 1839 at the age of 25, intent on being the first European to cross the country from south to north. After crossing the Flinders Ranges he came up against a huge, impassable horseshoe of salt lakes, and was forced to turn back. In 1840 Eyre tried again, eventually reaching the lake that now bears his name. Although it was dry, the treacherous mud floor prevented him from going farther.

Other explorers had similar experiences, yet reports of a great freshwater lake persisted. In 1922 Gerald Halligan surveyed Lake Eyre from the air and discovered water in the northern part. Yet when he visited the lake on foot the following year, he found barely enough water to float a boat.

Now it is clear that Lake Eyre can indeed be a vast expanse of fresh water – but only once in every eight or ten years. This cycle of events has been going on for some 20,000 years. Very occasionally heavy rains fall for two summers in succession. The first year's rain saturates the ground, so in the second year less is absorbed on the journey down from the mountains, and Lake Eyre is filled to its brim.

Port Campbell

OCEAN STORMS AND SWELLS HAVE CARVED OUT HUGE SEA STACKS FROM THE LIMESTONE CLIFFS OF AUSTRALIA'S SOUTH-EAST COAST

Once long ago, the Twelve Apostles – the huge rock stacks that stand offshore near Port Campbell in southeast Australia – were part of the jagged limestone cliffs. These stacks have resisted thousands of years of battering by relentless seas as the rock around them was slowly worn away. Now they stand alone, lonely markers of an earlier shoreline.

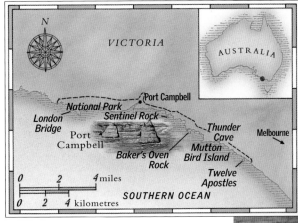

Huge waves continue to batter and reshape the cliffs, which stretch for nearly 20 miles (32km) and are a popular tourist spot. In 1990 a couple stood at the end of London Bridge – a natural pier jutting into the ocean, with two arches worn away by the action of the sea. As the couple prepared to take a photograph of the cliffs, the arch in front of them broke into pieces without warning and plunged into the sea, leaving them stranded. A police helicopter soon took them to safety, but 130ft (40m) of London Bridge, its link with the land, was gone for ever. In July 2005, one of the stacks (opposite page, foreground left) collapsed into the sea, leaving in its place a pile of rocks.

All along the Port Campbell shore, a national park, rocky islets of various shapes – wedges, stacks, grottoes, chimneys, arches – rise starkly from the ocean. Join them up like the dots in a giant puzzle, and the ghost of the now-vanished shoreline emerges. The Twelve Apostles and London Bridge, with neighbouring formations such as Sentinel Rock, Baker's Oven and Thunder Cave, are links in this ancient chain.

LIKE DOTS IN A GIANT PUZZLE, THE STACKS OUTLINE A VANISHED SHORE

The Port Campbell rock is limestone formed 26 million years ago, when the whole area was under the sea. As marine animals died, millions of tiny skeletons rich in calcium accumulated on the seabed. Slowly they built up an 850ft (260m) layer of limestone on top of the soft clay floor. About 20,000 years ago, during the last Ice Age, the sea level dropped and the rock was exposed. Wind, rain and waves began to pummel the soft bluffs, and the constant assault of centuries has sent chunks of land crashing into the ocean every 20 or 30 years. In some places, the coastline has retreated uniformly, leaving no clues to its original shape, but in others weaker sections gave way first, creating the stacks and arches of today.

The Southern Ocean is whipped up here by strong winds known as the 'Roaring Forties'; huge storm waves may cut ledges in the limestone some 200ft (60m) above the high tide mark. Near to Thunder Cave, The Blowhole illustrates how the sea exploits weaker beds in the rock to encroach on the land. Here the water thunders underground for 430yds (400m) along a wave-carved tunnel. Where the roof has caved in, visitors can peer down a 'blowhole' at the water churning below.

TALL AND TOUGH *Once the rock stacks called the Twelve Apostles were part of the coastal cliffs. Now they stand alone, some rising to 330ft (100m).*

The scenic stacks bring a steady stream of tourists all year round. Birds such as the Tasmanian mutton bird (or short-tailed shearwater) come here, too. They breed on the rocky outcrops of the largest stack, Mutton Bird Island, arriving in late September in their hundreds of thousands after making a perilous 9000 mile (14,400km) journey across the Pacific Ocean from Siberia.

ROCKY REFUGE

Nesting burrows are jammed side by side into every available crevice on the island. Here the birds can raise their chicks in peace, secure on the heights from predators such as rats and man.

Many other birds – albatrosses, gannets, cormorants and petrels – also come to feast on the rich supply of fish. Southern right whales pass by in winter, on the way from Antarctica to their breeding grounds off the Great Australian Bight – a few stop to breed here. But most of them pass by close to the shore, untroubled by the turbulent sea and its ruined rocks.

LONDON BRIDGE

Once this flat-topped rock had two arches linked to the cliffs, and looked so like London's old river bridge that it was named after it.

Now this London Bridge has fallen down, leaving its newly exposed edge clean and raw against the darker, weathered older rock. The first arch crashed unexpectedly into the sea in January 1990, leaving two tourists stranded above the second arch. In time, the relentless waves will bring down that one, too.

Fraser Island

RICH, VARIED FOREST CLOTHES AN ISLAND OFF AUSTRALIA'S EAST COAST – YET BENEATH LIES NOTHING BUT SAND

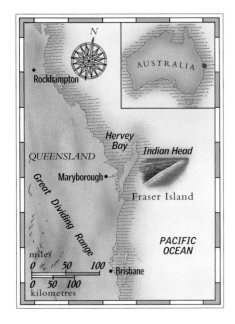

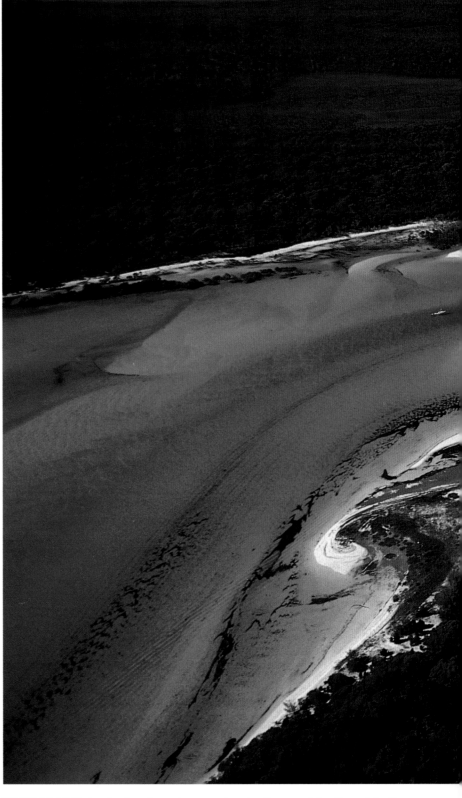

ISLAND OF SAND *A strip of sand stretches away into the distance, edging Fraser Island's Platypus Bay. An inlet breaks the shoreline on the left of the picture.*

Shaped like a well-worn thigh boot, Fraser Island, lying off the Queensland coast, is an island built of sand. There are beaches and dunes of golden sand along its shores, and in places the 77 mile (124km) long island has cliffs of yellow, red and brown formed of sand and carved by the elements into spires and pinnacles.

Yet behind the beaches and cliffs grows an astonishingly varied canopy of vegetation. Sand heaped up to 785ft (240m) high supports dense and sometimes luxuriant forest. Moisture-loving piccabeen palms and paperbark trees grow where the ground is almost waterlogged. Elsewhere are cypress pines and tall blackbutts, and stands of hoop pines and kauri pines that were much sought by 19th-century loggers.

Fraser Island began to take shape millions of years ago when mountains on the mainland to the south were eroded by wind and rain. Fine debris was swept into the ocean, carried northwards by currents and gradually accumulated on the ocean floor. Then, during Ice Age falls in sea level, the accumulating sand became dry land and was blown into massive dunes. During rises in sea level, ocean currents brought in more sand. After the Ice Ages, plants began to grow on the virgin sand, the seeds and spores carried there by birds and the wind. When they died back

they formed a layer of humus in which larger plants could put down roots, stabilising the dunes.

Now the island's high rainfall – over 60in (1500mm) a year – encourages a cycle of growth and decay on the sands. Arrow-straight satinay trees, found in few places in the world, grow here –

their trunks were used to line the Suez Canal in the 1920s. Scribbly gum trees – named after the marks left on their bark by burrowing insects – dominate the island's shrubby heathlands.

Fraser Island takes its name from the woman who brought it to the world's attention. In 1836 a group of ship-

wrecked Europeans struggled ashore from one of their ship's small boats. Among the party was the ship's captain and his wife Eliza Fraser, but by the time that rescue arrived two months later, several of the party, including the captain, were dead. Mrs Fraser alleged that her husband had

BARE SAND *A gnarled, solitary, coast banksia tree rises from wind-rippled sand on Fraser Island's north-east coast.*

been murdered by the island's Aborigines, the Butchulla people. In London she told increasingly lurid tales of her time on the island, describing them to the public, for a fee of sixpence, in a tent in Hyde Park. She related how she had been speared and tortured, and how the ship's mate had been roasted alive over a slow fire. Mrs Fraser's accounts of her

MEAL TIME *The Queensland blossom bat feeds exclusively on nectar and pollen.*

experiences have been the subject of a film and several books, including Patrick White's fictional account *A Fringe of Leaves*.

Not long afterwards, Fraser's fame also spread as a source of magnificent softwoods. Loggers moved in, and set up sawmills and tramlines to move out the timber. The Aborigines started to suffer from European diseases, the effects of opium and alcohol, and malnutrition as their food supplies were disrupted by land clearance. In 1904 the few remaining Butchulla people were moved to the mainland.

Among Fraser's forests and scrublands are more than 40 lakes. Although it is made up of sand, the island is far from being a giant, free-draining sandcastle.

Under the island the sand has cemented together with humus and minerals to form a water-tight pan that traps the island's plentiful rainfall.

Here and there the ground surface drops below this watertable to form crystal-clear lakes, such as Lake Wabby. Forested dunes surround the lake on three sides, while the fourth is a huge wall of wind-blown sand which is advancing into the water.

BY THE TIME THAT RESCUE ARRIVED, SEVERAL OF THE PARTY WERE DEAD

Higher up in the dunes are Fraser Island's many 'perched' lakes where rainwater is trapped in depressions by an impermeable saucer of bonded sand, humus and minerals. All the lakes are low in nutrients and have few fish. The island's lakes and streams provide watering holes for animals, including dingos and wallabies. Possums, flying foxes, echidnas and lizards can also all be found. A much smaller inhabitant is the diminutive Queensland blossom bat, which only weighs about half an ounce (15g). With so many different habitats leading one into the other, Fraser is a birdwatcher's paradise, and species as diverse as pelicans, sea eagles, kingfishers and lorikeets can be seen there.

Fraser Island is a fragile environment, affected by both natural and man-made forces. Vast sand-blows drift across the land, in places engulfing trees, shrubs and flowers. Small amounts of soap or detergent introduced into the perched lakes by visitors can contaminate the water, causing algae to proliferate and threatening fish, birds and reptiles. Before Fraser Island became a World Heritage Area and part of the Great Sandy National Park there was concern over the commercial felling of trees, but this industry has since been stopped and the future looks positive for this island.

Great Barrier Reef

THE LARGEST STRUCTURE ON EARTH IS THE JEWEL OF QUEENSLAND'S COAST. ITS ENGINEERS ARE TINY COUSINS OF THE JELLYFISH

Considering that it is one of the planet's loveliest ornaments – a jewel of azure, indigo, sapphire and purest white whose glories are apparent even from the Moon – it seems strange that the first Europeans to see the Great Barrier Reef should have been so sparing in their descriptions. Most, of course, were seamen who had other things on their minds than the beauties of nature.

In 1606 there was the Spaniard Luis Vaez de Torres, storm-driven round the tip of Queensland and through the strait now named after him. There was Captain Cook, whose HMS *Endeavour* was trapped and badly

RING OF BRIGHT WATER *Surf encircling one of the Bunker Group of cays stands out against the ocean's blue.*

holed between the outer reef and the mainland in 1770.

And there was Captain Bligh who, in 1789, brought his boatload of starving *Bounty* loyalists through the reef's breakers to the calm waters beyond.

Joseph Banks, the *Endeavour*'s botanist, was awed by the place. After the ship had been repaired, he wrote: 'A reef such as we have just passed is a thing scarcely known in Europe, or indeed anywhere but in these seas. It is a wall of coral rock, rising perpendicularly out of the unfathomable ocean'. Although coral in fact requires shallow, sunlit seas to thrive, Banks was right in proclaiming the uniqueness of the Great Barrier Reef. Running some 1260 miles (2030km) along the edge of the continental shelf of north-eastern Australia, it is the largest living entity on Earth.

Partly, it is grouped about real islands, actually the summits of a long-drowned mountain range. But its extraordinary richness comes from its 3000 coral reefs, islands, cays and lagoons, all at different stages of development. The reefs are the product of 10,000 years of labour, during which the oceans rose to their present level after the last Ice Age.

The engineers of this stupendous undertaking are millions of tiny coral polyps – some 350 different species of them. They are related to jellyfish and each has a mouth surrounded by a ring of tentacles on top. Each polyp can

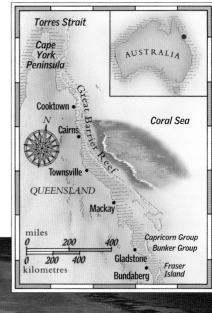

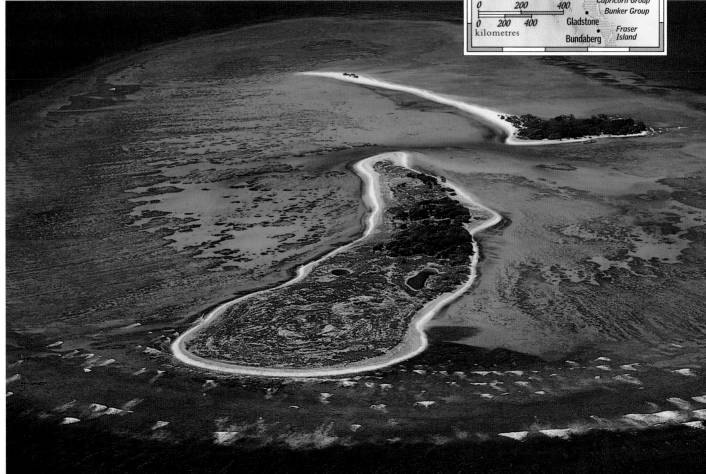

draw calcium carbonate from the sea and turn it into a casing of limestone that, multiplied by billions, forms the reef. But a polyp must share its limestone shelter with minute plants called zooxanthellae, which use light to convert carbon dioxide and water into carbohydrates and oxygen. These the polyp absorbs, presenting the plants in exchange with nitrates and other waste products. So coral reefs can grow only where sunlight can reach – in clear water up to about 130ft (40m) deep.

CORALS GALORE

To a visitor's eye the reef is a thing of beauty and serenity, but it is also a place of endless struggle as each creature within it competes for food and space. There are both soft and hard (reef-building) corals of various shapes and sizes – corals like stags' horns, like whips, like fans, corals tough enough to withstand the pounding of the surf, others so delicate they can live only in the stillest waters. Some species grow faster than their neighbours, so as to overshadow them and steal their light. Others use poisonous tentacles to sweep the area clear of rivals, or release deadly chemicals into the water.

Added to these hazards are predators such as parrot fish with coral-chewing jaws, and crown-of-thorns starfish that digest the coral by spreading their stomachs over it. These starfish have periodic population explosions and destroy entire reefs. Ocean storms and cyclones also grind, tear and pulverise.

Daytime in the reef's shallow waters is hardly quiescent, but night brings the greatest activity. At night the coral polyps feed, pushing out their multicoloured tentacles to entrap tiny creatures and plants called plankton. As billions of tentacles emerge, it is as if the reef has burst into flower – an action that would be impossible by day, as it would shade the zooxanthellae from vital sunlight.

On certain still nights in spring, the most remarkable display of all occurs. Then, all along the reef, triggered by who knows what message of chemistry or light, the entire polyp population releases orange and red, blue and green parcels of eggs and sperm. They float to the surface, covering it with a wash of colour. The parcels break up, and eggs and sperm mingle to produce infant polyps that swim away on the tide in

search of a suitable, vacant spot to begin building a new reef.

Other creatures adapted and attuned to life among the corals are sponges and anemones, sea slugs and sea cucumbers, shrimps, giant clams, sea squirts, sea snakes, jellyfish and fishes in endless, brilliantly hued array. Within and without the reef are sharks, and in the deeper waters beyond, such sea mammals as dolphins and whales.

The reef is forever growing. No sooner has a new speck of coral broken the surface of the sea than it acquires a cap of white sand with something growing in it. Some of these pioneer colonisers appear with miraculous speed – they have salt-tolerant fruits that may

REEF RESIDENTS *The 200lb (90kg) giant clam (above) releases at least a billion eggs at each spawning. (Inset) There are many kinds of both soft corals (top), which have limestone crystals in their tissues but do not form casings, and hard corals (bottom), which do.*

CAYS IN THE MAKING *(far right) Shallow, interconnecting lagoons, like these in the Capricorn Group, eventually fill with sand ground off their perimeter coral, forming islands known as cays.*

NEIGHBOURS IN PARADISE

REEF SHOAL *Among the thousands of colourful reef fishes are fairy basslets, which feed in large numbers in the plankton-rich waters of the reef's outer slopes.*

The Great Barrier Reef is the tropical rainforest of the ocean. Coral takes the place of trees and plants, and fishes and soft-bodied sea creatures replace animals and birds. But there is still the same rich diversity of life, and the same struggle to find a niche. With 150 species of fish alone – perhaps 100,000 individuals to every 2½ acres (1 hectare) of reef – competition is fierce.

Everywhere there is colour - colour to entice, to warn, to camouflage, to deceive. Creatures such as the white and crimson cowries or the blue-spotted, red coral trout, blend with their rocky background. Others, like the scarlet and silver harlequin tusk fish, are striped to mask their outlines. The trailing skirts of the red fire fish, brilliant as those of a Diaghilev dancer, warn of its venomous stings; vividly patterned angel fish flash flares of colour to deter intruders in their territory. Some, like the peacock sole which burrows into sand, can change colour to match their surroundings.

Ways of finding food are just as varied. Stone fish resemble the rocks they lie among, and kill with their deadly spikes. The carpet shark, its skin fringed like seaweed, also lies in wait for victims. Tirelessly voracious snappers hunt in shoals, devouring everything in their path. But the cleaner wrasse, which relieves other fish of damaged skin and parasites, is immune from all attack.

Shoals of herring and mullet hunt the small fry, and in turn fall prey to black-tip sharks, dolphins and barracuda. On the far side of the reef, the ultimate hunters – great white and tiger sharks - wait for dolphins and turtles.

DEADLY HAVEN *Anemone fish live safely among a sea anemone's tentacles, immune to their poison. The anemone profits from the fishes' food leftovers.*

bob about for months in the ocean before finding a suitable berth and germinating. They pave the way for more plants. Birds everywhere on the reef make a vital contribution to its well-being by distributing plant seeds and providing fertiliser to enrich the soil. Gulls have a fondness for night-shade berries, and spread their seeds all over the islands. Black noddies nest in pisonia trees, whose sticky seeds are distributed on the birds' wings.

The coral islands are the home of myriad sea birds – terns, noddies, gulls, shearwaters, frigate birds, gannets and lordly sea eagles that squabble and squawk over the rich harvest of the reefs. In summer, female turtles haul themselves ashore on the islands to lay eggs in the warm sand. About eight weeks later, thousands of baby turtles emerge to dash helter-skelter for the sea, harried by sea birds, crabs and rats.

THE GREATEST DANGERS

Altogether, the Great Barrier Reef is one of the world's most vigorous and best-integrated ecosystems. But it is also one of the most delicately balanced. Pressures on a single aspect can have disastrous effects upon the whole. The reef can take storms and the sea's rages in its stride, but now, in the 21st century, its greatest dangers are those induced by modern man.

Aborigines fished and hunted along the reef for centuries without damaging it. But in the past 100 years, guano (bird dung) diggings, overfishing, whaling, trade in bêche-de-mer (dried, smoked sea slugs) and hunting for mother-of-pearl, have left scars.

Declaring the area a National Park and World Heritage Area has put a stop to many dangers, and tourism is strictly controlled. Even so, some scientists blame resort sewage for an explosion in the crown-of-thorns starfish population, and hotel food scraps dumped in the sea led to an increase in gulls and a dramatic rise in predation on baby turtles. The run-off of phosphate-based fertilisers from sugar cane fields into the sea is another large threat to the reef.

In order to protect this exceptional area, no action is too small to help ensure that the Great Barrier Reef can continue on with its timeless affairs.

The Breadknife

A JAGGED BLADE OF ROCK SLICES UP
THROUGH THE EUCALYPTUS FORESTS OF
THE WARRUMBUNGLE MOUNTAINS

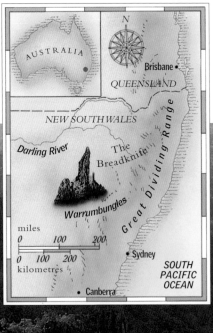

A narrow blade of rock stabs the clear air of the Warrumbungles – a range of mountains in New South Wales. Aptly called the Breadknife, it reaches skywards to a height of 300ft (90m), yet its summit is only about 3ft (1m) thick. The Breadknife is the most dramatic of several spectacular landforms in the thickly forested Warrumbungles, whose name means 'crooked mountains'. Rocky columns and spires rise abruptly from the surrounding plains, and tower above domes and ridges dissected by deep gorges. An early European explorer, Yorkshire-born John Oxley, described them as 'A most stupendous range of mountains, lifting their blue heads above the horizon'.

WALL OF ROCK *The Breadknife's bare blade rises from wooded, hummocky hills of the Warrumbungles. Climbing its sheer surface is forbidden.*

The origins of the Breadknife go back to volcanic upheavals that were at their peak between 17 and 13 million years ago. Lava filled cracks in the Earth's surface, and cooled to form walls of solidified lava embedded in rock. Millions of years of erosion have since worn down the rocks, but the solidified lava walls proved more resistant to the forces of wind and weather. The Breadknife now stands as a remnant of one of these walls, stripped of the rock in which it was embedded.

The Warrumbungles are often referred to as a place where east meets west, because of the contrasting climates on the opposite sides of the mountains. To the north and west the mountains slope down to hot, dry plains. On these sunny and drier slopes grow shrubby trees such as the quandong, which has edible bright red fruits. The cooler, wetter southern and eastern slopes are dominated by forests of tall eucalyptus trees and flowering shrubs. Sundews grow in damp spots in the forests, along with ferns, orchids and wonga vines with tubular, purple-throated flowers.

Parrots screech and dart around the forests. Red-rumped parrots from the inland plains join rosellas from the eastern coasts and mountains, lorikeets and pink and grey galahs, to make up a brilliant kaleidoscope of colour. At ground level, the flightless emu breeds in the seclusion of the northern grasslands, ready to make a long-legged dash for cover when disturbed.

Grey kangaroos abound in the more open areas, and koalas and the common brush-tailed possums live in the treetops. To move from tree to tree, koalas descend at night, cross the ground and scale another tree. Possums, however, climb from one tree to another, using the flap of skin between their front and hind limbs as wings.

For unknown numbers of years the Warrumbungles were part of the territory of the Kamilaroi people who lived in the adjacent plains. They gathered berries, roots and wild bees' honey, and hunted kangaroos, emus and wildfowl. But when European settlers arrived these Aborigines were moved on, leaving little to tell of their former presence, although a cave high on a hillside contains boulders with grooves created by axe-grinding. A rock shelter nearby held remains of organic material, which showed that macrozamia seeds – once a staple part of the Aborigines' diet – had been prepared there.

'A MOST STUPENDOUS RANGE OF MOUNTAINS'

TEMPTING FRUITS

Macrozamia belongs to a group of plants called cycads, which were once far more common than they are now. Their orange-red seeds are rich in starch, but are poisonous when eaten raw. Aboriginal people detoxified them by methods which included cracking, soaking, grinding and baking, and then ate the pulp raw, or roasted – when it resembled the taste of chestnut.

The appetising-looking seeds of macrozamia and other cycads gave early explorers considerable problems. The botanist Joseph Banks, who travelled with the British navigator Captain Cook on the *Endeavour*, recorded how men who tried to eat just a few cycad seeds 'were violently affected by them both upwards and downwards'.

In 1967, the Warrumbungles became a national park. Although some lower slopes were cleared by settlers, the forests are largely undisturbed by man, and stand out from a sea of heavily cultivated plains like a green island.

THE MANY AND VARIED GUM TREES

More than 500 species of eucalyptus tree - popularly known as gum trees – grow in Australia. Their timber is highly prized, and used for anything from flooring to wharves and railway sleepers.

The evergreen trees vary enormously in size and character, and there are species suited to most of Australia's climatic conditions. Giant trees more than 200ft (60m) tall grow in humid forests, and bushy mallees survive in drier areas because their extensive roots give them access to more water. Some trees are protected from grass fires - their bark is fire resistant and insulates the inner living parts from the heat. The snow gum of Australia's alpine regions can tolerate both freezing winter temperatures and the fierce heat of summer. The bark of some species is smooth - the result of an outer layer being shed in summer - and coloured anything from dull pink and yellow to cream, grey or orange. Fibrous, bristly bark covers other trees, and another variation is a hard and deeply furrowed bark.

COAT OF MANY COLOURS *During fires, the bark of blue gums (right) protects the trees' living tissues from very high temperatures. The salmon gum's bark (below) is shed each year.*

Wallaman Falls

EMERGING FROM MOUNTAIN HEIGHTS, A SMALL STREAM PLUMMETS BREATHTAKINGLY OVER A PRECIPICE INTO PRIMEVAL JUNGLE

In the heart of a steamy rainforest, Stony Creek winds a gently sloping course through tangled trees and shrubs. Still dripping from the night's rain, palm fronds jostle in the undergrowth, and high overhead a canopy of leaves filters the early morning light. Somewhere in the forest a black cockatoo is calling – an omen of more rain.

As the current quickens, the creek's meandering waters are disturbed by eddies and swirls. The water cascades down a winding gorge, then without warning plunges over a cliff to drop a sheer 912ft (278m) into the river below.

This is Wallaman Falls – a ribbon of silver pouring down through misty halos of ruby, azure and violet.

Stony Creek is one of many streams rising in North Queensland's coastal ranges and dropping off the edge of a plateau into the Herbert River Gorge. Here in the southern tip of Australia's largest rainforest, there are more different kinds of plants and animals than anywhere else in the country.

SHEER DROP *As they cascade down a forest cliff, Wallaman Falls cut into the rock and are slowly retreating upstream.*

Look carefully and you may spot a sleepy opossum, a giant green tree frog or a 20ft (6m) python. Here birds range from the tiny large-billed warbler to flightless, almost man-sized cassowaries, and the insect world includes blue caterpillars the length of your arm and moths with wings spanning 10in (250mm). This is platypus country, too; sit quietly by the water and you may hear the splash of a flat tail or catch a glimpse of silvery brown fur.

FURRY EGG-LAYER

If Nature had set out to create an enigma, she could not have done better than the platypus. A cat-sized egg-laying mammal with a beaver-like body and a duck's feet and bill, it looks like a bizarre experiment in anatomy.

In fact, the platypus is superbly adapted for its waterside life. Even the incongruous flat bill is a highly evolved food-finder, able to sense the tiniest electric currents in the muscles of its water-dwelling prey, such as crayfish.

Ball's Pyramid

AN ISOLATED PILLAR OF ROCK THRUSTING UP FROM THE SOUTHERN PACIFIC OCEAN IS THE HIGHEST ROCK PINNACLE IN THE WORLD

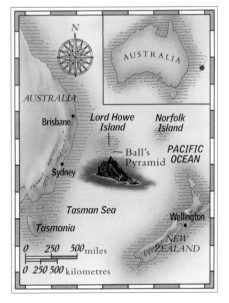

On the map, the tiny dot that marks Ball's Pyramid is almost lost in the surrounding ocean. But those who come face to face with the sea-stack in real life can hardly believe their eyes. It is an obelisk so tall that it seems to touch the sky. Although only 440yds (400m) across at its base, Ball's Pyramid reaches a height of more than 1800ft (550m) – almost twice the height of the Eiffel Tower. In the *Guinness Book*

of Records it is listed as the highest rock pinnacle in the world.

Lying off Australia's east coast, Ball's Pyramid is about 435 miles (700km) north-east of Sydney. The solo aviator Francis Chichester, looking down on the great rock during his trans-Tasman flight of 1931, described it as a 'broad primeval dagger of stone'. But this giant-sized Excalibur reveals its secrets not from the sky but under the sea.

OUT OF THE BLUE *Ball's Pyramid rises abruptly from the southern Pacific Ocean like the jagged ruins of an ancient abbey, full of power and mystery.*

Beneath the ocean's glassy surface, myriad brightly coloured fish dart round rock columns and under arches. Their playground is a plateau of volcanic rock, for Ball's Pyramid is a crumbling, long-extinct volcano with only its peak above the water. It is one of a series of volcanoes that became inactive 7 million years ago.

Ever since, the sea has waged war on the intrusive landmass that forced a way up through its depths. Waves have gnawed at the rocks for centuries and, thanks to their persistence and the help of the wind, they are winning. Only three per cent of the original landmass is left, reduced by the ocean's wear and tear to a chain of islands and outcrops.

BALL'S DISCOVERY

The first person known to have set eyes on the rock was Henry Lidgbird Ball, in command of HMS *Supply*, which passed by in 1788 with settlers for Norfolk Island. Ball named the pyramidal rock after himself, and on the way back anchored off the largest island in the chain, naming it after Lord Howe, Britain's First Lord of the Admiralty.

When Lieutenant Ball and his crew set foot on the crescent-shaped island, only 7 miles (11km) long, they found themselves in a forested paradise where wild animals showed no fear at their approach. But later other ships called, and hungry sailors hunted birds such as the white gallinule to extinction. By 1834, Lord Howe Island had been settled by people who made a living from trade with passing ships.

With the settlers came rats, which swam ashore from a sinking ship. The island offered the rats abundant food – the lizards, birds, and insects had no defences against them, and they wiped out five species of bird and pushed unique races of geckos, skinks and stick insects to the edge of extinction.

'IT STABBED THE AIR LIKE A BROAD PRIMEVAL DAGGER OF STONE'
Sir Francis Chichester

But Ball's Pyramid, about 12 miles (20km) south of Lord Howe Island, remains intact. Boats circle it while their passengers gaze upward in awe. Only the sea birds show no reverence as they wheel about the summit and perch on perilous ledges. For them, this windswept stack is an ideal home, and thousands, including masked boobies, providence petrels, noddies and red-tailed tropic birds, raise chicks here every year.

Lord Howe Island, where warm tropical southward currents meet the cool of the sub-Antarctic, has the most southerly coral reef. In the reef's nooks and crannies and the rock overhangs and galleries there are more than 400 kinds of tropical and cooler-water fish. A few, such as double-header wrasses 30in (760mm) long and named for the large bump on the male's forehead, are found nowhere else in the world.

For two centuries, Ball's Pyramid resisted the onslaught of man. There are no coves and beaches where boats can land – just one landing platform among the steep, rocky sides dashed by waves. Many boatloads of would-be climbers were beaten back by the sea; some

COLOUR MIXTURE *Both cool- and warm-water fish live in and around the Lord Howe Island coral reef. They include bespectacled angelfish, white-barred clownfish (darker bodied than their warmer-water cousins) and Spanish dancer sea slugs, like floating rose petals.*

braved waves and sharks by swimming to the rock with their gear.

As they struggled to find the few footholds on the brittle rock, sea birds swooped at their heads and centipedes 6in (150mm) long bit their flesh.

Described as 'Australia's Everest', Ball's Pyramid seemed destined to remain unclimbed. Success came in 1965, when Bryden Allen and John Davis led an Australian team to the top. They were almost defeated by the last 200ft (60m), where pieces of rock were balanced so precariously that some toppled seawards when touched – wind-blown holes had created a strange and hazardous sculpture. Other climbers have struggled up the rock and peered down from its lofty summit. Now Ball's Pyramid is protected as part of a World Heritage Site – a fitting fate for this lordly rock-stack.

New Zealand and the Pacific

Rotorua

A LAND OF STEAM, FIRE AND DEVASTATING VOLCANIC ERUPTIONS HAS A STRIKING BEAUTY OF ITS OWN

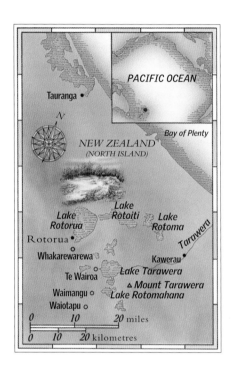

later, loved the mountain-girt chain of lakes centred on Lake Rotorua itself. The waters were full of succulent fish, wildfowl of various kinds were plentiful and the ground fertile and permanently warm. Most wonderful of all were the springs that provided water, not only hot enough for bathing, but for cooking, too. About them were geysers that periodically sent spouts of boiling water soaring high into the air.

The modern tourist resort of Rotorua, built by the lake shore, also depends upon these wonders, but suffers the attendant disadvantage of standing in the midst of the highly unstable Taupo Volcanic Zone which runs across much of North Island. Often, underfoot, the ground rumbles and steams threateningly, though the threats are seldom carried out. Instead, just beyond the resort's centre, at

To newcomers, the whiff of rotten eggs is at once pervasive and all-embracing. It emerges in wisps of steam from storm drains, cracks in the road, unusually deep, muddy hazards in the golf course, and even from flower beds in the garden. Rotoruans, tired of explaining that the reek is that of hydrogen sulphide, the very breath of volcanic activity, simply say that after a couple of days, you won't notice it. And you don't.

There are, in any case, many compensations. Since the Maori colonised what is now New Zealand in the 14th century, the Rotorua area has been the country of the great Arawa group of tribes. They, like the Europeans

FORCE OF NATURE *Colossal craters on Mount Tarawera recall the eruption that tore the area asunder in 1886.*

Whakarewarewa, there are such crowd pullers as Geyser Flat with its seven active geysers.

When underground water is heated by the underlying molten rock to pressurised steam, the geysers throw up columns of boiling water. Most spectacular is the Prince of Wales Feathers, a triple geyser that soars up to nearly 40ft (12m). This generally acts as a curtain-raiser for the 100ft (30m)

Pohutu, suggesting that the two are linked underground. Nearby pools of boiling mud bubble, writhe and coalesce into ever-changing patterns.

About 15 miles (24km) to the southeast lies Waiotapu, whose Lady Knox Geyser has been encouraged to rise to great heights by the insertion of an iron pipe. A dose of soap flakes, administered daily, triggers a fountain of suds that shoots up to treetop level.

Much less cheerful is Waimangu Valley, a silent, brooding desert of raw craters and boiling pools. Beyond it lie Lake Tarawera and Lake Rotomahana, above which once hung the renowned Pink and White Terraces, a delightful confection in silica exactly like water-filled tiers on a gigantic wedding cake. They vanished in the early morning of June 10, 1886, when nearby Mount Tarawera suddenly exploded with a roar that was heard over 100 miles (160km) away, and Lake Rotomahana dissolved into a towering pillar of mud and steam. There was no warning of the eruption – apart, it is said, from the appearance of a ghostly Maori war canoe that loomed upon the misty

A DAILY DOSE OF SOAP FLAKES TRIGGERS A FOUNTAIN OF SUDS

waters of Lake Tarawera a week or so earlier. The mighty explosion not only obliterated the terraces, but also buried three villages, killing 155 people. Evidence of the disaster is only too plentiful. A cratered rent, like a giant's footprints left in deep snow, stretches for about 12 miles (20km) across Mount Tarawera, and the cliffs above the enlarged Lake Rotomahana steam perpetually. One of the villages, Te Wairoa, has been excavated and attracts visitors like a mini Pompeii.

FREE FUEL SUPPLY *In a 19th-century photograph, Maori women cook their food in a hot spring near Rotorua.*

Milford Sound/ Piopiotahi

TOWERING MOUNTAINS
AND TUMBLING
WATERFALLS ENHANCE
THE GRANDEUR OF THE
MOST FAMOUS FJORD
IN NEW ZEALAND

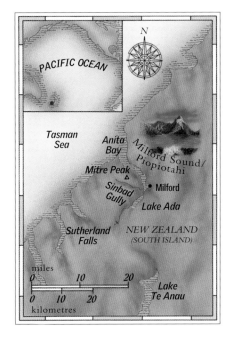

RUGGED ALLURE *The narrow entrance into Milford Sound, which Captain Cook passed by, conceals fjord and mountain scenery of unsurpassed splendour.*

Dawn on a still day is the best time to appreciate Milford Sound (also known as Piopiotahi). Mist tips the mountain peaks that rise steeply from the water's edge and are mirrored in the motionless blue of the sea. Captain James Cook, the first European to discover New Zealand's fjordland in the 1770s, missed the concealed entrance to Milford Sound altogether, so was denied a sight of its dazzling scenic splendour.

A finger of sea stretching 9 miles (15km) inland, the sound was given its European name by John Grono, the Welsh captain of a sealing vessel, in the 1820s. He called it after his home town of Milford Haven in South Wales. But to the Maori people who came to collect greenstone from the beach at Anita Bay, near the mouth of the sound,

it was known as *Piopio-tahi*, which means 'lone thrush'. Both names are now used for the area.

The thrush was said to be the companion of a legendary Maori folk hero, Maui, who sought immortality for the human race from the Goddess of Death by making love to her while she slept. But next morning she was awakened by the thrush's song, and in her fury crushed Maui to death between her thighs. The brokenhearted bird flew to Milford Sound to live in solitude and repentance.

Glaciers gouged out the hanging valleys and deep, steep-walled narrow troughs of Milford Sound and its fellow fjords on South Island's south-west coast

around a million years ago. The Tasman Sea took over as the ice melted some 10,000 years ago. Maori legend, however, has a more poetic tale. It tells how South Island was the hull of a partly sunken canoe that turned to stone, and was shaped into habitable land with an axe by the Sea God. He began his work in fjordland, and the jagged coast and islands at the extreme south around Dusky Sound are attributed to his initial inexperience. He improved as he worked northwards, and Milford Sound, the most northerly of the fjords, was his finest creation.

The Goddess of Death also took a hand, however. She was so alarmed by the attractions of the area that,

GREENSTONE TEARS

Milford greenstone is soft compared with the tough variety of greenstone – nephrite, or jade – that the Maori called *pounamu* and used for making adzes and weapons. The semi-translucent Milford stone is often flecked with black marks resembling water drops. The Maori called it *tangiwai* (meaning 'weeping tears'), and used it to fashion ornaments such as tikis – figurines that represent ancestors and are worn as talismans.

According to Maori folklore, the greenstone flecks may be the tears of the thrush that inadvertently betrayed their legendary folk hero, Maui.

TIKI *Milford Sound greenstone (above) was used for this Maori tiki (left).*

to discourage human visitors, she released insect pests – small black sand-flies that inflict itching bites. The place of release is said to be Sandfly Point in Milford Sound, where the insects are most troublesome.

Mitre Peak, 5550ft (1691m), which lies halfway along the southern shore of the sound, is one of the highest mountains to rise straight from the sea. It was named by Captain J.L. Stokes, commander of the British Navy survey ship *Acheron* in 1851, who thought the peak looked like a bishop's mitre. Captain Stokes was entranced by the towering cliffs of the sound which, he wrote, 'dwindled the *Acheron*'s masts

RAINFOREST CLINGS TO THE LOWER SLOPES OF THE MOUNTAINS ALONG THE SOUND

to nothing'. As with many of Milford Sound's mountains, verdant rainforest clings to Mitre Peak's lower slopes, encouraged by the high rainfall of one of the wettest parts of New Zealand.

Fierce, frequent winds and heavy rain make the sound a wonderland of fleeting waterfalls, some wind-blasted with such force that they soar skywards.

There are many impressive full-time waterfalls, too, such as Stirling Falls, which sluice 480ft (146m) straight into the sea from between two curiously shaped rocks known as the Lion and the Elephant. Bowen Falls, around 50ft (15m) higher, make a two-tier drop to

the sea, bouncing off the rocks as they go. But these waterfalls are just trickles compared with the magnificent Sutherland Falls, which cascade in three huge leaps down the mountainside from Lake Quill into the Arthur River, at the head of the sound. These falls are, at 1904ft (580m), the tenth highest in the world. Donald Sutherland discovered the falls while gold prospecting when he first visited the area in the 1860s.

'If I ever come to anchor, it will be here,' he vowed. He fulfilled that vow in 1877, and remained at Milford Sound until his death at 80 in 1919. Known as the Hermit of the Sound, Scots-born Sutherland built himself a cottage beside Freshwater Basin and explored alone for two years before being joined by a friend, John Mackay.

Together they came across the what was to be named the Sutherland Falls in November 1880, while exploring off-shoots from the Arthur River valley.

Until a track was cut by Sutherland in 1888, commissioned by the provincial government, the falls were inaccessible to all but the most determined visitors. Will Quill, one of the young surveyors with the job of mapping the track area, climbed to the top of the falls and came upon the lake that now bears his name.

Quill told colleagues: 'The outlet is a deep chasm about a hundred yards in length. The water rushes through this chasm with great force and swiftness, making a terrible noise.'

Quill died a year later in a fall from the Gertrude Saddle, not far away. The track cut by Sutherland became part of the Milford Track, a rugged, three-day walking route that stretches 30 miles (50km) north from Lake Te Anau to the head of Milford Sound.

Donald Sutherland married a fellow Scot, widow Elizabeth Samuel, in 1890. After an adventurous life – as

AWESOME DROP *The Sutherland Falls plunge nearly 2000ft (600m) down from Lake Quill in three long leaps – or just one huge leap after heavy rain.*

a stowaway at 12, a Red Shirt in the army of Garibaldi (the Italian guerrilla general) at 17, and as sailor, sealer, herring fisherman and gold prospector – he became a hotelier upon his marriage. As tourists flocked to the falls, the couple set up the John O'Groats Hotel at Milford which stands at the head of the sound.

Visitors today can appreciate the magnificence of the Sutherland Falls from the air, or cruise in comfort along Milford Sound. Or they can approach from the south, not only along the Milford Track for walkers but also along

PIONEER COUNTRY *Storm clouds and snow (above) cast an eerie enchantment over Milford Sound. The first settlers there were Donald Sutherland (left, centre) and his wife Elizabeth (right).*

the motor road through unsurpassed scenery between Te Anau and Milford.

One of the world's rarest birds, a flightless rail known as the takahe, lives in the Fjordland mountains. Thought to have been extinct for 50 years, the 24in (610mm) tall bird was rediscovered in the area in 1948.

RARE PARROT

Sinbad Gully at the southern foot of Mitre Peak, where Sutherland once went in search of gold (without success), is one of the last-known habitats of the rare kakapo – a large, flightless nocturnal parrot that is in danger of becoming extinct. Once the yellowish-green kakapos were numerous, and the booming calls of the male birds kept explorers awake at night. However, stoats and ship rats, introduced in the late 19th century, devastated the population.

Seldom seen by visitors are the night-foraging, flightless kiwis that are common in the region. But their plaintive cries, shortly after dusk and just before dawn, are part of the haunting attractions of Milford Sound.

Mt Taranaki or Mt Egmont

ON A JUTTING HEADLAND, A VOLCANIC MOUNTAIN STANDS LIKE A LONE GIANT ABOVE THE TASMAN SEA

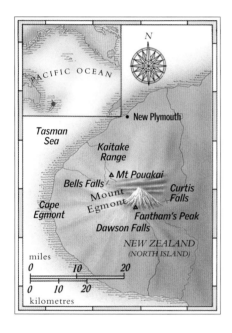

REACHING FOR THE SKY *Mount Taranaki or Mount Egmont's snowy peak soars above the clouds, but on its lower slopes the trees are constantly competing for light.*

Rising like an island from a sea of pastureland, Mount Taranaki or Mount Egmont often seems like a mirage – sometimes there, sometimes not. Here on the south-west coast of New Zealand's North Island, mist and clouds often hide the mountain completely.

But in clear weather, the mountain's dignified peak pierces the skyline, and its great bulk is visible from afar. From the snowscapes of its 8183ft (2494m) summit to the rainforest of its lower slopes, the mountain offers dazzling scenery and breathtaking views.

The Maori say that a lover's tiff brought Mount Taranaki or Mount Egmont to this spot on Cape Egmont. Once Taranaki lived in the centre of North Island, but fought with another male mountain, Tongariro, over a female

mountain, Pihanga. Taranaki was vanquished. He stamped off to the south-west, gouging out the gorge of the Whanganui River on his way.

Jagged scars on the mountain's upper flanks tell another story – they were made by lava, for this mountain is a volcano. It exploded into existence about 70,000 years ago, after the Pouakai and Kaitake volcanoes to the north-west had died down. Ever since, Mount Taranaki or Mount Egmont has periodically boiled over, sending stony

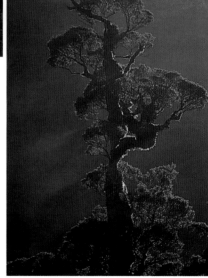

GIANT STRUGGLE *A rimu pine often has a vine-like rata growing up it. In time the rata may shade out the rimu.*

When you enter the maze of vegetation covering the lower slopes up to about 3000ft (900m) you are lost in a rainforest where rimu trees nearly 30 times a man's height reach for the sunlight. Rata trees, which also vie for the light, start life on rimu branches, clinging like vines. They do not feed on rimu sap, but send their roots down to the ground for sustenance. In time the rata may rob the rimu of light. But rimu and rata are both gradually disappearing and kamahi trees are spreading.

Shorter, tougher trees take over higher up the mountain - some of the kaikawaka (mountain cedars) are 400-year-old survivors of the 1665 eruption. Above about 3500ft (1070m) there is dense, head-high leatherwood scrub. Beyond, alpine flowers light up the crags and screes. Finally at the summit, there is nothing but mosses and lichens.

LAST STRONGHOLD

For centuries only Maori set foot on the mountain. Its river valleys gave them red ochre to mix with shark oil for body paint. Its forests hid them from their enemies. Its caves were tombs for dead chiefs. When the Dutch navigator Abel Tasman sailed by in 1642, it must have been a cloudy day, for he made no mention of the mountain. Not until the evening of January 10, 1770, was Mount Taranaki or Mount Egmont revealed to European eyes – those of the British explorer Captain James Cook, who named it Mount Egmont after a former First Lord of the Admiralty.

In 1839 Maori guides led two men – Dr Ernst Dieffenbach, a German naturalist, and James Heberley, an English whaler – on the first European expedition to the summit. They were following in the footsteps of Tahurangi, a Maori chief said to have climbed to the top centuries earlier. The wispy cloud often seen swirling round the summit is said to be smoke from his fire. Because of the belief that spirits and mythical reptiles stalked these lofty heights, the Maori guides would not venture beyond the snow line. The two Europeans scrambled alone to the top.

FROM SNOWSCAPES TO FOREST, THE MOUNTAIN SCENERY DAZZLES THE EYE

Today, about 150 years later, Mount Taranaki or Mount Egmont is the country's most-climbed peak. At least 200,000 people visit it every year, many taking the well trodden path to the top. All land within a radius of just under 6 miles (10km) from the summit has been protected since 1881. The boundary is easy to see – trees inside and fields outside.

Mount Taranaki or Mount Egmont is the last stronghold of the forests that once covered this region. Like its greenery, the mountain remains untamed. Its sudden changes of mood can catch visitors unawares – when the wind whips up from nowhere or mist drops without warning. And the volcano is dormant, not extinct. At any moment Taranaki could wake up.

FOREST ORCHID

Luxuriant ferns and creepers flourish in the forests of Mount Egmont, and often the trees are hung with long garlands of pale green moss.

Sometimes among the branches of trees such as kamahi and rimu, the delicate pink-tinged petals of the tiny, sweet-smelling bamboo orchid (below) may be seen peeping out. This orchid is found on the underside of tree branches, and is an epiphyte - it uses tree branches for support, but does not feed on their sap. Instead, its roots take their food from decaying matter and moisture on the surface of a branch.

mud-flows, known as lahars, streaming down its sides. The most ferocious eruption of recent times occurred in 1500, when enough rocks hurtled down to flatten a forest on the slopes. The last big flare-up was in 1665, and there was a lesser eruption in 1775.

But a volcano's violence can nurture as well as destroy. Farmers working in its shadow can thank the volcanic ash for the fertile soil that, along with high rainfall, gives Mount Taranaki or Mount Egmont's slopes a profuse plant and insect life. Some species are unknown elsewhere, for in its isolation distinct varieties have developed here including two kinds of mountain daisy, a unique fern and two rare moths.

Tongariro's Volcanoes

AT THE HEART OF NORTH ISLAND ARE THREE ACTIVE VOLCANOES, ONE OF WHICH GIVES FREQUENT AND IMPRESSIVE DISPLAYS

A giant white plume of steam and gas rises almost continuously from the crater of Mount Ngauruhoe, a 7516ft (2291m) volcano in the heart of New Zealand's North Island. It is one of a trio of active volcanoes. To the north is Mount Tongariro, a complex mass of truncated peaks, cones and craters, and to the south stands Mount Ruapehu, at 9176ft (2797m) the highest of North Island's peaks. The three volcanoes form the nucleus of the Tongariro National Park.

Mount Ngauruhoe – pronounced 'Narahoce' – is the most spectacular of the three. It is the classic volcano, a steep-sided cone topped by a crater 1300ft (400m) across, and has

HOT AND COLD *The snow-bound crater of Mount Ruapehu, North Island's highest peak, holds a sulphurous lake that is hot, despite its icy surround.*

been continually active at least since Europeans first settled in New Zealand in the late 1830s. Every few years it stirs into more dramatic action, and spouts ash which then rains down over the surrounding countryside.

Less frequently, Mount Ngauruhoe explodes with colourful violence, sending lava flowing down the mountain and reshaping its profile. In 1954 red-hot lava spouted into the air and, a witness reported, made 'continual grating and clanking noises' as it moved.

Eruptions also bring changes to the crater itself, and secondary cones form and reform within the main crater.

Snow covers the top of Ngauruhoe's cone in winter. Ruapehu, however, is snow-capped all year and is a magnet for skiers who combine the excitement of the sport with the risks of skiing on an active volcano. The dangers are real. Ruapehu's crater lake breached its rim in 1953, cascaded down the mountainside carrying boulders and ice, and swept away a railway bridge, causing a train crash that killed 151 people. A similar flow in 1969 crossed a skiing area – but at night.

On the flank of the many-cratered Mount Tongariro is a bizarre landscape

known as Ketetahi Springs. Here geysers throw fountains of boiling water into the air, pools of boiling mud bubble and plop like a giant witches' cauldron, blow-holes thunder

SPRING FLOWERS *Giant mountain buttercups grow on the volcanoes' higher slopes, and produce abundant pure white flowers in spring and early summer.*

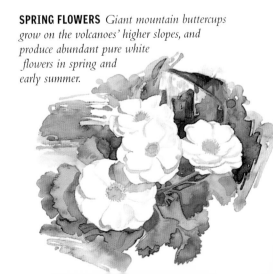

deafeningly and the heavy, pungent smell of sulphur hangs in the air.

As volcanoes go, Ngauruhoe is young. It is thought that volcanic activity began in the area about 2 million years ago, but Ngauruhoe, actually an offshoot of nearby Tongariro, was formed a mere 2500 years ago.

In Maori legend, volcanic activity was brought to North Island by a *tohunga* – a person with special powers. The tohunga Ngatoro-i-rangi is said to have travelled southwards from his warm Polynesian home, noticed the snow covered peak in the distance and set out to climb it. He took with him his female slave Auruhoe and told the rest of his party to fast while he was away. Ngatoro's companions, however, disobeyed him and broke the fast, and the gods, in their anger, sent blizzards to the mountain. Ngatoro prayed to his gods, and they replied with fire which revived Ngatoro. But it came too late to save Auruhoe, and Ngatoro hurled her frozen body into the crater at the peak which now takes her name.

The three volcanoes were sacred to the Maori. They buried their chiefs in craves on the mountainsides, and tried to deter Europeans from climbing them. The English botanist J.C. Bidwill reached Ngauruhoe's summit in 1839, and tried to explain to an angry local chief afterwards that he had done no harm because although the mountain was sacred to Maoris, the taboo did not apply to white men.

'A THICK COLUMN OF SMOKE SPREAD OUT LIKE A MUSHROOM'
J.C. Bidwill

Ngauruhoe came to life during Bidwill's ascent. He heard a noise 'not unlike that of a safety-valve of a steam-engine' that lasted about half an hour, and saw 'a thick column of black smoke [that] rose up for some distance, and then spread out like a mushroom'. When he reached the crater the volcano emitted a great roar, and Bidwill beat a hasty retreat, as he 'did not wish to see an eruption near enough to be either boiled or steamed to death'.

In 1887 the Maori chief Te Heuheu Tukino IV gave Ngauruhoe, Tongariro and Ruapehu to the government as a gift to all New Zealand's people, because it was feared that the sacred mountains would be taken over by European settlers.

The volcanoes rise up from a varied landscape. In places it is barren and lunar, yet in the wetter, lower areas there are forests with tall trees, orchids and ferns. Heather and tussock shrub-lands grow higher up, and higher still mountain buttercups and everlasting daisies scatter the upper slopes of the three spectacular volcanoes.

ROUGH AND SMOOTH *Winter snow streaks Ngauruhoe's smooth cone, and in the distance, Mount Ruapehu's irregular summit rises above the clouds.*

Haleakala Crater

MASSIVE AND MAJESTIC, THE WORLD'S LARGEST DORMANT VOLCANO TOWERS ABOVE THE HAWAIIAN ISLAND OF MAUI

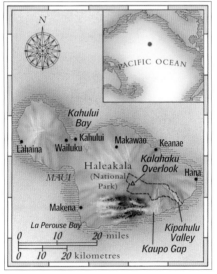

So immense is the Haleakala Crater on the Hawaiian island of Maui that the American writer Mark Twain wrote: 'If it had a level bottom it would make a fine site for a city like London.' The crater of Vesuvius, he said, was a 'modest pit' by comparison.

Haleakala's vast bowl is 21 miles (34km) round and more than ½ mile (800m) deep – large enough, in fact, to accommodate the New York island of Manhattan. Within lies a stark landscape of tumbled rocks, multicoloured cinder cones and bizarre lava formations resembling grotesque statues. But on a mountain 10,023ft (3055m) high, the crater is often cloaked in cloud. Mark Twain, after watching from the rim as

the sun rose over the cloud-filled crater, wrote: 'I felt like the Last Man ... left pinnacled in mid-heaven, a forgotten relic of a vanished world.' It was, he said, the most sublime spectacle that he had ever witnessed. Today, visitors can join organised trips to view the Haleakala sunrise, when the pink and purple shadows and filmy clouds are slowly suffused with bars of burning yellow and gold.

The name Haleakala means 'House of the Sun'. According to Hawaiian legend, the demi-god Maui crept to the

HOUSE OF THE SUN *Strong sunlight highlights the multihued cinder cones within Haleakala's massive crater.*

summit before sunrise and roped the rays of the sun one by one as they appeared over the rim. He made the sun promise to cross the sky more slowly so that there was more daylight for crops to grow and fishermen to fish.

In 1790, according to local stories, Haleakala spat a spurt of lava from a side vent down to La Perouse Bay. This was its last eruption, although scientists think it could erupt again.

CENTURIES OF WEATHERING

The volcano's huge, barren crater is not entirely the result of volcanic action. It has been carved out over thousands of years by erosion – wind, rain and down-cutting streams such as Kaupo and Keanae have all played a part.

But the multicoloured cinder cones, such as Pu'u o Maui (Hill of Maui), almost 1000ft (300m) high, result from volcanic action 800–1000

MAGIC MOMENT *(overleaf) Sunset floods the silent crater, bringing a scene of fiery desolation as the cones flush crimson before darkness envelops them.*

They are fragments of molten lava that cooled before striking the ground.

There is some greenery amid the ash and cinders within the crater – bracken fields carpet parts of the southern slopes. But the most remarkable plants are the gleaming grey silverswords. Their succulent leaves are covered with a mat of fibreglass-like hairs that act as mirrors to reflect the scorching sun, and they grow in a spiky rosette that protects the plant's roots from the sun by day and from freezing cold by night.

SHORT-LIVED SPLENDOUR

When the silversword flowers, only once in 10–15 years, its magnificent column of maroon florets grows to the height of a man. After flowering and fruiting it dies, leaving a sun-bleached skeleton. Another rarity, the ground-nesting Hawaiian wild goose, or nene (pronounced nay-nay), may be seen in the crater. Introduced animals such as rats and mongooses destroyed the original Maui nene population, but the bird was reintroduced in the 1960s.

Greenery abounds on the crater's outer slopes, below the alpine bogs of the rim. In the lovely Kipahulu Valley stretching down the eastern slopes, rainforest and bamboo thickets are broken by the Ohe'o Stream – a series of sparkling pools linked by short waterfalls that cascade towards the sea. Volcano and valley form a national park. As with the crater, the valley is sometimes shrouded in swirling mist.

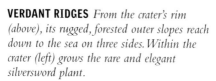

VERDANT RIDGES *From the crater's rim (above), its rugged, forested outer slopes reach down to the sea on three sides. Within the crater (left) grows the rare and elegant silversword plant.*

years ago, long after Haleakala had pushed its peak high above the sea. Sulphur and iron spewed out with the burning lava account for their predominant yellow and red streaks. The cones include Bottomless Pit and Pele's Paint Pot, named after the goddess Pele – said to have created the volcanoes. Hawaiians once threw umbilical cords into the 70ft (20m) deep core of Bottomless Pit, so that the newborn babies would grow up to be worthy adults. Strewn across the crater floor are volcanic 'bombs', which range from fist-sized to car-sized.

Mount Waialeale

THIS IS THE WETTEST PLACE IN THE WORLD – THE JUNGLE-COVERED SLOPES OF AN EXTINCT HAWAIIAN VOLCANO

As the shipwrecked but glamorous Jessica Lange approaches a towering, jungly island in the 1976 remake of *King Kong*, she murmurs silkily, 'I feel this is going to be the biggest thing in my life'. A pedantic viewer might add:

'And the wettest.' The setting for her encounter with the giant ape was Kauai, a Hawaiian island whose central mountain is the rainiest place in the world.

The island is certainly dramatic enough to be the home of Hollywood's most famous beast. An extinct volcano called Mount Waialeale – pronounced 'why-alley-alley' – rises from the ocean, its vast crater almost permanently covered in clouds. Knife-edge ridges separate deep ravines carved by millennia of rain, and luxuriant greenery tumbles down to golden beaches. Not surprisingly, Kauai is a popular location for film-makers:

EARTH'S WETTEST PLACE *Ribbons of water cascade down from Mount Waialeale's rain-battered summit.*

part of *South Pacific* was shot here, as were the opening sequences of *Raiders of the Lost Ark*.

Waialeale is one of a string of volcanoes that rise from the ocean floor, 18,000ft (5500m) below. They were

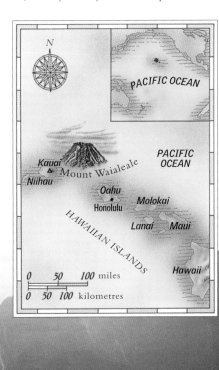

formed one by one as lava rose to the ocean floor from a 'hot spot' deep within the Earth. The ocean floor here is constantly moving north-westwards at about 4in (100mm) a year as one of the Earth's plates glides over the semi-molten layer below. The hot spot, however, remains where it is.

Each volcano was gradually carried by the gliding crust away from its spring of molten rock and became extinct, allowing another to form above the hot spot. Waialeale, the volcano on Kauai, began to be formed in this way nearly 6 million years ago, and Hawaii, the newest of the islands, is still forming.

Waialeale is well-named, for it means 'over-flowing water'. The rain falling on its summit averages 486in (12,350mm) a year, almost 20 times that of London. This is the average figure – in 1948 the rainfall totalled almost a third as much again. This deluge of rain is dumped by moisture-laden winds that sweep across the Pacific Ocean from the north-east. As the air strikes Waialeale's flanks, it howls up its ravines, condenses and releases its watery burden.

One result of this vast amount of water is the mountain's hot-house vegetation. The Alakai Swamp, a peaty depression on its flanks, sustains a jungle of rare plants and birds in a misty morass of tea-coloured waters and black mud bogs. Trees that loom like ghosts through Alakai's mists include the

BEAKS MADE FOR A PURPOSE

Amakihi

Iiwi

Apapane

About 5 million years ago, ancestors of the Hawaiian honeycreeper flew 2000 miles (3200km) across the Pacific Ocean from North America and landed on Kauai and the other Hawaiian Islands. Groups of birds, however, were isolated from each other – on islands, on coral atolls and in remote valleys. They fed on locally abundant food, and those whose beaks were best suited to the food survived and bred.

In a short time – in evolutionary terms – different species of honeycreeper with varying beak shapes evolved. A long and slender, highly curved beak, such as the iiwi's, can probe into tubular flowers for nectar. A short stout beak is ideal for cracking nuts and seeds; a powerful one can chisel into bark and extract larvae.

Most of the 15 species known to be surviving are now rare, and only the predominantly insect-and-nectar eating apapane and amakihi are widely found.

lapalapa, whose leaves flutter in the slightest breeze, and the ohia, which bears bright red blooms. All trees are upholstered in sodden layers of moss, which turns finger-thin branches into green 'sponges' as thick as an arm.

Waialeale has few large animals. The only land mammal to arrive on the island with no human help was the bat; all others have been introduced by the succession of peoples who have come to live in this subtropical paradise. Polynesians arrived here in about AD 750, after a journey across 2400 miles (4000km) of ocean in double-hulled canoes. In the 19th century, Japanese, Americans, Filipinos, Chinese and Europeans from many countries came to Kauai, many of them drawn by the island's sugar plantations.

The Polynesians brought pigs to the island, and today intrepid biologists forcing their way through waist-deep mud and down precipitous ravines encounter occasional wild pigs. Goats, introduced by the British navigator Captain Cook, who visited the island in 1778, also roam the mountain slopes. Their hooves get little support in the mud and soggy peat, and have become splayed to the size of saucers.

Throughout the Hawaiian Islands, many birds have become extinct for reasons that include the destruction of their forest homes and competition from birds introduced to the islands. On Kauai, however, birds have fared better than on other islands, and one particular reason may be that the mongoose was not introduced there. During the 19th century, the Hawaiian Islands became an evermore important source of sugar cane. The plants were attacked by rats, and in 1883 mongooses were brought in to control the pests. The mongooses not only attacked rats, but also ate the eggs and chicks of ground-nesting birds.

Some birds are found only on Kauai. The anianiau, a 4in (100mm) long honeycreeper, lives only in the island's uplands, in ohia trees. Other birds are restricted to the Alakai Swamp – the Kauai oo, with its eerie whistling call, lives there and nowhere else.

A MISTY MORASS OF TEA-COLOURED WATERS AND BLACK MUD BOGS

GOING FISHING

A very rare sea bird of Kauai's mountains is the pigeon-sized ao. It nests in burrows like a puffin, and consequently fell easy victim to the mongoose on other islands. These ungainly little birds make loud braying calls as they return from fishing trips, crash land through dense vegetation, and claw their way through the undergrowth to their burrows. To take off, the birds climb a plant and then rely on the fierce updraughts of air to give them the lift that they need.

Rain, mud and vertiginous slopes discourage visitors, and this has preserved Waialeale from the trappings of tourism that encroach on this and other Hawaiian islands. Provided that the mongooses are kept at bay, Waialeale should remain the Garden of Eden so dear to film-makers.

FOREST FALLS *Mount Waialeale's huge quantity of rain results in waterfalls (left) that cut deep into its flanks, and dense forest where plants such as the intensely coloured ieie (above) grow.*

Bora-Bora

THIS IDYLLIC TROPICAL ISLAND HAS DAZZLING BEACHES, SWAYING PALMS AND AN ENCHANTING BLUE LAGOON

Pearl of the Pacific, the nearest thing to paradise on Earth, the island of dreams – all these names have been given to Bora-Bora. For American author James Michener it was the most beautiful island in the world and the model for his magic island of Bali-h'ai, mentioned in *Tales of the*

South Pacific and featured in song in the Rodgers and Hammerstein musical, *South Pacific*, in 1949.

Bora–Bora is an island of dream-like tranquillity in the heart of French Polynesia, one of the loveliest of the Leeward group of Society Islands. White, glistening beaches, backed by palm groves, viridian hills and profusions of bright hibiscus, stretch beside a crystal clear lagoon. The tropical temperatures, ranging from 24°C (75°F) to 28°C (82°F), are moderated by fresh breezes from easterly trade winds.

There is only one navigable inlet through the ring of coral islands – known locally as *motus* – so the lagoon is a natural harbour. As well as the main island, which is about twice the size of Gibraltar, there are two smaller islands, Toopua and Toopuaiti – all remnants of

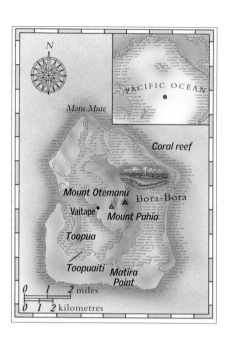

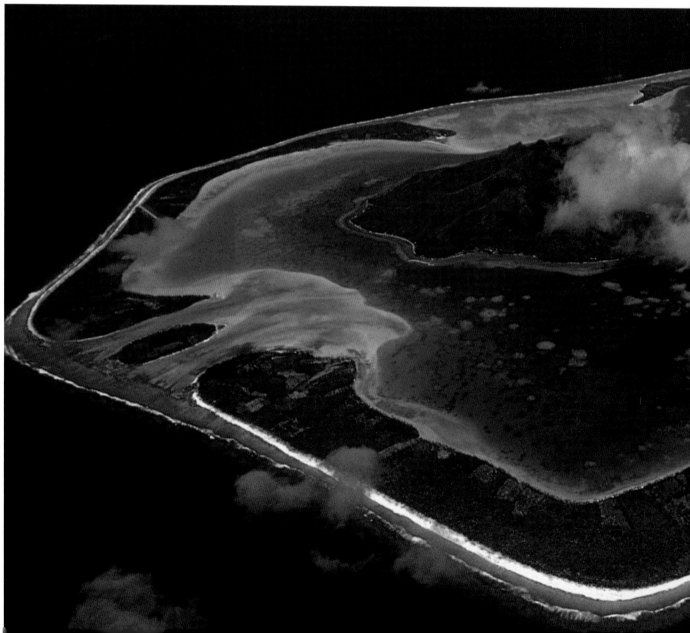

an eroded volcanic crater. Two sharp, craggy twin peaks dominate Bora-Bora – Mount Pahia, 2165ft (660m) and Mount Otemanu, 2379ft (725m). Polynesians colonised the island about 1100 years ago, and there are several ancient temples. One of them has stone slabs carved with sacred turtles.

Jacob Roggeveen, the Dutch explorer, visited Bora-Bora in 1722, the first European to do so. Captain James Cook, the British explorer and navigator, sighted the island in 1769, and dropped anchor at the harbour entrance in December 1777. Cook

PACIFIC JEWEL *Bora-Bora's sparkling lagoon lies serene within an enclosing necklet of coral reefs, which keep at bay the pounding breakers of the Pacific.*

recorded the island name as Bola Bola (meaning First Born), but Pora Pora might have been more accurate, as the native Polynesians were unable to pronounce either 'b' or 'l'.

The first European settler was James Connor, a survivor from the wreck of a British whaler, the *Matilda*, in 1792. He married a Polynesian woman and settled on the southernmost tip, calling it Matilda Point; today it is known as Matira Point. The island became part of French Polynesia in 1895.

MODERN TIMES

Bora-Bora plunged headlong into Western 20th-century ways in 1928–9, with its first American 'invasion' – a film crew making a silent movie called *Tabu*, the tragic love story of a Tahitian pearl fisherman who transgressed the taboo

laws. This was a prelude to the coming of the Americans during World War II, when for four years the island was an air and naval base for 6000 men – *Tales of the South Pacific* is about the experiences of American servicemen in the 1940s.

Italian film-makers arrived on Bora-Bora in 1979 to shoot Dino De Laurentis's film *Hurricane*, a remake of a 1930s melodrama.

The wartime airstrip built at Motu Mute is part of the modern airport, from where today's tourists are transported by boat across the lagoon to Vaitape, the main village.

After a day of sun, sand and sparkling water, Bora-Bora's sunset is fiery and shortlived. It leaves the island to an inky darkness that amplifies the sighing of the wind in the palm trees and the pounding of the waves on the reef.

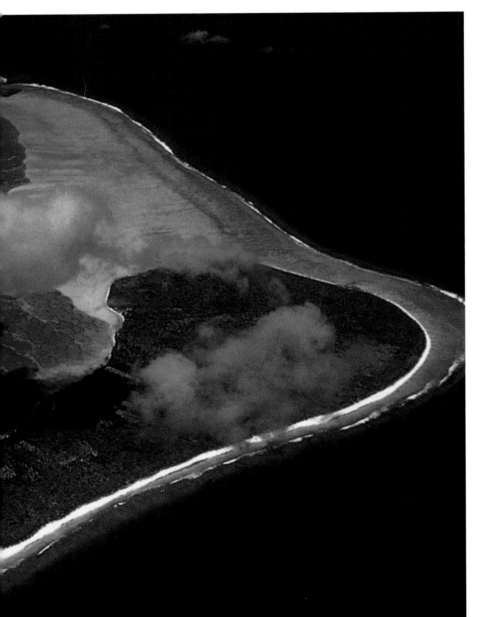

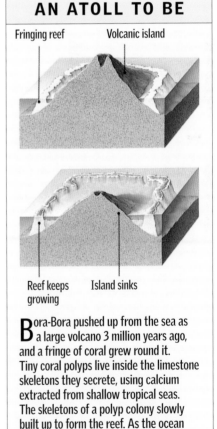

AN ATOLL TO BE

Fringing reef   Volcanic island

Reef keeps growing   Island sinks

Bora-Bora pushed up from the sea as a large volcano 3 million years ago, and a fringe of coral grew round it. Tiny coral polyps live inside the limestone skeletons they secrete, using calcium extracted from shallow tropical seas. The skeletons of a polyp colony slowly built up to form the reef. As the ocean crust cooled the volcano began to sink but the coral still grew upwards, leaving an island and lagoon within the encircling reef. In time the island will disappear, leaving only an atoll – a lagoon ringed by a coral reef.

North America

Ellesmere Island

A LONELY AND ICY
DESERT ISLAND AT THE
TOP OF THE WORLD
HAS NO SUNRISE FOR
NEARLY HALF THE YEAR

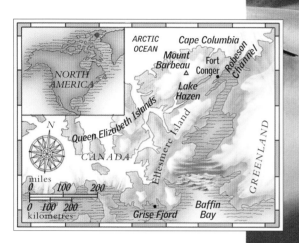

A loof from the hubbub of the world, Ellesmere Island is so remote and in such a harsh setting that it seems purified by the rigours of its climate. Even the air is so pure that the whole landscape – the vast icefields, bare mountains and mighty glaciers – stands out in crisp detail, giving the disconcerting impression of both distance and closeness at the same time.

LIGHT AND DARKNESS

In summer the sun circles permanently over the horizon and casts bewildering shadows. But for nearly five months from about early November to the end of March, there is no sunlight at all.

Ellesmere is about twice the size of Iceland. Its northernmost point, Cape Columbia, is just 470 miles (756km) short of the North Pole. Where the sun melts the snow on south-facing slopes, the mountains stand a sober grey-black against the dazzling white around them. Some are rounded in shape, smoothed by ice over thousands of years. Their shape disguises their height. Mount

Barbeau in the Grant Land Mountains in the north rises to some 8540ft (2600m), making it the highest peak in eastern North America.

The coastline is ragged with fjords, ground out by glaciers. Some, such as Archer Fjord, have deep ravines with cliffs plunging 2300ft (700m) to the sea. For much of the year the sea round the island is thick with ice, bringing a permanent chill to the air. In winter temperatures can plummet to about

JOURNEY'S END *As the weak sun breaks through the clouds, sculptured shapes at the foot of a glacier eventually break free and drift off to sea as icebergs.*

−45°C (−49°F). Even in summer – from late June to late August – the temperature is often below 7°C (45°F), but on cloudless days it can reach 21°C (70°F). In spite of its iciness, the island is not, as you might expect, deep in snow. It is in fact a desert – its precipitation (snow, rain and condensation) amounts to only 2⅜in (60mm) a year, because there is not enough warmth to bring about much surface evaporation.

Small wonder that, despite its size, Ellesmere Island is thinly populated. There is only one settlement, at Grise Fjord in the south. This is Canada's most northerly community, inhabited by 100 or so Inuits. It was founded in 1953,

WHITE SILENCE *Utterly remote, the windswept Grant Land Mountains in the north of Ellesmere Island show dark against a mantle of ice and clouds.*

mainly to underpin Canada's claim to the island. But Grise Fjord was not the first settlement on lonely Ellesmere Island.

Settlers came here 4000 years ago – the hardy descendants of the first Americans who crossed into Alaska from Siberia. Ancient remains, such as a camp site encircled by boulders, can still be seen – the landscape is little touched by time. Waves of new settlers known as the Thule people, ancestors of the Inuit,

SMALL BUT TOUGH *Peary caribou have thicker coats and shorter legs than other caribou. This reduces the loss of body heat in their icy Ellesmere homeland.*

began coming around 1250. But years of harsh winters took their toll, and until 1953 no Inuit had lived on the island for about 200 years.

Ellesmere has no trees – the nearest are about 1250 miles (2000km) south in mainland Canada. In summer, most areas are free of snow, and wild flowers such as arctic poppies flourish in sheltered spots – beside creeks, for example. The Lake Hazen area is the largest of these green oases in the vast wilderness. In summer its borders burst into life with greenery such as sedges, prostrate willows, heathers and saxifrages.

Thousands of snow-white arctic hares and herds of musk oxen graze in the summer meadows along with herds of Peary caribou. These island caribou are smaller and whiter than mainland caribou, and cannot migrate south for winter. Like the musk oxen and arctic hares, they survive as best they can by digging up and feeding on the lichens and any greenery they can find under the snow. In winter or summer, they are preyed on by arctic foxes and wolves. Many of the birds seen on the island in summer, such as the snowy owl, fly south to warmer climates in winter. Arctic terns fly half-way across the world to the Antarctic to spend the summer there. Snow buntings and rock ptarmigans survive on the island on winter vegetation as best they can.

SENSITIVE ENVIRONMENT

For the wildlife of Ellesmere Island, the balance between survival and extinction is delicate. Some 90 of the caribou were killed between 1891 and 1906 by Robert Peary's North Pole expeditions. Now named after Peary, these caribou are a threatened species, with only a few left in existence.

In recognition of its fragile nature, part of the the island was made into a national park in 1988. The park, which covers an area only slightly smaller than Switzerland, includes the 44 mile (70km) long Lake Hazen, the largest lake within the Arctic Circle. Visitors are flown in during summer to hike through the park and see its unique splendours. Whether this is likely to damage the fragile natural environment is open to question and under constant review.

FIRST AT THE NORTH POLE

Fort Conger on Ellesmere Island was the base from which Robert Peary (1856–1920), a US naval officer, led the first party to reach the North Pole in April 1909 – his fourth attempt. The fort's huts and cast-iron stoves, preserved in the dry climate, are haunting reminders of the old explorers.

Commander Peary used relays of Inuit and their dog sleds to lay out a route with supply points. With Matthew Henson, his companion, he covered the last 155 miles (250km), and the return of more than 450 miles (720km), in 16 days. Their victory was clouded by the rival claim (eventually discredited) of a naval surgeon, Dr Frederick Cook, who declared he had reached the Pole in 1908. A postcard (shown below) named both as conquerors.

PIONEERS *Matthew Henson (centre) with Inuits at the North Pole (above).*

Glacier Bay

AS ICE AGE GLACIERS IN ALASKA GRADUALLY RETREAT, THEY GIVE GROUND FOR THE RETURN OF PLANTS AND ANIMALS

BLUE GROTTO *(overleaf) Meltwater has carved this cave from the dense ice of a glacier. Soon the cave could collapse to join the debris littered on the floor.*

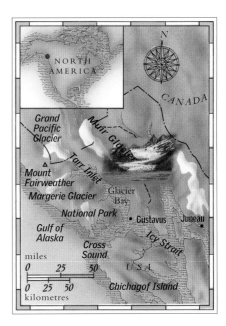

Every summer's day in Glacier Bay resounds to the crash and splash of falling masses of ice, some the size of office blocks. They are breaking off from the towering walls of ice that meet the frigid waters of the bay, which lies off Icy Strait in the Gulf of Alaska. Slowly the land is sloughing off its icy shell to reveal bare rocks, and plants and animals are reclaiming territory lost to them during the 'Little Ice Age' that began about 4000 years ago.

When the British navigator Captain George Vancouver of HMS *Discovery* visited Icy Strait in 1794, Glacier Bay did not exist. He saw only the end of a massive glacier – an ice wall over 10 miles (16km) long and 300ft (100m) high. But when John Muir, the American naturalist and writer, arrived 85 years later, he found an extensive bay. The ice had retreated inland some 48 miles (77km) towards the mountains.

Now, in what has become the Glacier Bay National Park, ice-gouged

ICE WORLD *In a glittering landscape of blue and white, Margerie Glacier winds its way down from the Fairweather Range into the Tarr Inlet in Glacier Bay. Year by year, the glacier is slowly shrinking as more snow melts in summer than falls in winter.*

fjords reach up to 65 miles (100km) inland past rich forests, until they meet bare rock or one of the 16 glaciers that grind down from the heights straddling the US–Canadian border. Lofty peaks line the horizon; the highest, Mount Fairweather, is 15,300ft (4663m). The peaks overlook vast fields of snow and ice that feed the glaciers. John Muir climbed into the cloud-covered Fairweather Range in 1879. He wrote of the beauty of the wing-shaped cloud masses gathered around the peaks, with sunshine streaming through their luminous fringes to fall on the green waters of the fjords, and of the intensely white, far-spreading fields of ice. He described the unearthly splendour of the dawn, appearing as a red light burning on the topmost peak. 'The glorious vision passed away,' wrote the entranced Muir, 'in a gradual, fading change through a thousand tones of colour to pale yellow and white.'

GREEN FJORDS AND INTENSELY WHITE, FAR-SPREADING FIELDS OF ICE

Such scenes can still be seen today as the glaciers crack and groan their way downward from the icy heights.

In summer, meltwater thunders deep within them, carving out caves and tunnels that eventually collapse with a deep rumble when the melting ice is too thin to span the voids. For the last few centuries, winter snowfall has not matched the summer melt, so the glaciers are retreating, and combining this with the effect of global warming, the speed at which the glaciers are retreating is increasing. However, the retreating ice does allow scientists to study the sequence of returning life.

At first the newly exposed rocks support only a crust of algae (minute

WILDERNESS SUNSET *As day fades, the sunset illuminates the 'chaste and spiritual beauty' of Glacier Bay described by the American naturalist John Muir.*

GIANT LEAP *Watching a humpback whale breaching – throwing its 30-ton bulk almost clear of the water – is one of the thrills of Glacier Bay. Whales breach most when seas are rough, and may be making sound signals more easily heard than their voices.*

plants) that make way for mosses and lichens. Then delicate yellow dryads form dense mats in debris from the glacier, which has traces of ancient forests that existed before the Ice Age.

Gradually a soil layer forms, enriched by nitrogen-fixing bacteria in the dryads' roots. Thickets of dwarf alder and willow appear, and are in turn overshadowed by black cottonwoods, which finally give way to the forests of spruce and hemlock that now line many of the shores. Once vegetation is established, plant-eating animals move in, followed by predators such as wolves. In summer, the giant icebergs carved from the glacier snouts provide

nurseries for harbour seals. Other summer visitors are the humpback whales, around 45ft (14m) long, that lunge and leap in the waters of the bay after wintering around Hawaii.

John Muir watched fascinated at the birth of countless icebergs, describing how they 'heave and plunge again and again before they settle in poise and sail away as blue crystal islands, free at last after being held fast as part of a slow-crawling glacier for centuries'.

ALASKAN HIGHLIGHT *In northern latitudes, the aurora borealis, or northern lights, may light up the night sky with bands or streamers of red or green light.*

Brooks Range

THE HAND OF MAN HAS PLAYED LITTLE PART IN THIS WILD MOUNTAIN RANGE IN THE FAR NORTH OF ALASKA

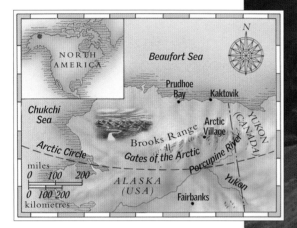

It is known as the 'Last Great Wilderness', this untamed landscape of rugged, treeless peaks, deep valleys and icy lakes and rivers. Human activity has hardly touched the central and eastern parts of Brooks Range – the tip of the Rocky Mountains that spreads across northern Alaska for 600 miles (1000km). Grizzly bears, wolverines and moose are the mountains' inhabitants, along with horned Dall sheep, arctic foxes and caribous.

Brooks Range forms a great wall across this northern tip of the United States. On its south side grow forests of spindly trees, whose trunks can take 300 years to grow 3in (75mm) wider.

BRIEFEST OF SUMMERS

To the north of the mountain wall lies the Alaskan North Slope, a vast wasteland of frozen ground. During the few months of warmth and daylight it bursts into life, with flowers blooming among lichens, sedges, mosses and stunted willows (see right).

Few people live in this barren land. In midwinter it is dark all day and the temperature, which routinely falls to a numbing −30°C (−22°F), can fall as low as −45°C (−49°F). Settlements can be very isolated. Arctic Village, on the south side of Brooks Range, is accessible only by air, and by snow-mobiles or dog-sleigh teams.

The people of this area hunt the Porcupine caribou. These arctic deer spend the winter south of Brooks Range, in valleys leading to the Porcupine River that gives them their name. Each spring the 160,000-strong herd leaves its winter grounds and migrates across Brooks Range to the coastal plains. There, the calves are born and the caribous graze on lichens and

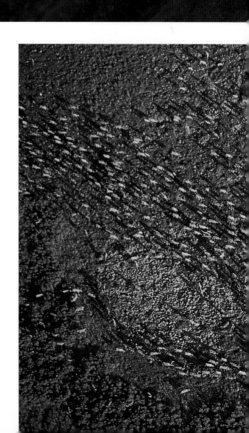

ON THE MOVE *Groups of caribou join together to migrate to the coastal plains where females give birth. Most calves are born during the same week.*

grasses that fatten them ready for the bitterly cold winter. The area has been dubbed 'America's Serengeti', for the caribous' migration recalls the great migration of wildebeests, zebras and gazelles that takes place in east Africa's Serengeti National Park.

PROTECTING THE WILDERNESS

A national park and other protected land encompass most of the central and eastern parts of Brooks Range, and also the eastern part of the North Slope. Gates of the Arctic National Park, in the heart of the mountains, takes its name from the pass between Boreal Mountain and Frigid Crags.

The area was described as 'Gates of the Arctic' by Bob Marshall, a forester and explorer. He had a fascination for places visited by no-one else and, in the 1930s, explored the valleys of Brooks Range and scaled many of its mountains. 'There is something glorious,' he said, 'in travelling beyond the ends of the Earth, in living in a different world which men have not discovered.' And so far, only a few determined and hardy visitors have discovered the unique wilderness areas of Brooks Range.

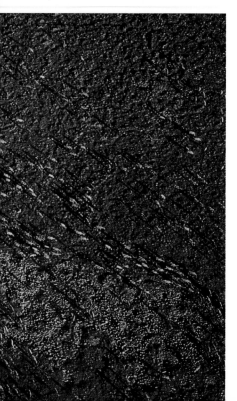

SURVIVORS IN A TOUGH WORLD

Plants that grow in the frozen land north of Brooks Range must have special qualities to survive the cold, wind and low rainfall. All plants grow close to the ground, minimising the battering effects of cold, desiccating winds – the polar willow, for example, grows flat on the ground. Heat is trapped in clumped plants – the temperature in the centre of a clump of moss campion may be 22°C (40°F) higher than the surrounding air. Moss campion's narrow leaves cut down moisture loss, and so do leaves pressed close to a stem, such as the arctic bell heather's. Only at flowering time do stems reach above the tundra carpet, and then they bend in the wind.

PINK CUSHION
Masses of flowers cover low clumps of moss campion.

Mount Katmai

ONE OF THE 20TH CENTURY'S GREATEST VOLCANIC EXPLOSIONS BEHEADED THIS MOUNTAIN IN THE VAST ALASKAN WILDERNESS

Few of the great news stories of the early 20th century enjoyed such immediate reportage as the Katmai mountain story. On the steamship *Dora*, bound for the port of Kodiak on Kodiak Island, Alaska, on June 6, 1912, the captain logged, at precisely 1pm: 'Sighted heavy column of smoke directly astern, rising from the Alaska Peninsula. I took a bearing of same, which I made out to be Mount Katmai, distance about 55 miles (88km) away.'

SMOKE, ASH AND EXPLOSIONS
Accompanied by fierce winds and lightning flashes, the smoke overtook the ship two hours later, smothering it in white ash that blotted out even the surface of the sea. Ash covered Kodiak, too, roofs collapsing under its weight.

At Cold Bay on the Alaska Peninsula, a severe earthquake was followed by a tremendous explosion that was also noted on the British Columbian border

nearly 800 miles (1300km) away. More explosions reverberated through the night and following day, culminating at 10.40pm on June 7 with a flash of yellow light from a mountain of incandescent volcanic ash that lit up the area 'like sunshine'. Next day, the familiar silhouettes of distant peaks confirmed a witness's statement: 'The top of Katmai mountain blowed off.'

Later estimates suggested that some 33 billion tons of Earth's crust had been spread as dust and ash over vast areas of

the American north-west, and also shot up into the stratosphere. There, during the next year or so, the material encircled the Northern Hemisphere, deflecting some ten per cent of the sun's energy and causing cooler summers and colder winters everywhere.

Not until 1915 was an American botanist, Dr Robert F. Griggs, able to lead an expedition to the Katmai Valley. There they found a wasteland of mud, quicksand and pumice dust, with not a tree or blade of grass left alive. The

COLLAPSED MOUNTAIN *Drained of molten rock by a nearby eruption, Mount Katmai collapsed inwards. Its summit was replaced by a vast crater, or caldera, that filled with water.*

ALASKAN GIANT *Undeterred by the area's volcanic catastrophes, a Kodiak brown bear – bigger than the average grizzly – fishes for migratory salmon.*

ground rang hollow beneath their feet and, when struck hard, it gave way to reveal steaming sulphurous fissures. Wisely, the party retreated. But they returned the following year, when they cautiously skirted new, yawning ravines to reach the top of Mount Katmai.

The summit had been replaced by a pit 2½ miles (4km) long and more than 2000ft (600m) deep. At the bottom gleamed a lake of vitriolic blue-green. Farther on, the expedition encountered a valley whose fissured floor emitted thousands of columns of steam that climbed high into the sky. The awed Griggs named it the Valley of Ten Thousand Smokes. At the upper end, about 6 miles (10km) from Mount

Katmai, he discovered a new, small, volcano; it was christened Novarupta.

This was the clue to the disaster. Katmai had not blown up at all – it was the new volcano that had exploded, draining molten rock from Katmai by way of underground fissures and so causing the unsupported summit to collapse inwards. Novarupta then buried

the bogs, snowfields and rivers of the valley under 700ft (215m) of ash; the the columns of steam from the boiling water gave rise to the 10,000 smokes.

The valley no longer smokes. It remains a pastel-hued desert, fantastically eroded by 80 years of frost, wind, and snow-melt rivers – a glimpse of the world as it was when it was young.

PRESSURE COOKING
Dr Griggs's expedition prepares breakfast over a volcanic steam fumarole. This not only fries the bacon, but also lifts up the pan.

Mackenzie Delta

NORTH OF THE ARCTIC CIRCLE, A WEB OF
WATERWAYS TWISTS BETWEEN WOODED ISLANDS
IN CANADA'S LARGEST RIVER DELTA

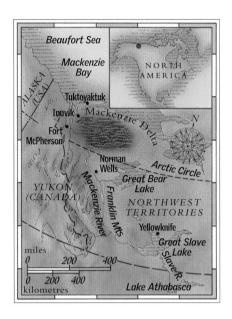

For nearly six months of the year, the Mackenzie Delta on the north-west coast of Canada is barely recognisable as a river delta. It is blanketed by an icy mantle that merges its islands and waterways with the frozen coastal plain. Biting winds scour this flat Arctic wilderness, which for several weeks in the depths of winter is cloaked in darkness, with no sunrise.

At this time, the only light comes from the eerie, ever-present moon and the spectacular northern lights, or aurora borealis – sky-filling curtains and streamers of mainly green and crimson light. The Inuit thought the northern lights were reflections from the dance fires of ghosts.

Spring arrives dramatically in the Mackenzie Delta. As the long winter draws to a close, isolated communities of delta dwellers wait eagerly for the welcome crash and splinter of melting ice. As huge ice blocks break off and hurtle seawards, buffeting the river

banks on their way, life on the delta begins anew. Within hours, the noisy thaw reveals an extensive fan-shaped network of channels and lakes separated by countless small islands.

FLAT AND LOW-LYING

The full extent of the Delta's complex tracery – which stretches north about 100 miles (160km) to the Beaufort Sea and spans 50 miles (80km) of coast – can be seen only from the air. The land is low-lying, and most of the islands barely clear the water. Here and there, as if to emphasise its flatness, the landscape is punctuated by conical hillocks known as pingos, from an Inuit word for mound. Each mound has a frozen mass of ice at its core. There are more than 1000 pingos in the Mackenzie Delta – the greatest concentration of them anywhere in the world.

In summer, the Delta is constantly being shaped and reshaped by the force of its powerful, mud-laden waters, which alternately erode and build up its banks, season after season. In the Americas, only the Amazon and the Mississippi discharge a greater flow of water than the Mackenzie, which drains three lakes – the Athabasca, the Great Bear, and the Great Slave. The main stream flows from the Great Slave Lake, which is about the size of Albania.

It is North America's deepest lake, being some 2015ft (614m) deep. Even though the Mackenzie flows for only about 1100 miles (180km) from the lake to the sea, its basin covers an area that is almost as big as France, Germany, Italy, Spain and Portugal combined, for it has several direct tributaries as well as a number of indirect ones that flow into the lakes. A Scot named Alexander Mackenzie opened up the river and its delta to fur trappers in the late 18th

THE SPRING THAW REVEALS A VAST MAZE OF CHANNELS AND ISLANDS

century. Mackenzie, who was employed by the North-West Fur Company, was chosen by them to explore the north-west in June 1789. He set out from Fort Chipewyan, on Lake Athabasca, with a party that included native Americans and Canadian voyageurs (boatmen). They travelled in birch-bark canoes.

Mackenzie hoped to discover a route leading westwards to the Pacific, and was delighted when he found a river flowing westwards from the Great Slave Lake. But as he continued navigating its churning waters, he realised that it turned northwards towards the Arctic Ocean instead of continuing to the Pacific. Now the river is named after

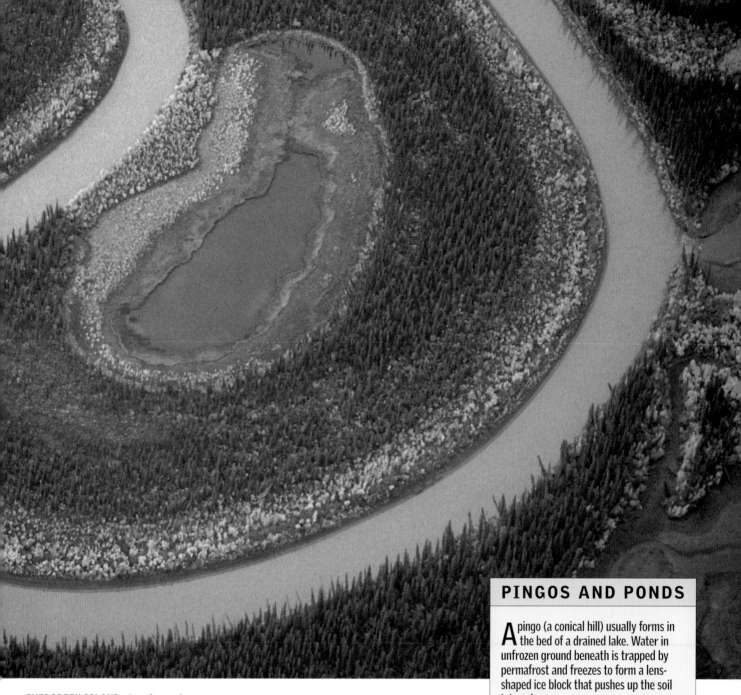

EVERGREEN ISLAND *Conifers such as spruce and pine blanket many of the Mackenzie Delta's innumerable islands.*

him, but Mackenzie himself gave it the name 'River of Disappointment'.

His party reached the sea in less than three weeks, expertly negotiating stretches of rapids such as the Rampart Rapids, which run through a gorge 7 miles (11km) long between cliffs 200ft (60m) high. By September they had returned to Fort Chipewyan, having travelled 3000 miles (4800km).

The Mackenzie Delta became the haunt – during the three short months of summer – of fur trappers hunting muskrats and beavers, of whalers after belugas (white whales) and bowhead whales, of gold seekers and, more recently, of oilmen. Mackenzie later became the first European to cross the Rocky Mountains. He wrote a book about his exploration in the north-west, and was knighted in 1802.

Today the Delta in summer is busy with boats and barges chugging downstream to deliver supplies, as well as excursion boats and canoeists and the occasional light aircraft overhead. The northernmost port of call is the coastal village of Tuktoyaktuk, once a thriving whaling centre and now a place for the transfer of cargoes such as timber and fish from ocean to river vessels.

PINGOS AND PONDS

A pingo (a conical hill) usually forms in the bed of a drained lake. Water in unfrozen ground beneath is trapped by permafrost and freezes to form a lens-shaped ice block that pushes up the soil into a dome.

A pingo may grow yearly – one of the largest recorded was more than 1300 years old and some 160ft (50m) high. But most pingos stretch, crack and collapse long before they reach such a size, leaving a high-rimmed pond filled with water in summer, as the exposed ice core melts.

WATERY WILDERNESS *In summer, there are three main navigable channels through the maze of waterways and low-lying islands that form the Mackenzie Delta. They enable supply boats to reach isolated communities cut off by ice for nearly half the year.*

Underlying the watery world of the Delta is a bed of permafrost – permanently frozen ground where only the surface layer thaws in summer. The thawed layer reaches down to about 4ft (1.2m) at its deepest. The permafrost prevents surface water from seeping into the ground, and so gives the Delta its lush, boggy summer vegetation.

Nature works overtime in the short summer, when the land is bathed in permanent daylight for several weeks. On the northernmost islands of the Delta, where the topsoil thaws least, only dwarf trees such as willow and alder thrive, along with mosses, lichens, sedges, tussock grasses and wild flowers such as fireweed. Southwards, as the soil layer deepens, the islands support spruce, pine, poplar and tamarack (a North American larch species).

TREE FELLER
A beaver uses its sharp teeth to fell a tree, which it will take to repair its dam. The dam creates the pond in which its lodge is built.

Summer also brings dense clouds of mosquitoes hanging above the water, and wildfowl such as snow geese and Canada geese come in their thousands to raise their broods before flying south for winter. Muskrats scurry among the marshes, beavers repair their lodges and dams, and caribou drift north from the evergreen forests to calve and feed on the flush of lichens and sedges. Like other creatures, the foxes and wolves are busy fattening themselves and their young for winter, on prey such as spruce grouse, lemmings and caribou.

THE GRIP OF WINTER

Winter grips fast, the ice taking hold as speedily as it thawed. River traffic must leave before ice seals the channels and locks the landing stages. Then, for months on end, the only transport will be snowmobiles and dog sleds. Human settlements and animals alike will be left in isolation until the spring thaw opens up their icy world again.

Nahanni River

DEEP IN CANADA'S NORTHWEST TERRITORIES LIES A REMOTE, LEGEND-HAUNTED LAND OF WILD AND CAPTIVATING BEAUTY

If your heart is still young enough to quicken at stories of a faraway, secret land where verdant valleys bloom amid arctic snows, and lost gold mines are guarded by wild men and spirits of the forest, then the Nahanni River may be able to offer the holiday of a lifetime. Add to this places with names like Deadmen Valley, Headless Range, Funeral Range, Valley of No Return, each with its own legend and fascinating stories, and your bags are halfway packed.

Remoteness is guaranteed to the area by the Canadian Government and UNESCO, who placed the river and its surroundings on the World Heritage list, allowing access only by boat or light aircraft. It was a wise decision, for the splendours of the river country, the magnificence of its dark canyons and towering waterfalls, owe much to its aloofness. In part, this has been assured by sheer size – the Nahanni drains a wilderness half the size of Scotland. But it is also because of the reputation it has

held since the beginning of the 20th century, when gold prospectors began to penetrate its hinterland.

In 1905, two brothers were rumoured to have struck it rich. A year later, their headless skeletons were discovered near the river. Then, in 1915, the headless corpse of another prospector, a tough Swede, was found in the woods, and the body of yet another was discovered

DOUBLE THUNDER *Far from any tourist track, two arms of the Nahanni River plunge 294ft (90m) over Virginia Falls into the turbulent waters of Hell's Gate.*

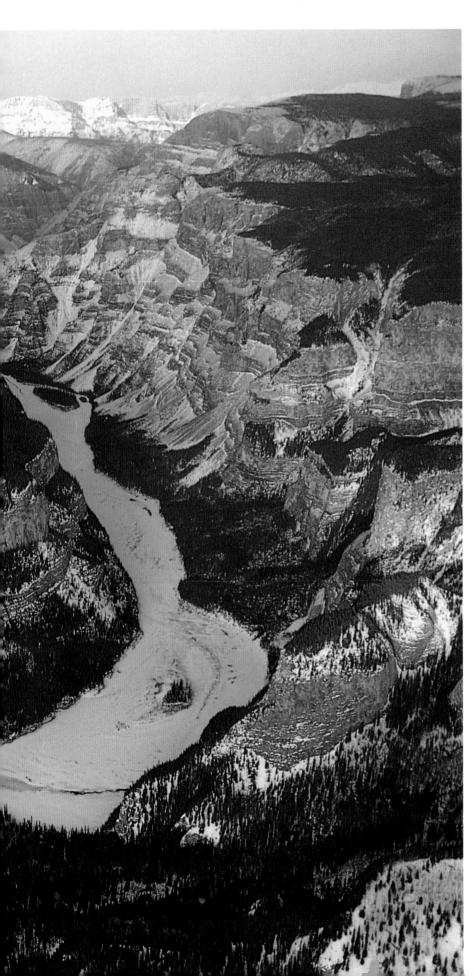

DEEP CHILL *At First Canyon, the Nahanni River has carved a steep-walled path through the wild Mackenzie Mountains. The winter freeze up starts in October and lasts until May.*

frozen to death while kneeling by the ashes of his long-dead camp fire.

The fates of still more were suggested by upturned canoes drifting in the river. Altogether, some 50 either died or disappeared – in such wild country probably by accident or starvation, but legends of evil spirits grew, along with tales of treasure guarded by half-human monsters that lived in fertile, hidden valleys where snow never fell.

DRAMATIC CANYONS

All great wildernesses have a touch of the uncanny, but nowadays on the Nahanni, this is largely forgotten in the overwhelming majesty of the place. For most visitors, the only way to see it is to take the guided motorboat trip 130 miles (210km) upriver from Nahanni Butte to Virginia Falls – fighting a 17¼ mph (28km/h) current all the way.

A DREAM COME TRUE

In 1924, a young clerk named Raymond Patterson quit his job in London's Bank of England. Three years later, having fought his way up the wild waters of Canada's Nahanni River, he found himself gazing at the thundering Virginia Falls – one of the first Europeans ever to do so.

This was the culmination of a childhood dream – to explore the north-lands of Canada, one of the last great wildernesses on Earth.

Much later, Patterson wrote a book. *Dangerous River,* which told of his experiences in this wilderness, and recounted the legends he had heard from trappers and prospectors – tales of lost Indian tribes ruled by a White Queen, and of Wild Men who cut off the heads of intruders.

But his book also extolled the beauties of the place, paving the way for the adoption of the Nahanni River country as a national park.

YEAR-ROUND SPRING *Throughout the chill sub-arctic year, the warm, mineral-laden Rabbitkettle Hotsprings bubble forth to create mounds of fragile stone called tufa. It offers a precarious foothold for mosses, butterworts (inset) and other flowers.*

At the mouth of First Canyon, the warm waters of Kraus Hotsprings have created a microclimate where small, lush meadows glow with asters, violets and golden rod – could this be the origin of the secret valleys of the old prospectors' stories?

As the boat enters First Canyon, dramatic limestone walls striped yellow, brown and orange climb to some 4000ft (1200m) on either side, their faces pocked by caves. In one of these caves, Valerie Grotto, are the bones of more than 100 Dall (or Thinhorn) sheep that at various times over the past 2000 years sought winter shelter in its depths and

starved to death. At the upstream end, the canyon meets Deadmen Valley, named after the headless skeletons discovered there in 1906.

Second Canyon, which cuts through the Headless Range, offers the best chances of seeing Dall mountain sheep perched on dizzying ledges, black bears turning over rocks at the water's edge and moose browsing in the shallows. Jagged, rocky Third Canyon, the narrowest of the three, slices through the Funeral Range. Its narrowness gives the impression of greater depth than its 3000ft (900m) or more, and makes it a suitable curtain-raiser for Hell's Gate, a double hairpin boat-killer of white water that spins into whirlpools. Round the next bend you come face to face with Virginia Falls, the truly astounding climax of the whole trip. High above, the Nahanni swirls

royally round a spruce-capped rocky tower to plunge down on each side in twin cataracts that shake the earth with their thunder. The drop from the rim is 294ft (90m) – almost twice as high as Niagara Falls.

Rabbitkettle Hotsprings lies some way upstream beyond the falls – the only way to get there is by light aircraft. One of the great sights of Canada's north-west, its wide, spreading terraces of delicately hued stone, each cover an area of 250sq ft (23m^2) or so. They may have been 10,000 years in the making, as the hot springs deposited minerals to form tufa, a type of limestone. Each terrace has a mirror-like pool of steaming water, with fringes of emerald green moss and tiny flowers, so it is easy to see that some wistful old trapper might have thought he had discovered an arctic paradise.

SPREADING TERRACES OF DELICATELY HUED LIMESTONE WITH MIRROR-LIKE POOLS

Western Brook Pond

A NEWFOUNDLAND LAKE LIES AT THE BOTTOM OF A WINDING CANYON CUT DEEP INTO FLAT-TOPPED MOUNTAINS

To the eye of the osprey soaring overhead, Western Brook Pond looks like a shimmering jewel dropped by a giant hand. The jewel's landing place is the bottom of a 2000ft (600m) deep canyon, cut into the Long Range Mountains of the Canadian island of Newfoundland.

To describe this lake as a 'pond' is misleading, for Western Brook Pond snakes for 10 miles (16km) into the mountains, and is 544ft (166m) deep. The gorge containing it was cut during the Ice Age. A glacier moved down an existing river valley, deepening and widening it before stopping short of the coast. When the ice finally retreated about 11,000 years ago, Western Brook Pond formed in the bottom of the gash.

It was some 6000 years after the Ice Age ended that people started to move into this area, the earliest of whom hunted seals, fish, birds and caribou. The later Dorset Inuits settled along the

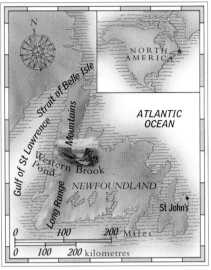

coast near Western Brook Pond in the early centuries of the Christian era. They built houses with earth walls and fireplaces, and may have used wood and hide boats similar to kayaks.

VIEW FROM THE BOTTOM

Now pleasure boats take summer visitors along Western Brook Pond, past the waterfalls that tumble down the canyon's sides, and the scree that litters the lower slopes. To reach the lake, visitors cross a boggy plain where the insectivorous pitcher plant, Newfoundland's floral emblem, grows.

DEEP CLEFT *A glacier cut the chasm that contains Western Brook Pond. Thick ice covers the lake in winter.*

INSECT EATER
The pitcher plant's jug-like leaves contain water and enzymes that drown and digest insects that crawl into them.

The Banff Lakelands

A SPARKLING ARRAY OF GLACIER-FED, JEWEL-LIKE LAKES GLITTERS AGAINST THE BACKDROP OF THE ROCKY MOUNTAINS

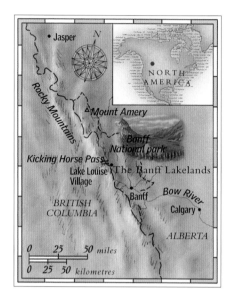

Doctor James Hector, a geologist exploring the Bow Valley in the Canadian Rocky Mountains in 1858, was kicked violently in the chest by a packhorse while he helped the horse across a river. When Hector was found unconscious by his Stoney Indian guides they thought he was dead and prepared to bury him. But the doctor awoke, refusing his grave – and the incident gave the river, and the pass at its head, the name Kicking Horse.

The Bow Valley cuts through the mountainous lakelands of Banff National Park – established in 1885 and Canada's oldest. Then 'Hotsprings Reserve' covered a mere 10sq miles (26km²). Now Banff National Park is 2580sq miles (6680km²) of peaks, meadows, lakes and glaciers running for 150 miles (240km) along the easternmost ridges of the Rocky Mountains in southern Alberta. It and the adjoining parks of Jasper, Yoho and Kootenay form a vast and protected wilderness.

ICY ORIGINS

The park's mountains are young, pushed up some 70 million years ago – a geological eyeblink. Their youthful restiveness, combined with the awesome power of shifting ice, has created a land of astonishing contrasts.

In the north, the Columbia Icefield, 125sq miles (325km²) in area, is the largest icefield in North America. Its meltwaters form rivers that eventually flow into three different oceans – the Pacific, the Arctic and the Atlantic.

From the icefield, huge glaciers ooze down, grinding the rocks to powder. The debris – 'rock flour' – clouds the icy lakes. Lake Louise, a place of legendary beauty, is a stunning example of a glacier-fed lake. The glacial silt, suspended in the water, refracts the light, giving the lake a brilliant emerald hue.

LOFTY PEAK *Mount Amery is in the wild and less accessible north of Banff Park.*

Cold above is matched by heat below. Icy meltwater seeps through rock and into cracks in the Earth's crust. Here it is pressurised, heated and percolated back to the surface to form the mineral hot springs that drew the first tourists to Banff a century ago.

The varied landscape creates a matching variety of plants. In the valleys, glittering lakes lap thick forests of aspen, pine, fir and spruce. Higher up, meadows and gnarled alpine trees give

ALPINE GEM *Lake Louise's iridescent water is 'distilled from peacocks' tails', in the words of a 1920s writer.*

way to barren, wind-scoured heights. Timbered mountains are splashed with meadows of bluebells and heathers. In summer, wild strawberries and blueberries grow beside rugged trails, and yellow glacier lilies push through melting snows.

Animal life is just as varied – there are 225 species of birds, from hummingbirds to eagles, and 53 species of mammal, including moose. The best-known residents are grizzly bears and black bears. Grizzlies are wary and rare

(there are around 80–100 in the park) but black bears often scavenge on roads and campsites. If attacked, visitors are advised to play dead.

Although bear attacks are rare, sightings are not, especially for those who roam and ride the 930 miles (1500km) of trails, that range from easy lake-side rambles to gruelling, poorly marked routes. All of the trails let visitors immerse themselves in the sharp sweet air of stunning mountainscapes.

> ## THE BEST-KNOWN RESIDENTS ARE GRIZZLY BEARS AND BLACK BEARS

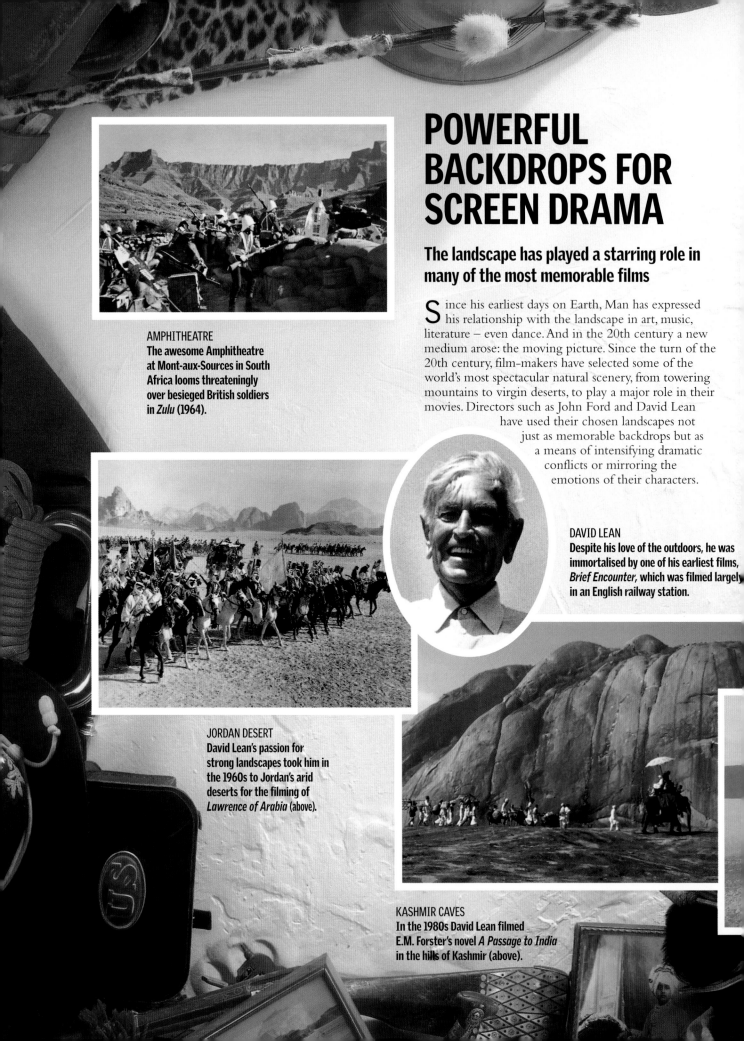

POWERFUL BACKDROPS FOR SCREEN DRAMA

The landscape has played a starring role in many of the most memorable films

Since his earliest days on Earth, Man has expressed his relationship with the landscape in art, music, literature – even dance. And in the 20th century a new medium arose: the moving picture. Since the turn of the 20th century, film-makers have selected some of the world's most spectacular natural scenery, from towering mountains to virgin deserts, to play a major role in their movies. Directors such as John Ford and David Lean have used their chosen landscapes not just as memorable backdrops but as a means of intensifying dramatic conflicts or mirroring the emotions of their characters.

AMPHITHEATRE
The awesome Amphitheatre at Mont-aux-Sources in South Africa looms threateningly over besieged British soldiers in *Zulu* (1964).

DAVID LEAN
Despite his love of the outdoors, he was immortalised by one of his earliest films, *Brief Encounter,* which was filmed largely in an English railway station.

JORDAN DESERT
David Lean's passion for strong landscapes took him in the 1960s to Jordan's arid deserts for the filming of *Lawrence of Arabia* (above).

KASHMIR CAVES
In the 1980s David Lean filmed E.M. Forster's novel *A Passage to India* in the hills of Kashmir (above).

PLAINS OF AFRICA
Meryl Streep and Robert Redford picnic against a backdrop of the Kenyan plains in *Out of Africa* (1985).

MONUMENT VALLEY
The desert buttes of Monument Valley, bordering Arizona and Utah, were used as a backdrop by John Ford in the classic Western drama *Stagecoach* (right), which was made in 1939.

SNOW-COVERED STEPPES
The desolate wastes of Russia's steppes, re-created in David Lean's epic of the Russian Revolution, *Doctor Zhivago,* were actually filmed in Finland (below).

SYMBOL OF DANGER
For John Ford (right), the desert symbolised hardship and danger.

Niagara Falls

TWIN WATERFALLS SEPARATED BY AN ISLAND HANG MAJESTICALLY ABOVE A MISTY CURTAIN OF FOAMING SPRAY

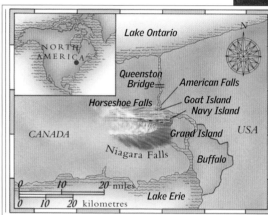

IN RETREAT *Most of Niagara's water crashes over the Canadian Horseshoe Falls, which are slowly being undercut at the centre to leave a projecting ledge.*

Niagara, meaning 'thunder water', was the name the native Americans gave to the mighty waterfall that today forms a spectacular boundary between the USA and Canada. From Lake Erie, the Niagara River flows placidly for almost 35 miles (56km), but near Lake Ontario runs into rapids that surge towards the cataract in a mist of spray and rainbows. Then a dramatic drop of about 180ft (55m) sends a torrent of water roaring down into a fury of foam as if into a bottomless chasm.

Goat Island, on the brink of the cascade, separates the river into two. The American Falls on the eastern side form a straight line about 1000ft (300m) long; the Canadian Horseshoe Falls are twice as long and, as their name indicates, form a horseshoe shape.

OVERALL VIEW

The falls look magnificent from both sides, but the Canadian shore offers the best overall view of both. For a really close look, the Horseshoe Falls can be braved in a small boat, the *Maid of the Mist*, which sails into the swirling spray.

Niagara Falls were born about 12,500 years ago at the end of the last Ice Age. With the melting of a massive glacier, water spilt out of Lake Erie and rushed northwards to form what is now Lake Ontario in a basin about 320ft (100m) lower. Originally, the ridge over which the water falls was some 7 miles (11km) farther north – where Queenston now stands – but over the centuries it has been cut back by the action of around 7000 tons of water a second crashing over it. At a rate of retreat of about 4ft (1.2m) a year, it will take 25,000 years for the ridge to be cut back to Lake Erie.

Queenston Heights rang to the roar of battle when Britain and the USA clashed in the war of 1812. Later in the 1800s, voices roaring around the falls were those of onlookers watching one of the many daredevil stunts that became a feature of the falls, such as leaping into the maelstrom below!

The first to take this death-defying risk was Sam Patch of Passaic Falls, New Jersey, who jumped from Goat Island in October 1829, and survived.In 1901, 43-year-old Mrs Annie Edson

TWO ON A TIGHTROPE

Charles Blondin, a French acrobat whose real name was Jean-François Gravelet, was the first to cross Niagara Falls on a tightrope – on June 30, 1859. On the way along the 1100ft (335m) rope, he hauled up a bottle from a boat 160ft (49m) below and took a drink. A month later Blondin carried his terrified manager, Harry Colcord, across (left).

Signor Farini (actually an American named William Leonard Hunt) copied the feat in August 1860. Two weeks later, he and Blondin made a twin moonlight crossing, each carrying a passenger. Others who copied the stunt included an Italian, Maria Spelterini, who shuffled across with her feet in baskets.

Taylor, a schoolteacher from Bay City, Michigan, and a non-swimmer, was the first to go over the falls in a barrel and live. The fall took three seconds. She made a lecture tour as 'Queen of the Mist', hoping to make her fortune, but died a pauper 20 years later.

Of those who tried to emulate her feat in the next 60 years, three succeeded and three died. They included George Stathakis of Buffalo, New York, in 1930. He survived the plunge but suffocated when the barrel was caught behind the falls for 22 hours – he had only carried enough oxygen for three hours.

Badlands

ARID GULLIES WIND
AMONG ROCKY RIDGES
AND RANKS OF
CRUMBLING PINNACLES
AMID THE SOUTH
DAKOTA PLAINS

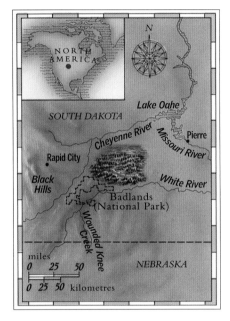

From the green of the surrounding farmland, with its vast stretches of nodding grain, you come abruptly upon the Badlands of South Dakota. The arid hills and ridges do not rise up from the plain – they stand below it, like a landscape carved in relief.

STONE HAYSTACKS

Spread suddenly before your feet is a startling panorama of jagged and windswept rock – crumbling pinnacles and ramparts cleft by winding gullies, and endless haystack mounds that change from pink to glowing red as the sun moves across the sky.

Rugged and austere, the Badlands were for centuries the haunt of the Sioux, who named them *mako* 'bad' *siko*

WILDERNESS SANCTUARY *Bleak as it seems, Sage Creek in the South Dakota Badlands has grasslands that sustain buffalo (bison) and prairie dogs.*

BUFFALO HUNT *This Sioux buffalo hunt was painted in 1835 by American artist George Catlin. Badlands hunters sometimes drove the animals over a cliff.*

'lands'. This 100 mile (160km) long swathe of broken country, 50 miles (80km) wide, is parched in summer except for rare torrential rainstorms, and freezing cold in winter. But the Badlands are not quite as stark as they initially sound, for a few junipers cling to the rocky slopes, and tough grasses flourish in creeks and basins, along with cotton-woods and wild flowers.

The Badlands owe their beginning to the pine-clad Black Hills to the south-west, rising to 7242ft (2207m). The Black Hills were pushed up out of an inland sea about 65 million years ago. As time went by, soil and fine stone was continually flushed down the hill slopes to form a layered, swampy plain on the flat land to the east. About 30 million years ago there was a change of climate, and the swamp slowly turned into grassland.

As time went on, wind and water eroded part of this grassland, gnawing into the layers of frail soil and soft stone – erosion that still continues. Grass torn up by the roots in rainstorms left a sludge of exposed soil that was washed away in rivulets, carving the stone into pinnacles and domes that baked hard under the searing sun.

The pale stripes that run horizontally across the soft rocks mark the layers of sediment flushed down from the hills aeons ago. Revealed in these layers and the bedrock are fossils millions of years old – marine turtles, for example, and the rhinoceros-like titanothere of the forested swamp; the Sioux called its giant fossil the Thunderhorse.

THE BADLANDS STAND BELOW THE PLAIN, LIKE A LANDSCAPE IN RELIEF

With the coming of European settlers in the 1870s there was an invasion of buffalo hunters. The great herds of buffalo (or bison) of the plains were almost wiped out, and the Sioux, whose lives depended on them, were in despair. In 1890 the South Dakota Badlands became a centre for Ghost Dances – the focus of a new religious cult that promised a revival of native American fortunes and the return of the buffalo.

One buffalo hunting technique sometimes used by the Sioux was to drive a herd over the edge of a cliff. The Badlands was a suitable spot for such mass killings, and the carcasses were butchered at the base of the cliff. The Sioux made use of every part of the buffalo – the flesh and fat were used for food; the hides for lodge walls, blankets, clothing, saddles and thongs; the horns for ladles; the bones for clubs, saddle trees and sledge runners; and the bladders for water carriers.

During the unrest that occurred as a result of the Ghost Dances, the US Seventh Cavalry intercepted Chief Big Foot and a group of 350 Sioux as they crossed the Badlands in 1890. The incident led to the tragic killings at Wounded Knee Creek.

WILDLIFE RETURNS

Many settlers tried to farm the Badlands, but drought and erosion caused repeated crop failures. Wildlife revived in 1930, after the setting up of the Badlands National Monument, which became a National Park in 1978. It covers about 380sq miles (980km²) in the heart of the area, and is home to lizards, rattlesnakes, many kinds of bird, bats, ever-busy colonies of tunnelling prairie dogs and small herds of bison and pronghorn antelopes.

BADLANDS BEAUTY

Not only its bright and refreshing appearance makes the sego lily a boon to wanderers in the Dakota Badlands. The flower grows from a nutty flavoured edible bulb that can be eaten raw or cooked like a potato.

Native Americans ate the bulb, and so did the Mormon settlers of Utah when their crops failed. The sego lily blooms in summer, growing up to 20in (510mm) tall and thriving on dry slopes or grasslands.

Yosemite

A SPLENDID WILDERNESS WHERE SHINING WATERFALLS PLUNGE DOWN MASSIVE CLIFFS OF POLISHED GRANITE

One of the tallest unbroken cliffs in the world, El Capitan (The Chief) towers above the gentle, wooded shores of the Merced River in the Yosemite Valley. It rises a sheer 3000ft (900m) near the valley entrance, just one of Yosemite's many incomparable splendours. Yosemite Falls, the sixth highest in the world, plummet 2425ft (739m) down the neighbouring cliff in three giant leaps. At the other end of the valley rises the granite bulk of Half Dome – so named because it has a rounded back and a vertical rock wall 2200ft (670m) high on the valley side.

Several of the highest waterfalls in North America are found within the Yosemite National Park, an area slightly bigger than Luxembourg in the heart of California's Sierra Nevada range.

SCENIC WONDERLAND

Rivers roar among giant boulders and wooded, flower-filled meadows lie below the park's massive granite cliffs, with the snow-capped peaks of the High Sierras as a glittering backdrop. Of all this outstanding scenery, the most impressive is the Yosemite Valley.

Yosemite, pronounced 'Yohsemittee', is derived from a native American word for grizzly bear, the tribal totem of the people who lived there. Until 1851, they had the whole of the Yosemite wilderness to themselves.

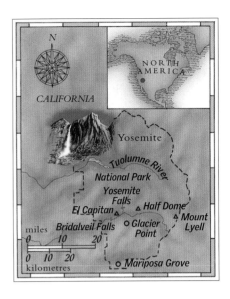

Then a troop of cavalry, California Volunteers of the Mariposa Battalion, pursued a band of braves into the valley, and set eyes on its scenic glories – such

PURPLE SHADOWS *Half Dome, its flat face cut by Ice Age glaciers, stands out above its granite fellows as sunset splashes the sky above the shadowed Yosemite Valley. John Muir (right) inspired the establishment of the Yosemite National Park.*

309

VISITING THE WILDERNESS

Walkers sauntered through the Yosemite Valley on the first organised High Trip in 1901. The party of 96 was led by Will Colby, secretary of the Sierra Club. Formed in 1892 with John Muir as its president, the Club's aims were to keep the wilderness unspoilt and to help people to both enjoy and appreciate it.

A permanent camp was set up in the Tuolumne Meadows, from where parties set out to climb, fish and explore. The three-week trip was so successful it became an annual event. Writing about the trip in the club bulletin, Ella M. Sexton stated: 'A man's attire is indispensable ... Any sort of skirt would make the struggle through the brush simply hopeless.' Before long the Yosemite became popular for summer holidays and for winter sports, and travel companies featured it on their brochures (right).

SNAPSHOT *Members of the Sierra Club pictured on the first High Trip in 1901.*

GIANT ROCK *Clouds brush the granite face of El Capitan (left) as its mighty form is reflected in the river below. Winter sunlight (above) caps the rock with a golden glow.*

as Bridalveil Falls, opposite El Capitan, plunging 620ft (190m) and then hanging in the air like a misty veil. The soldiers were overwhelmed by the grandeur of the valley. Their stories of its beauty led to the region being opened up to tourists and to its establishment as a national park. This was created in 1890, largely at the inspiration of John Muir, a Scottish-born naturalist who worked tirelessly for its conservation. He wrote: 'No temple made with hands can compare with Yosemite ... Every rock in its walls seems to glow with life ... as if into this mountain mansion Nature had gathered her choicest treasures.'

About 10 million years ago the Yosemite was a land of low rolling hills, but then earth movements pushed the hills higher and rivers carved their valleys deeper. Many of the white or blue-grey granite domes are the cores left when the rocks above expanded and cracked as the erosion of surface rocks relieved the pressure on them.

About 3 million years ago, the Ice Ages began. Slow-moving glaciers plucked the jointed rock walls and scoured the valleys even deeper, cutting off side canyons to create hanging valleys. When the ice finally melted some 10,000 years ago, a large lake filled the deep Yosemite Valley.

Slowly the lake silted up, until it became a fertile valley floor amid the granite cliffs. The Grand Canyon of the Tuolumne, which lies to the north of the Yosemite Valley, also cuts through the park from east to west, and was shaped in the same way.

Among more than 1000 kinds of wild flower are the Californian poppies that light up the lower grasslands in spring and the fragrant western azaleas that brighten the valley meadows in summer. California lilac and purple-barked manzanita cover the hillsides.

Yosemite in autumn is ablaze with the reds and yellows of turning leaves. Trees found there include the black oak, incense cedar and ponderosa pine, and the king of them all, the giant sequoia – the world's largest living tree. Although not as tall as the related giant redwood of the California coast, the

ROOT POWER *A wizened Jeffrey pine clings tenaciously to the rocky edge of Sentinel Dome in the Yosemite Valley.*

sequoia's height and girth combined give it more bulk than any other tree.

All the sequoias in the park are to be found only in three separate groves – silent cathedrals of yellowish-brown columns soaring to 200ft (60m) or more. In the largest, the Mariposa Grove, is a gnarled, lightning-blasted veteran – the 'Grizzly Giant'. Estimated to be 2700 years old, the Grizzly Giant must have been well grown before the Iron Age reached Europe.

The American black bear is Yosemite's largest mammal – grizzlies are no longer found there. The bears forage mostly at night, struggling to fatten up for the long winter on a diet that includes bulbs, shoots, fish, honey, nuts and berries. Mule deer, named for their large ears, are easily picked out by their rusty red summer coats as they browse in wood and meadow.

AN UNFORGETTABLE VIEW

Today Yosemite attracts 3 million visitors a year. In summer, Glacier Point offers a stupendous bird's eye view of the Yosemite Valley 3300ft (1000m) below, with the Yosemite Falls seen opposite in their full glory. It is a sight never to be forgotten, most magical at sunset or by moonlight.

DANCING WATERS *Upper and Lower Yosemite Falls, together the highest waterfall in North America, thunder down the cliff in a torrent of spray.*

Yellowstone

A LANDSCAPE OF STEAM HEAT, WHERE BOILING GEYSERS MAY SPOUT FAR HIGHER THAN THE OLD-TIMERS' TALLEST TALES

SANCTUARY
Moose are among the many large animal species that find a haven in Yellowstone National Park.

Long ago, when the United States was hardly out of its teens, you could sometimes find leathery backwoodsmen who told tales of a fabulous land to the west where fountains of boiling water rose high above the trees as the ground trembled to their roaring. There were,

they said, mountains of glass and mountains of sulphur, places where you could catch a trout and cook it straight away in a pool of boiling water. There were lakes like bubbling paint pots, and tiers of porcelain baths where a man could wash at whatever temperature he chose.

As for rivers – some set off for the distant Pacific while their neighbours flowed away to the Atlantic, others flowed so fast that the friction heated

their beds, and the greatest river of all plunged down a canyon the colour of purest gold. There were even, they said, forests of 'petrified stone trees' where 'petrified birds sang petrified songs'. No one believed them, of course, but the stories persisted. In 1871

COLD COMFORT *(overleaf) A bison herd treks through Yellowstone Park in winter to find grazing near hot springs. Hot water keeps the river free of ice.*

GRAND PRISMATIC *The colours in the largest of Yellowstone's hot springs are produced by heat-resistant algae (minute plants) that live in the near-boiling water.*

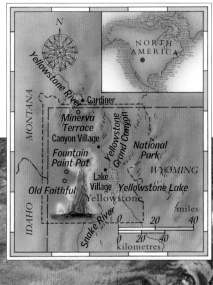

a government expedition went to investigate; its report led President Grant in 1872 to declare the whole area, 3500sq miles (9000km²) in extent, the world's first ever National Park: 'Withdrawn from settlement or sale ... for the benefit and enjoyment of the people.' The name Yellowstone is from the native American name for its mightiest river.

TALES WERE NOT SO FAR-FETCHED

Since then, millions of visitors have discovered that, in general, the old-timers were right. Streams do drain to each side of the Continental Divide within the park, and there is a glass mountain – Obsidian Cliff, composed of volcanic glass that Shoshone warriors once chipped into arrowheads. On the Minerva Terrace, natural calcite baths rise in steaming tiers, and at Fountain Paint Pot there are boiling mud pools stained by minerals to all the colours of the rainbow. But it is something of a disappointment to learn that the Firehole River owes its warmth not

WATER SCULPTURE *Hot springs raise limestone solutions to the Minerva Terrace, new rock being deposited as the water cools. Two tons of limestone are added to the terraces every day.*

to friction but to the hot rocks beneath.

Yellowstone's most talked-about feature is still its geysers – awesome waterspouts such as Old Faithful, which every 1¼ hours or so climbs boiling and roaring up to 200ft (60m) into the sky. The many others, all different, include Grotto Geyser emerging from a white silica cave, Riverside Geyser arching a

plume of boiling water over the Firehole River, and Steamboat – the tallest in the world – with eruptions nearly twice as high as Old Faithful's but erratic, spouting at intervals of anything from four days to four years.

The geysers' performance depends on the chance meeting of three things – an abundant water supply, a powerful heat source and a rock structure that lends itself to a natural plumbing system. The heat source is molten rock from the core of the continent, which at Yellowstone is little more than about 3 miles (5km) below the surface.

chambers from underneath, the cycle starts again.

Altogether there are some 10,000 thermal features in the park. As well as geysers, there are pots of bubbling, broth-like mud, gushes of sulphurous steam from vents called fumaroles and hot springs often stained emerald or turquoise by algae that have adapted to live in their near-boiling temperatures.

All this activity owes its existence to the great blister of molten rock shifting beneath this thin-crusted area, forever threatening to erupt. About 600,000 years ago erupt it did, lifting some 1000sq miles (2590km²) of the Rocky Mountains in a paroxysm of violent eruptions that deposited a huge pile of ash and spread a thin layer of volcanic dust over much of North America. Then the unsupported crust collapsed into the emptied chamber to leave a 1200sq mile (3100km²) caldera (crater).

Later, less-violent eruptions almost filled the caldera with ash and lava, blocking the ancestral Yellowstone River and creating Yellowstone Lake. But the river, aided by the glaciers of three Ice Ages and even more by hot water and steam that softened and yellowed the caldera's rock rim, slowly whittled out today's Grand Canyon of the Yellowstone that descends in a series of majestic falls from the lake.

TREES TURNED TO STONE

Nowhere does the evidence of past eruptions surface more dramatically than on Specimen Ridge. There stand the petrified trees, still recognisable as sycamores, walnuts, oaks, dogwoods and magnolias. Millions of years ago they were buried in volcanic ash and cinders that cut off oxygen from the wood and prevented it burning.

Then, over aeons, cell by cell, the organic material of the trees was replaced by minerals from the rocks so that when at last their covering was eroded away, they stood as stone replicas of themselves. If the imagination cannot grasp how long this process must have taken, consider this: on parts of the ridge there are the remains of 27 such forests, one on top of the other. Each grew for hundreds of years in the same place, and each in succession was buried and turned to stone.

WATER POWER *Yellowstone River carves its Grand Canyon through the pale rocks after which it is named.*

The park's plentiful rainfall seeps down through the porous rock to a depth of about 5000ft (1500m). There, under pressure, it is superheated to a temperature far above boiling. In a round trip taking centuries, hot water rises towards the surface, and near ground level some of the hottest turns to steam. It blasts out the column of water above it, starting a chain reaction in which the reduced pressure lets more superheated water flash into steam – maintaining the geyser eruption until the plumbing system is empty. When hot water refills the underground

Devils Tower

A GIANT PILLAR LOOMING OVER WYOMING'S CATTLE COUNTRY MADE AN IDEAL FILM SETTING FOR A SPACESHIP'S LANDING

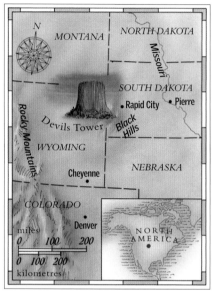

A solitary monolith like a massive tree stump thrusts up from the rolling cattle-ranch country of north-east Wyoming. A legend of the Kiowa people who lived in the region says Devils Tower was created when seven little girls were chased by an angry bear. The girls jumped onto a low rock, which started to stretch upwards from the ground, carrying them beyond the bear's reach. As the bear tried to get to the girls it clawed at the rock, leaving grooves down its sides. Eventually the bear died from exhaustion, but the girls live forever as the seven stars visible in the Pleiades cluster.

Devils Tower, the United States's first National Monument, is a massive cluster of multisided columns, that rises 865ft (265m) above the forested mound at its base. It measures 1000ft (300m) across at the base and tapers to 275ft (85m) across at the summit.

UNDERGROUND ORIGINS

Geologists say that the tower started to form about 50 million years ago, when hot molten material deep in the Earth rose towards the surface through weaknesses in the rocks above. This mass of molten material slowly cooled and solidified within the surrounding rock, and as it cooled it contracted and fractured to form multi-sided columns, like mud that cracks as it dries out. Over many millions of years, the softer rocks surrounding the solidified material were worn away, slowly uncovering the cluster of many-sided columns.

The distinctive bulk of Devils Tower may be seen from 100 miles (160km) away, the colour of its lichen-encrusted sides changing with the light

WATCHDOG *A prairie dog stands on guard, ready to bark a warning of danger.*

and time of day. It was a landmark for early European settlers, who turned the area into cattle-ranch country. More recently, the tower was seen by millions in the 1977 film *Close Encounters of the Third Kind*, when it featured as the landing site for the aliens' spaceship.

Near the foot of Devils Tower are the

A SKYDIVER WAS MAROONED ON THE SUMMIT FOR SIX DAYS

underground tunnels and chambers of prairie dogs – rodents the size of small rabbits that bark like dogs. Now they are protected, but once many were killed because they were thought to be depriving cattle and sheep of grass.

'Inaccessible to anything without wings' was how Colonel Richard I. Dodge described the tower's summit in 1875, when he escorted a US Geological Survey party there. It was he who gave the tower its name, after he heard that the Cheyenne people knew it as Bad God's Tower because of an evil god who lived at the top and beat drums that made the roar of thunder.

It was not long before someone set out to prove Dodge wrong. On July 4, 1893, a crowd of a thousand people watched local rancher William Rogers haul himself up using his 'ladder' – wooden pegs driven into a vertical crack and joined together for stability.

From the summit, climbers see five states spread out before them – Wyoming, Montana, North Dakota, South Dakota and Nebraska. Prickly pear cacti and sage grow at the top – the seeds probably carried by birds – and rattlesnakes and chipmunks have made their way up. A skydiver who landed on the summit in the 1940s had ample time to study both the view and the wildlife. He lost his rope and could not climb down, and was marooned there for six days before rescue arrived.

DIZZY HEIGHTS *The sheer sides of Devils Tower present climbers with an irresistible challenge. Fritz Weissner (inset), pausing on a broken column in 1937, was the first climber to reach the top using only a rope.*

319

Arches

STONE ARCHES BY THE SCORE AND PILLARS BY THE THOUSAND BRING A RAINBOW OF COLOURS TO UTAH'S DESERTS

The barren rockscape of south-eastern Utah resembles the surface of some fantastic planet. Rugged pillars of rock, sculpted to every imaginable shape and size, jut up from the desert floor. But far more astonishing are the 200 or so stone arches that span openings in walls of rock and give the area its name.

Landscape Arch is the world's longest natural arch – a ribbon of stone, barely 6ft (1.8m) thick at one point, that stretches 291ft (89m) between massive buttresses. Eye of the Whale is an elongated slit beneath a huge span of rock. The most distinctive arch, however, is the freestanding Delicate Arch. Shaped something like an inverted letter 'U' with splayed sides, it stands on the rim of a great natural amphitheatre.

Equally evocative names have been given to other landforms of Arches, which is one of the United States's national parks. Some bear a freakish likeness to humans, objects or animals. The Dark Angel, a pinnacle of black rock 125ft (38m) high, presides over an area known as the Devil's Gardens, and the Tower of Babel is a soaring 500ft (150m) slab of ribbed rock.

NATURE'S SCULPTURES

The rock formations of Arches are carved out of sandstone – grains of quartz held together by a cement of silica or calcium carbonate and coated with iron compounds that give the rock its many colours. The sandstone of the Arches area lies on top of a thick layer of salt. Under pressure from the overlying rock, the salt can move into weaker areas in the rock and itself apply pressure to those weaknesses.

In the Arches area, moving salt has forced the sandstone upwards into a dome, stretching and cracking it and resulting in hundreds of parallel joints 10–20ft (3–6m) apart. Water seeped into the joints, and the rock of the intervening fins was easily weathered, although more easily in some places than others. Some fins were weathered more in their lower layers, until the rock broke through to leave an arch (see right).

Normally, arches take shape imperceptibly slowly, but occasionally there is a dramatic change, such as the one at Skyline Arch in 1940. The arch was known as 'Arch in the Making' until a gigantic slab of sandstone tumbled from the opening, doubling its size.

BOW-LEGGED *Delicate Arch was known to early settlers as 'Old Maid's Bloomers' or 'Cowboy Chaps'. One 'knee' is only 6ft (1.8m) thick.*

FRAMED *North Window, one of a pair of arches called The Spectacles, makes a lens-shaped surround for Turret Arch, which itself frames the desert beyond.*

This part of Utah is known as 'red rock country', but almost every hue is present in this semi-desert where little vegetation obscures the rocks. Some of the rock forms are draped with 'desert varnish' - a glossy coating of minerals left behind as seepage water evaporates. The Ute people etched drawings of men on horseback into the varnish, some time after horses, brought to America by the Spaniards, had reached this area during the 17th century.

The climate of Arches is harsh. Less than 10in (250mm) of rain falls each year, and the temperature, which drops below freezing in winter, can rise to 38°C (100°F) or more in summer, with the rock a searing 66°C (150°F). Yet ferns and orchids flourish in cool overhangs and moist alcoves.

Most animals of the area rarely emerge during the day, but after nightfall the desert comes to life, as animals including bobcats and long-eared mule deer hunt or forage amid the monstrous shadows of the moonlit rocks.

CREATIONS OF THE DESERT'S WATER

Although Arches has little rain, it is water that is mainly responsible for the landforms. Rain and melting snow dissolve the cement that binds the sandstone, allowing the grains to be washed away. In winter, water in the rock freezes and expands as it turns into ice, forcing off grains or flakes of rock.

The cement is patchily distributed. Less well-cemented rocks are worn away faster than solidly bound ones, and the uneven weathering leaves the surviving stronger

rocks shaped as fins, arches and towers. The combination of thin fins of rock and patchy weathering accounts for the profusion of arches in this area.

Narrow fin of rock

Base of a rock followed by weathering

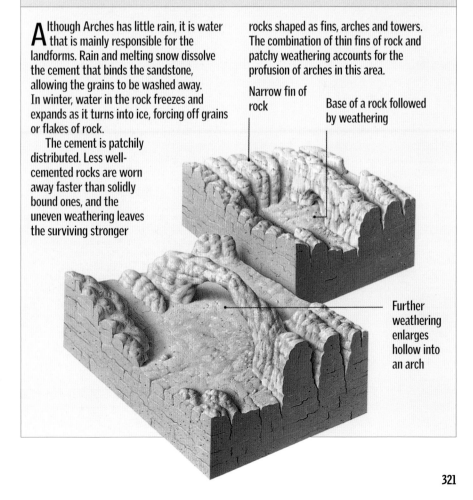

Further weathering enlarges hollow into an arch

Crater Lake

A CLEAR BLUE LAKE
IN OREGON FILLS THE
GAPING HOLE LEFT
AFTER A MOUNTAIN
TOP COLLAPSED
7000 YEARS AGO

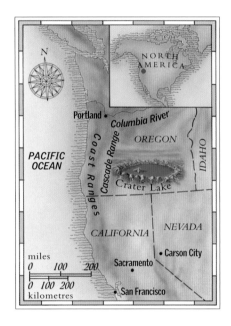

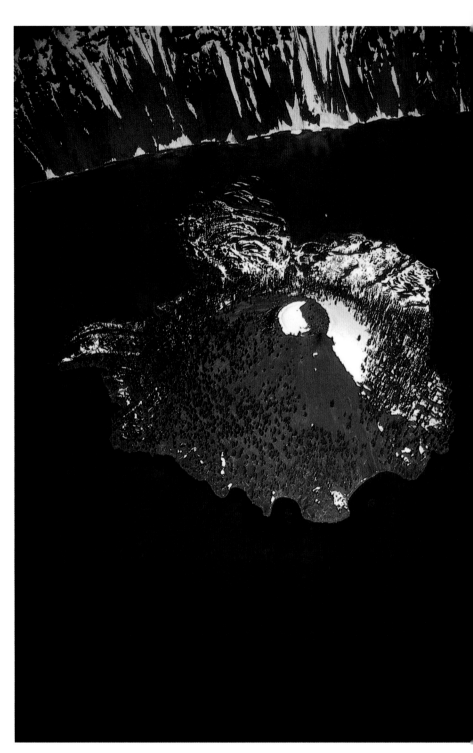

LAKE VOLCANO *Wizard Island is a cone of lava and ash that tapers up from the floor of Crater Lake. All but its tip is drowned by the waters of the lake.*

In 1870, a Kansas schoolboy read a short article – in the newspaper wrapped round his lunch – about a lake that lay high in the Oregon mountains, encircled by sheer walls and containing an extinct volcano. The article triggered William Gladstone Steel's lifelong interest in Crater Lake. He campaigned tirelessly to protect it from the changes that man's activities could bring and his work bore fruit in 1902, when Crater Lake became the United States's fifth national park.

The lake that Steel worked so hard to protect lies in the vast hole left after the top of Mount Mazama collapsed during violent volcanic eruptions 7000 years ago. The lake, 5 miles (8km) across, is surrounded by multicoloured cliffs which rise steeply from the water to form a jagged rim that in places is almost 2000ft (600m) high – twice the height of the Eiffel Tower.

Two small but contrasting islands punctuate the surface of the lake. One,

known as Wizard Island, is an almost perfect volcanic cone. The other, named Phantom Ship, sails forth from the south side of the lake, with masts, sails and rigging formed by pinnacles of rock and spiky conifer trees.

Crater Lake lies high in the Cascade Range, 6176ft (1882m) above sea level. Winters are long and hard – snowfalls totalling 50ft (15m) a year start in September and last until July, and the lake broods beneath swathes of fog.

WRATH OF LLAO *Thunderstorms, once thought to be the god venting his anger, interrupt spells of dry, tranquil summer weather.*

As the snow melts in spring, Nature emerges from its winter retreat. Wild flowers bring colour to the slopes, black bears wake from their winter sleep, and mule deer and moose migrate to the meadowland to graze.

The native American peoples who lived in the area – the Klamaths and the earlier Maklaks – held Crater Lake in awe. To the Klamaths, it was a place of unnerving magic, to be visited only by healers and holy men who went there to refresh their powers.

In Maklak legend Mount Mazama was the site of a battle between the Chief of the World Above, Skell, and Llao, the Chief of the World Below, who lived on the mountain with his monstrous disciples. During the battle, massive rocks hurtled across the sky, fire swept through forests and the land trembled until Llao lay dead and the mountain top was in ruins. Skell cast Llao's quartered body into the massive pit that had formed in the ruined mountain, and

THE CENTRE OF THE VOLCANO BEGAN TO COLLAPSE

the tears of his disciples filled it to form Crater Lake. Llao's head remained where it fell, and was later called Wizard Island by European settlers.

The legend's battle scene resemble actual events. Before its eruption in about 5000 BC, Mount Mazama was a many-coned volcano that could have been 12,000ft (3600m) high. Then the main central vent and a host of subsidiary vents started to blast out huge quantities of incandescent ash that swept down the volcano's flanks. The eruptions increased in power, and eventually so much rock had been lost that the centre of the volcano began to collapse, leaving the huge caldera 4000ft (1200m) deep that now contains Crater Lake. Mazama's final paroxysm, as it continued to fall in on itself, discharged ash that fell over a vast area from Nevada to Saskatchewan, more than 750 miles (1200km) away.

Over thousands of years water settled in the hollow to form a lake 1932ft (589m) deep – the United States's deepest. No streams flow into Crater Lake and none flow out, and water lost through seepage and evaporation is neatly balanced by snow and rainfall.

After the major eruption, volcanic activity continued on a diminished scale and volcanic cones, including Wizard Island, formed on the lake bed. Phantom Ship's jagged spikes, however, are much older, and are weathered from a vertical sheet of hard rock filling a fissure that fed a much earlier volcanic vent.

The area has been inhabited continuously for 12,000 years, and there may have been witnesses to Mount Mazama's eruption. Tools and sandals predating it have been found near Crater Lake, buried beneath a layer of ash – a product of the cataclysmic events that created this treasure of extraordinary natural beauty.

EVENING COLOURS *(overleaf)*
The setting sun gives a rosy tinge to the sky above Crater Lake, and casts the lake's rim, and Wizard Island, into shade.

Bryce Canyon

FANTASTIC STONE
PINNACLES GLOWING
IN MANY SHADES OF
RED STAND IN SERRIED
RANKS IN THE BADLANDS
OF UTAH

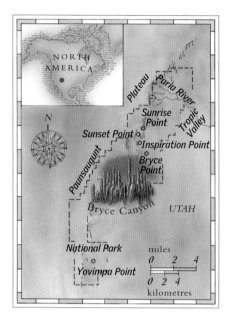

An architectural fantasy of sandstone and limestone, the spires and pinnacles of Bryce Canyon rise from its shadowed depths like the disinterred ruins of an ancient city. When an American surveyor named T.C. Bailey first set eyes on the beautiful and mysterious stone sculptures in 1876, he was enchanted – he thought it was 'the wildest and most wonderful scene that the eyes of man ever beheld'.

EVER-CHANGING COLOURS

The Paiute people who lived in the area for centuries were, however, less romantic about the place, calling it 'Red rocks standing up like men in a bowl-shaped canyon'. They believed the rocks to be men who had been turned to stone by the wrath of the gods.

Bailey described the 'thousands of red, white, purple, and vermilion coloured rocks, of all sizes, resembling sentinels on the walls of castles, monks and priests in their robes, attendants, cathedrals and congregations'. Modern names given to some of the rock formations, such as 'Wall of Windows', 'Thor's Hammer', 'Tower Bridge', 'Hat Shop' and 'Atomic Cloud', indicate their strangeness and diversity.

Bryce Canyon is not truly a canyon but a series of natural rock amphitheatres some 500ft (150m) deep. Its red-brown rocks range through shades of rust red, salmon pink, lemon and almost white – due to the weathering of different mineral blends, mostly iron oxides, in the rock layers. Blues and purples indicate manganese oxide.

Changing light brings ever-changing colours and new perspectives to the surreal and silent stones. Dawn and dusk are the best times to view them, for at these times the sun's slanting rays reflect richer hues and cast darker shadows that accentuate the rock shapes. In winter, the stones are flecked with white where snow gathers in odd corners, and in shady places lingers until late spring.

BRAVING THE BADLANDS

Early pioneers found travel through Bryce Canyon difficult because of the debris underfoot and the maze of ravines. The heat and glare from the bare rocks added to their discomfort, and the thin air – the altitude is up to 9000ft (2750m) – soon sapped their strength.

This is why such areas were known as badlands – or 'bad lands to cross'.

SNOW AND SUNLIGHT *From Inspiration Point, sunrise brings a glow to the snow-flecked rocks of Silent City, a series of gullies in Bryce Canyon.*

Ebenezer Bryce, a 19th-century pioneer who settled near the Paria River, north of the canyon, described the badlands as 'a hell of a place to lose a cow!'

Bryce, from whom the canyon gets its name, was a Scottish-born settler who joined the Mormon community of Salt Lake City as a carpenter and sawmill operator. He moved south to set up the Paria River homestead with his wife and ten children in the 1860s, hoping that the warmer climate would be good for his wife's health. Bryce sold out in 1880, after failing in an attempt

to irrigate the valley by diverting water from the River Sevier, a project that was successfully completed 12 years later.

The rocks are grooved horizontally, each groove marking the edge of one of the layers of rock-building sediment, for 60 million years ago Bryce Canyon was at the bottom of a lake covering much of Utah. Layer upon layer of silt, sand and shell debris settled on the bottom, each layer varying according to the material washed in and the life present in the water. Gradually the grains were glued together by chemical cements to form layers of limestone and sandstone of different strengths.

THE GRAND STAIRWAY

By the time a rock layer about 2000ft (600m) thick had built up some 15 million years ago, earth movements pushed the lake bed high above the water to build the Paunsaugunt Plateau, which is the youngest and highest of a series of plateaus known as the Grand Stairway that descends south-wards to the rim of the famous Arizona Grand Canyon.

The highest point of Paunsaugunt Plateau is its southern tip, 9000ft (2750m) above sea level. Northwards it drops some 2000ft (600m) in height. The rock amphitheatres of Bryce Canyon stretch for 21 miles (34km) along the plateau's eastern edge, carved out from its cliffs.

Water has shaped this wild, bizarre landscape, and is still doing so. Although the terrain is dry in summer, winter snowfall is heavy, and in spring meltwater seeps into the rocks by day and freezes by night. Expanding ice breaks up the surface rock, leaving it to be swept away by the meltwater torrents and summer storms.

The floodwaters carve through the softer parts of the layered limestone, creating gullies, arches and tunnels, and scouring the canyon ever deeper. As the process continues, the canyon rim is reckoned to be receding at the rate

SUN SEEKER *A Douglas fir, which can grow taller than 300ft (90m), reaches skywards between the vertical rocks of Wall Street in Bryce Amphitheatre.*

of about 12in (300mm) every 50–65 years. Trees growing on the rim tell the tale – they are left standing on 'tiptoe', with their roots exposed.

Paunsaugunt Plateau's wooded greenness, interspersed with open

BIG CAT *The Bryce Canyon rock country and the plateau adjoining are one of the last haunts of the elusive cougar.*

OLDEST RESIDENTS

Some of the world's oldest living trees have survived for centuries on the bare, unfriendly soil of Bryce Canyon's most exposed ridges. They are twisted, low-growing bristlecone pines, which are super-efficient at making use of what little moisture is available to them.

In times of drought the pines feed only a few roots and branches, and do not grow any new needles. In fact, they hardly ever shed their needles at any time. The trees grow far enough apart not to spread fire, should it occur, and their resinous wood keeps fungi and insects at bay.

So successful is this survival strategy that some of the Bryce Canyon bristlecone pines are 1200–1600 years old. Yet they are not the oldest of their kind – 'Methuselah,' a bristlecone pine in California's White Mountains, is 4700 years old.

WEIRD AND WONDERFUL *In the last rays of evening sunlight, the ranks of rock spires viewed from Sunset Point seem strange and surreal beneath the rising full moon.*

HANGING ON *An age-old bristlecone pine clings to a ridge in Bryce Canyon, its roots exposed by the washing away of the frost-shattered rim rock.*

meadows and sagebrush, contrasts dramatically with the bare red rocks of its fretted edge. The plateau takes its name from the Paiute language – Paunsaugunt means 'Home of the beaver'. But beavers were a prime target for 19th-century fur trappers, and are no longer part of the local wildlife.

Fir and spruce thrive on shady slopes at the higher levels, giving way mainly to ponderosa pine as the land drops northwards. In summer, mule deer browse here at dawn and dusk and are preyed upon by cougars (also known as pumas and mountain lions), which are, however, seldom seen.

This area is one of the last refuges of these big cats. One adult cougar kills up to 50 deer a year, helping to keep the deer numbers at a sustainable level – that is, just enough of them to flourish on the available vegetation without destroying it.

Early pioneers mistook the low-branched junipers clothing the lower, eastern slopes of the plateau for cedars. This accounts for some of the local names, such as Cedar City, Cedar Breaks and Cedar Mountain.

Woodland clothes the floor of the amphitheatres, but few trees and shrubs manage to survive on the higher slopes,

which are powder-dry for much of the time. Yet bristlecone pines, the world's oldest living trees, are found on some of the desolate ridges, and the yellow-flowered rabbitbrush brightens open, sunny spots, providing food for small creatures such as marmots that live among the rocks.

THE SIGHT OF A LIFETIME

Sunrise Point and Sunset Point overlooking Bryce Amphitheatre – the most spectacular of the natural amphitheatres – are just two of the viewing points along the canyon rim. Today, the canyon and part of Paunsaugunt Plateau together form the 56sq mile (145km²) Bryce Canyon National Park and hundreds of thousands of visitors come here every year.

From the various viewing points, they can gaze in wonder at the incredible panorama of coloured rock spires, ridges and pinnacles – for many the favourite view among all the spectacular views of the American West. Those who are feeling slightly more energetic can follow trails down into the ravines and gullies. Seen from below, the rock spires look different again and even more fantastic.

Lechuguilla Cave

A NEW MEXICO
CAVE CONTAINS A
TREASURE TROVE OF
FABULOUS AND
INFINITELY VARIED
DECORATIONS

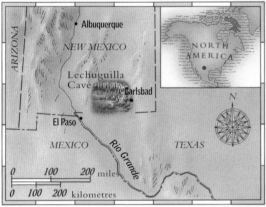

Incredulity is a constant companion
to those who explore Lechuguilla
Cave in New Mexico. So far, around
101 miles (156.5km) of caverns and
passageways have been discovered
underneath the desert mountains of the
southern United States, making it one
of the world's longest caves. Within are
cave 'decorations' – encrusted minerals
that hang from the ceilings and
embellish the walls and floors.

The beauty and variety of the
decorations is stunning. Hollow
stalactites like drinking straws up to
15ft (4.5m) long hang from cave roofs.
Shelves shaped like birdbaths are
supported by knobbly pedestals and
suspended from the roof by columnar
stalactites, and strands of gypsum as fine
as human hair reach 20ft (6m) in
length. There are formations resembling
pearls, popcorn, balloons and minute

PRECARIOUS PATH *Cavers make their way
along the massive Prickly Ice Cube Passage,
where water has carved the gypsum floor into
spiky-edged blocks.*

ORNATELY FASHIONED *In Tower Place cavern, majestic 50ft (15m) columns rise from floor to ceiling.*

rime-covered fir trees, and others that look rather like elegantly draped cloths.

It seems strange that this extraordinary wonderland was not discovered until the 1980s. In 1914 some local men made short-lived attempts to mine the bat guano (droppings), found just inside the cave entrance, for use as a fertiliser. Over the years, the occasional curious caver ventured in, but not until 1986 did a group of cavers make the final breakthrough. They had been intrigued by strong winds that blew in the entrance, signalling the existence of much larger caves deeper down. After digging away some floor debris they found an almost vertical shaft which they named Boulder Falls after the boulders which fell as they descended. Beyond lay the maze of beautifully decorated caves.

Exploration of Lechuguilla has been slow and meticulous, and not just because of the difficult terrain and deep lakes to be negotiated. The cavers are also intensely aware of how fragile the decorations are, and the changes that they themselves could introduce, such as draughts and temperature increases.

HUMAN HAZARDS

No matter how carefully the cavers place their feet, it is impossible not to crush or dirty some of the pristine surfaces. The many decorations that are made from gypsum (used in making plaster of Paris) are exceptionally fragile – a careless move could damage or destroy a formation that has taken several million years to develop. Even the slight drying out of the atmosphere caused by enlarging the cave entrance could decay the glittering gypsum decorations, and may ultimately weaken them to the point where they collapse.

The cavers have a strict code of conduct. Wherever possible, they walk barefoot to avoid dirtying the cave floors, but they have to be careful not to cut their feet where the floor is jagged in case they leave bloodstains. All waste is removed in plastic bags, and no-one

washes in the pools of pure water.

Most limestone caves form when slightly acidic rainwater seeps down through the ground, but Lechuguilla seems to have been formed from the bottom up. Gas from deep oil deposits rose through cracks in the rocks and mixed with oxygen and water. The result was sulphuric acid that reacted with the limestone, dissolving out the warren of passages and creating gypsum in the same reaction. Over several million years, the caves have been decorated with minerals carried through the labyrinth dissolved in water – both calcite stalactites and stalagmites and the many gypsum decorations. Gypsum formations of breathtaking beauty hang in the Chandelier Ballroom. They formed when deposits of the mineral higher up in the cave system were dissolved by water, which

STRANDS OF GYPSUM, AS FINE AS HUMAN HAIR AND 20FT (6M) LONG

GEMS *Cave pearls – smooth spheres of calcite – have been formed in a cavern known as the Pearlsian Gulf (right).*

seeped down through the cave roof and evaporated, leaving growths of crystals.

Cave experts have argued that the Lechuguilla Cave should be open only to researchers, and not to the public, to preserve this Aladdin's Cave of treasures in an unspoiled state.

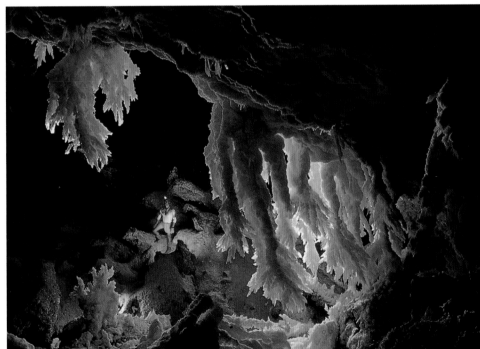

LIGHT FANTASTIC *Delicate creations of gypsum hang from the Chandelier Ballroom's roof. Some of these uniquely large chandeliers are 20ft (6m) long.*

Grand Canyon

THE STRIPED ROCKS OF
THE COLORADO RIVER'S
PLUNGING CHASM
RECORD 2 BILLION YEARS
OF EARTH'S HISTORY

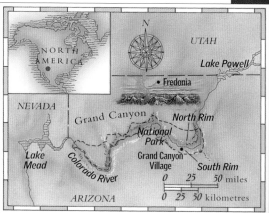

A little blue biplane bumping over the floor of a featureless desert is depicted in a film made to illustrate the capabilities of IMAX – the ultramodern cinema with the five-storey, wrap-around screen. Suddenly, shockingly, the biplane reaches the rim of Grand Canyon and goes down over the edge. And you go with it, twisting and tumbling into that incredible abyss.

But no film can prepare you for the awesome impact of the canyon itself. Even blasé busloads of teenagers are muted by the existence of something so vast, so old, so serene and so silent. This tremendous trench carved by the Colorado River is a dizzying 1 mile (1.6km) deep and 9 miles (15km) wide, on average, and stretches for some 280 miles (450km). At any given 13 mile (21km) stretch, you could drop in the entire island of Manhattan and still need field glasses to inspect the tops of the skyscrapers beneath you.

Its moods and colours change with the hours and the seasons. At dawn, the

SUNSET SPECTACULAR *An electrical storm dances along the edge of the canyon's South Rim. Such summer displays often cause brush fires.*

striped rocks on the opposite rim – far distant yet seemingly close enough to touch – are lacquered silver-gold above the blue chasms below. Spring mornings fill the depths with mist that looks solid enough to snowshoe on; moonlight floods the distances with white and indigo; and sunset flushes the upper cliffs to deepest rose.

Most rain evaporates before it reaches the bottom of the chasm, so

COLORADO TRIBUTARY *For centuries, the Havasupai have lived beside the falls in Havasu Creek (left). The tribal name means 'Blue-green water people'.*

down beside the river the terrain is arid desert. By contrast, the North Rim, which is considerably higher than the South Rim, is covered by Arctic snows until well into May. Between these two extremes the climatic shadings range through tundra, temperate woodland and coniferous forest. As when climbing a mountain, every 1000ft (300m) of elevation produces a climatic change comparable to a 300 mile (500km) journey northwards over the flat.

This variation allows a rich range of wildlife – mountain animals such as bighorn sheep become near neighbours of such desert creatures as rattlesnakes. And the canyon's great divide ensures that certain animals never meet – tassel-eared squirrels of the North Rim are a quite different subspecies from those of the South Rim.

UPLIFT AND EROSION

Years ago, they say, a wandering cowboy peered down into the canyon's fearsome depths and exclaimed: 'Something sure happened here!' Like many a visitor since, he could not credit that the canyon was shaped mainly by the ribbon of river at its base. Only closer inspection reveals that here the Colorado can be a raging torrent, bearing with it tens of thousands of tons of sediment a day – 'Too thick to drink, too thin to plough', the old settlers used to complain. The valley's width is largely due to tributaries fed by melting snow, aided by 5 million years of erosion by wind, frost and rain. The deep, central slash is the work of the Colorado.

It is reasonable to assume, as did the early explorers, that the river, over aeons, simply burrowed its way down to its present depth. In fact, the river stands more or less where it always did, at about 2000ft (600m) above sea level. It was the land that gradually rose, but so slowly that the scouring power of the Colorado enabled it to maintain its original place while the walls of the chasm climbed high on either bank.

The canyon's story is written in the differing ages of rocks as they emerge

CANYON WALLS *From the heights of Toroweap Overlook on the North Rim, the Colorado River can be seen winding its way nearly 3000ft (900m) below.*

layer upon layer from the depths. Lowest of all is the Inner Gorge, where the Colorado runs. Two billion years ago, the dark rock here was part of a mountain range as high as the Himalayas. The mountains were worn down to a plain and replaced by a shallow sea. Limestone deposited on the sea floor contains the fossils of plankton that are 1 billion years old.

Upwards, the diary of the rocks tells of ancient cataclysms in which mountains were worn away to be drowned by muddy flood plains where amphibians and reptiles left their footprints. There are layers that were once marshes and desert and further ancient seas in which corals lived. The river did not begin its scouring until 6 million years ago. Yet when lava spread down one end of the gorge less than a million years ago, the canyon was already within 50ft (15m) of its present depth.

Visitors who study the layered pages of this diary of Earth may find the subject matter too enormous to comprehend. Most will feel an awed glow at seeing its secrets revealed.

WINTRY DAYBREAK *Sunrise lights up the snow at Mather Point on the canyon's South Rim, where heavy snow is rarer than on the North Rim.*

DEFYING THE CANYON'S DANGERS

The name of Major John Wesley Powell, a one-armed American Civil War veteran, will always be associated with Grand Canyon. He led the first expedition down the Colorado River in May 1869 – a small party of nine men in four boats. One boat, carrying most of the provisions, was sunk in the first week, but the explorers pressed on and entered Grand Canyon on August 4.

There followed exhausting days of fighting rapids and fending off rocks, the hazards made worse by the sense of moving always into the unknown. On August 28, three of the men would go no farther and climbed out of the canyon, only to be killed by Native Americans. Ironically, next day the boats emerged into the calm waters of the lower Colorado. The river had been conquered – but at a price.

WESTERNERS *The Major and a Paiute brave.*

RIDING THE RIVER *Powell's boats lunge through the canyon on their epic Colorado journey.*

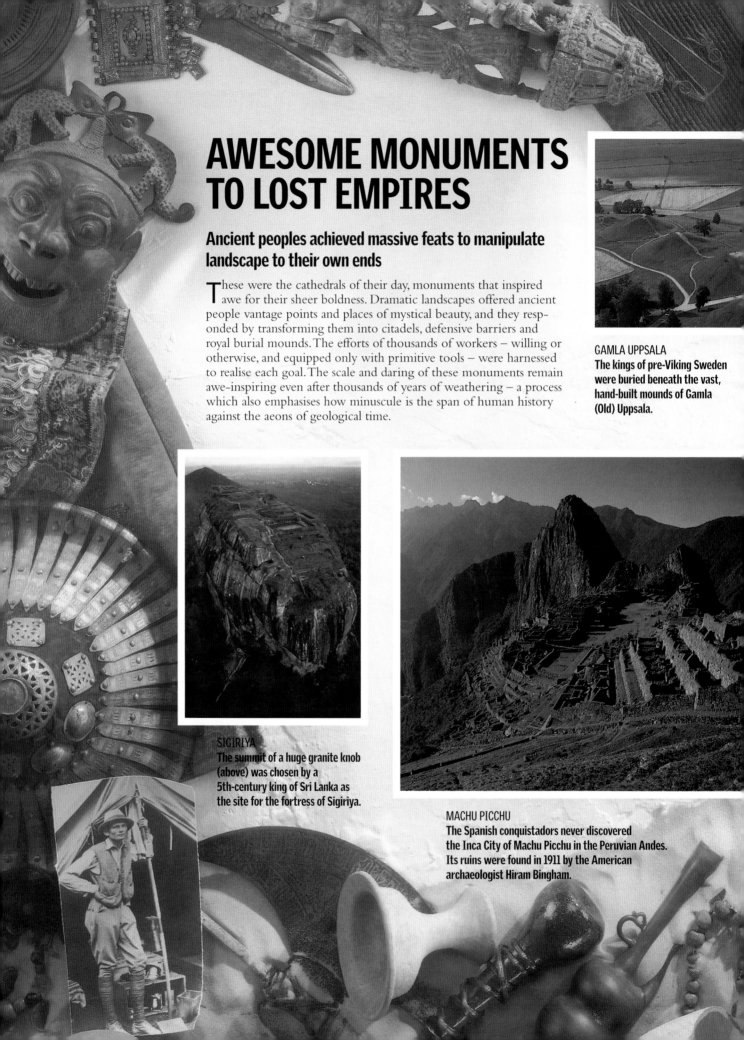

AWESOME MONUMENTS TO LOST EMPIRES

Ancient peoples achieved massive feats to manipulate landscape to their own ends

These were the cathedrals of their day, monuments that inspired awe for their sheer boldness. Dramatic landscapes offered ancient people vantage points and places of mystical beauty, and they responded by transforming them into citadels, defensive barriers and royal burial mounds. The efforts of thousands of workers – willing or otherwise, and equipped only with primitive tools – were harnessed to realise each goal. The scale and daring of these monuments remain awe-inspiring even after thousands of years of weathering – a process which also emphasises how minuscule is the span of human history against the aeons of geological time.

GAMLA UPPSALA
The kings of pre-Viking Sweden were buried beneath the vast, hand-built mounds of Gamla (Old) Uppsala.

SIGIRIYA
The summit of a huge granite knob (above) was chosen by a 5th-century king of Sri Lanka as the site for the fortress of Sigiriya.

MACHU PICCHU
The Spanish conquistadors never discovered the Inca City of Machu Picchu in the Peruvian Andes. Its ruins were found in 1911 by the American archaeologist Hiram Bingham.

MAIDEN CASTLE
Earth ramparts were built round the Iron-Age Maiden Castle in southern England about 100 BC (above).

RELIGIOUS SYMBOL
Great Serpent Mound in Ohio (above) was probably a religious symbol of the Adena people 2000 years ago.

HADRIAN'S WALL
The Romans exploited the crest of a natural rock sill (above) when they built Hadrian's Wall in AD 122–9, creating a barrier across the neck of England.

DUN AENGUS FORT
A prehistoric fort, Dun Aengus in Ireland (right), perches on the edge of a cliff 250ft (75m) above the Atlantic.

Meteor Crater

ABOUT 50,000 YEARS AGO
A MASSIVE METEORITE
BLEW A GIANT HOLE IN
THE EARTH IN THE
ARIZONA WILDERNESS

STAR SCAR *The crater was gouged into the Arizona plains by a meteorite four times as heavy as any ocean liner.*

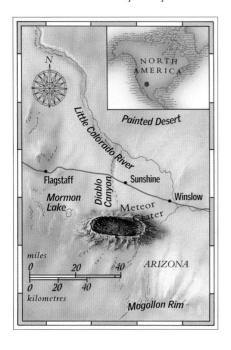

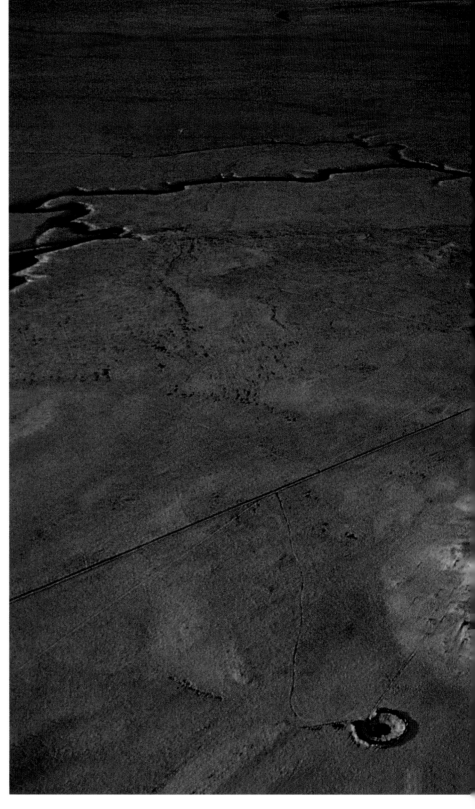

From the plains beside it, the rim of Meteor Crater looks like a low hill, giving no hint of the immense hollow it surrounds. Blasted out when a giant meteorite struck the ground here around 50,000 years ago, the crater is about ¾ mile (1.2km) across and 600ft (180m) deep, with a rim rising 150ft (45m) above the plain. Its floor is so like the Moon's terrain that Apollo astronauts trained there, and it was a testing ground for lunar vehicles.

Scientists estimate the meteorite's speed as 45,000mph (72,000km/h), and that on impact it exploded with a force a thousand times greater than the nuclear bomb dropped on Hiroshima in 1945. It sent 5 or 6 million tons of rock and earth hurtling heavenwards and blocked out the sunlight. After the

impact, the meteorite – a mass of nickel-iron reckoned to be some 130ft (40m) across and more than 300,000 tons in weight – disintegrated and melted. Remnants have been found within a 6 mile (10km) radius.

The crater was once thought to be volcanic, but a Philadelphian mining

engineer named Daniel Barringer was one of the first to recognise it as a meteorite crater. In the belief that it was rich in nickel and iron, he staked a claim there in 1902 and spent a fortune trying unsuccessfully to mine it. Today the crater is also known as the Barringer Crater, and is still owned by his family.

On average, large meteorites fall to Earth about once every 1300 years. The world's largest intact meteorite, which probably also fell in prehistoric times, weighs 60 tons and lies near the town of Grootfontein in Namibia. The second largest, 30 tons, fell in west Greenland.

'BOMB' DISPOSAL
A 30-ton meteorite was removed from Greenland by the Arctic explorer Robert E. Peary in the late 1890s. It is now in the Museum of Natural History, New York.

Canyon de Chelly

TOWERING ROCK WALLS THAT NURTURED THE BELIEFS OF THE NAVAJOS ALSO GUARD THE MYSTERY OF A LONG-VANISHED PEOPLE

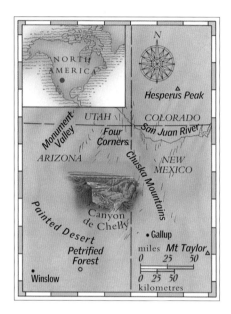

In the land of Four Corners, where Utah, Colorado, Arizona and New Mexico meet, geological extravaganzas are the norm – hence the many national parks and monuments that dot the map. Even among these, the Canyon de Chelly (pronounced 'de Shay') is special because of its serenity, its seclusion and the profound effect it has had on the lives and beliefs of the peoples who have lived there.

The Canyon is not a single valley but a labyrinth of canyons, which were carved by slow-moving rivers deep into the red sandstone of the Defiance Plateau. The canyon walls, varying in depth anywhere between 30ft (9m) and 1000ft (300m), are not only sheer but incredibly smooth. They look exactly as though a confectioner, working with red icing, had finished off the job with a single expert sweep of a palette knife. The dark streaks resembling paint runs that mark the canyon walls are known

NIGHT AND DAY *Sunset gilds the canyon rim while its floor is already deep in shadow. (Inset) Nanaja sheep follow a centuries-old trail.*

as 'desert varnish'. They have been left by centuries of mineral-laden water flowing down the rock face.

Although frost erodes the canyon rims, sending boulders crashing to the bottom, there is little debris – after a while the boulders disintegrate into their component sand, which simply blows away. So the broad canyon floors have a spruce and well-kempt appearance, especially in spring when silver streams wind in and out among their sandbanks, and the small orchards of the Navajo people who live here are bright with apple and peach blossom.

Despite its chilly winters, the Canyon de Chelly has always invited settlement. At the foot of the towering cliffs there are often deep recesses. In a few of them

stand the ruined stone buildings of an ancient race that vanished around AD 1300. They are known only as the Anasazi – a name given to them by the Navajo, who arrived after them, and which means 'the Ancient Ones'.

HOLY HOMELAND

It was the Spanish who came in the 1500s who gave the tough, resourceful local people the name Navajo. They call themselves Dineh, simply 'The People'. Their sacred homeland is all of the country round

about, bounded by the four holy peaks of San Francisco, Hesperus, Blanca and Mount Taylor.

The canyon's odd name is a corruption of a Navajo word meaning rock valley. Here, beside the Anasazi inscriptions, the Navajo have recorded their own version of Creation, tales of the Yei – holy beings who inhabited Earth before First Woman and First Man emerged from the underworld. The stories are painted or incised in pictures on the walls of caves and on walls above rock ledges.

SILVER BELT *A Navajo silversmith of the 1870s shows a hammered silver shell belt (above). The Navajo took up the craft in the 1860s, flattening US coins.*

Tucked into recesses in the cliffs of Canyon de Chelly are the still imposing ruins of complex stone buildings with tall towers and underground ceremonial chambers. The builders, known only by the Navajo term Anasazi, lived in the area from about AD 100 to about 1300.

Not only were the Anasazi accomplished builders, they were also great farmers, weavers of cotton, basket-makers and potters, who traded as far away as Mexico and the Pacific coast. The reason why they vanished late in the 13th century will never be known, perhaps it was because they faced drought and starvation. Only their buildings mark their passing.

NICHE IN TIME *The White House has sheltered in a large rock cave for nearly a thousand years.*

ROCK TOWER *Spider Rock is the Navajo name for this 800ft (244m) sandstone pillar in Canyon de Chelly. It is said to be the home of the holy Spider Woman.*

Here, too, from the stronghold of the canyon, the Navajo waged war on successive invaders – first the Spanish, who retaliated by massacring 115 Navajo men, women and children in one of the canyon's caves in 1805, and then US settlers. The response of the US government was, in 1863, to send cavalry units under Colonel Kit Carson. They starved the Navajo into submission, and some 7000 of them were marched into captivity in New Mexico, a journey of 200 miles (320km) still bitterly remembered as the Long Walk.

Four years later, the government relented, and the Navajo were returned to their homeland, now officially allocated as the Navajo Reservation. It is a land in which every rock, every natural object is woven into Navajo beliefs.

Chief among them is the conviction that all Creation is one, and that by being in harmony with his surroundings, Man can achieve the ultimate goal of unification with the beauty of the whole. In the serenity of the canyon, it is easy to see how such beliefs might arise.

Not far from the Canyon de Chelly is the Petrified Forest National Park, a desert landscape littered with tree trunks that have been lying there for 225 million years. They grew, flourished, and eventually died early in the Age of Dinosaurs, when this part of Arizona was tropical marsh.

The fallen logs, buried in sediment, absorbed silica from the ground water, which gradually replaced their organic matter with hard, rainbow-coloured agate. Gradually the petrified trees were eroded out of their soft stone covering, along with the fossilised remains of ferns, fishes and reptiles – a striking catalogue of the world when young.

Death Valley

THIS DESERT FRYING PAN HOLDS NOT ONE RECORD
BUT THREE – IT IS THE HOTTEST, DRIEST AND LOWEST
PLACE IN NORTH AMERICA

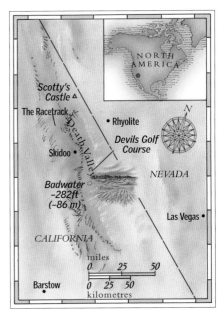

Deadman Pass, Dry Bone Canyon, Funeral Mountains – the very place names of California's Death Valley are sinister. This is North America's hottest, driest area – a place of baking summer heat where a whole year can pass without a drop of rain.

On summer days, the thermometer routinely rises to 43°C (110°F), and temperatures reaching more than 49°C (120°F) have been recorded daily for a period of just over six weeks. When rain comes, it is often in sudden downpours that flood the heat-baked ground with torrents of water and mud.

SHIFTING SANDS *Death Valley's brisk wind blows sand into intricate patterns (left). Yet the desert primrose (above) can flourish even in this barren land.*

343

Death Valley claims another record at its lowest point, 282ft (86m) below sea level, it is the lowest place on the North American continent. It formed when huge blocks of land sank downwards along fault lines, while adjacent blocks rose to form the neighbouring mountains. This deep trench, with its very low-lying floor, acts as a sheltered sun trap within an area that is already hot and dry, and in the rain shadow of the Sierra Nevada mountains.

Everywhere there is evidence that the climate was once much wetter. Canyons cut into the valley walls were created by torrents of running water,

CRAZY PAVING *Rare outbursts of rain leave a layer of mud that cracks as it dries out under the fierce sun.*

and there are great fans of sediment that was washed down from the surrounding peaks. Salt deposits on the valley floor were left behind after lakes evaporated, and at the Devil's Golf Course salt has been eroded by wind and rain into jagged spires.

Yet despite the hostile surroundings, Death Valley is far from devoid of life. Bighorn sheep can live on very little water, sidewinder snakes move in 'jumps' that keep their bodies clear of the hot ground, and the stems and leaves of the rare, white-flowered rocklady are covered with hairs that insulate them from the desiccating wind. Even the few brackish streams and ponds support life – tiny pupfish that can cope with salty water.

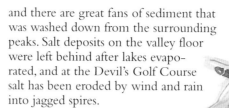

SURVIVORS *Bighorn sheep that live in the valley need very little water – even in the scorching heat of summer they need to drink only once every three days.*

A party of gold prospectors bound for California visited Death Valley by accident in 1849, and their experiences gave the place its name. They left the trail, hoping to find a short cut, but instead found themselves struggling down a barren, almost waterless valley which had no obvious way out. One woman wrote later of how her little boys 'bore up bravely, though they could barely talk, so dry and swollen were their lips and tongues'.

Two of the group found a route out of the valley and returned to guide their companions to safety. As they left, one of them delivered the parting shot, 'Goodbye, Death Valley'.

A myth grew up about the horrors of Death Valley. Greatly embellished stories were told of wagon trains of people dying in torments of thirst, yet prospectors were still drawn there by rumours of gold and silver.

In the boom and bust days that followed, fortunes were made, but more often lost, in short-lived mining ventures. Settlements mushroomed and were deserted a few years later when the mines ran out – Skidoo, site of a very profitable gold mine, had 500 inhabitants at its peak in the early 1900s. It had a telephone link with Rhyolite, just outside the valley, which in 1906 had a swimming pool, an opera house and 56 saloons. By 1911 Rhyolite had been abandoned, and slowly decayed into a ghost town.

Though gold mining had little long-term success in Death Valley, the same was not true of borax. During the 1880s, the 'white gold', one of whose many uses was in pottery glazes, was scraped from the valley floor. Mule teams then hauled it to the railhead, 165 miles (265km) away from the harsh, yet austerely beautiful Death Valley.

HARSH LAND *Rugged hills with deeply etched gullies rise on either side of Death Valley's floor. There is little vegetation to soften the severe outlines.*

ROCKS THAT SLIDE

A track over parched ground leads to a boulder and stops. This track is straight; others trace wandering curves or zigzag over the ground. The tracks are on a dried lake bed called The Racetrack, where randomly scattered boulders have all moved over a completely level surface. The most likely explanation is that the ground becomes slippery after rain, strong winds push the boulders along and paths form in their wake.

White Sands

BLONDE MICE AND
WHITE LIZARDS BLEND
INTO THE BACKGROUND
IN A DESERT OF MILK-
WHITE DUNES

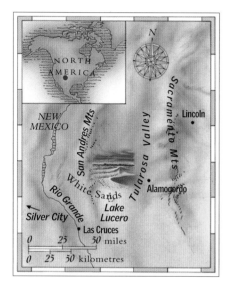

SHADOW SHOW *Evening light (above) colours the dunes a mysterious blue. Sunset shadows (right) show up the wave formation of the wind-rippled sands.*

Shimmering white dunes, shaped and contoured by the wind into smoothly rounded crescents, stretch endlessly before the eyes of wanderers in the White Sands. But this is unusual sand – not the usual quartz, but gypsum. White Sands is the world's most impressive gypsum desert. About 300sq miles (780km²) in extent, it lies in the flat-floored Tularosa Valley in New Mexico, and much of it has been a US National Monument since 1933. No one ever exploited its gypsum; the area was too remote, and gypsum was too plentiful elsewhere.

Gypsum is a white mineral used in cement and plaster manufacture, and massive layers of gypsum rock exist in the mountains that surround White Sands. Centuries of erosion by rain and melting snow have carried rock debris down to Lake Lucero, the lowest part of the basin, to mix with water that seeps up from the valley floor. Sun and wind evaporate the water to leave a dry bed of coarse encrusted gypsum, and this is ground by the wind into fine particles.

These are blown into dunes that can grow 100ft (30m) high. Slowly the wind shifts the dunes north-east, sometimes at the rate of about 20ft (6m) a year.

This arid, dazzling landscape below a wide, blue sky and relentless sun evokes the Old West – the Rio Grande is not far away. Mescalero Apaches came here to gather on the alkali flats, and there are still plaster casts of their campfires – the heated gypsum formed plaster of Paris, which was set by rain.

Silver City, west of the San Andres Mountains, was the birthplace in 1859 of William H. Bonney, better known as Billy the Kid. The outlaw was only 21 years old when he was shot dead by Sheriff Pat Garrett after escaping from jail in Lincoln, New Mexico. White Sands also features in another footnote to the history of conflict. During World War II, the Tularosa Basin was a bomb range. On July 16, 1945, the first nuclear bomb, made at Los Alamos to the north, was tested near Alamogordo.

Some plants succeed in scratching sustenance from this shifting wilderness. Cottonwood trees thrust defiantly skywards, sometimes with just their heads above a dune. When the dune

moves on, they may be left encased in a plaster cast. Similarly, skunkbush sumacs sit on stools of hardened gypsum. Soaptree yuccas survive by pushing snake-like stems through the dunes. Their creamy, bell-shaped flowers, known as 'Candle of the Lord', are New Mexico's State flower. Native Americans ate the shoots and flowers and made porridge from their seeds.

BLEACHED COLOURING

Few large animals venture into the white desert – it offers little food and no shelter from the killing midday heat. Sands pocket gophers thrive because they burrow into the sand away from the heat. Apache pocket mice shelter in gopher burrows. Along with three kinds of lizard – particularly the bleached earless lizard – these pocket mice have developed bleached white colouring that camouflages them from predators such as owls and hawks.

Unlike the Westerners of old, who braved the heat and the sandstorms on foot or horseback, modern visitors to White Sands can drive through the area along a signposted route. But sandstorms sometimes slow traffic, and drifting dunes may bury the road.

CAMOUFLAGE EXPERT *When hunting near an ants nest, the bleached earless lizard can make its skin so white it is hard to see against the white dunes. But it can darken its body again in shady areas.*

Mammoth Cave

THIS GIGANTIC LIMESTONE LABYRINTH, THE WORLD'S LONGEST CAVE, HAS UNDERGROUND RIVERS, LAKES AND 'FROZEN STONE WATERFALLS'

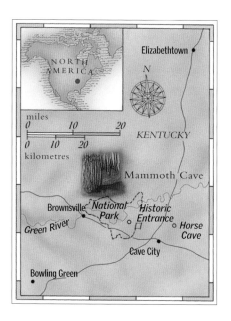

Mammoth Cave owes its name to its size, not to relics of long-gone mammoths. Carved from limestone hills in Kentucky by trickles of acidic water over millions of years, the cave has some 330 miles (530km) of passages, possibly more, on five levels.

Native Americans knew this fantastic underground world some 4000 years ago – stone spearheads and burial remains have been found there. The earliest cavers lit the way with cane reed torches. Visitors today can view some of the scenery by electric light. It varies from vast halls such as the Rotunda, as spacious as New York's Grand Central Station, to narrow passages such as Fat Man's Misery, only 18in (460mm) wide. Boat trippers on the Echo River, 360ft (110m) below ground, can test its resonant echoes. Frozen Niagara is a series of chambers where colourful stalagmites and stalactites look like waterfalls turned to stone.

European settlers first came to Mammoth Cave in the 1790s, and during the War of 1812 between the US and Britain its nitrate deposits were mined to make gunpowder. In 1843 the cave was briefly and unsuccessfully used as a tuberculosis hospital because of its dry climate and equable temperature – around 12°C (54°F). By then it had become a tourist attraction; its first guide and explorer was a slave named Stephen Bishop, who lit the way with a kerosene lantern. Now the cave is part of an 80sq mile (207km²) national park, with guided underground tours.

SUBTERRANEAN SCENERY *Mammoth Cave's cathedral-like caverns, intriguing rock formations and natural stone sculptures (left), were popular with late 19th-century tourists. Outings often included an underground picnic (below).*

Everglades

RARE PANTHERS,
CROCODILES AND OTTERS
SURVIVE IN THE
DEPTHS OF FLORIDA'S
WARM AND WATERY
WILDERNESS

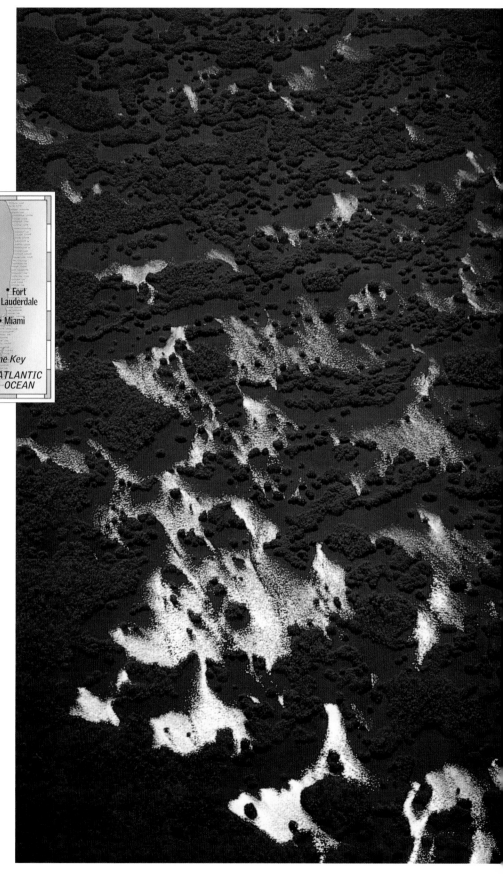

American writer Marjory Stoneman
Douglas has described Florida's
Everglades as 'one of the unique regions
of the earth, remote, never wholly
known'. She tells of 'their vast glittering
openness ... the racing free saltness and
sweetness of their massive winds, under
the dazzling blue heights of space', and
the 'miracle of the light ... over the green
and brown expanse of saw grass and of
water, shining and slow – moving below'.

The Native Americans of southern
Florida, the Seminoles, called the
Everglades Pa-hay-okee, or 'grassy
waters'. Much of the area is flat, low-
lying and waterlogged, a prairie of saw
grass (tooth-edged sedge) that grows up
to 12ft (4m) high. But there are also
trees – dense subtropical forest and dark
cypress swamps that give the feeling a
dinosaur might still be lurking in their
silent, secret depths. The largest of the
many creatures that dwell here,
however, are alligators and crocodiles,
panthers, black bears, river otters and

MANGROVE MAZE *Countless clumps of
mangroves flourish in the Ten Thousand
Islands of the Everglades estuary.
Their roots shelter many sea creatures.*

STEAMY SWAMP *Snakes and alligators live among the bald cypresses of the Big Cypress Swamp. It also shelters the very rare Florida panther.*

white-tailed deer. Since 1947 part of the area has been a national park.

The heart of the Everglades is a shallow river some 100 miles (160km) long and about half as wide, dotted with low-lying islands, or hammocks. The river's source is Lake Okeechobee, which is less than knee-deep but about 720sq miles (1865km²) in extent. At the height of the June–October rainy season, as much as 12in (300mm) of rain can fall in a day, and the lake overflow (controlled by dykes) feeds the river. Other springs and streams top up the river, too, and its limestone bed tilts gently down to Florida Bay at the tip of the peninsula.

The profuse greenery of the hammocks includes trees such as live oak (an evergreen), mahogany, cocoplum, cabbage palm and gumbo limbo (a type of pine). The bark of the gumbo limbo is red and peeling, like sunburnt skin, earning it the nickname

> ### 'VAST GLITTERING OPENNESS … THE DAZZLING BLUE HEIGHTS OF SPACE'
> Marjory Stoneman Douglas

of 'tourist tree'. When the saw grass disappears beneath the floods, or when drought dries up the river, these islands are refuges for many animals. The area has also been a refuge for people.

Until the early 1800s, neither the 16th-century Spanish explorers nor the early American settlers had ventured far into the Everglades. Native Americans lived there in thatched houses on raised platforms. They were hunter-gatherers and also planted gardens on the hammocks, a name derived from their word for garden place. The Seminole Indian Wars began about 1817, when settlers from Europe began to encroach on the area. In 1835 the US government tried to get the Seminoles to move to Oklahoma, and sparked off the Second Seminole War. Under the leadership of Osceola, many fought a guerrilla war in the swamps and marshes. But in 1837 Osceola was

imprisoned when he went with other chiefs to parley under a flag of truce. He died a year later and resistance faded.

The saw-grass prairies teem with life. On one sedge blade you may see a bright green frog, on another what looks like a large black seed pod that breaks open to reveal a cluster of grasshoppers. Tropical zebra butterflies frequent the hammocks in summer, and the sparkling waters are alive with fish, tadpoles and molluscs such as snails the size of golf balls.

The abundant waterlife makes the Everglades one of the world's best bird sanctuaries. In the 1880s, as more settlers came in, thousands of birds were killed for their feathers, but in 1905 a law was passed protecting non-game birds in the region. More than 350 species of bird now live in these marshes or visit them regularly, including roseate spoonbills, spindly

REDCOATS *Cypress trees clothed in red by harmless baton rouge lichens give an exotic air to the eerie forest. Air plants and ferns add to the jungle atmosphere.*

their 'knees' – clusters of small stumps that grow from the roots. They are thought to be the means by which the tree roots take in oxygen. The wooded ridge of Long Pine Key, east of the river, is all that remains of a palm and pine forest.

As the river crawls southwards, the sea comes to meet it, as if impatient with its dawdling pace. Together they make a singular brew of saltwater and freshwater. Red mangroves thrive in the saltwater because their roots rise above the ooze, so can take in air. Their inter-locking roots form a water-level barrier that traps so much silt, flotsam and jetsam that it forms new islands.

Fish, terrapins, dolphins and young sharks seek these sultry waters and shelter among the mangrove roots. Olive-green American crocodiles, which have longer, narrower snouts than alligators, live here, too, but all you are likely to see is a shadow in the water. This is now their sole habitat in the USA.

TURN OF THE TIDE

More graceful shapes glide through the seas flanking the Florida peninsula, and some find their way into the mangrove swamps of Whitewater Bay. They are manatees, or sea cows, around 10ft (3m) long and weighing nearly half a ton. The bustling water traffic around the coast has been the death of many sea cows, and many more bear scars from motor-boat propellers. Only about 3000 manatees are left in Florida, and protection schemes are under way.

Not only the manatees bear the scars of civilisation. In the early 1900s the settlers discovered that the layers of dead saw grass, known as muck, made excellent compost, and irrigating and draining began. Now nearly a quarter of the Everglades is farmland, and canals divert and control the water. This disturbs the delicately balanced natural rhythms of water and wildlife. But the tide of destruction is turning and Lake Okeechobee, poisoned by agricultural pollution, is being cleaned up.

legged fishers such as herons, snowy egrets, white ibises, and the cormorant-like anhinga, or snakebird. Lurking alligators up to 16ft (5m) long eat everything from snails to deer. But in the dry season they also provide life-saving drinks for other thirsty animals when they dig themselves water holes by thrashing with their heads and tails.

On its western flank the river passes the Big Cypress Swamp, which borders the Gulf of Mexico and covers an area about half the size of Jamaica. Bald cypress trees rise tall from the water. Sticking up around them are

FRIENDLY FLORIDIANS
Placid manatees graze on plants under water, eating up to 200lb (90kg) a day. They go to the surface regularly to breathe.

Mono Lake

FAIRY-TALE ROCK TOWERS RISE FROM A VAST AND SALTY LAKE RINGED BY CALIFORNIA'S SNOW-CAPPED MOUNTAINS

Weird pinnacles of rock seem to float like a mirage on the brilliant blue waters of Mono Lake, which gleams like a jewel in a setting of sand flats and sage brush ringed by mountains. 'A country of wonderful contrasts, hot deserts bordered by snow-laden mountains,' was how the area was described by John Muir, the 19th-century American naturalist.

Nearly three times saltier than the sea, Mono Lake takes its name from a native American word for brine flies, which it supports by the million – it is too salty

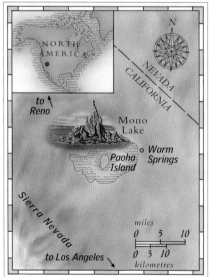

for fish. Local people who ate the fly larvae were known in Shoshone language as Monachi, or fly eaters. The water has a soapy feel and is very buoyant to swim in. After visiting Mono

Lake, the 19th-century American writer Mark Twain said the water was so strong with alkali that even a hopelessly soiled garment could be washed clean.

A party of fur-trappers led by Captain Joseph Walker, who was a well-known mountain man of the time, were the first Europeans to describe the lake. They were heading west for the mountains from Wyoming, and according to Zenas Leonard, one of the party, they came upon it in October 1833 as they stood on a high ridge so they could survey the 'frightening grandeur' of the Sierras.

Below them was a vast blue bowl of water sitting in the middle of a desert; they went down for a closer inspection, and found the water bitter. There was no sign of life except for millions of worm-like creatures wriggling about in the water and the drifts of flies along the shore. Rafts of hard but sponge-like rock floated on the surface, and there were strange spires and columns of a

different soft rock, which had a Swiss cheese appearance, underneath the water and rising just above it. Hot water springs rose along the shore, and there were blackened, pitted rocks from volcanic action to the south.

Mono Lake is some 60sq miles (155km²) in extent and more than 700,000 years old. Its basin was formed by earth movements and volcanic action during the birth of the Sierra Nevada Mountains. The steam vents and hot springs in the lake basin show that there is still some volcanic activity. Paoha Island in the middle of the lake was formed by volcanic action about 200 years ago.

Freshwater springs and melting snow feed the lake with water. It has no natural outlet, and its saltiness results from the salts and minerals washed in over thousands of years. The pinnacles jutting from the lake surface are of tufa (pronounced toofah), a type of limestone. It slowly builds up in columns above the freshwater springs in the lake bottom as calcium from the spring water combines with carbonates in the alkaline lake water. The tufa columns stop growing when the water level drops and they become exposed.

CONFLICT OF INTERESTS

Since 1941, the lake's water level has dropped nearly 40ft (12m). This is because four of the seven meltwater streams that flow in from the mountains have been diverted to supply water to Los Angeles, 275 miles (443km) to the south. This has robbed Mono Lake of more than half of its water supply. Consequently it has shrunk and become saltier, and the dry, dusty alkali flats around it have become more extensive.

Scientists fear that further draining will harm both the lake and its wildlife. Along with the brine flies the water teems with brine shrimps, but increasing salinity could kill them off. Both flies and shrimps feed on the algae (microscopic plants) that flourish there and turn the water from blue to green when they bloom in winter. Nesting California gulls and snowy plovers feast on the flies and shrimps, as do millions of migratory birds – some 80 species in all, including eared grebes, Wilson's phalaropes and red-necked phalaropes.

Mark Twain, who in 1863 nearly drowned in Lake Mono in a storm, was not impressed with it at all. He dubbed it the Dead Sea of California, and wrote: 'This solemn, silent, sailless sea – this lonely tenant of the loneliest spot on earth – is little graced with the picturesque.' Few who have seen the lake share this view. Most are captivated by its stunning setting and haunting beauty.

Bisti Wilderness

WEIRDLY SCULPTED ROCKS STAND IN A HARSH MOONSCAPE WHERE DINOSAURS ONCE LUMBERED THROUGH SWAMPY RAINFOREST

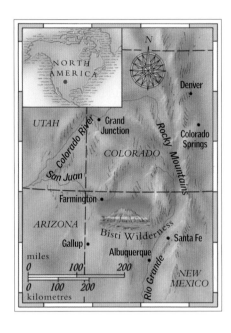

Midnight. Total silence – not even the sound of crickets or frogs. The sky above the high New Mexico plateau in the southern United States is so clear that the Moon and the Milky Way drench the landscape in an eerie light. Then a coyote howls out across the Bisti Wilderness, followed by another and another, rising to a full chorus. One by one the voices fall silent, leaving only the originator of this ghostly performance. In their nightly serenade, 'song dogs' add an uncanny dimension to an already bizarre scene.

Amid the Bisti's rolling dunes and dried-up riverbeds stands a natural art gallery rich in fantasy rock sculptures. Armless stone monsters balance their ill-proportioned heads upon spindly necks. Enormous mushrooms might have escaped from Alice's Wonderland, and outlandish pillars and spires look like creations for a Salvador Dali theme park. Appropriately, the figures are called *hoodoos* – an African word that means 'spirit'. And scattered among them are 80-million-year-old fossils of cypress tree stumps, palm fronds and dinosaurs.

Looking around this silent and barren landscape with little trace of plant or animal life, it is hard to imagine that it was once a humid swamp teeming with life that lay near the edge of a vast inland sea. Dinosaurs crashed their way through the steamy rainforests thick with huge trees and ferns – among them dinosaurs with duck-bills, five-horned giants, and fierce carnivorous tyrannosaurs that feasted on smaller reptiles. The first mammals lived there, too – opossum-like creatures the size of rats.

Animal bones and remains of plants were buried in the swamp's sand and mud, which compacted over millions of years to form sandstone and shale.

FIERCE CARNIVOROUS TYRANNOSAURS FEASTED ON SMALLER REPTILES

Rotting vegetation was gradually transformed into peat and coal. Shifts in the Earth's plates and changes in climate later led to the rocks being raised to form a high and dry plateau. Wind and occasional downpours of torrential rain then sculpted the rocks into the hoodoos that now populate the Bisti, and exposed the fossilised remains of more than 200 plant and animal species.

The Bisti Wilderness has provided scientists with a snapshot of a dramatic turning point in the Earth's history. The fossils uncovered there include remains of both dinosaurs and mammals, and record the end of the 140-million-year dynasty of dinosaurs and the beginning of the Earth's domination by furry, warm-blooded mammals.

MOONLIT SCENE *Hoodoos of the Bisti Wilderness stand about like strangely silent late-night revellers, wearing their capstones of more weather-resistant rock.*

It is only relatively recently that man has played any part in this weird landscape. From about 6000 BC, hunters and gatherers, and later the Anasazi people, visited the Bisti area's springs and chipped tools from the rocks to help them hunt for food.

SACRED LAND

Much more recently, Navajo people made their homes in the area. Driven out of their original lands by rival groups of Native Americans, the pastoral Navajo retreated towards the Bisti and by about 1850 families had settled around springs. They lived in hogans (wood-framed, earth-covered homes) and grazed their sheep on the nearby grassy plateau. Today's Navajo regard the land as sacred. They gather the Bisti's coloured sands to make sand paintings used in healing ceremonies, and make ceremonial body paint from its chalky white clay.

As the sunlight breaks over this astonishing place, vivid colours strike the eye – pale pinks, rich maroons and tiger-striped oranges of the shales and sandstones; sombre greys of exposed coal seams, and rich creams and lemon yellows of the sands. Like a techni-colour three-dimensional puzzle, Bisti demonstrates above all else that Nature has a sense of fun.

PALM PRINT *A palm frond fossilised in Bisti's sandstone (above) grew in a warm, wet climate 80 million years ago.*

WATERCOURSE *Several dried-up stream beds (left) weave through the Bisti.*

Copper Canyon

IMMENSE CANYONS MAKE DEEP AND JAGGED CUTS INTO THE MOUNTAINS OF NORTHERN MEXICO

The railway journey up into the high mountains of Mexico's backbone seems stupendous enough. On its ascent towards the Copper Canyon, the train swings round hairpin bends and crosses bridges raised high above the ground. It plunges into the darkness of one tunnel after another, emerging to offer its passengers new vistas of dizzying drops down steep-sided valleys.

But the journey's scenic rewards pale in comparison with the prize to be found at Divisadero, a railway station more than 7500ft (2300m) up in the mountains. The view it offers down the Barranca del Cobre, or Copper Canyon, is mesmerising. A vast trench stretches away for some 30 miles (50km), and plunges some 4600ft (1400m) to the Urique River that flows in shadowy blackness far below. Gullies cut deeply into the canyon's walls, their steep sides meeting at knife-edge ridges. In the distance, waves of ridges and pinnacles ripple away like a petrified sea.

Copper Canyon – named after long-abandoned mines – is one of at least 12 huge gorges that gash Mexico's Sierra Madre Occidental. At the top of the canyons, the rocky land is often snow-covered in winter, but the steep descent into a canyon takes the visitor through a series of ever warmer worlds.

The open pine and cedar forest of the higher ground gives way to mesquite and acacia trees, and tall branching cacti. On the canyons' floors the scene changes again to one of well-

RUNNING KIT *The fleet-footed Tarahumara go barefoot or wear the simplest of shoes, together with loose tunics and brightly coloured headbands.*

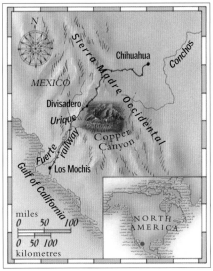

ANGULAR SPLENDOUR *Nothing smooth or gentle softens the harsh outlines of the canyon cut by the Urique River, which winds along far below the rugged peaks.*

watered, balmy valleys where oranges, bananas and wild orchids grow. As one 19th-century explorer wrote:
'In a little over four hours we dropped from the land of the pine to the land of the palm.'

Despite the canyons' uninviting appearance, they are the home of 70,000 Tarahumara people. Before the arrival of Europeans in the 17th century, the Tarahumara lived in a much larger area, but as the Spaniards encroached on their territory they retreated deeper and deeper into the canyons in order to retain their own way of life. Now they keep cattle, sheep and goats, and grow corn, apples and peaches on what little flat land there is. The Tarahumara call themselves 'rarámuri' – running people – for they have an astonishing capacity for running, in a land where almost every step they take is either uphill or down. They hold competitions in which teams dribble a wooden ball along a course that can take several days and nights to complete – a feat of endurance that staggers visitors drained by the mere sight of the awesome Copper Canyon.

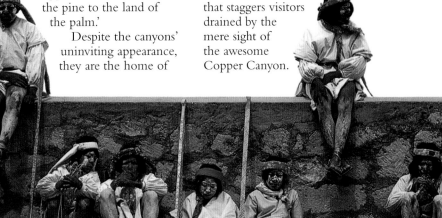

Volcán Poás

A THREE-CRATERED VOLCANO IN CENTRAL AMERICA IS THE MOST POWERFUL GEYSER IN THE WORLD

Volcán Poás in Costa Rica achieved fame in 1910, when it threw a column of steam 4 miles (6.4km) into the sky, thus with ease capturing the world's geyser record. On other occasions since then, this volcano has hurled columns of boiling water to a height of 1000ft (300m).

Geyser-like behaviour such as this is thought to be a sign of a volcano in decline. It is caused when surface water filters down to meet the heat source of very hot, though cooling, molten rock.

The volcano possesses three craters, two of them long dormant. One dormant crater contains a lake. The other is covered with dwarf forest that is almost permanently shrouded in clouds. Here, mosses, lichens and orchids abound in the damp shade, along with the broad-leaved plant known as poor man's umbrella. The bird life too is magnificent – fiery-throated hummingbirds, sooty robins and the gorgeous quetzal.

The lowest and still-active crater, however, retains a hellish aspect – a barren moonscape 1 mile (1.6km) across and 1000ft (300m) deep. Rain-slicked ash forms the floor, interspersed with smoking cones of cinder and

lumps of lava washed off the steaming walls. A hot, muddy lake fumes at the bottom, changing colour from white to green as sulphurous vapours are forced in from below, turning the water into a sulphuric acid solution.

During the past few years, Poás has shown signs of increasing geyser-like activity. Intervals between eruptions have lessened, and the accompanying sulphur gas and steam have given rise to acid rain.

This in turn has wreaked havoc on the local coffee crop, as well as causing skin and respiratory complaints among the farming population.

Of particular interest to scientists is the recent discovery of pools of molten sulphur in the crater, thought to be the only ones on the planet. They were formed when the underlying molten rock boiled off the surface water.

Volcán Poás is just one of more than

HELL AND HEAVEN *The summit of Poás has three craters – a sullenly steaming cauldron of hot water, a dark mirror of cold water and a third hidden by a rich growth of tropical foliage.*

SAFETY VALVE

Fumaroles (steam vents) like the ones below serve to release the pressure of gas welling up in a volcano. The gases emitted in Poás's active crater have a high content of sulphur which crystallises, as the gases emerge, into piles of pure sulphur.

It has been noted recently that occasionally, and under certain circumstances, these piles collapse to form pits of bubbling sulphur that later enlarge into pools. The phenomenon is unique on the surface of this planet, but from images sent back by the Voyager spacecraft, it is suspected that similar activity may take place in other parts of the solar system.

DEVIL'S BREATH *Choking fumes from a fumarole in Poás's crater floor form heaps of yellow sulphur.*

60 volcanoes dominating the landscape in this part of Central America. In 1835, Nicaragua's Cosiguina blew up in an explosion more violent than the largest nuclear bomb. In Guatemala, Pacaya pours out rivers of lava and Fuego buries villages in ash. Poás's symmetrical neighbour Turrialba occasionally throws out vast quantities of fine sand, and incidentally offers views of both the Atlantic and the Pacific.

In Managua, the capital of neighbouring Nicaragua, you may see half a dozen sets of footprints – of men, women and children – indented in a now rock-like mixture of mud and volcanic ash. The spacing of the prints suggests that they were made by people who were running hard – running, indeed, for their lives, for the prints were made during an eruption of the nearby volcano Masaya that took place some 10,000 years ago.

It seems that the Pacific coast of Central America has for a long time been a land of fire, and of awesome tremblings in the depths of the Earth. Geologically, this land is young, and the forces that created it are by no means at rest. One of the plates of the Earth's crust has thrust against the adjacent one and is still on the move, promising volcanic eruptions and earthquakes far into the future.

South America

The Amazon

THE WORLD'S MIGHTIEST RIVER SYSTEM DRAINS ONE-THIRD OF SOUTH AMERICA AND WAS NAMED AFTER WARRIOR WOMEN

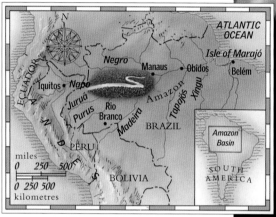

NEARING THE SEA *Clouds cast shadows over the Amazon as it approaches the Atlantic Ocean towards the end of its 4000 mile (6440km) journey. In the vast Amazonian rainforest slender trees (right) reach for sunlight.*

Trying to imagine the vastness of the River Amazon is almost as difficult as trying to comprehend infinity – the mind reels at its staggering immensity. With its countless tributaries, the Amazon drains an area of South America almost the size of Australia, and is deep enough for ocean-going ships to sail inland from the Atlantic to Iquitos in Peru – half the river's length. It disgorges ten times more water into the sea than the Mississippi.

The Amazon crosses virtually the entire continent. Its most far-flung tributaries begin in glacier-fed lakes high in the Peruvian Andes, just 120 miles (190km) from the Pacific. Thundering down from the mountains, the tributaries carve out dramatic gorges in the eastern slopes, churning up clay that turns the water the colour of milky coffee. Yet these are known as white waters. There are also black-water tributaries, whose water is coloured by decomposed plant matter from the swamps they drain, yet very clear. As the gradients slacken, the rushing waters slow to a more stately pace before reaching the plain below – the immense Amazon basin.

Tropical rainforest in the Amazon basin covers an area nearly twice the size of India, with hardly any ground more than 650ft (200m) high once it has left the mountains. Melting snow in the Andes and heavy rains bring flooding for much of the year. An extent of forest the size of Iceland, known as the *várzea*, is inundated to a depth of around 30ft (9m) for months, and some parts, the *igapós*, are under water most of the time. For most of the time, too, the forest is hot, wet and

FOREST DWELLER *The cat-sized kinkajou feeds on ants which have made their nest in a tree. The kinkajou can use its tail to hang from branches.*

RED WATER
Sunlight passing through the dark red water of the Rio Negro (right) lights up a white sandbar.

BLACK WATER
A giant swirl is created by the dark water of the Rio Xingu (above) as it joins the Amazon.

sticky, with temperatures around 33°C (91°F) by day and 23°C (73°F) by night. Near Manaus in Brazil – 750 miles (1200km) from the Atlantic – is the 'wedding of the waters', where the black-water River Negro, here 3 miles (5km) wide, converges with the white-water main stream. To the Brazilians, the Amazon proper begins at this confluence – they call the river upstream from here the Solimões.

So flat are the Amazon's lower reaches that the river is tidal for 600 miles (966km) inland from the Atlantic, as far as Obidos. Before it finally discharges into the ocean, it forms a massive maze of channels, along with two other rivers (Tocantins and Pará) that join it on the south side. Overall, the mouth spans some 200 miles (320km); two of its channels are separated by Marajó island – the size of Switzerland.

WARRIOR WOMEN

Vicente Yañez Pinzón, a Spanish captain who had sailed with Columbus, is the first European known to have scouted the Amazon mouth, in 1500. He thought it was a freshwater sea. Another Spaniard, Francisco de Orellana was the first to sail much of the way down the river in 1541–2, starting in Peru on the River Napo. Orellana had set out from Ecuador as part of Gonzalo Pizarro's Spanish expedition in search of gold and spices and the fabled golden city of El Dorado. When the expedition foundered in the Peruvian jungle, they built a ship, the *San Pedro*, and dispatched it, with Orellana in command, to search for food. He never returned. Pizarro and his men struggled back overland to Ecuador, but Orellana sailed east to the Amazon delta, and eventually reached the Caribbean.

Hostile tribes were among the many hazards faced by Orellana and his men

A GIANT AMONG SNAKES

No snake in the world is larger or heavier than the Amazonian anaconda. It can grow up to about 33ft (10m) long, weigh 500lb (225kg) or more, and have a girth the size of a man's torso. On average, however, most anacondas reach a length of no more than a modest 18ft (5.5m).

At home in the water, these giant snakes lie in ambush on muddy banks or in shallow pools, ready to catch prey such as water birds, turtles, capybaras and tapirs. An anaconda will even take an 8ft (2.5m) long cayman, which it suffocates to death and swallows whole – after a feast like this, the anaconda can go without a meal for weeks on end.

Only in maturity is the snake the most fearsome of predators. Young anacondas are born live – sometimes about 70 at a time – and only about 2ft 6in (760mm) long. Many of them are snapped up by caymans. Those that survive to maturity can get their own back.

GIANT STRUGGLE *An anaconda can kill and eat a large animal such as a crocodile-like cayman. Despite tales to the contrary, it rarely attacks humans.*

on their journey, among them a tribe that appeared to be all women. Later, when the tale was told, it so captured public imagination that the warrior women were dubbed Amazons – after a tribe of fierce female fighters in Ancient Greek myth. This is how the river came to be named the Amazon. But Orellana himself called the river El Rio Mar, River Sea, because of its enormous scale.

Nowhere in the world has a larger variety of plants than the Amazon. Trees towering to 200ft (60m) shade out the sunlight, so that in dry forest the floor is often barely more than a carpet of rotting vegetation. In flooded forest, shrubs and trees have buttressed roots to help them survive. In all parts, the storeyed canopy of branches bursts with life – lianas, orchids and bromeliads vie for holds in the upper branches that also shelter creatures such as monkeys, sloths, hummingbirds, macaws, huge butterflies and innumerable bats.

Caymans and river turtles live in the water, as do water-dwelling mammals such as manatees and botos (freshwater dolphins). Land animals include jaguars, jaguarondis, peccaries, tapirs, capybaras and armadillos. There are around 2500 species of fish and more than 1600 species of bird.

Some parts of the Amazon rainforest are preserved, including the Amazonias National Park that borders the River Tapajós in Brazil and covers almost 4000sq miles (10,000km²). But if deforestation continues at the present rate, this vast forest – which totals one-third of the world's tropical rainforest – will have virtually disappeared by the end of the 21st century.

AMAZING AMAZON

- The Amazon, 4000 miles (6440km) long, is the second longest river in the world; the Nile is 4160 miles (6695km) long.
- It discharges an average of 116 thousand tons of water into the Atlantic every second – nearly three times more than the Zaire (Congo), ten times more than the Mississippi and 60 times more than the Nile.
- It contributes one-fifth of all the water poured into the world's oceans by rivers.
- It meets the Atlantic with such force that its freshwater stream can be located for a distance of up to 100 miles (160km) from shore.
- Seven of the Amazon's tributaries are more than 1000 miles (1600km) long; the longest of them, the Madeira, is more than 2000 miles (3200km) long.

Angel Falls

A BUSH PILOT IN SEARCH OF GOLD DISCOVERED THE WORLD'S HIGHEST WATERFALL IN VENEZUELA'S DENSE JUNGLE

One of the most satisfying ways of achieving greatness must be to stumble across it while you are searching for something else – take Christopher Columbus and the New World, for instance. Another such was Jimmy Angel, an American ex-World War I pilot and wanderer.

In 1935 Angel was quartering the vast Venezuelan plateau of Auyan Tepuí – Devil's Mountain – in search of a river. An old prospector had introduced him to it and its dazzlingly high gold content some years before, and he had been trying to find it again ever since. Looking down from his biplane, Angel saw stream after stream tumbling over the edge of the plateau to be lost in the rainforest below. Then, turning the corner of a towering rocky buttress, he froze at the controls.

From high above, almost in the clouds, an entire river poured out of the summit of the dark pink edge of the escarpment, falling past him to crash

FLIGHTS OF ANGEL *From a halo of cloud, the rain-fed cataracts of Angel Falls leap down to explode among the stones of the Churún river.*

into the valley far below with a roar that overwhelmed the noise of his engine. Diving down, he knew, even then, that he had discovered the mightiest cataract in the world.

Back in Caracas, the Venezuelan capital, he interested a pair of mountain explorers, Gustavo Heny and Felix Cardona, in his story and volunteered to fly them in from his base camp below Auyan Tepuí. While Cardona manned the radio at base, Angel, with his wife Marie and Heny, took off to find a landing place on the plateau.

They chose a spot that turned out to be a bog, and although no-one was hurt there was no chance of the plane flying them out again. The terrain was atrocious – yawning gullies and fissures eroded into the plateau over millennia and covered with close-knit forest. To reach the top of the falls was impossible, and besides, the party's immediate problem was to extricate themselves from their predicament. Miraculously, they did so, turning up tattered and starving at the base camp two weeks later, after hope for their safety had been abandoned.

SOURCE OF THE FALLS

Angel and his companions had, however, solved the problem of the falls' water supply. The cracks and ravines of the plateau – 300sq miles (770km²) in extent – collect an enormous rainfall of 300in (7620mm) a year, throwing it down the cataract to feed the River Churún, a tributary of the Carrao.

AN AMPHITHEATRE CARVED OUT BY THE WATER'S ABRASIVE HAMMERING

Angel's claim to have found the highest waterfall in the world was not confirmed until 1949, when an expedition led by Ruth Robertson, an American ex-war correspondent, ventured up the canyon of the Churún in motorised canoes. Moonlight illuminated her first glimpse of the falls – a long sliver of silver knifing through an orange glow.

Instruments set up in the following days showed the waterfall's height to be 3212ft (979m), nearly 18 times higher than Niagara Falls. Its flow, however, is by no means constant. In the wet season, spray exploding from the foot of the falls drenches the forest for a wide area. But in the dry season, the diminished flow may dissolve into mist before it reaches the river. This reveals an enormous amphitheatre around the falls, carved out over millions of years by the water's abrasive hammering.

Jimmy Angel had earned his place in atlases and record books, though it has been said that a rubber gatherer named Ernesto Sanchez La Cruz was the first outsider to see the falls, in 1910. And, of course, the local people had always known of them. When Jimmy was killed in an air crash in 1956, his ashes were scattered over the falls named after him. His aircraft, extracted from its lofty eyrie, now has an honoured place in the Ciudad Bolivar Museum.

DIZZYING DROP *(overleaf) The remarkable view from above the falls reveals that the water pours from deep gullies in the plateau's fissured sandstone.*

RECORD RODENT
The world's biggest rodent, the capybara, lives in the rivers around Angel Falls. It weights up to 175lb (80kg).

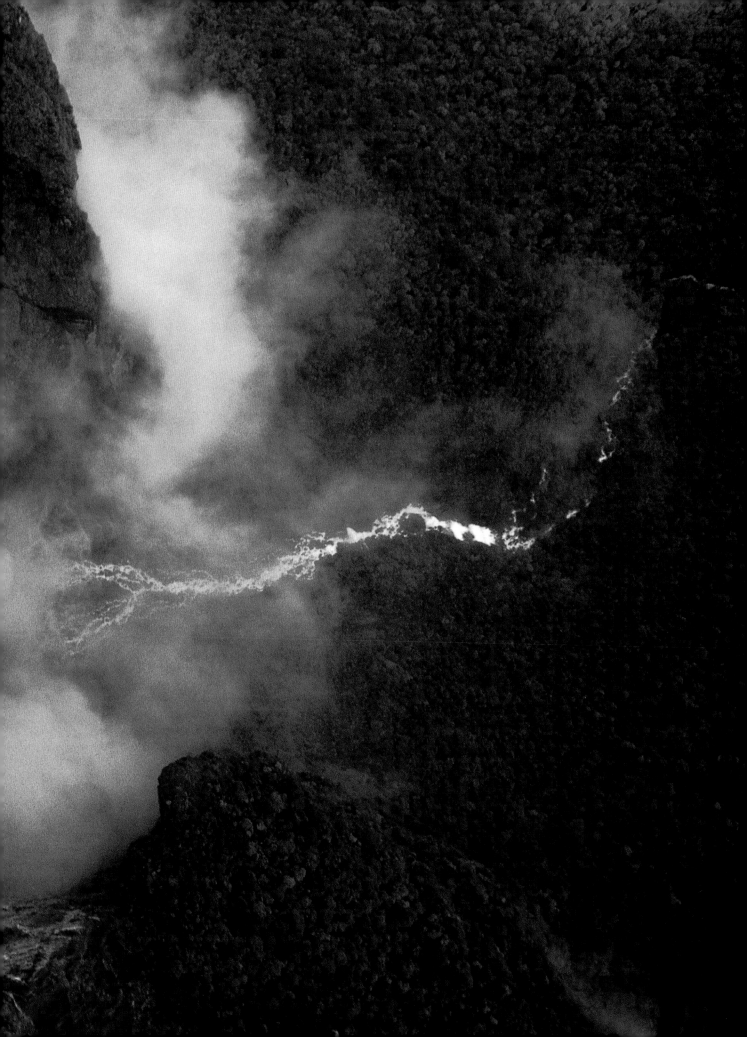

Venezuela's Lost Worlds

ISOLATED TABLE MOUNTAINS TOWER ABOVE VENEZUELA'S TROPICAL RAINFOREST LIKE SCATTERED ISLANDS IN A VAST OCEAN OF GREEN

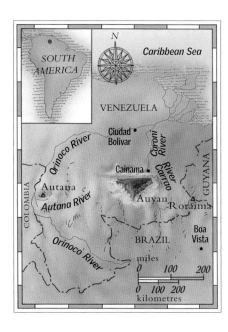

There are two quite separate worlds in south-east Venezuela's remote tropical rainforest. Massive, flat-topped sandstone mountains loom like impregnable citadels above the lush jungle – a mysterious, cloud-wrapped overworld surrounded by a noisy underworld alive with chattering monkeys and screeching macaws. Called tepuís by the Pemón people of the area, the sheer-walled mountains were the inspiration for Sir Arthur Conan Doyle's adventure story, *The Lost World*.

Nearly 2 billion years ago, when South America and Africa were still part of the supercontinent Gondwanaland, debris from eroding mountains formed a vast bed of sandstone. This was lifted up by earth movements and rent with fissures, and as years went by relentless scouring by weather and water gradually wore away the weaker spots. Now only the towering table mountains remain, some 3300ft (1000m) high and physically isolated from the land below. The temperature in the rainforest is around 27°C (80°F), but on the high, cloud-shrouded table mountain tops it is nearly 10°C (18°F) cooler.

These 'islands' – more than 100 of them – have been more or less inaccessible for millions of years. The only way to reach the top of some, such as Auyan (where Angel Falls cascades down a sandstone precipice), is by helicopter.

This can be risky because of treacherous whirlwind currents, low clouds and sudden rainstorms. The terrain, too, is daunting – caves, labyrinths, bogs, torrential rivers, impassable piles of

boulders and deep, seemingly bottomless, fissures.

Sir Walter Raleigh, the English navigator and explorer, visited the area in 1595 in search of El Dorado, a fabled land of great riches. He told of a sparkling crystal mountain from which flowed 'a mighty river which toucheth no parte of the side of the mountain, but falleth to the grounde with a terrible noyse and clamor, as if 1000 great belles were knockt one against another.' This description fits the Valle de los Cristales, a fairytale canyon shimmering with pink and white crystals on the summit of the tallest table mountain – Mount Roraima, 9094ft (2772m) above sea level and 17sq miles (44km²) in extent. Climbers have forced a route up its sheer cliff wall.

LAND OF MYSTERY *More than 100 table mountains rise above the forest in Venezuela's Guiana Highlands. Autana (left of centre below, and overleaf) has huge caves carved in its sheer sides.*

THE LOST WORLD OF CONAN DOYLE

Everard Im Thurn, a British botanist, scaled Mount Roraima in 1884, and returned with previously unknown plants. His descriptions of the mist-enshrouded rock labyrinths and impenetrable terrain fired the imagination of Arthur Conan Doyle, later to become famous as the creator of the fictional master detective, Sherlock Holmes. As a result, Conan Doyle wrote a bestseller, *The Lost World*, in which the irascible Professor Challenger leads a party of explorers to a mysterious table mountain. They find a world untouched by millions of years of evolution, with prehistoric dinosaurs, vicious apemen and friendly Indians. They also stumble upon 'a rookery of pterodactyls' (giant, flesh-eating, flying reptiles), and manage to take one back to London!

HIGH ADVENTURE *Arthur Conan Doyle (inset) featured rampaging prehistoric monsters in his novel (right), which was first published in 1912.*

FINE FEATHERS *Scarlet macaws feed on fruit and leaves in the forest, and roost on tepui ledges.*

Because of their age-long isolation, the plants, and many of the animals, on the tepuís have flourished unmixed with others and virtually undisturbed by man. This so excited Conan Doyle that he imagined a world of prehistoric monsters still surviving.

But scientists exploring the tepuís' tops have found no animal larger than a mountain lion. Their chief interest has been in studying how plants and animals of the 'overworld' have developed in comparison with similar 'underworld' species. Oddities include a primitive, warty toad that is barely 1in (25mm) in length and cannot hop or swim. It crawls clumsily, its black skin camouflaging it against Roraima's algae-blackened rocks.

AT LEAST HALF THE PLANTS FOUND ON THE TABLE MOUNTAIN TOPS ARE UNIQUE

Each tepuí has its own particular mixture of plants – of the estimated 10,000 or so species found there, at least half are unique, including several kinds of insect-digesting pitcher plants and some bromeliads. Because the rain leaches through the soil very fast, plants suffer from both soil and nutrient shortages. Bromeliads root in mosses and lichens and on branches, and some 900 orchid species, many no larger than a pin, root in rock crevices and moss tufts. There are also unique fungi that kill their insect and plant food by injecting it with poison.

FLOATING PLATEAU *Mist clings around the sheer walls of Mount Roraima like a surrounding ocean.*

Lake Titicaca

ON THE GREAT INLAND SEA OF THE HIGH ANDES, THE GODS, HISTORY AND LEGEND ARE FOREVER INTERTWINED

Nowhere in history can there be found a more fruitful marriage of sublime courage and naked greed than in the personalities of the *conquistadores*, the Spanish conquerors of Central and South America. In 1535, with Peru subjugated, and already rich beyond all dreams of riches, Diego de Almagro left his partner Francisco Pizarro in Cuzco, the Inca capital, and marched south into the unknown. His quest, and that of the 570 troops who accompanied him, was for yet more gold.

Their route took them across the high arid plateaus of what is now Bolivia and Argentina, over the Andes, and down to the coastal jungles of Chile. Men and horses froze to death in the mountain passes, choked in the rarified air of the plateaus, roasted within their armour in deserts. And there was no gold.

That they had accomplished one of the great exploratory adventures was of little consolation and less interest. However, along the way, even for those single-minded men, there were things that filled them with wonder. High on the plateau where Peru and Bolivia now meet, they encountered a vast inland sea of an incredible blue, beyond which were glacier-shouldered mountains glittering against a perfect sky. People sailed its waters in strange boats made out of reeds.

That was how outsiders first came to Lake Titicaca, in its splendid setting against the 21,000ft (6400m) range of the Cordillera Real. But if even the hard-bitten Spanish were moved by the

HOLY ISLE *Lake Titicaca's Island of the Sun is still revered – as the place where the gods landed to found the Inca dynasty and bring wisdom to the Aymara people who live by the lake.*

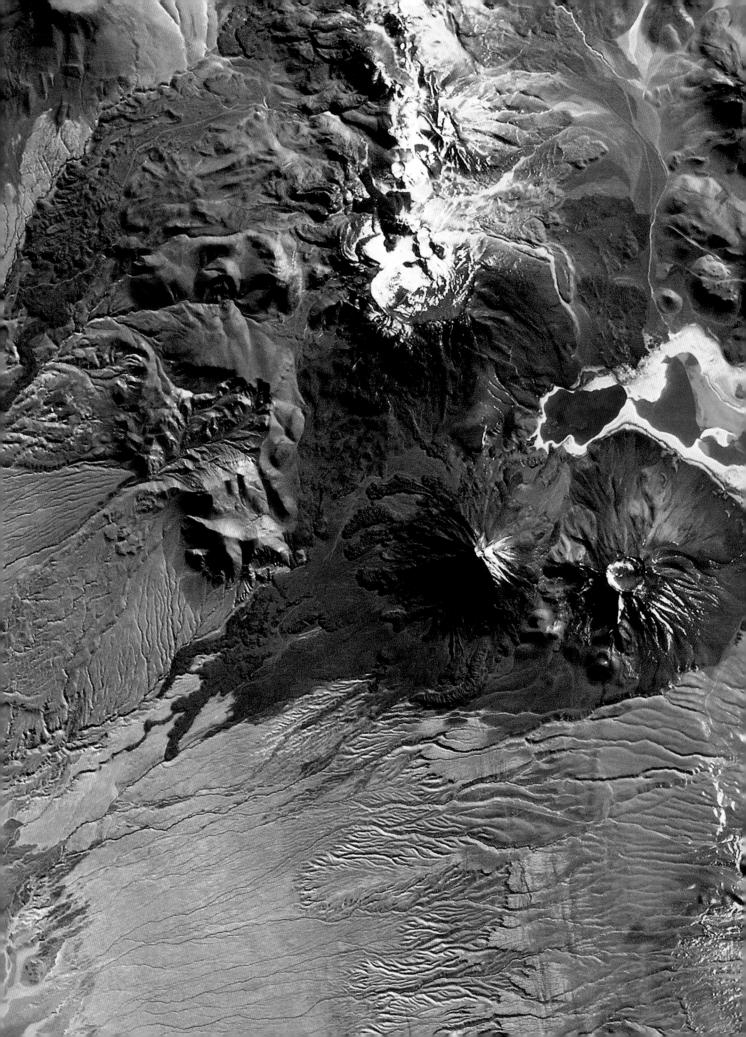

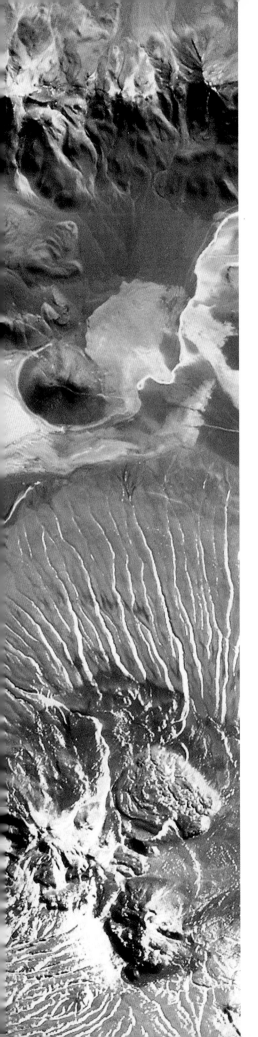

SPACEMAN'S VIEW *A satellite image shows Lake Titicaca cupped among the ice-covered peaks of the Andes on the border of Bolivia and Peru.*

scene, to the peoples native to the place, it was, and is, sacred. The high peaks are the abodes of gods, or are perhaps deities themselves. To the Aymara people, who live by the lake, its waters are the womb from which Viracocha, the white and bearded representative of the Sun on Earth, emerged to teach men how to build, grow food and make reed boats.

THE AYMARA PEOPLE HAVE LARGER HEARTS AND LUNGS THAN NORMAL

Lake Titicaca is the largest of South America's lakes, with an area of 3200sq miles (8300km²). It lies 12,505ft (3812m) above sea level, but even then it is not the world's highest lake; there are much higher ones in the Himalayas. But it is the world's highest navigable waterway for large vessels, and has been since 1862, when a steamer was carried up in sections and reassembled on the shore. After a century of service, this venerable craft was retired and replaced by hydrofoils that ply between Puno in Peru and destinations in Bolivia.

Lake Titicaca marks a division in the Andes – to the north, the climate becomes steadily more temperate, and to the south, progressively more harsh. Its shores are about the southern limit of year-round human habitation, and of successful crop-raising. Potatoes are grown there; maize and barley, which do not ripen, are grown for animal feed.

LIFE IN THE LAKE'S DEPTHS

Fishing in the lake is now poor. Introduced rainbow trout devoured the native catfish and were themselves overfished in turn. The chief native denizen of the lake is a frog, reported to be the size of a rat. But as it breathes only by extracting oxygen from the water through its skin and cannot survive in the air, it is seldom seen.

Many of the Aymara people still live much as their forefathers did when they were glimpsed by the conquistadores. Unlike the Spanish and later visitors, they do not suffer from mountain sickness, for they have larger hearts and

lungs than normal, and more red blood corpuscles to counteract the effects of oxygen deficiency. They construct rafts of totora reed by the shore, and on them build houses of the same material, and even plant vegetable plots upon them. Totora is also used to make their boats which, despite their frail appearance, are immensely tough. Larger versions would be perfectly seaworthy.

This very point struck the voyager Thor Heyerdahl. He had seen very similar but much larger craft in Egyptian tomb paintings, and put forward the theory that South American peoples owed their Sun worship, and the skills that enabled them to build their ancient cities, to Egyptian visitors of long, long ago. To prove the possibility, Heyerdahl imported several Aymara boat builders to Morocco, and there constructed *Ra II*, a seagoing reed ship.

Heyerdahl sailed the ship, without mishap, across the Atlantic from Morocco to Barbados, following in the wake of who knows what far-off adventurers. Could they have anything to do with Viracocha, the Sun's representative, credited with pale skin and a beard in a land where both are unknown? If Heyerdahl is right, then the conquistadores were late arrivals indeed.

LAST JOURNEY *A ribbon-decked llama is carried to the Island of the Sun to be sacrificed, in order to ensure good crops.*

Iguazú Falls

WHERE ARGENTINA AND BRAZIL MEET, A LINE OF WATERFALLS CASCADES OVER A CRESCENT OF CLIFFS INTO A NARROW GORGE

In a welter of foam, the Iguazú River hurls itself off the edge of the Paraná Plateau into the gorge below, whipping up clouds of spray that hang high above the falls. Dozens of rainbows dance a colourful ballet in the misty veil as the sunlight streams through.

The waters swirl and tumble from the crescent-shaped cliffs in a long line of some 275 cascades separated by islets and rock outcrops. Some plunge sheer down the cliff and others crash over stepped ledges – 'an ocean pouring into an abyss' is how a Swiss botanist, Robert Chodat, described it.

The river makes a sweeping bend and widens out on its approach to the falls, where the roar of the water is like the sound of rolling thunder and can be heard 15 miles (24km) away. In January and February, at the height of the summer rainy season, enough water rushes over the cliffs every second to fill about four Olympic swimming pools.

Union Falls, the highest of the Iguazú cascades, plunges into a spectacular chasm known as the Devil's Throat. This has been cut by the river

along a geological fault, and at its end the river's course is turned at right angles before it rushes on through rapids to join the Paraná River.

Thousands of swifts wheel and dive low and fast above the water, chasing the swarms of insects that can be found there. Lichen-like water plants grow on the rock ledges behind the water curtain, and hot, humid rainforest – with filmy ferns, bamboos and trees such as palms and pines – borders the gorge and drapes over its stepped ledges like huge green shawls.

BRIGHT FOREST

Mosses, trumpet-flowered lianas and bromeliads festoon the trees, and brilliantly plumed macaws and parrots, as well as hundreds of different types of butterflies, flit among the foliage. Their bright colours vie with the masses of wild orchids, which can be found at their best in the cool of spring (August–October).

The chattering of capuchin monkeys rivals the raucous calls and screeching of the birds, and the roaring of black howler monkeys adds to the din. Deer and pig-like peccaries roam the forest depths, as do hoofed, heavy-bodied

THE GREAT WATER

- On its 820 mile (1320km) journey to the falls from its source near Brazil's Atlantic coast, the Iguazú River is fed by 30 tributaries and has 70 waterfalls.
- The falls are 2½ miles (4km) wide, with a 279ft (85m) drop at their highest point – Union Falls.
- They are four times as wide as Niagara Falls in North America, and half as high again.
- In summer they spill around 58,000 tons of water a second – about twice as much as Niagara.

tapirs and shy, solitary big cats – ocelots and jaguars. But the commonest mammals are the rabbit-sized agouti and two cat-sized rodents – the white-spotted paca and the long-tailed coatimundi.

A Spanish explorer, Alvar Núñez Cabeza de Vaca, was the first European to see the falls, in 1541. Being a pious man, he named them Salto de Santa Maria, the Falls of Saint Mary. The name soon reverted to Iguazú – which was what the local people, the Guarani, called them and which in their language means 'Great Water'.

According to their legends, Taroba, the son of a tribal chief, stood on the river bank to plead with the gods to restore the sight of the blind princess he loved. The gods replied by ripping open the gorge. The river then plunged in, taking Taroba with it. But the princess

BIRD SANCTUARY *Dusky swifts rest on the ledges behind the waterfall (below). They wait for gaps in the flow of falling water, then fly quickly through.*

WATER DIVIDER *This rocky outcrop perched precariously on the brink of the gorge is just one of many outcrops and islets that divert the Iguazú River into a series of separate cataracts and churn it into a teeming torrent of foam and spray.*

FAST FLY CATCHERS

All day long hundreds of dusky swifts wheel and dive on their long, curved wings above the river gorge at the Iguazú Falls. Frequently they disappear, flying behind the falls through the tumbling wall of water.

The dusky swifts, which are around 7in (180mm) long, breed here in summer, building their mossy nests on the ledges behind the falls. It takes about three weeks for the eggs to hatch, and it is another 5-8 weeks - depending on the supply of food available - before the nestlings launch themselves from their nursery through the watery curtain. The parent birds are kept busy feeding their brood. They catch insects on the wing in their gaping mouths, and carry bundles of them back to their youngsters in a sticky ball of saliva.

regained her sight and was the first person ever to see Iguazú Falls.

De Vaca was not impressed by the Iguazú Falls. He reported them merely as 'considerable', noting that 'the spray rises to two spear throws and more above the fall'. On the heels of the Spanish explorer came Jesuit priests, who built missions and began to convert the local people to Christianity.

Later on the Jesuits established settlements to protect the Guaranis from marauding slavers, who kidnapped them to supply workers for Portuguese and Spanish plantations. But the landowners doubtlessly had the ear of King Charles III of Spain, and in 1767 he expelled the Jesuits from South America because he thought the order was becoming too powerful. One of the old Jesuit missions still standing is San Ignacio Miní (1696), near Posadas in Argentina, a centre for visiting the falls.

THE BEST VIEWS

Brazil and Argentina both have a national park bordering the falls. In general, the Brazilian park, which is approached from Curitiba near the Atlantic coast, gives the most stunning panorama of the whole falls – at their most impressive in the morning light. Closer views are possible on the Argentinian side – such as the San Martin Falls that make two 100ft (30m) leaps, and the dramatic Devil's Throat, reached along a catwalk and best seen in the evening when the swifts are returning to their roosts.

Not only can park visitors enjoy the falls, they have a rare opportunity to walk through a rainforest similar to that found in the Amazon, but along waymarked trails.

Salt Lakes of the Andes

COLOUR AND WONDER
LIE ABOVE THE CLOUDS
IN THE STRANGE AND
SECRET WORLD OF
BOLIVIA'S HIGH PLAINS

Cradled between the eastern and western ranges, or cordilleras, of the Andes mountains is a series of high plateaus stretching some 1500 miles (2400km) from central Peru into Argentina. Nowhere do they drop below 10,000ft (3000m), and generally they lie much higher. It is a strange run of country in which nothing is quite what it seems, a little topsy-turvy. The sun burns, yet the deserts on which it shines are often icy cold. Skies by day are violet rather than blue, and at night the stars do not twinkle but glow in a pall of velvety blackness.

Distant mountains seem almost close enough to touch, and lake water can be any colour from jade green to rosy red, sometimes with water life to match. Or what at first appears to be a lake may not be water at all, but a dazzling plain of salt. Add to this clumps of sullenly smoking volcanoes, pools of bubbling mud, and rocks eroded into the shapes of nightmare beasts, and the picture begins to look familiar. It is an old-fashioned sci-fi illustrator's idea of the surface of Mars.

HIGH AND DRY

The overwhelming thing about the plateaus, though, is their sheer scale. The Altiplano – the 'high plain' between the two arms of the Andes in west Bolivia and south-east Peru – lies below peaks that have been awarded no more than a light dusting of snow by the dry air, although they are pushing up towards 20,000ft (6000m) above sea level. Towards the end of the last Ice Age, the Altiplano was covered by two huge lakes; Titicaca, vast though it is, is just a tiny remaining fragment of the northern one.

DREAM WORLD *The red waters of Laguna Colorada seem contrary to nature, but are in fact the result of a rich content of microscopic plant life.*

ISLES IN A SALT SEA

Vegetation is non-existent in the wide salt plain of Salar de Uyuni, apart from some cacti, such as the Browningia (below), that have established themselves on its few rocky islets. Their thick skins protect them from extremes of heat and cold and some, too, are able to store water in their expansible stems.

Both lakes were fed by run-off from glaciers and snowfields in the cordilleras, but when the ice retreated and the water supply decreased, the lakes began to evaporate. In the burning sun and clear atmosphere of those high altitudes, the process was relatively swift. Now nothing remains of the southern lake but some brackish lagoons and

IN FLIGHT *(overleaf) Flamingos, including the rare James's flamingo, cast shadows over the salt reefs that stretch out into Laguna Colorada.*

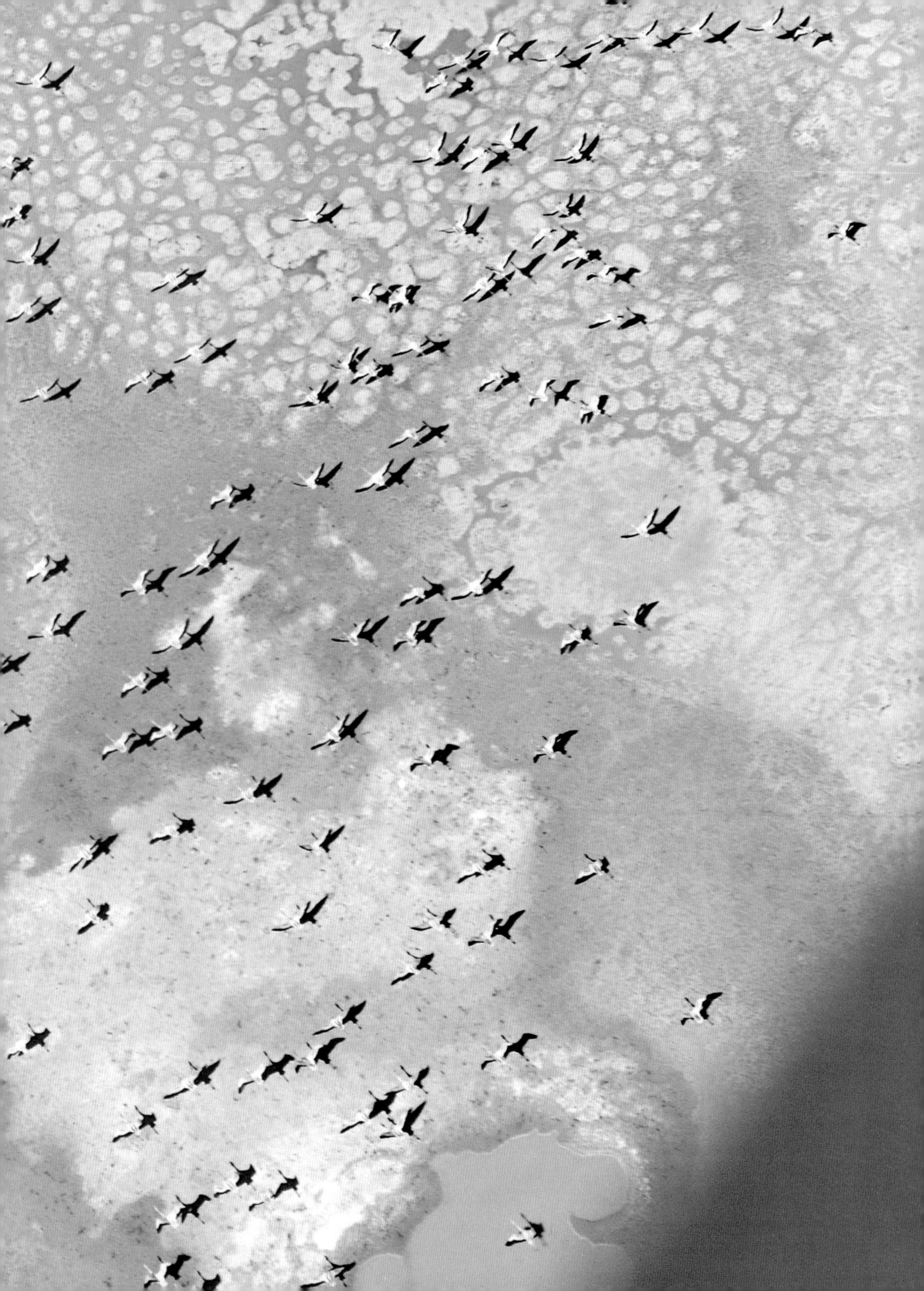

marshes – these and the salt lakes, or salars, king among them being the awesome Salar de Uyuni.

For most of the time, this salt lake is a blinding plain of pure white salt extending over an area about the size of Cyprus. Ever since the death of the Ice Age lake some 10,000 years ago, the process of evaporation has been sucking up moisture and minerals to Uyuni's

CONTRASTS *Laguna Verde, its water muted shades of green, stands out against the surrounding barren land. Behind the lake are at least 20 volcanoes.*

surface from the mud below. Each year, winter rains form a large shallow lake which evaporates during the summer. All this evaporation creates a crust of minerals, chiefly salt, up to 20ft (6m) deep. Except at the edges, that is, where it is thin enough to collapse and deposit the unwary into the sludge below.

To drive a more rugged kind of car across the salt lake is one of the world's great driving experiences, as well as being a considerable short cut across the

LAGUNA COLORADA
GLOWS BRICK RED
IN ITS GREAT CUP
OF MOUNTAINS

plateau. You take to the salt by one of the safe entrances marked by long-distance truckers, line up on some far-away peak and, in theory, simply go. In fact, the great white plain tends to disorientate direction, and mountain tops seem to float up into the sky. After rain it is even worse. The film of water overlying the salt reflects the blue sky, the horizon vanishes, and drivers start to feel as though they are ants sliding across the face of a gigantic mirror.

Landmarks are rare, although here and there a rocky islet lifts above the salt. Quite often, broken flamingo eggshells and polished stone arrowheads are found there, but whether they were abandoned centuries or millennia ago is undetermined. Bones are found, too, of animals that somehow managed to reach the islets but died there of thirst and hunger before they could return across the salt desert to the shore.

South of Uyuni, the plateau climbs still higher to the Puna de Atacama, becoming ever colder and more desolate. It is nevertheless a landscape of grandeur and unexpectedness, with

ancient outcrops of grey-green and maroon lava sandblasted into surrealistic images, and remote salars embracing glaciers of salt. The most successful plant is the outlandish llareta, a relative of parsley, that covers large boulders with a smooth coating of tiny, bright green leaves, and whose closely woven mat of iron-hard roots is the only fuel the country offers.

The really startling feature of the Puna de Atacama though, is its patches of bright water, like splashes fallen from a painter's palette. These lagoons too are rich in minerals, but have not yet dried out. Some are turquoise, others silver-grey, or, like the little Laguna Verde, green – each lake's colour depends on its chemical mixture. But the sight to take the breath away, if you have any left at this altitude, is the Laguna Colorada, glowing brick red in its great cup of mountains. Salt reefs protrude into the water, emphasising the redness even more strongly.

As you approach, the surprises are multiplied, as the surface suddenly lifts off and takes to the air. It is composed

of thousands of James's flamingos, whose plumage precisely matches the lake. These rare birds, the rarest of all flamingos, forage in briny water that is only just above freezing, and feed on the algae (microscopic plants) that give Colorada its astonishing hue. Accompanying them are taller, less colourful Andean and Chilean flamingos.

The three species of flamingo mingle quite happily together, but do not compete for food – the black-and-yellow-beaked James's have very fine beak filters and take smaller organisms than the other two. From time to time all go off to freshwater pools nearby to wash salt off their legs.

James's flamingos are linked to Colorada's bitter waters by a strong bond. When a number of the birds were taken to the New York Zoo in the 1960s, with gratifying alacrity they took to a diet of chicken feed and baby cereal, but began to lose their colour. It was apparent that their brilliance, like that of the lake, was derived from the algae. Fortunately, a daily ration of carrot oil did much to redress the balance.

FLAMINGOS IN THEIR THOUSANDS LIFT OFF AND TAKE TO THE AIR

MANY-FACETED SALARS *Each salt lake has its own characteristics. These polygons are created when moisture evaporates from the mud, causing it to shrink and crack.*

The Pantanal

WIDESPREAD SWAMPLANDS IN THE HEART OF SOUTH AMERICA ARE ONE OF THE GREATEST WILDLIFE HAVENS ON EARTH

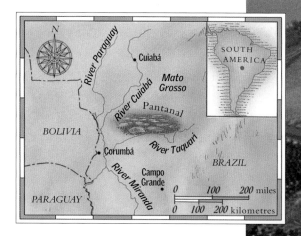

Water birds by the million flourish in the Pantanal – a watery world of lagoons and pastures in the centre of South America, mainly in Brazil. The air resounds to their calls, and huge flocks on the wing are like clouds in the sky, while on the ground ostrich-like rheas graze amid the deer. Many kinds of animal live in the Pantanal – jacaré (Brazilian alligators), furry capybaras (also known as water pigs), giant otters and shy jaguars, all part of perhaps the largest wildlife concentration found outside Africa.

Between November and March each year there is 80-120in (2000-3000mm) of rain, at its heaviest in February. Gradually the River Paraguay and its many tributaries overflow their banks to flood the surrounding plain that covers an area slightly larger than Great Britain. The water can be 10ft (3m) deep or more, and the land becomes a vast expanse of water dotted with small islands where palms and small trees flourish. Many animals and birds move south to drier ground, but some, such as deer, are marooned on the islands – easy prey for hunting jaguars.

DRY SEASON *The receding floods leave countless shallow lakes and pools that teem with fish, making the Pantanal an ideal breeding site for water birds.*

In April, as the rains cease and the floods start to drain away, rich, tree-scattered grassland is revealed around thousands of pools and water holes. Animals and birds return again to breed during the May-October dry season. The shrinking pools teem with trapped fish and other water creatures, providing a rich source of food for many flesh-eating birds and animals.

The harsh, piercing cries of goose-like crested screamers compete with the screeches of the many kinds of jewel-coloured parrots, and long-toed acanas step lightly over the water lilies as they forage for snails and insects. Egrets feed alongside roseate spoonbills and Muscovy ducks, and cormorants and waders such as sandpipers and finfoots abound.

SPECTACULAR STORK

The most striking of all the Pantanal birds is the jabiru – a kind of stork that stands shoulder-high to a man and glides on wings that span 10ft (3m). It has a bald black head and neck with a red dog-collar above cream-coloured body plumage. The Tupi-Guarani, the earliest Pantanal inhabitants, called it the *tuiuiu*, which means 'driven by the wind'.

More sinister inhabitants are the crocodile-like caymans that sun themselves beside the pools, and the anacondas – 20ft (6m) long snakes that lurk submerged in the swampy shallows and squeeze their prey to death.

For centuries the Tupi-Guarani thrived by farming (growing maize and cassava), hunting and fishing. When Spanish and Portuguese explorers and settlers arrived in the 17th century, they intermixed with the local people. A century later came the cattle ranchers, ready to exploit the Pantanal's rich pastures. Now herds of cattle graze alongside the deer, and much of the area is taken up with extensive ranches that are known as *fazendas*.

There is one national park covering about 500sq miles (1300km²) in the north of the area. One of the first people to plead for the protection of these wetlands was former US President Theodore Roosevelt, who visited the Pantanal in 1913-14. He said it offered 'extraordinary opportunities for the study of the life histories of birds'. Today the Pantanal is opening up to tourists. Hunting is forbidden, but fishing with a rod is allowed. The Pantanal is not easy to reach; its inaccessibility may be its greatest protection.

FROG EATS FROG

The brightly coloured horned frog, which lives in the Pantanal marshes, has a large head and powerful jaws with which to eat any animal small enough to swallow. Its diet ranges from snails to mice, and includes other smaller frogs. A horn-like skin flap above each eye gives the frog its name. Because of its colouring, and its aggressiveness if attacked, it is often thought wrongly to be poisonous.

SKIN HORNS
A flap above each eye looks like a horn.

Atacama Desert

THIS COOL, BARREN DESERT ON A WINDSWEPT PLATEAU BESIDE CHILE'S NORTHERN COAST IS THE DRIEST PLACE ON EARTH

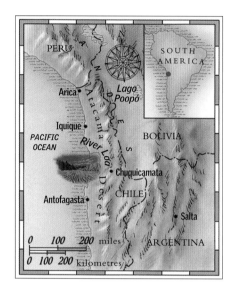

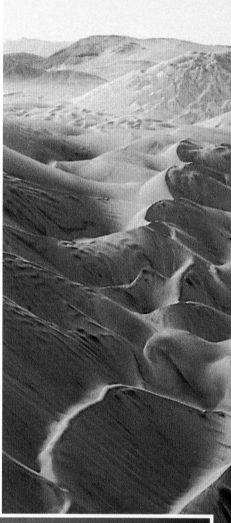

Few birds wheel above the Atacama Desert, the driest place on Earth, and you can see no hint of green from the one paved road that crosses it, the Pan American Highway. An empty landscape of sunbaked rock, gravel and shifting dunes, the desert stretches for some 600 miles (1000km) beside the coast of northern Chile. And, with changes of name, it continues for another 1400 miles (2250km) both north and south. About 60 miles (96km) inland, the desert gives way to the bleak and windswept foothills of the Andes.

SHIFTING SANDS

Empty and silent though it may be, the desert is not inert. Where there is sand, crescent dunes ripple across the landscape, formed and reformed by the wind. In rocky areas, scudding dust devils of wind-whipped sand, and the infrequent downpour, have scoured the hills into soft curves. In the evening light, the mineral-rich rocks glow with colour – browns, reds, purples, greens.

As deserts go, the Atacama is cool. Summer temperatures are generally around 18°C (65°F), but at midday the ground can be as hot as 50°C (122°F). At night the temperature can drop by 40°C (70°F) in little more than an hour. A sound like a pistol shot at twilight may be a rock splitting, distorted by the swift temperature change.

Only one permanent river, the Loa, winds through the heart of the desert from the Andean foothills, its course cut so deep that desert travellers barely see it until they are on top of it. There are said to be areas of desert where it never rains – no-one knows for sure. In the ports of Iquique and Antofagasta it rains no more than four times in a century – and when it does rain the results are devastating. Most moisture comes from the mist that often shades the sun in the northern and southern fringes of the desert, where a few cacti survive.

The Atacama is starved of rain by the circumstances of its surroundings. Rain cannot reach it from the Amazon basin

SMOKING MOUNTAIN *Sulphur lies around a smoking vent (below) on snow-capped Tocorpuri, 19,136ft (5833m), on the desert's eastern edge.*

because easterly winds drop all their rain on the eastern slopes of the Andes. In the Pacific to the west, the cool Humboldt Current sweeps north from the Antarctic. Whereas onshore winds are normally warm and moist, bringing rain, here they are cooled by the chilly current, so on passing over the warmer land they take up moisture and form mist. Known locally as *camanchaca*, the mist clings to the coast below 1000ft (300m). It does not reach the heart of the desert above the cliffs. Its dry air makes the Atacama a place where traces of human activity are long preserved.

Cart tracks made about 100 years ago can still be seen in the crust of soft 'costra' formed from sun-baked rock fragments and salt crystals. Most intriguing are the earth-pictures (or geoglyphs) of patterns and stylised figures outlined in stones. The 400ft (120m) long Giant of Atacama on a hill near Iquique is the largest. Although the earth-pictures look as fresh as new, they were created maybe 1000 years ago by a long-vanished people.

The Atacameños, the area's original inhabitants, were conquered by the Incas of Peru not long before the 16th

DESERT DUNES *In the northern extension of the Atacama Desert, near Nasca, Peru, dunes are blown into patterns similar to tide-washed sand.*

century, when the Spaniards came. Prospectors followed in the Spaniards' wake, seeking gold and silver – even, maybe, in the many well-preserved ancient graves. They told tales of being guided by the Alicante, a legendary bird that glowed with the colour of the precious metal it devoured. But the Alicante vanished if threatened, leaving the prospector lost, starving, sweltering by day and shivering by night.

DESERT EDGE *Where the Atacama Desert meets the Pacific Ocean, the steep and arid cliffs are traced with gullies where streams pour down their flanks after rainfall. Generally, however, rainfall occurs here no more than a few times in a century.*

In the 1830s, wealth of an entirely different kind was discovered in the Atacama's wastes inland from Iquique – the world's largest deposits of sodium nitrate, once vital for making gun-powder and fertiliser. These deposits were originally in Peru, and the industry that developed led to the 1879-84 War of the Pacific in which Chile fought Peru and Bolivia. Chile was victorious – Peru lost its mines and Bolivia its coastline.

MINES AND MEMORIALS

For the next 30 years, Chile's wealth came almost entirely from sodium nitrate, but after World War I the industry collapsed as artificial chemicals replaced the natural ones. Now the desert winds blow round the skeletal remains of buildings, smokestacks and railways, and the innumerable crosses that poke up through the shifting veils of dust and sand and mark the graves of dead miners. But there is still mining in

the area – one of the largest-known copper deposits is now being mined in the foothills around Chuquicamata.

Where the coastline is low, foxes and hog-nosed skunks survive on a diet of sea birds and seashore creatures such as crabs. Grey gulls, too, feast on the crabs, but in summer fly up to 50 miles (80km) inland to nest in the desert in scrapes in the ground – perhaps to avoid predators. By day, nestlings are shielded from the sun by their mother's outspread wings. Vampire bats dwell in coastal caves. They usually feed at night, biting a small cut in the flesh of prey,

BABY BITER *A vampire bat snatches a quick meal of blood from the flipper of a southern sea lion pup.*

then lapping its blood – often without disturbing the victim.

Unlike the desert, the neighbouring coastal waters are rich with life. Water upwelling from the sea's depths brings up minerals and plankton (minute animals and plants) that provide food for hosts of fish; they in turn are eaten by immense flocks of sea birds. Millions of them nest on rocky islets off the coast, where fur seals and southern sea lions also come ashore to bask or breed.

Colca Canyon

A CANYON THAT IS TWICE AS DEEP AS THE GRAND CANYON CUTS AN AWESOME GASH IN THE TOWERING NORTHERN ANDES

High in the Peruvian Andes lies Colca Canyon, described in the *Guinness Book of Records* as the world's deepest gorge. Yet few people have even heard of it. And despite its status as a world record holder, and its stunning grandeur, mere handfuls of travellers venture into these mountains to look at the seemingly bottomless chasm that the Colca River has incised into the Earth's surface.

Other extraordinary discoveries can be made in this corner of Peru. Extinct volcanoes lie strewn along a valley, boulders bear mysterious etchings, and tales are told of people with pointed heads. On their travels, the few visitors follow dusty roads across treeless grasslands and stony deserts where the sun blazes down, and cross mountains more than 13,000ft (4000m) high with icy torrents tumbling down the sides.

Cut off from the outside world, this part of the Andes keeps its secrets to itself. Those who eventually reach Colca Canyon are rewarded by a most breathtaking sight – a slit in the mountains that looks as though it was made by one slice of a knife. At the bottom is the Colca River, wild and

DEEP CUT *The sides of Peru's Colca Canyon fall sheer from the photographer's viewpoint to the river at the very bottom of the picture.*

MOONSCAPE *Symmetrical cinder hills, neatly circled by man-made paths, loom over a small settlement in the Valley of the Volcanoes. Cacti grow on some of the cones.*

muddy in the wet season. At the top – a whole 2 miles (3.2km) above the river – are lofty mountains whose snowy white heads are frequently lost in clouds.

Yet for centuries people have eked a living in these difficult mountains, terracing the lower slopes for crops and keeping llamas. Ask them how they

came to live here, and they will tell you that their ancestors moved here from a snow-covered conical volcano called Collaguata. They called themselves Collaguas after their sacred mountain, and even shaped themselves in its image, wearing pointed hats and binding their children's heads to make

them conical – until Spanish conquerors banned the practice in the 1570s.

Over the mountains from Colca Canyon, conical hills taper up from a valley floor to terminate in more or less circular craters. This eerie lunar landscape is the Valley of the Volcanoes, and the 86 cones, some of them approaching 1000ft (300m) high, are extinct volcanoes. In some parts of the 40 mile (64km) long valley, the cones

FLOWER CANDLES *When it is about 100 years old, the puya bursts into bloom by sending up a 13–20ft (4–6m) candle-like spike packed with spirals of flowers. Puyas are related to the pineapple.*

rise from fields; elsewhere, swirls of solidified black lava lap at their feet.

Between the Valley of the Volcanoes and the Pacific Ocean, thousands of white boulders lie scattered over Toro Muerto, a hot and sandy gully. Many of the boulders have been engraved with geometric shapes, sun discs, snakes and llamas, and with people wearing what look like space helmets. The boulders were probably left after some volcanic upheaval, but who engraved them remains a mystery. Some have speculated that the helmeted figures represent spacemen. With no other remains of past peoples to go with the engravings, more down-to-earth explanations of their origins are scanty.

One suggestion is that migrating tribes passed by more than a thousand years ago on their way from the mountains to the coast, and stopped to make their marks.

Sprouting from the bare slopes of this harsh land are balls of 4ft (1.2m) long spikes. They are puya plants, whose sword-like leaves radiate from a thick trunk and are edged with curved hooks that fend off browsing animals. Shelter is so scarce here that small birds brave the barbs and build nests among the puyas' leaves, although the number of corpses shows how many homes turn into death traps. Some biologists speculate that the puya 'eats' the birds by absorbing chemicals leaching out of the corpses.

Bird corpses, and those of animals, are the food of the mighty Andean condor. Yet this vulture, with a wing-span of 10½ft (3.2m), is less invincible than it looks. The food supply in the mountains is meagre and unreliable, and, because condors normally breed only when there is a glut of food, their future survival is constantly under threat. Devastating storms every five or more years provide abundant carrion – they kill weaker animals and bring insects that cause disease. Only then do the condors lay their single eggs. Yet if any living creature knows all the secrets of these mountains it is this magnificent bird, which casts a shadow on the slopes as it glides above with such effortless ease.

AN EERIE LUNAR LANDSCAPE, WITH THE CONES OF 86 EXTINCT VOLCANOES

Los Glaciares

A GLACIER DAMS AN
ARGENTINIAN LAKE,
AND THEN BREAKS UP IN
A POWERFUL DISPLAY OF
SPLINTERING ICE

Massive blocks of ice collapsing in frenzied confusion, together with raging torrents of water, are part of an ice cataclysm that occurs about once every two or three years in Los Glaciares National Park in southern Argentina. The arena where this drama takes place is Lake Argentino, and the performer is the Moreno Glacier.

Lake Argentino lies below the high Patagonia ice cap, near the southern tip of the Andes. At the head of the lake, tentacle-like arms of water wander deep into the mountains. The Moreno Glacier, one of the ice cap's offspring, crawls down the mountain towards one of the lake's arms. When it reaches the water's edge, the deeply crevassed glacier does not stop but keeps on going, forwards through the lake and onto the opposite shore. In some of its advances it has pushed on relentlessly into the lakeside forest, uprooting trees and gouging rocks out of the ground.

A wall of bluish-white ice up to 200ft (60m) high now straddles the lake, damming back the water that flows into it. The water level upstream from the ice dam rises to as much as 120ft (37m) higher than that below the

LAZY BONES *The mylodon whose remains were found in Los Glaciares was a smaller relation of the giant ground sloth Megatherium (left), which was about the size of an elephant.*

dam, before the pressure becomes so great that the dammed water breaks through the barrier with immense force and a deafening roar (see opposite). When the dam broke in 1972, so much water was trapped behind it that several weeks elapsed before the water levels above and below the dam reached equilibrium.

GLACIERS' BIRTHPLACE

Moreno is one of nine glaciers in Los Glaciares. The Patagonia ice cap where they are born is a vast icy waste on the border of Argentina and Chile. This ice cap spawns glaciers that flow towards both the Pacific and Atlantic Oceans. The largest of the nine glaciers is the 30 mile (48km) long Upsala,

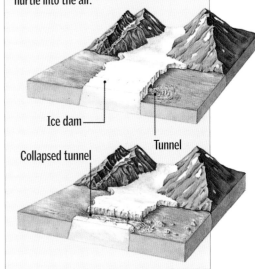

which grinds down to Lake Argentino's northern arm and constantly disgorges huge blue icebergs into it.

In 1893, local landowner Herman Eberhard explored a deep cave near the ice cap. He found a piece of hairy skin, about 4ft (1.2m) long, that had once covered a mylodon – an extinct ground sloth with massive claws and a long tongue. The 10ft (3m) tall animal's skin was so well preserved that at first it was thought to have come from a species that is still in existence.

Climbers are drawn to Los Glaciares, to scale the 11,073ft (3375m) Cerro Fitzroy. This challenging peak rises sharply from grassy plains in the north of the park, providing a rival sight to the Moreno Glacier in the south.

CLOSING IN *Like a vast frozen tongue, the Moreno Glacier (top) advances inexorably through Patagonia's Lake Argentino. The surface of the glacier (above), and its cliff-like sides that rise sheer from the water, are broken by a jumble of deep crevasses.*

Paine Horns

SPECTACULAR, HORN-LIKE MOUNTAIN PEAKS RISE ABOVE AZURE BLUE LAKES AT THE TAIL END OF THE ANDES

Two striking peaks of pinkish–grey granite tipped with black slate rise at the southern tip of the Andes, overlooking the Patagonian steppes. These strange 8350ft (2545m) peaks are Paine Horns, part of the Paine (pronounced Pienay) Massif that lies in southern Chile. The massif was described by Padre Agostini, a Roman Catholic priest who travelled through Patagonia in 1945, as 'an impregnable fortress, crowned with towers, pinnacles and monstrous horns surging boldly to the sky.' Michael Andrews, in *The Flight of*

the Condor (1982) wrote, 'I could not forget their vertical spires, the clarity of the light, the raging wind, and the myriad of flowers.'

The horns are not the only strange peaks in these mountains. Not far

STORMY SETTING *A lowering sky provides a backdrop for Paine Horns, the twin peaks on the left of the picture.*

away are three sheer-sided peaks known as Paine Towers. When Lady Florence Dixie, a British traveller, visited Patagonia in 1879 she saw, against a background of thickly wooded hills, 'three tall peaks of a reddish hue, and in shape exact facsimiles of Cleopatra's Needle'.

WORK OF GLACIERS

A chain of volcanoes running down the Andes gave birth to the granite masses. They solidified underground, and were thrown aloft by subterranean upheavals, breaking through the surface crust of slate that now crowns the peaks. Glaciers shaped the curves of the horns and the steep sides of the towers, and glacier meltwater formed the area's gleaming azure lakes and colourful bogs carpeted with mosses of red, yellow and green.

SADDLEBACK SAFARI

A 19th-century traveller, Lady Florence Dixie (below), saw Paine Towers during a 250 mile (400km) horseback trek from Punta Arenas. On the journey, her party experienced an earthquake, drenching rains and blasting winds, and dined on llama-like guanaco and ostrich-like rheas, with calafaté (berberis) berries as dessert.

The sight of the three peaks was well worth the journey. 'Their white glaciers,' she wrote, 'with the white clouds resting on them, were all mirrored to marvellous perfection in the motionless lake, whose crystal waters were of the most extraordinarily brilliant blue I have ever beheld.'

No-one knows for certain where the name Paine came from. Some say that the word meant pink in the language of the now-vanished Tehuelche people, others that it was the name of a settler in the area. Until the 1950s, few people visited these parts, and the peaks, battered by storms and the fierce Pacific westerlies, remained unclimbed. Italian climbers in Guido Monzino's team scaled the north tower of Paine Towers in 1958 and, in 1963, British mountaineers Chris Bonington and Don Whillans were the first to climb the central tower, the highest and most formidable of the three.

Wildlife abounds in the lakes, forests and meadows, and eagles search the mountain ridges for prey. And the Andean condor, a giant vulture, soars high above on widespread wings – lord of the skies and keeper of the towers.

GRANITE TRIO *Colossal, glacier-carved granite obelisks known as Paine Towers rise near the southern tip of the Andes.*

Penitentes

ROWS OF SPARKLING
SNOW PINNACLES RANGE
BESIDE A HIGH ANDEAN
PASS BETWEEN CHILE
AND ARGENTINA

Silent and eerie, the Agua Negra Pass
high in the remote Andes links
La Serena in Chile with San Juan
Province in Argentina. At an altitude
of 15,633ft (4765m) it is one of the
world's highest motoring passes – a
tough 12-hour drive with a high risk of
plunging into a ravine or of being swept
away by a landslide. The sky is dark in
the thin air, and the shadowy ranks of
the Penitentes – pinnacles of frozen
snow 620ft (1.8-6m) tall – lining the
steep slopes like white hooded figures,
add to the spine-chilling atmosphere.

In 1835, the British naturalist Charles
Darwin thought that the pinnacles were
formed by wind action. But in 1926,
the Argentinian geologist Luciano
Roque Catalano regarded their form to
be the result of electrical effects caused
by intense ultraviolet radiation and dry
air. As the tips melt by day and freeze by
night, the snow crystals are attracted by
electrical fields at right angles to the
Earth's magnetic field, which accounts
for their uniform east-west slant.

SILENT PENITENTS *The snow pinnacles
are named after white-cloaked penitents in
Christian Holy Week processions.*

399

Antarctica

Zavodovski Island

FOR A FEW MONTHS EACH YEAR, PENGUINS SHATTER THE PEACE OF A REMOTE ISLAND IN THE SOUTH ATLANTIC OCEAN

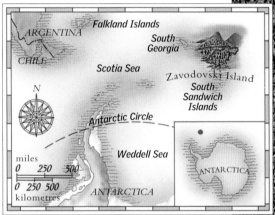

The noise is deafening, the smell overpowering, but at least they are all smartly dressed. This is one of the world's largest gatherings of penguins, and it takes place on a tiny island 1100 miles (1800km) east of the tip of the Antarctic Peninsula.

Zavodovski Island, one of the South Sandwich Islands, is dominated by the volcanic cone of Mount Asphyxia. The island measures hardly 4 miles (6km) across, yet each spring some 14 million pairs of chinstrap penguins arrive there to nest in the volcanic ash. The thigh-high birds, named for the black band under their chins, are joined by yellow-plumed macaroni penguins.

Chinstrap penguins seem to be increasing in number. Their main food, the shrimp-like krill, is in lavish supply. Baleen whales, which also eat krill, are declining in number, and the penguins may be multiplying on the surplus.

STANDING ROOM ONLY *Penguins by the million jostle noisily on Zavodovski Island, discovered by Russians in 1819.*

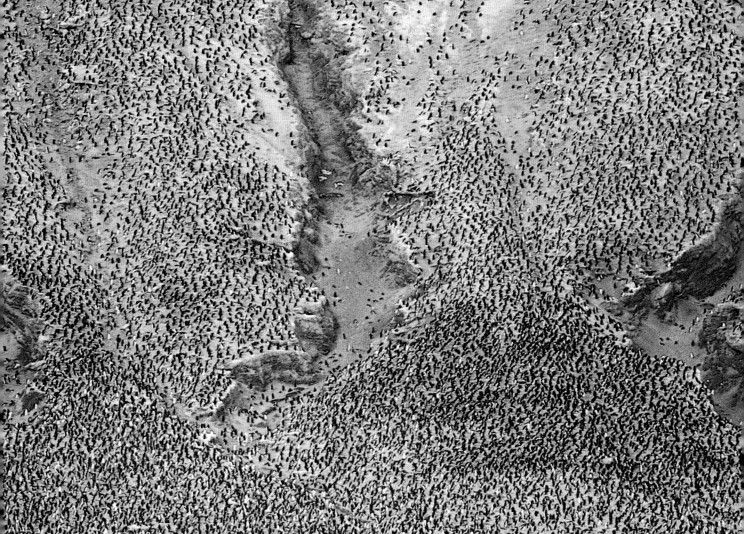

Antarctica's Dry Valleys

NOT A FLAKE OF SNOW LIES IN THE DRY VALLEYS,
IN STARK CONTRAST TO MOST OF THE CONTINENT'S
GLARING WHITENESS

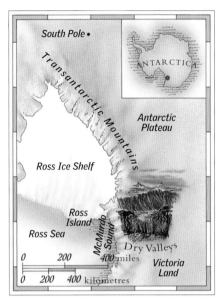

As you fly over Antarctica towards McMurdo Sound, endless white wastes give way suddenly to the browns and blacks of land completely free of snow. Sunk into this unexpected, ice-free area are the Dry Valleys – three massive, steep-sided basins gouged out by long-gone glaciers.

Although ice covers almost all of Antarctica, most of the continent has very low snowfall – the ice accumulated over millions of years. In the Dry Valleys – Taylor, Wright and Victoria – snow equivalent to barely 1in (25mm) of rain falls each year, and the ground is kept free of even this meagre covering by dry winds which blow the snow away, and by the heat that the dark, exposed rocks absorb from the sun.

Each valley has a few curious salty lakes. The largest, Lake Vanda, is more than 200ft (60m) deep and topped by a layer of ice 13ft (4m) thick. Yet the temperature at the bottom of the lake is 25°C (77°F), because the ice acts like a greenhouse and warms the water.

Mummified seal carcasses are scattered over the Dry Valleys. In the cold, dry air decay is extremely slow, and some of the seals may have found their way to the valleys and died hundreds, or even thousands, of years ago.

ICE FREE *'A bare stony trough' wrote Griffith Taylor, of Captain Scott's 1910–12 polar expedition, after seeing the Dry Valley that takes his name.*

Mount Erebus

A GUARDIAN OF FIRE AND ICE WATCHES OVER THE THRESHOLD OF THE EARTH'S LEAST-TRODDEN CONTINENT

Glowing rose-red and turquoise in the midnight sun, and trailing a long banner of steam over Ross Island's miles of snow and ice, Mount Erebus is the very symbol and beacon of Antarctic exploration. At its feet lies the modern sprawl of the US McMurdo Base and, not far off, the huts that once sheltered the expeditions commanded by Robert Scott and Ernest Shackleton.

These huts are shabby now, but otherwise, from tinned food to phonographs, they remain exactly as they were left, unchanged and timeless in the deep preserving cold. It was to those early 20th-century explorers particularly that the 12,261ft (3743m) Mount Erebus was mentor and friend, witness of their triumphs and tragedies, the guide that beckoned them home from a score of mapping or scientific forays.

THROUGH THE PACK ICE

Christening the two peaks that guard the end of the known world Terror and Erebus suggests a nice poetic touch on the part of their discoverer – especially Erebus, for it was the name the Greeks gave to the dark realm through which all the dead must pass. But in fact, the names were simply those of the ships that Captain James Clark Ross RN led into the pack ice in January 1841, in search of the South Magnetic Pole.

As the expedition pressed on southwards, they saw one morning a large and shapely mountain rising above the clouds ahead. From its top there flew a scarf of what at first they took to be blown snow. At this very moment of introduction, the mountain revealed itself as a volcano, letting forth one of its rarish, full-scale eruptions of fire and

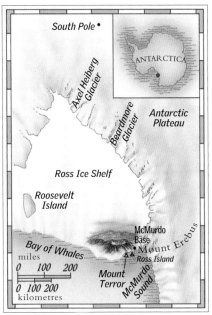

South Pole

Axel Heiberg Glacier

ANTARCTICA

Beardmore Glacier

Antarctic Plateau

Ross Ice Shelf

Roosevelt Island

McMurdo Base
Mount Erebus
Ross Island

Bay of Whales

miles
0   100   200

Mount Terror

McMurdo Sound

0   100 200
kilometres

steam – an astonishing sight in that icy waste. Captain Ross named it Erebus after his own ship, and the smaller, inactive volcano nearby was called Terror, after the companion vessel.

Ross never reached the magnetic pole. His way south was blocked by the vast ice shelf, the size of France, that would later be named after him. Nevertheless, the voyage was accounted

POLAR CAULDRON *Deep in Erebus's crater lies a lake of molten lava that heaves and bubbles, and throws lava bombs far beyond the crater rim.*

a great success, and he returned to England full of honours.

The next explorers to pass by were the men of Captain Scott's expedition of 1901–4. But not until Ernest Shackleton attempted to reach the magnetic and geographical poles in 1907–9 was the first attack made on the summit. The climbers were inexperienced and conditions were frightful – near-vertical plates of blue ice thinly overlaid by snow and temperatures that dropped to −33°C (−28°F). Breathing was difficult in the thin air, and one of the party developed frostbite in the foot.

But at last they gained the summit, and found it to be a very peculiar place indeed, with four craters superimposed one on top of the other. The ground was littered with perfectly formed feldspar crystals, and all about stood an array of ghost-like fantastical shapes that

BEAUTY OF ICE *(overleaf) Seen across the fangs of Ross Island's icefields, Mount Erebus glows with unearthly loveliness as it picks up the dawn rays.*

appeared to be waiting in welcome. These greatly puzzled the party until it was realised that they were fumaroles, or columns of steam that had seeped up through cracks in the ground and frozen solid as they rose. The active crater, 900ft (275m) deep, poured out clouds of sulphurous smoke and spat lava bombs high into the air.

Displays of volcanic artillery are a regular feature at the summit of Mount Erebus, as Colin Monteath, survival expert at New Zealand's Antarctic Scott Base, reported in 1978. 'Dozens of

spinning, molten missiles corkscrew high above us, seemingly in slow motion. Some thud down out of the sky while others hurtle between us, low and fast. Most are about the size of a teapot; however, some very much larger …bombs poured into the main crater floor to send up hissing geysers of steam as they melt into the snow.'

POLAR 'WHITEOUT'

Despite its alarming displays, Mount Erebus had never harmed anyone until a tragic day in November 1979, when a

New Zealand plane on a sightseeing tour flew into the mountainside, killing all 257 passengers and crew aboard. Largely, they were victims of 'whiteout', a polar hazard in which all horizon definition between white land and pale, overcast sky abruptly vanishes. Much of the wreckage is still strewn over the ice – a reminder that Antarctica, although fascinating and beautiful in its own way, is always a dangerous place.

ICE COLUMN *High on Erebus (right), a scientist examines a frozen fumarole – volcanic steam stilled by the cold.*

THE RACE TO THE END OF THE WORLD

Carved on a monument below Mount Erebus are Tennyson's words: 'To strive, to seek, to find, and not to yield' – a tribute to the courage that drove the race for the South Pole in the Antarctic summer of 1911–12. The chief competitors were the British naval captain Robert Falcon Scott and the Norwegian explorer Roald Amundsen.

The two groups' base camps were some 500 miles (800km) apart – the Norwegians in the Bay of Whales and the British on Ross Island. Amundsen favoured dog teams for his sledges, but Scott believed that the team making the final assault on the Pole should haul the sledge all the way. Partly this was due to lack of experience in dog handling. But there was a touch of mysticism in it, too – that the Pole should only be won through personal effort overcoming all hazards.

SECOND PLACE *Beaten by a month, the British team reach the Pole. Eight weeks later all of them were dead.*

'GREAT GOD,' SCOTT CONFIDED TO HIS DIARY, 'THIS IS A TERRIBLE PLACE.'

On October 19, the Norwegians set off with four sledges. A month later came the toughest part of the journey – the climb up the icy chaos of the Axel Heiberg Glacier.

At the top lay the flat run of the Antarctic Plateau. Then on December 14 at 3pm, the drivers, anxiously watching their sledge meters, simultaneously cried 'Halt!' Dead reckoning showed that they had reached the South Pole.

Scott's team of five men, hauling their laden sledge, reached the South Pole on January 17, 1912. In the snowy wastes, the black speck of a tent bearing the Norwegian flag told them they were too late. 'Great God,' Scott confided to his diary, 'this is a terrible place.'

They turned for home. Already, both Petty Officer Evans and Captain Oates were badly frostbitten, and on February 17 Evans died. The other four marched on, but blizzards set in. Aware that he was holding his companions back, Oates walked out into the snow, and was never seen again. Trapped by the blizzard towards the end of March, the remaining three died in their tent. When a search party found them in November, they looked to be no more than asleep.

THE WINNER *Roald Amundsen, first to reach the South Pole, poses there with huskies, and the Norwegian flag behind.*

The forces that shape the Earth

THREE TYPES OF ENERGY – HEAT FROM THE EARTH'S INTERIOR, HEAT FROM THE SUN, AND THE FORCE OF GRAVITY – GIVE THE PLANET ITS FASCINATING FEATURES

The perpetual cycle of change which has created the face of the Earth, with all its rugged and fascinating variety, usually happens too slowly to be noticed. But occasionally it is rapid and violent. Volcanoes disgorge molten lava, earthquakes rip open the landscape, landslides carry away whole mountain-sides. Then human beings become aware of the awesome forces that are shaping their planet.

These forces are fuelled by three powerful sources of energy – heat from within the Earth, heat from the Sun, and the force of gravity. Every landform in the world has been shaped by these three energy sources.

The continents that drift across the surface of the globe, setting off volcanoes and earth-quakes and building mountains, are driven by heat from the Earth's interior which has a temperature of about 5000°C (9000°F). Most of this heat is created by the breakdown of radioactive elements.

Earth is unique among the planets of the Solar System in having liquid water on the surface. And water has a major role in shaping the planet. The warmth of the Sun evaporates water from seas and lakes. The vapour rises and condenses to form clouds and then falls again as rain and snow. It is then that its landscaping powers begin, weathering rocks and washing away the loose material, or grinding down the landscape under the power of a glacier. The Sun's heat also produces the wind and the waves that scour the land.

The third force – gravity – causes the tides, which nibble away at the edges of continents, and landslides, which alter the shape of mountains. Under the influence of gravity, rain works its way downwards as streams and rivers, carving the terrain. On its journey, it carries frag-ments of rock and sand to be deposited on the ocean floor. And over thousands of years this sediment turns back into more rock which may then be buckled and lifted up by movements of the Earth's crust to form new mountains.

STORM CLOUDS *Over the mountains of Arizona, a thunderstorm illustrates one of the forces that mould the planet – the weather, which is driven by the Sun.*

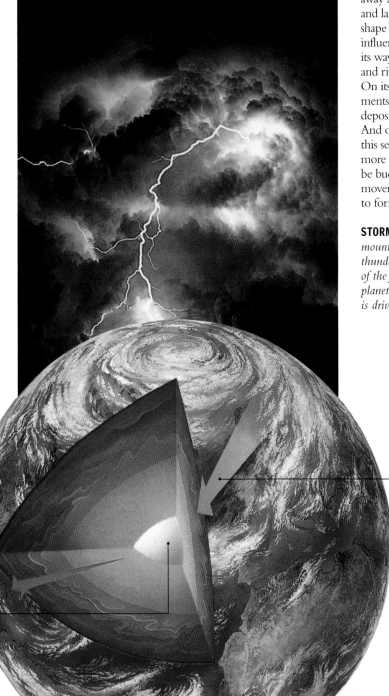

HEAT FROM THE SUN
Water from the oceans is evaporated by the Sun's heat. The vapour forms clouds which then produce rain to make rivers – among the major forces that shape the landscape. The wind, too, is a product of the Sun's warmth.

HOT INTERIOR
The interior of the planet provides much of the heat that causes volcanoes and earthquakes. The heat has been generated since Earth's earliest days, 4500 million years ago.

GRAVITY
Over millions of years mountains are reduced to hills. Frost and water break them up, then rivers – pulled by gravity – carry the fragments to the oceans. At the same time, other forces build new mountains.

Why the continents are drifting across the globe

THE MOST VIOLENT FORCE SHAPING THE SURFACE OF THE EARTH IS THE IRRESISTIBLE MOVEMENT OF THE MAJOR PLATES THAT MAKE UP THE PLANET'S CRUST

MAJOR PLATES *The world is divided into seven main plates, each containing continents and oceans. Some boundaries are pulling apart (divergent), some coming together (convergent) and others sliding past each other (transform).*

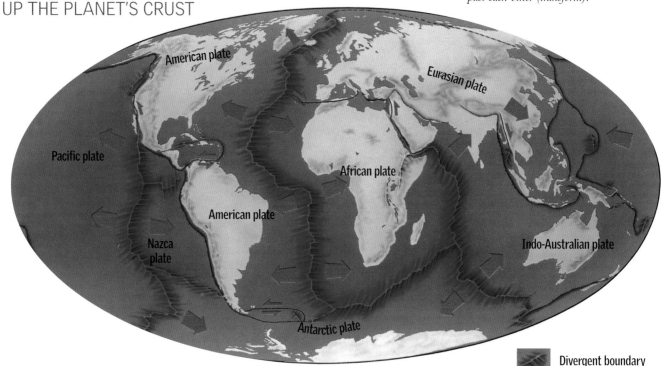

Divergent boundary
Convergent boundary
Transform boundary
Uncertain

 t the speed of a growing fingernail but with a power that defeats human imagination, all the continents are continually drifting across the surface of the planet.

The seven major segments, or plates, which make up the Earth's crust, jostle about the globe, travelling never more than a few centimetres a year. But over the aeons of geological time, parts of the crust have travelled from one side of the world to the other.

This phenomenon, which is known as plate tectonics, is the most important force involved in the shaping of our planet.

Two types of crust make up the Earth's surface – continental crust which we live on and the heavier crust that makes up the floor of the oceans. The continental crust is very much thicker, often more than 25 miles (40km), but the oceanic crust is rarely more than 5 miles (8km) thick.

THE HEAT THAT DRIVES THE PLATES

Underneath both types of crust is the mantle, the thick layer of dense material which separates the crust from the white-hot metal core that forms the centre of the Earth.

The mantle is made up of rock, but because of its great heat it is semi-liquid in places – soft enough to flow sluggishly, like treacle taken from the refrigerator. The even greater heat of the molten core has the same effect on the mantle as a lighted gas ring has under a pan of porridge. It sets up convection currents that cause the mantle to rise, spread out at the top where it loses some of its heat, and then sink down again. It is these convection currents in the mantle that drive the continents around the globe.

The convection currents rise beneath the Earth's great oceans. The heat causes the rock on the ocean floor to melt and to rise in liquid form, reaching the surface as volcanic lava. The

molten rock slowly oozes up through the sea floor, creating underwater volcanic ridges. Sometimes it pushes up sufficiently high to form volcanic islands, such as Iceland and its satellite island, Surtsey, which was born in 1963.

As the currents in the mantle move outwards from the ridge, they take with them – floating on top – the rigid plates of the crust, together with the topmost layer of the mantle. The underwater volcanoes of the mid-ocean ridges are continually

411

creating new crust as their lava solidifies, replacing the crust that moves outwards. So, as new ocean crust is being formed, these ocean plates are growing all the time.

THE ATLANTIC WAS NARROWER WHEN COLUMBUS SAILED ACROSS

The continents on each side of the Atlantic Ocean – the Americas on the west, Africa and Europe on the east – are being pushed apart at about 1in (25mm) a year. When Columbus crossed the Atlantic in 1492 it was about 40ft (12m) narrower than it is today.

If all the oceans of the world carried on spreading, the whole Earth would have to get bigger, and this is clearly not happening. The Pacific Ocean is, in fact, shrinking. At the edges of the Pacific, crust is diving beneath the continental crust of Asia and the Americas as it follows the convection currents down into the mantle. This has produced a 'ring of fire'

of volcanoes and earthquakes in the lands bordering the Pacific.

The regions where the ocean plates disappear into the mantle, called subduction zones, are marked by deep ocean trenches. The deepest is the Mariana Trench in the Philippine Sea which is 36,197ft (11,033m) deep – more than 7000ft (2100m) deeper than Mount Everest is high.

The Atlantic will not keep on expanding for ever; subduction zones will develop at its margins, and South America and Africa will eventually draw together again and then meet to create one great continent, just as they were 150 million years ago. This is nothing new in the long history of the planet, which is 4600 million years old. Countless oceans have opened and closed, shunting the continents about. They will continue to do so as long as Planet Earth survives.

THE MAN THEY DIDN'T BELIEVE

A German astronomer and meteorologist, Alfred Wegener, introduced the theory of continental drift –

MINERAL CHIMNEYS *Fantastic towers rise from the Atlantic floor (right) as water, heated in deep cracks along the plate boundary, deposits minerals.*

RICH HARVEST *Shrimps cluster around the mineral chimneys to feed on bacteria living near the hot springs.*

yet his ideas were ridiculed during his lifetime.

Born in Berlin in 1880, Wegener became interested in maps that had been published in France pointing out the matching shapes of the Americas and Africa. As a meteorologist, Wegener built on the idea by examining past climates and fossil records.

His theory, published in 1915, proposed that the continents are drifting over the surface of the Earth. Although Wegener found

MID-OCEAN RIDGE
Volcanic lava oozes through the ocean floor along the dividing line between two plates. The lava creates new crust to fill the space as the plates separate.

SHELL MYSTERY *Shells in mountain rocks perplexed early geologists. Plate tectonics finally explained how the sea floor had risen.*

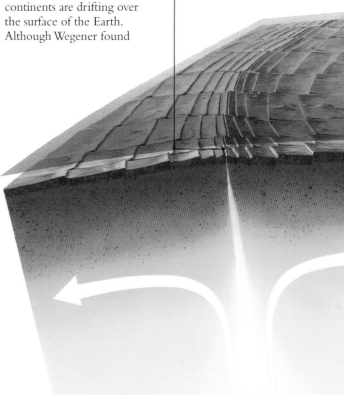

OCEANIC CRUST

The crust that makes up the ocean floor forms a thin layer over the mantle. It is heavier than continental crust.

SUBDUCTION ZONE

Following the convection currents, ocean crust dives beneath a continent. It then melts, creating areas of volcanoes and earthquakes.

CONTINENTAL CRUST

The sections of crust that make up the continents float like thick rafts in the top of the mantle. They are often more that 25 miles (40km) deep.

MANTLE

A layer of rock that has been made semi-liquid by the heat of the Earth's core.

CONVECTION CURRENT

Heated by the core, currents in the mantle rise, spread out at the top and sink again. As they move outwards they carry the crust with them.

RIDGE OF FIRE *The Mid Atlantic Ridge rises above the sea in Iceland where a series of spectacular eruptions occurred between 1975 and 1981 as lava burst to the surface.*

THE OCEANS' DEEPEST PLACES

PACIFIC Mariana Trench (Challenger Deep), 36,197ft (11,033m)

ATLANTIC Puerto Rico Trench, 30,200ft (9200m)

INDIAN Java (Sunda) Trench, 26,400ft (8047m)

ARCTIC Angara Basin, 17,850ft (5440m)

ANTARCTIC *(Southern)* South Sandwich Trench (Meteor Deep), 27,651ft (8428m)

The lowest known place on Earth has never been visited by humans. It is the Challenger Deep, part of the Mariana Trench in the western Pacific, east of the Philippines. It was discovered in 1951 by the British survey ship *Challenger*, and the depth of 36,197ft (11,033m) was later established by a Russian survey ship using echo soundings. In 1960 a manned US bathyscaph descended to 35,810ft (10,915m), which is almost 7000ft (2100m) further than the height of Mount Everest.

evidence that the continents had split apart and moved from their original positions, he was unable to explain the vast forces that were needed to make it happen. He believed that the 'fit' of Africa with the east coast of South America was not a coincidence. And he was convinced that all the continents were once lumped together in a supercontinent called Pangaea (Greek for 'all lands'), surrounded by an ocean.

Wegener found related rocks and fossils on continents separated by oceans. For example, fossils of the glossopteris fern have been found in both Brazil and South Africa, suggesting that 200 million years ago the Atlantic did not separate the two land masses. He pointed to coal deposits in Siberia that must have formed in the tropics, and ancient glacial deposits in Africa, as evidence that continents had drifted from one climatic zone to another.

Wegener's fossil evidence was compelling, because

Charles Darwin had shown that if species become isolated from each other, they will evolve differently. So diversification from an apparently common ancestor must imply that some form of physical separation had taken place far back in the past. Other geologists argued that a land bridge had once existed between Africa and South America, and that when it broke up animals could no longer get across.

Wegener also suggested that colliding continents would explain the crumpling of rocks into mountain chains. But this was dismissed by geologists in favour of the theory that the Earth had shrunk, and wrinkled into mountain chains.

Wegener died on an expedition in Greenland in 1930 at the age of 50, more than 20 years before his theory became accepted. In 1931 a British geologist, Arthur Holmes, put forward the idea that convection currents in the Earth's semi-liquid mantle could cause sections of the crust to move.

Then in 1963 came evidence that the floor of the oceans was spreading, and pushing the continents around as it did so.

When molten rocks solidify they take up the magnetic field of the Earth. The Earth's field has reversed many times in the past, and it was discovered that the patterns of magnetic change either side of the mid-ocean ridges were symmetrical, and that the rocks increased in age away from ridges. Clearly, the crust was forming at the ridges and moving sideways. The force behind Wegener's theory had been found.

ARCTIC COMFORT *On an expedition to Greenland in 1912–13, Alfred Wegener took a collection of pipes to see him through the Arctic winter. He died in Greenland in 1930.*

The fiery, active youth of volcanoes

WHETHER BORN IN MID-OCEAN OR ON THE EDGES OF CONTINENTS, ACTIVE VOLCANOES PROVIDE THE EARTH'S GREATEST SPECTACLES

On February 20, 1943, a Mexican farmer saw gas and dust rising from a crack that had opened up in his field. During the night, the fissure erupted and by morning a cone 30ft (9m) high was hurling out ash and lumps of rock. At the end of a year the cone had grown to 1000ft (300m) and had buried the nearby village of Paricutin. Then lava poured from the side of the newly formed mountain and engulfed a town 6 miles (10km) away.

After nine years of destruction, the volcano died down and has been quiet ever since.

Paricutin volcano was the first to be studied by scientists almost from the moment of its birth. Its remarkably short life cycle makes it highly unusual among volcanoes which can often remain active for millions of years. Of course, Paricutin – which lies in an active volcanic region – could surge back to life at any moment.

Active volcanoes are the most dramatic of the world's natural wonders. They are born when rock melts deep down in the Earth's crust – or even deeper down in the mantle – then is squeezed upwards and bursts through the surface.

A volcano's shape depends on the lava it produces. Thin, runny lava spreads out in sheets and builds up into a wide, flattish mound called a shield volcano. Thick, sticky lava forms a much taller cone shape, like Mount Fuji. The runny lava consists of molten mantle; the thick lava is molten crust. The world has 1300 active volcanoes, most of them along the edges of the plates.

HOT SPOTS

Volcanoes can also form in the middle of plates above isolated 'hot spots' in the mantle. The Hawaiian Islands are the best example. They are a string of huge shield volcanoes that have formed as the Pacific plate has moved over the hot spot.

The world's biggest active volcano, Mauna Loa on Hawaii itself, is currently moving just off the hot spot. To the south-east, right over the hot spot, lies Kilauea volcano whose activity is increasing while Mauna Loa's declines. The other islands in the chain are formed from older volcanoes that have now been carried well away from the hot spot by the movement of the plate.

All the volcanoes in the Hawaiian Islands are made of a hard, dark rock called basalt which is formed from molten material derived from the upper mantle and is the commonest type of lava. The Hawaiian lava is the runny type, and the volcanoes have built up from the long succession of lava flows that have issued from them. Basalt lava is so runny that the hot streams – which are coloured orange – can sometimes move as fast as 60mph (100km/h). Some of the flows come from the central vents at the top of the volcano, but most pour out from long fissures on the flanks.

Frequently a lava flow disappears underground for a while, down a lava tube. Tubes are formed when the top of a lava flow cools and solidifies but the inside remains hot and continues to flow. When the eruption stops, a long hollow tube remains. Later flows may run down the same tube.

Hawaiian basalt solidifies into two types. One is known by the Hawaiian name *pahoehoe*, referring to its smooth surface which is formed from a stretched skin of cooling lava. The skin may sometimes become wrinkled into the common ropey variety.

The other type of lava, called *aa*, has a thicker crust of cooled lava which gets sheared and broken by the movement of hot lava beneath, so that it forms a surface of jagged, loose blocks.

FIERY FOUNTAIN *Lava erupts from the flank of Kilauea volcano, Hawaii. The island is the youngest of the Hawaiian chain, created as the Pacific plate creeps north-west over a hot spot.*

BIZARRE LANDSCAPES *Smooth pahoehoe lava on Mauna Loa (left) contrasts with jagged aa lava on Kilauea (above).*

VOLCANOES ON THE OCEAN FLOOR

The ridges which stretch across the floor of the world's oceans, dividing one tectonic plate from another, are littered with volcanoes. Quietly and unobserved by human beings, they are continually pouring out lava. The emerging lava is quickly chilled by the water and becomes encased in a skin, so that it forms football-size lumps which break off and pile up one on top of the other, giving them their name 'pillow lavas'.

Occasionally deep-sea volcanoes grow tall enough to poke up above the waves, and sometimes they are tall enough to form substantial islands. Iceland is a cluster of such volcanoes, perched right on top of the Mid Atlantic Ridge.

In 1963 the world watched a new island, Surtsey, form off Iceland. Born amid clouds of steam and gas as the lava made the ocean boil, Surtsey was a glimpse of the immense heat engine that drives the Earth's active crust. As the sea floor spreads, Surtsey will travel to one side of the ridge. It will eventually become extinct and waves will erode it down to an underwater guyot, just as the Hawaiian volcanoes will one day be eroded by the Pacific Ocean.

THE RING OF FIRE

The region around the Pacific Ocean is named the 'ring of fire' from the volcanoes that encircle its shores. They are among the most violent in the world – formed above subduction zones where the ocean plates are diving down beneath the continental plates. They spew out ash, lava, steam and gas, produced by the melting of continental crust as it is carried down into the hot depths.

Most of the ring-of-fire volcanoes are classic cone-shaped mountains with a central pipe and possibly a few secondary fissures on the side. They usually produce lava that is much thicker than the basalt lava of the ocean volcanoes. This is because they contain a large amount of silica from the molten continental crust. The runny lava of Hawaii, which is formed from molten mantle and oceanic crust, contains less silica. The combination of the thick lava and the masses of ash and other explosion debris piled up around the vents gives the ring-of-fire volcanoes their conical profile.

The highest volcano in the world is on the ring of fire. Ojos del Salado rises to 22,595ft (6887m) in the Andes on the border of Argentina and Chile.

Ring-of-fire volcanoes are more violent than oceanic ones because steam in the thick lava cannot escape. It is trapped in the lava like the bubbles in champagne, and it may explode, perhaps producing frothy lava called pumice.

If volcanoes have lain dormant for many years, cooled lava in the neck acts like a cork, sealing in the remaining lava and the gases. The pressure mounts and the volcano's sides may even swell slightly as more lava fills the chamber. Eventually the volcano reaches bursting point, and the explosion that follows can be so violent that the whole mountain is blown apart.

On May 18, 1980, the top and side of Mount St Helens in Washington State, USA, was blown apart, devastating a large area. A fiery cloud of ash, gas and steam rose 16 miles (25km) into the air. But St Helens was a modest explosion in the history of volcanoes.

When Tambora volcano in Indonesia erupted in April 1815, it hurled 40cu miles (165km³) of rock and lava into the sky, leaving a crater 7 miles (11km) across. More than 90,000 people died.

Tambora in turn was a mere firework compared to eruptions in the distant past that have left mighty scars on the landscape such as the Yellowstone caldera (giant crater) in Wyoming that covers 1000sq miles (2500km²).

SURPRISE GUEST *Paricutin appeared in a Mexican cornfield in 1943. In a year it built a cone of cinders 1000ft (300m) high.*

VOLCANIC SHAKE-OUT *In 1980, an earthquake shook loose a landslide on the north flank of Mount St Helens. This released a blast which devastated the pine forests up to 12 miles (20km) away.*

MID-OCEAN RIDGE
Along the boundary where two plates are moving apart, lava rises to fill the gap, sometimes forming volcanic islands.

GUYOT
As the plate moves, the volcano travels away from the ridge and becomes extinct. Waves wear it down.

HOT SPOT
Molten rock rises from a 'hot spot' in the mantle to form a volcano on the ocean floor. It may build up until it protrudes above sea level to form islands such as Hawaii. As the lava is very fluid the volcanoes are wide and fairly flat. They are called 'shield volcanoes'.

EXTINCT VOLCANO
The hot spot remains stationary while the plate moves. As the volcano is carried away from the hot spot, it becomes extinct. But it remains as an island, perhaps one of a chain.

PLATE MOVEMENT

SUBDUCTION ZONE

'RING OF FIRE' VOLCANOES
Cone-shaped volcanoes are formed out of thick lava above subduction zones where ocean plates dive beneath continental plates. Because of the stickiness of the lava, and the steam it contains, they are highly explosive.

EXPLOSIVE SPECTACLE *Curtains of liquid rock, belching out of fissures in the ground, are typical of an Hawaiian eruption. Gases in the lava expand explosively to produce the spectacle.*

THE WORLD'S WORST ERUPTIONS

TAMBORA, INDONESIA, 1815
Deaths: 92,000

KRAKATOA, INDONESIA, 1883
Deaths: 36,000

MT PELEE, MARTINIQUE, 1902
Deaths: 30,00.

NEVADO DEL RUIZ, COLOMBIA, 1985
Deaths: 22,000

MT ETNA, SICILY, 1669
Deaths: 20,000

VESUVIUS, ITALY, AD 79
Deaths: 16,000

MT ETNA, SICILY, 1169
Deaths: 15,000

UNZEN-DAKE, JAPAN, 1792
Deaths: 10,400

LAKI, ICELAND, 1783
Deaths: 10,000

KELUT, INDONESIA, 1919
Deaths: 5000

Volcanoes in old age

WHEN VOLCANOES LOSE THEIR YOUTHFUL FIRE, THEY MAY LEAVE LANDSCAPES OF HOT SPRINGS, BUBBLING MUD AND SKELETONS OF THEIR INTERNAL WORKINGS

The most dramatic landforms created by volcanoes are giant calderas – great circular scars, often many miles across, which were left behind when huge volcanoes of the past blew apart.

Lake Taupo in New Zealand is a typical caldera. Two thousand years ago a large volcano lay dormant while lava built up beneath it. Then in AD 186 it erupted so violently that the whole centre of the mountain collapsed into the magma chamber. Where a majestic mountain once stood, with its summit in the clouds, there is now a wide lake fringed by a circle of low cliffs that mark the boundary of the huge caldera collapse.

Sometime around 1645 BC, the central part of the Greek island of Santorini collapsed during a massive eruption which destroyed the ancient city of Akrotiri. Santorini may be the site of the mythical island of Atlantis described by Plato as having been engulfed by waves. The circle of islands that make up modern Santorini are the rim of the caldera left behind after the explosion. A new volcano has appeared in the lagoon.

As active volcanoes fade into dormancy, they may leave a landscape of gas-emitting vents, hot springs and mud pools, often inside a caldera.

Hot springs are formed when ground water percolates down towards a body of molten rock, called magma, then heats up and rises to the surface again. If the water gets hot enough it will boil, and steam will eject it towards the surface with great force to form a geyser. Old Faithful in Yellowstone Park gushes forth regularly every 1¼ hours or so – the time it takes for the steam pressure to build up in underground reservoirs.

The molten rock in the roots of a volcano may take millions of years to cool and solidify, because the overlying rock acts like an insulating tea cosy.

CALDERA *Faial volcano on the Azores in the Atlantic has collapsed to form a caldera. The caldera's floor lies 1000ft (300m) below the rim.*

FLOOD BASALT
Lava pours out of fissures in the ground and builds up layer by layer.

CALDERA
Remains of a volcano which collapsed into its magma chamber.

LACCOLITH
When molten rock from the magma chamber forces older rock upwards, it cools into a mushroom shape.

GAS VENTS AND MUD POOLS
Sulphurous gas gushes out of the ground, coating rocks with yellow deposits. Hot water rises and mixes with decayed rock to form bubbling mud.

DYKE
Lava that flows into a vertical crack underground cools to form walls of rock which become exposed by erosion.

VOLCANIC PLUG
Molten rock solidifies in the feeder pipe of a volcano and is later exposed by erosion.

HOT SPRINGS AND GEYSERS
Rainwater percolates down into the hot rock where it is heated and rises again as hot springs. If it boils, the steam will shoot it out as a geyser.

STOCK
A dome-like offshoot of the magma chamber, called a stock, may eventually be exposed on the surface after the softer rock above has been eroded away.

RING DYKES

VOLCANIC PLUG *Lava which hardened inside a volcano's feeder pipe has been exposed by erosion in Cameroon, West Africa.*

EXPOSED DYKE *Molten rock oozed into a crack and solidified underground to form this dyke on the Aleutian Islands in the North Pacific.*

A dormant volcano will eventually become extinct, although no volcano above an active plate margin can ever be said to be truly extinct. The wind and weather then erode away the ash and the softer rocks through which the volcano erupted, to expose the internal feeder pipes which are now choked and solid with old magma. Because rock that is formed from cooled magma is usually very hard, the pipes and plugs of old volcanoes resist weathering and are left as protrusions in the landscape.

Devils Tower in Wyoming, USA, which was made famous in the film *Close Encounters of the Third Kind*, is a volcanic plug. The original volcano profile has long been eroded away, leaving intact the solidified lava that was inside the pipe. This has revealed the internal structure of six-sided basalt columns that were formed when the lava shrank as it cooled.

Basalt columns are more common in lava flows, like

SILL

Molten rock that penetrates between horizontal layers of sedimentary rocks solidifies to form a flat sill.

the Giant's Causeway in Northern Ireland, than in volcanic plugs. Rows of columns side-by-side like organ pipes stand perpendicular to the flow. Very often

PIPES AND PLUGS ARE LEFT AS PROTRUSIONS IN THE LANDSCAPE

lava of this sort has erupted from a fissure in the ground rather than from a volcano, with lava pouring out and flooding the land. These lava flows, also called flood basalts, may form high plateaus built up from successive lava sheets. The Deccan plateau, which makes up a fifth of India, was one of the largest outpourings of lava in the Earth's history.

As lava is squeezed to the surface it makes use of any fracture or weakness in the rock. Often it does not reach the surface but solidifies underground. In vertical cracks, molten rock congeals to make dykes – long straight walls of rock which may resist erosion. A dyke 9 miles (15km) long stretches out from Ship Rock in the New Mexico desert.

If the molten rock worms its way between horizontal cracks it hardens to make a sill. The

Whin Sill in northern England was left as a long escarpment after the softer rock above was eroded away. It was used by the Romans as a barrier between Scotland and England, and they built part of Hadrian's Wall along the top of it.

Molten rock injected into layers of sedimentary rock may bend the sedimentary rock upwards, forming a mushroom shape called a laccolith. Sometimes, laccoliths are stacked one on top of the other as the lava bursts up in successive layers and forms a 'Christmas tree' laccolith. The Judith Mountains in The US state of Montana take their shape from laccoliths.

Beneath every volcano, there

is – or was – a magma chamber. Often, the magma cooled underground, usually forming crystalline rock such as granite. Later Earth movements and erosion may strip off the rock which covered these batholiths, and expose the granite on the surface. In Cornwall, round offshoots of a magma chamber called stocks protrude above the surface to make granite moorland such as Bodmin Moor. The Sierra Nevada in California is composed of a huge batholith which has been exposed to form a range of mountains. The granite walls of Yosemite Valley are cut in just a tiny fragment of them.

BASALT COLUMNS
The Gorge of Alcantara River in Sicily is cut through basalt columns of amazing regularity. The six-sided columns were formed by lava which shrank and cracked as it slowly cooled.

The cracks where the Earth divides

AS TECTONIC PLATES MOVE, THE EARTH'S SURFACE SHIFTS ALONG FAULT LINES

The whole of the Earth's surface is criss-crossed with cracks where brittle rocks have fractured under the immense forces exerted by the Earth's moving plates.

Some of these cracks are clearly visible, others are not. Some are small enough to be seen in a pebble, others stretch across whole continents.

If the rocks on either side of a crack move, or have moved at some time in the past, the crack is called a fault. Some faults are active. They move from time to time – sometimes every few years or decades – with a sudden shunting and scraping of the rocks which releases vast amounts of energy. The shock waves from the movement shake the ground and cause earthquakes, which can range from barely noticeable tremors to disastrous

upheavals (see overleaf). The most famous scar on the face of the Earth – and the most dangerously active – is the San Andreas Fault in California which runs right through the city of San Francisco.

WHEN PLATES SLIDE PAST EACH OTHER

The most active and fast-moving faults are caused by sections of crust sliding past one another. These faults sometimes occur along plate boundaries and are usually extremely deep, running from the surface down to the bottom of the Earth's crust. They are called transform faults.

The San Andreas Fault is the line along which the Pacific plate is sliding against the North American plate. The western edge of California is attached to the Pacific plate and is slowly moving, earthquake by earth-

quake, up the coast and past the rest of North America.

Sections of the Earth's crust have been moving along transform faults for the past 3 or 4 billion years. So the landscape on either side of a fault may show a stark contrast. This is clearly seen in Scotland, where a transform fault called the Great Glen Fault forms a gash right across the country and contains a line of lakes including Loch Ness. The Grampians to the south of the fault are younger and more rounded, and have an average height of 2800ft (850m). The Northwest Highlands to the north are older and more rugged but are lower, with a height of about 2100ft (650m).

WHEN CONTINENTS STRETCH AND TEAR

When two moving plates pull apart, a continent can become stretched. Under the enormous stress the crust tears, and faults are formed. Then rocks on one side of a fault may drop below the level of the other.

These 'normal' faults seldom occur singly. Swarms of near-parallel faults can be traced in the Greek islands. They are still moving, and indicate that the Aegean Sea

PACIFIC PLATE
The western edge of California is attached to the plate, which is moving at about 2in (50mm) a year relative to the rest of North America.

is slowly becoming wider, causing earthquakes in the eastern Mediterranean.

The most famous pair of normal faults runs through Israel, down both sides of the Dead Sea Valley, then south through the Red Sea and all the way down East Africa as far as Mozambique. The two faults are mirror images of each other, and the land between has dropped to form the Rift Valley which is about 30 miles (50km) wide. The faults are marked by lines of hills – in places forming a sharp escarpment about 10,000ft (3000m) high.

The valley floor contains a string of seas and lakes – the

WIDENING RIVER *The Rio Grande in New Mexico, USA, flows along a fault which is widening as two plates move apart.*

DIVIDED COUNTRY *Iceland is being torn in two by 1in (25mm) a year as two plates pull apart along the Mid Atlantic Ridge.*

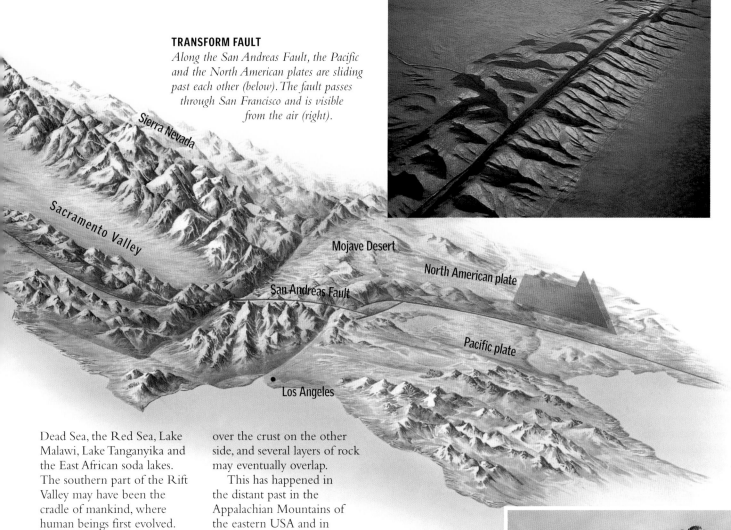

TRANSFORM FAULT
Along the San Andreas Fault, the Pacific and the North American plates are sliding past each other (below). The fault passes through San Francisco and is visible from the air (right).

Dead Sea, the Red Sea, Lake Malawi, Lake Tanganyika and the East African soda lakes. The southern part of the Rift Valley may have been the cradle of mankind, where human beings first evolved.

WHEN CONTINENTS COLLIDE

If two land masses crash into each other, the vast forces of the collision create reverse (or thrust) faults. The crust on one side of the fault rides up over the crust on the other side, and several layers of rock may eventually overlap.

This has happened in the distant past in the Appalachian Mountains of the eastern USA and in Brittany in France. In the recent geological past – 25–30 million years ago – it occurred in the European Alps. And it is still happening in the Himalayas as India drives up into the heart of Asia.

REVERSE FAULT
When two continental plates collide (right), one may ride up over the other, as at Culan Peak in the Swiss Alps.

NORMAL FAULT
As two continental plates pull apart, faults develop in the Earth's crust. A steep-sided valley may form between two faults as the ground between them subsides. Along the Great Rift Valley in East Africa, the land has sunk between two parallel faults. In Tanzania (right), the cliffs marking the line of the faults tower 1500ft (460m) above the valley floor.

Lurching rocks that can wreak terrible destruction

EARTHQUAKES USUALLY OCCUR ALONG PLATE BOUNDARIES, BUT NOWHERE ON EARTH IS REALLY SAFE FROM THEIR DEVASTATION

The most destructive earthquakes occur at the boundaries of the Earth's plates. As the plates move and grind against each other at the speed of a growing fingernail, enormous stresses slowly build up over decades or centuries until – often without warning and sometimes with terrible violence – the rocks suddenly lurch along fault lines.

In the devastating 1906 earthquake which destroyed large parts of San Francisco, one section of the San Andreas Fault moved 20ft (6m) in 48 seconds.

SHOCK WAVES

When the rocks move, shock waves travel through the Earth and shake the ground at the surface. Sometimes this causes no more than a tremor that rattles kitchen crockery, but sometimes it destroys entire towns, with terrible loss of life.

The intensity of the earthquake depends on three things: the amount of energy released (as measured on the Richter scale), the depth at which the movement happens, and the nature of the surface.

In the San Francisco earthquake of October 1989, which measured 7 on the Richter scale, 70 people died, yet an earthquake of the same magnitude in Armenia in December 1988 killed 25,000 people. The Armenian earthquake took place only 3 miles (5km) below the surface, compared to 10 miles (16km) in the San Francisco earthquake.

The devastation in 1985 of the Mexico City earthquake which killed 2000 people was due largely to the city being built on the soft sediments of an old lake. Because of their poor foundations, many buildings collapsed.

The San Andreas Fault is clearly visible on the surface, but most plate boundaries are not. In fact, the subduction zones where ocean crust takes a nose dive back into the mantle were only discovered by the pattern of earthquakes and volcanoes that they

OUT OF LINE *Earthquakes in California caused kinks in two streams where they crossed a fault and jolted an orange grove out of alignment.*

produce. Plotted on a map, an intense concentration of volcanoes and earthquakes was seen to form a 'ring of fire' around the Pacific Ocean.

One of the most devastating earthquakes in living memory was caused by the subduction of the Pacific plate under Alaska in 1964. It was so violent that soils and clays on the surface of the ground behaved like a liquid, losing all their solidity and 'swallowing' buildings. Great chasms opened up, and landslides crashed down hillsides. A giant wave swept inland, carrying ships and everything else in its path.

NOWHERE IS FREE OF RISK

It is tempting to think that if you live away from plate margins you are immune from earthquakes. But nowhere is free of risk. The constant pushing and shunting in the crust frequently causes rocks around ancient faults to build up stress which eventually gives way.

In 1884, New York – which is far from any plate boundary – suffered an earthquake which measured 7 on the Richter scale, although no-one was killed. And in the same year an earthquake was felt over half of Britain, also far from any plate boundary. In the town of Colchester in Essex, 400 buildings were damaged, but once again there were no deaths.

Smaller, often imperceptible, earth tremors occur all the time throughout the world, each one playing its own small part in the constant slow shuffle of the Earth's ever-changing crust.

FLOODING
If the earthquake occurs near a coast, low-lying land may be flooded by fast-moving waves ('tsunamis').

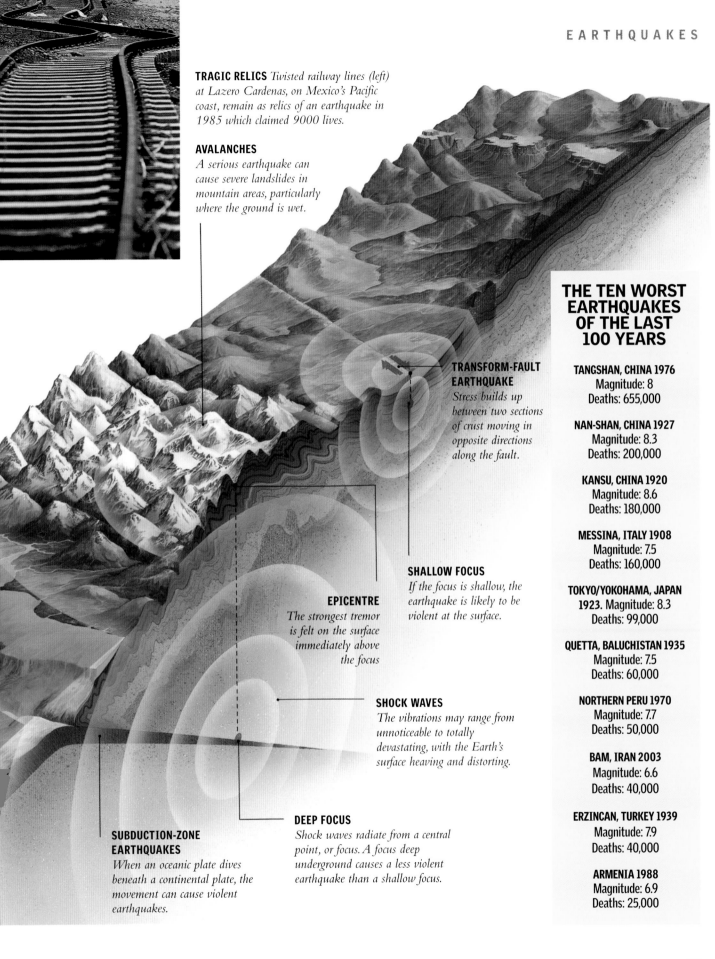

TRAGIC RELICS *Twisted railway lines (left) at Lazero Cardenas, on Mexico's Pacific coast, remain as relics of an earthquake in 1985 which claimed 9000 lives.*

AVALANCHES

A serious earthquake can cause severe landslides in mountain areas, particularly where the ground is wet.

TRANSFORM-FAULT EARTHQUAKE

Stress builds up between two sections of crust moving in opposite directions along the fault.

SHALLOW FOCUS

If the focus is shallow, the earthquake is likely to be violent at the surface.

EPICENTRE

The strongest tremor is felt on the surface immediately above the focus

SHOCK WAVES

The vibrations may range from unnoticeable to totally devastating, with the Earth's surface heaving and distorting.

SUBDUCTION-ZONE EARTHQUAKES

When an oceanic plate dives beneath a continental plate, the movement can cause violent earthquakes.

DEEP FOCUS

Shock waves radiate from a central point, or focus. A focus deep underground causes a less violent earthquake than a shallow focus.

THE TEN WORST EARTHQUAKES OF THE LAST 100 YEARS

TANGSHAN, CHINA 1976
Magnitude: 8
Deaths: 655,000

NAN-SHAN, CHINA 1927
Magnitude: 8.3
Deaths: 200,000

KANSU, CHINA 1920
Magnitude: 8.6
Deaths: 180,000

MESSINA, ITALY 1908
Magnitude: 7.5
Deaths: 160,000

TOKYO/YOKOHAMA, JAPAN 1923. Magnitude: 8.3
Deaths: 99,000

QUETTA, BALUCHISTAN 1935
Magnitude: 7.5
Deaths: 60,000

NORTHERN PERU 1970
Magnitude: 7.7
Deaths: 50,000

BAM, IRAN 2003
Magnitude: 6.6
Deaths: 40,000

ERZINCAN, TURKEY 1939
Magnitude: 7.9
Deaths: 40,000

ARMENIA 1988
Magnitude: 6.9
Deaths: 25,000

The violent birth of mountains

IN THEIR NEVER-ENDING JOURNEY AROUND THE GLOBE, THE EARTH'S PLATES THROW UP CHAINS OF MOUNTAINS AS THEY COLLIDE WITH DEVASTATING FORCE

Don't be misled by the apparent permanence and great age of mountains. In the Earth's long history, mountains have continually come and gone, rising in splendour only to be eroded down to remnant hills. The highest are the youngest. Mt Everest itself didn't begin to take shape until about 15 million years ago, when the apes that fathered mankind already had a firm foothold on the planet.

As the plates carrying the Earth's oceans and continents move endlessly around the globe, they jostle each other like gigantic dodgem cars, sometimes getting involved in head-on collisions. And it is these collisions that bring about the birth of the great mountain chains.

When an ocean plate slides beneath a continental plate, its rocks melt as they are forced down into the hotter depths of the Earth, and some of that molten rock creates a string of volcanoes up above. At the same time, the overriding continental plate crumples along its leading edge to create more mountains.

When two continental plates meet head-on, huge quantities of the Earth's crust are squeezed upwards like a train crash in slow motion.

Once mountains have been raised, however, Nature's other forces set about eroding them down until the whole process begins all over again,

taking millions of years. Mountain-building is a never-ending cycle, and mountains at many different stages of the cycle can be found all over the globe.

A RING OF FIRE

While the plates are moving around, driven by convection currents in the Earth's mantle, sediment accumulates on the floors of the seas and oceans. The sediment consists of fragments of old rock washed down from the surrounding continents, as well as the skeletons of millions of tiny creatures that live and die in the sea. These sediments, astonishingly, may be destined to become part of the mountains of the future.

Eventually, the edges of the oceanic plate are forced down beneath the plates carrying the continents. Temperatures are so high at these depths that the oceanic plate melts, together with some of the

sediment and the rocks in the continental plate above.

Liquid rock, being lighter than solid rock, rises through the Earth's crust to form a line of volcanoes along the edge of the continent. Volcanoes produced in this way form chains of young mountains such as the Andes on the western coast of South America and the Cascades on the western coast of North America.

The young volcanoes erupt at frequent intervals. And, though young, they may reach great heights. Mount Aconcagua in the Andes is the highest point in North or South America at 22,835ft (6960m).

Under the enormous pressure, faults can also develop in the continental crust, and

THE HIGHEST PEAK

The farthest point from the centre of the Earth is the top of a dormant volcano in Ecuador - Mount Chimborazo. Because the Earth bulges at the equator, Chimborazo stands 7050ft (2150m) 'higher' - from the Earth's centre - than Mt Everest. But measured from sea level Mt Chimborazo is only 20,560ft (6267m) high compared to Mt Everest's 29,028ft (8848m).

CHIMBORAZO *Its peak (below) is farther from the Earth's centre than Everest.*

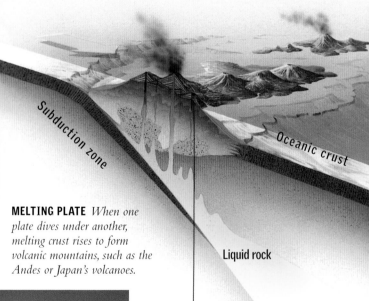

MELTING PLATE *When one plate dives under another, melting crust rises to form volcanic mountains, such as the Andes or Japan's volcanoes.*

Liquid rock

VOLCANIC MOUNTAINS
Rocks from both plates melt when they reach higher temperatures at the greater depths. Some of the liquid rock rises to the surface.

VOLCANIC PEAKS *Mount Jefferson in the American Cascade Range is in a line of peaks that reveal the volcanic origin of the mountains.*

blocks of crust are thrust on top of each other, separated by huge, nearly horizontal fault lines. In the Himalayas, Annapurna – the world's eighth highest mountain – is formed of ancient limestones that were thrust up over younger rocks.

ISLAND ARCS
Strings of islands are formed largely of volcanoes generated by the melting of the sinking plate.

The same pressures cause severe folding of the rocks, and all the world's great mountain chains are formed of rocks folded and faulted on a grand scale. The intensity of the folding declines away from the collision zone to create marginal fold mountains such as the outer ranges of the Appalachians in the eastern United States.

FOLD MOUNTAINS
Sedimentary rocks have more gentle folds on the fringes of the main compression zone.

SEDIMENTARY ROCK
Particles of old rock washed into the sea by rivers settle on the ocean floor, together with the remains of marine animals, and turn into layers of new rock.

Continental crust

SUBDUCTION ZONE
Oceanic crust dives beneath continental crust, as is happening on the west coast of South America.

HORSTS
Low mountains called horsts remain from earlier movements. When a plate was stretched, faults occurred, producing rift valleys with the horsts between them.

Liquid rock

ALPINE JUMBLE *The Alps are still being pushed up in a complex jumble of folded rocks as the African plate and Europe collide.*

They were formed when Africa and America collided about 300 million years ago.

The mountains of Wales were produced by these processes 450 million years ago, but aeons of erosion have since reduced them to their present modest size.

COLLIDING CONTINENTS

When an oceanic plate no longer has an active construction zone above a rising convection current, the ocean is doomed to close up. The continents on each side drift together and finally collide with a devastating impact.

Slices of continental crust concertina and pile on top of each other. Slabs of ocean floor get scooped up into the pile, and rocks at the bottom of the heap melt to form granite. The force of the collision may be so great that one continent pushes its way under the other. This is what is happening today under the Himalayas as the Indian subcontinent forces its way beneath the rest of Asia. The Himalayas are being pushed upwards at about ⅛in (3mm) a year. The crumpled rocks of the Himalayan Mountains and the Tibetan plateau represent the remains of the two continental margins and an intervening ocean which were originally more than 1250 miles (2000km) across.

As the forces within the Earth give birth to new mountain ranges, the world's existing mountains are slowly being eaten away by the power of gravity and erosion. In about 40 million years, rivers and glaciers will have reduced the mighty Himalayas to the proportions of the American Rockies. And in 400 million years they will be down to the level of the Scottish Highlands. But the continuing dynamo of plate movement will eventually create another great mountain range to succeed the Himalayas. Such is the rise and fall of all great mountain chains.

WHY MOUNTAINS FOLD LIKE A BLANKET

When continents collide, some rocks get pushed up into folds which can vary in width from a fraction of an inch to several miles. Folding occurs in deeply buried rocks that are so hot they are soft and malleable. At cooler temperatures, most rocks are brittle, consequently they crack along faults instead of folding.

Folds in rocks are formed in the same way as if you put a blanket on a shiny table and push it from both sides. More compression creates stronger folds, which eventually topple over on top of each other.

The stacking of folded rocks is enhanced as one plate pushes over another in a collision zone. Mountain chains are built of fold upon fold, which may be difficult to distinguish as individual features within a region that has been dissected by faults. Farther away from the main area of compression, however, gentler folds are formed

ERODED FOLD *Sheep Mountain, Wyoming, is the remnant of a fold mountain that has been eroded away, revealing its layers.*

which can be seen in the shape of the land. The Jura Mountains of Europe reveal their folds clearly, away from the complex deformations in the core of the Alps.

PLATE IMPACT *As two continents collide, they concertina into a gigantic pile of folded and fractured rocks, such as the Himalayas.*

OVERRIDING CONTINENT

Under the intense pressure, one continent may force its way under the other — as is happening now in the Himalayas where India is diving under the rest of Asia.

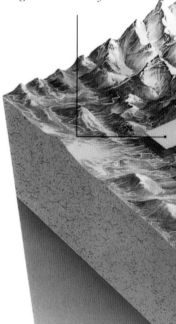

HIGHEST POINTS ON THE CONTINENTS

AFRICA, KILIMANJARO (TANZANIA)
19,340ft (5895m)

ANTARCTICA, VINSON MASSIF
16,863ft (5140m)

ASIA, EVEREST (NEPAL/CHINA)
29,028ft (8848m)

AUSTRALIA, KOSCIUSZKO (NSW)
7316ft (2230m)

EUROPE, MONT BLANC (FRANCE)
15,770ft (4807m)

NORTH AMERICA, MCKINLEY (ALASKA)
20,320ft (6194m)

SOUTH AMERICA, ACONCAGUA (ARGENTINA/CHILE)
22,835ft (6960m)

RISING ROCK *A sweeping curve of rock rose up in the Zagros Mountains of Iran as the Arabian and Eurasian plates collided.*

THRUST FAULTS
The continental crust cracks under the impact, and blocks of crust slide up over each other.

EROSION
Even as the mountains are born, wind and water begin to wear them down. Fragments are swept into the ocean by rivers to form sedimentary rock that will become mountains in the distant future.

FOLDED SEDIMENTS
As two continents come together, sediments on the ocean floor between them are squeezed into folds.

GRANITE
At the bottom of the pile, rocks start to melt and form granite.

OCEAN FLOOR
Slabs of deformed ocean floor basalt are caught up in the chaotic pile.

LIMESTONE ARCH *Thin sheets of limestone have been contorted into a 65ft (20m) multilayered arch on the south-west coast of Wales.*

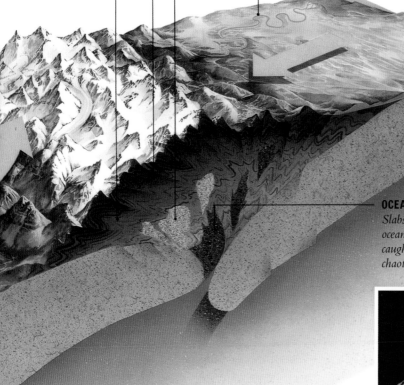

YOUTHFUL PEAKS *Lhotse in Nepal, the world's fourth highest mountain, displays the pointed peaks and sharp ridges that are characteristic of young mountains.*

Sun and gravity: forces of erosion

THE ENERGY OF THE SUN, WHICH CREATES THE WEATHER, COMBINES WITH THE FORCE OF GRAVITY TO FLATTEN THE HIGHEST MOUNTAINS

High in he Andes mountains of Peru, it had been snowing steadily for several days, but January 10, 1962, was warm. At 6pm all was quiet in the nine villages around Mount Huascaran. But by 6.20pm eight of the villages had been wiped out and at

least 3500 people had died. A vast mass of snow and ice, loosened by the Sun's warmth, had crashed down from the mountain, picking up rocks, trees and buildings on its 12½ mile (20km) journey.

Eight years later, on May 31, 1970, an earthquake shook the same region. Near the summit of Mount

Huascaran a huge slab of ice and rock was shaken free. It hurtled down the mountain at 300mph (480km/h), killing 21,000 people and wiping out the only village that survived the previous catastrophe.

The power of the Sun – the creator of weather – had caused the snow to fall on the fatal mountain. Then its

warmth began to melt the snow, causing the mass to become unstable before the first disaster. On both occasions, once the mass was loose, the force of gravity took over.

These two great forces – the heat energy of the Sun and the pull of gravity – play major roles in shaping the Earth's surface.

ENERGY FROM GRAVITY

Landslides occur when a slope becomes unstable, perhaps because chemical reactions have eroded the underlying rock, and the rock is no longer able to support its own weight. Sometimes

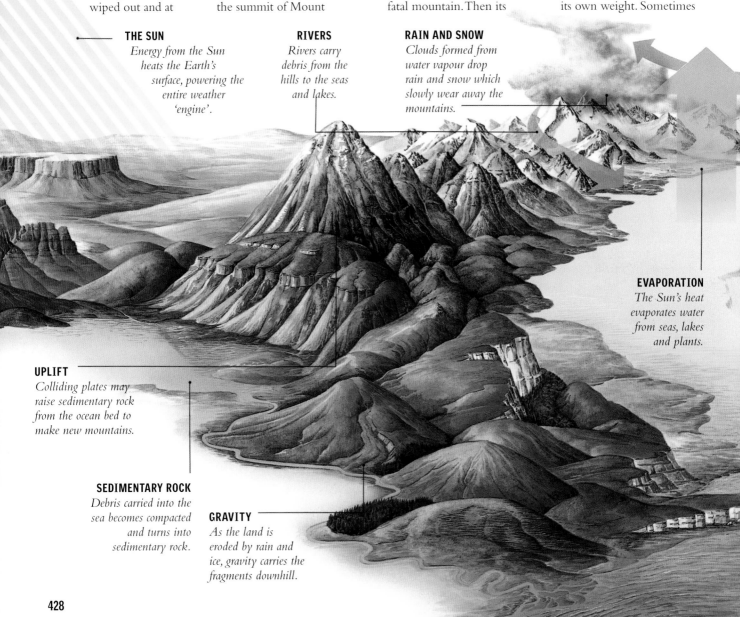

THE SUN
Energy from the Sun heats the Earth's surface, powering the entire weather 'engine'.

RIVERS
Rivers carry debris from the hills to the seas and lakes.

RAIN AND SNOW
Clouds formed from water vapour drop rain and snow which slowly wear away the mountains.

EVAPORATION
The Sun's heat evaporates water from seas, lakes and plants.

UPLIFT
Colliding plates may raise sedimentary rock from the ocean bed to make new mountains.

SEDIMENTARY ROCK
Debris carried into the sea becomes compacted and turns into sedimentary rock.

GRAVITY
As the land is eroded by rain and ice, gravity carries the fragments downhill.

heavy rain can trigger land-slides by simply adding more weight. Or water flowing through the soil and rock may reduce their grip and set off sudden movement.

Earthquakes can set off landslides in active mountain regions such as the Himalayas and the Andes where the rocks are under stress as the Earth's plates collide.

Rockfalls on a much smaller scale frequently create typical mountain features called scree. Steep cliffs, which rarely have plants growing on them, are open to all weathers. As the rain beats against the rock, water seeps into the cracks. When the temperature falls below freezing point, the water turns to ice and expands, splitting the rock further. Pieces of rock fall from the cliff face and collect lower down the slope in a loose pile (the scree).

Gravity also has a role in forming 'quick clay', which is similar in effect to quicksand, and can destroy whole towns. Very fine particles of rock eroded by glaciers are carried downhill by gravity and deposited in lakes. If the water later drains away, the fine silt becomes solid, but if it should become waterlogged again or be shaken by an earthquake it will lose its strength and 'liquefy'. In the Alaskan earthquake of 1964, part of the city of Anchorage was destroyed because it had been built on quick clay which liquefied under the shock. As the ground became unstable, buildings toppled and some sank up to first floor level in the clay.

On a much larger scale, the crust of the Earth can be bent when huge layers of ice build up. This happened in northern Europe during the last Ice Age when glaciers more than 1 mile

SCREE BEDS *On the Arctic islands of Svalbard, frost crumbles the cliffs, and gravity pulls the fragments down to form piles of scree.*

WIND POWER *North Sea storms, driven by the Sun's energy, swamp the German island of Gröde, which in summer is grazing land.*

CLIFF COLLAPSE *California's Route 1 was buried by a landslide during a disastrous earthquake in 1989.*

(1.6km) thick moved across Scandinavia. When the ice melted 10,000 years ago, the Baltic Sea flooded the land, but the loss of weight allowed the land to rise slowly until it formed a multitude of islands – the Stockholm Archipelago – which are still rising at about 20in (510mm) each century.

At the most commonplace level, gravity is seen at work every day as it sculpts the landscape. Without it, water would not flow downhill, producing dramatic waterfalls and shaping the hills and valleys into the forms that human beings find so beautiful.

ENERGY FROM THE SUN

The world's weather, which is constantly eroding the landscape into its multitude of curious shapes, is caused by the energy of the Sun.

The Sun's radiation heats the Earth's surface which then warms the air at ground level. The air expands as it gets warmer, becoming lighter. It then rises, forming areas of low pressure. Colder air moves in from areas of higher pressure to fill the 'space', and this movement produces the winds. As less of the Sun's energy reaches the Earth at the poles than at the equator, large-scale air circulation takes place

RAIN LEAVES BILLIONS OF TINY PITS IN THE SOIL

between these two areas of high and low temperature.

Warm air evaporates water from lakes, seas and plants. This moist air, driven by the winds, is forced to rise as it crosses hills and mountains. At the higher altitude it cools and water vapour condenses to form clouds of water droplets. Within the clouds the tiny droplets combine to form raindrops,

RAVAGED LAND *The red soil of Madagascar is bleeding away down the country's rivers, staining them a matching red. Tree felling has left the hillsides vulnerable to erosion by rain.*

or – in freezing conditions – hailstones or snow.

Ordinary raindrops falling on bare ground will cause the soil to splash upwards and outwards, leaving tiny pits. Billions of raindrops will move huge amounts of soil or rock debris, and on a slope most of the particles will fall a little farther down the hill. Over long periods of geological time whole mountain ranges can be worn away by rain combined with the shattering effect of frost on rocks. Rivers and glaciers then carry the debris away, causing more erosion on their way.

Where soil is formed from small particles mixed with large rocks, curious earth pillars, such as the Ritten Pillars of north-eastern Italy, can be formed. Rain washes away the finer material, leaving the bigger rocks

perched on top of a pinnacle of sand and clay, acting like an umbrella to protect the material beneath. The pillars at Ritten are as high as 130ft (40m). Eventually the capstone topples off and the pillar is then rapidly eroded. Earth pillars are also found in the Cappadocia region

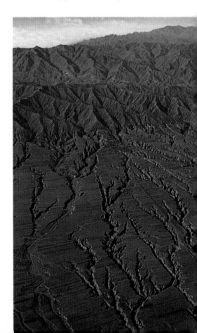

BADLANDS *Erosion by wind and rain has stripped the land to its bare bones on the coast of Santa Cruz Island, southern California. Such ravaged landscapes are known as badlands.*

of Turkey and the badlands of the USA.

In deserts, wind can shape rocks by bombarding them with sand, acting like a sand-blasting machine. Softer rocks are worn away more quickly than hard ones, creating weird shapes that are characteristic of desert scenery.

The wind is also capable of carrying the eroded dust great distances. The fine-grained soil of northern China, called loess, is formed from dust blown out of the dry, cold lands of central Asia. It has been deposited in layers more than 1000ft (300m) thick.

Heating and cooling are powerful agents of erosion in dry areas where plants do not protect the rock surfaces. Travellers have reported hearing desert rocks crack during the night as they cool, perhaps to near freezing, after daytime temperatures of 50°C (120°F). Dew may then soak in and start a chemical reaction in the rock, causing it to split.

Despite all the forces of erosion that are created by the Sun's energy and the pull of gravity, the Earth is not being reduced to a flat landscape.

The relentless movement of plates that make up the Earth's crust ensures that new mountain ranges rise up to replace the peaks that have been reduced to rolling hills.

TOR *Granite blocks have been shaped by weather to form the Cheesewring tor on Bodmin Moor, Cornwall.*

SCARRED PLATEAU *Water erodes the thick soil called loess, which was deposited by wind in northern China.*

Limestone country: land of caves and dry valleys

SKELETONS OF UNTOLD NUMBERS OF SEA CREATURES HAVE FORMED A TYPE OF ROCK THAT BECOMES HONEYCOMBED BY RUNNING WATER

On May 10, 1981, a large sycamore tree disappeared down a hole that suddenly opened up in a suburban garden in Florida. Over the next few hours, the hole grew and the tree was followed by a three-bedroom house, five cars, a parking lot and much of the municipal swimming pool. The hole, in the Winter Park district of Orlando, ended up the length of a football field and the depth of an eight-storey office block.

The Winter Park sinkhole was nothing new to Florida; it was just bigger than usual.

Central Florida stands on a bed of limestone 1000ft (300m) thick. Water has eroded the limestone to create cavities that are normally filled up with water

or mud. But when the water table drops, as it did during the 1981 drought, the thin roofs of the empty caverns may collapse, creating enormous sinkholes.

Limestone areas, which are typically riddled with caves, sinkholes and dry gorges, are also known as karst scenery, after a limestone region on the border of north-eastern Italy and Slovenia.

Karst scenery is formed when water from rain and streams percolates down through the limestone rock, following the natural joints. The water has become a weak form of carbonic acid after absorbing carbon dioxide gas from the air and the soil. The acid slowly eats away the limestone, like a gigantic attack of tooth decay taking place over hundreds

of thousands of years.

Nearly all the world's limestone was created from the shells and skeletons of countless millions of creatures which lived and died in the sea many millions of years ago. The tiny skeletons settled on the bottom of the sea and hardened into rock. Over millions of years the sediments built up into layers that may, occasionally, be as thick as the height of Mt Everest. Upheavals of the Earth's crust later pushed the limestone above sea level.

Among the creatures that helped to form the limestone were corals, related to the coral which today forms reefs off Australia, the West Indies and some of the islands in the Indian and Pacific Oceans. Today's coral reefs may become part of the limestone landscapes of the distant future. You can often recognise limestone country by the limestone pavements on the surface. Pavements are irregular, bare stone broken up by joints and blocks. There is probably no water on the surface because rain drains down through the joints to form underground streams.

As the water follows the joints in the limestone, it

LIMESTONE PINNACLES *Slightly acidic rainwater dissolves the limestone of Mount Api, Borneo, to create razor-sharp pinnacles.*

IMMORTALISED IN STONE

In the late 18th century a French scientist, Déodat de Dolomieu, discovered that the mountains in the northeast of Italy were made of a limestone rich in magnesium. The rock is much harder than the surrounding shale and clay. After the Alps were formed 50 million years ago, erosion began wearing away the softer rock, eventually leaving behind the spectacular steep-sided range of today.

Similar magnesium-rich limestones are found in the Appalachian Mountains in the eastern United States.

Now the name of the French scientist, Dolomieu, has been immortalised in the term dolomitic limestone, and the Dolomite Mountains of Europe.

STALAGMITE *Temple of the Sun stalagmite rises from the floor of the Big Room chamber in Carlsbad Caverns, New Mexico.*

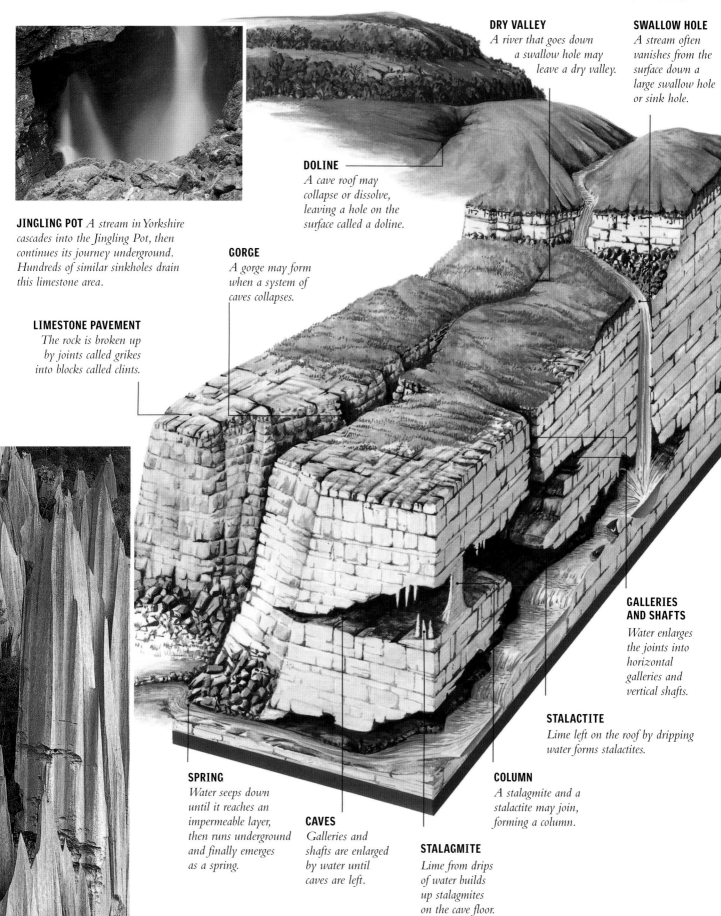

DRY VALLEY
A river that goes down a swallow hole may leave a dry valley.

SWALLOW HOLE
A stream often vanishes from the surface down a large swallow hole or sink hole.

DOLINE
A cave roof may collapse or dissolve, leaving a hole on the surface called a doline.

JINGLING POT *A stream in Yorkshire cascades into the Jingling Pot, then continues its journey underground. Hundreds of similar sinkholes drain this limestone area.*

GORGE
A gorge may form when a system of caves collapses.

LIMESTONE PAVEMENT
The rock is broken up by joints called grikes into blocks called clints.

GALLERIES AND SHAFTS
Water enlarges the joints into horizontal galleries and vertical shafts.

STALACTITE
Lime left on the roof by dripping water forms stalactites.

SPRING
Water seeps down until it reaches an impermeable layer, then runs underground and finally emerges as a spring.

CAVES
Galleries and shafts are enlarged by water until caves are left.

STALAGMITE
Lime from drips of water builds up stalagmites on the cave floor.

COLUMN
A stalagmite and a stalactite may join, forming a column.

433

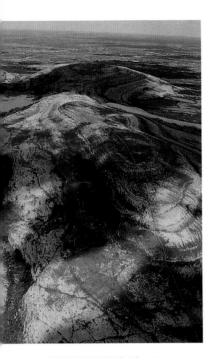

ROUNDED HILLS *The Burren in Ireland was scraped clean by glaciers 15,000 years ago, leaving stark limestone hills.*

LIMESTONE PAVEMENT *At Malham, North Yorkshire, limestone has been eroded by the weather into bare rock pavement.*

slowly dissolves the rock and enlarges the joints into horizontal galleries and vertical shafts, also called potholes. Over many thousands of years, galleries and shafts become enlarged by rock falls to form caves that can develop into enormous caverns. The world's biggest cave, the Sarawak Chamber in Borneo, is 3½ times as long as St Peter's Basilica in Rome and twice as wide.

The interiors of many caves are a wonderland of bizarre limestone formations. Stalactites hang from the ceiling, formed by dripping water that leaves behind tiny deposits of lime (calcium carbonate). Over the millennia stalactites can grow to astonishing sizes. The longest in the world descends 21½ft (6.5m) in the Poll an Ionain cave in County Clare, Republic of Ireland.

On the floor of a cave, stalagmites grow upwards as

the slowly dripping water falls from the stalactites above. Eventually the two may join to form a column of limestone stretching from floor to ceiling. The shapes are often strange, ghostly and many-coloured, stained by chemicals such as iron and copper which have dissolved from the rocks above.

CAVE POOLS

In some caves pools form on the floor as the flowing water is dammed behind some natural obstruction. When the water evaporates, the calcium carbonate is deposited along the 'shore' forming a low ridge. This ridge follows the outline of the water and eventually becomes a natural dam supporting a subterranean lake. Because the air is almost motionless underground, the surface of the water acts like a mirror, perfectly reflecting all the stalactites and the other structures on the roof of the cave.

If the calcium-rich water flows over moss or any other plants in the open air, limestone is deposited, a process

SCULPTED GORGE *The Vikos Gorge in Greece has been carved over the years by water running through the limestone.*

called petrification.

In southern China in the provinces of Guangxi and Yunnan, the same processes that form karst scenery have produced sheer-sided towers of limestone up to 330ft (100m) high. Because the grey limestone blocks in Yunnan look like old tree stumps, the area is called the Stone Forest.

THE WORLD'S TEN DEEPEST CAVES

KRUBERA (VORONJA) CAVE, GEORGIA 6824ft (2080m)

LAMPRECHTSOFEN VOGELSCHACHT WEG SCHACHT, AUSTRIA 5354ft (1632m)

GOUFFRE MIROLDA/LUCIEN BOUCLIER, FRANCE 5335ft (1626m)

RESEAU JEAN BERNARD, FRANCE 5256ft (1602m)

TORCA DEL CERRO DEL CUEVON, SPAIN 5213ft (1589m)

SARMA, GEORGIA 5062ft (1543m)

CEHI 2, SLOVENIA 5030ft (1533m)

SHAKTA V. PANTJUKHINA, GEORGIA 4948ft (1508m)

SISTEMA CHEVE (CUICATECO), MEXICO 4869ft (1484m)

SISTEMA HUAUTLA, MEXICO 4839ft (1475m)

Coasts: where land and sea battle for supremacy

THE COMPETING FORCES OF WAVES, TIDES AND RIVERS MAKE THE SHORELINE AN EVER-CHANGING LANDSCAPE OF CURIOUS SHAPES

The frontier between land and sea is one of the most violent, rapidly changing zones on Earth. It is a battleground where wind and waves assault the shoreline, often with enormous ferocity. It is also a region where new land is constantly being created as rivers deposit sediment in the sea to form deltas and islands. Consequently, the coastal fringe is often moving and altering its appearance.

Every day most of the seas of the world have two tides which rise and fall in an apparently gentle motion. But the strength of the tides varies from month to month and from year to year, and they possess great destructive power. During the last weekend of January 1953, high tides in the North Sea coincided with hurricane-force winds to produce tides more than 7ft (2m) higher than expected. The waves poured over sea walls in eastern England and Holland, flooding nearly 1200sq miles (3000kkm²) of coastal land. A total of 2107 people were drowned in the two countries.

DEMOLITION BY WAVES

The relentless and destructive power of the sea can be seen in the steady demolition of an apparently rock-solid headland. Any cape or promontory that projects out from the coast into the sea is likely to be made of stronger rock than the rest of the shoreline, and has been formed by the sea eroding away the surrounding land more easily. The face of the headland then takes the full force of the pounding waves.

The sea will seek out the weakest points in the cliffs, and gradually erode them away to form caves. Sometimes the caves will break right through to create a sea arch. As the sea continues to attack the headland, the supports of the arch grow thinner until they collapse, leaving the end of the promontory as a solitary sea stack. One such stack is the Old Man of Hoy which rises 445ft (136m) on the coast of the Orkney Islands, north of Scotland. It has stood in isolated splendour since the sea arch which joined it to the Island of Hoy collapsed 300 years ago.

Eventually, the stack itself will be demolished by the sea's bombardment.

The weather and waves are not the only factors that affect the shape and form of the coastline. The rocks themselves exert a strong influence. Hard rocks like granite or old limestones form towering cliffs. On Molokai, Hawaii, volcanic rocks soar above the sea nearly three times the height of the Empire State Building.

Softer clay, mud or shale form the collapsing cliffs of California and eastern England. Rotted, ground-down and eroded rocks form the sandy beaches of eastern Australia, Florida and South Wales.

THE LAND SINKS AND RISES AGAIN

The position of coastal rocks, however, is not permanently fixed in relation to the level of the sea. Around the northern end of the Gulf of Bothnia, on the western shores of Finland, the land is rising. Twenty thousand years ago, during the last Ice Age, this whole area was covered in ice several kilometres thick. The weight of the ice

ANCIENT SEABED *Australia's Nullarbor Plain ends abruptly in limestone cliffs. Rocks pounded today by the ocean were laid down on the sea floor 20 million years ago.*

435

sheet was so great that the land sank.

Now that the ice has gone, the land is slowly rising again. Boulders with metal rings in them have been found in the middle of farm fields in northern Finland. About 100 years ago these rocks were on the shoreline and boats used to be tied up to the rings.

Today, Greenland still bears its load of ice. If the ice melts, Greenland may begin to rise again. Perhaps the great, great grandchildren of today's Greenlanders will see new coastlines, with today's beaches well inland.

Similar 'raised beaches' can be seen today around the Island of Arran in Scotland. Old cliffs, caves and sand are raised above the present sea level by 25ft (7.5m) and more.

In other parts of the world, which were not under the ice, the coastlines were drowned when the sea rose by about 410ft (125m) as the Ice Age came to an end 10,000 years ago. Most of the water from the melting ice flowed into the sea until it submerged low-lying coasts and filled river mouths to form rias, like Sydney Harbour in Australia. Rising water also flooded valleys cut by glaciers to form the fjords of Norway, Chile, New Zealand and Canada.

GLOBAL WARMING

Another change in sea level may take place in the future because of 'global warming'. If the world is getting warmer, as many scientists believe, the seas will get warmer, too. Warm water takes up more space than cold water, as you can see if you fill a cup to the brim with hot coffee and let it go cold. The cold coffee will be below the top of the cup. If the world's oceans warm

ROCK STALKS *In the Bay of Fundy, Nova Scotia, the tide falls 45ft (14m), exposing rocks eroded by the water.*

DELTA
Silt deposited at a river mouth. The river enters the sea along several channels.

FJORD
Deep inlet carved by a glacier and later flooded.

RIA
Former river valley that was flooded when the sea rose after the Ice Age. Can make an excellent harbour.

COVE
Carved out when the sea penetrates a weakness and erodes rocks behind.

BEACHES
Consist of sand and gravel formed from rock broken up by the sea or carried by rivers.

LOW CLIFFS
Composed of chalk, soft limestone, sand or clay. Waves undermine them.

TOMBOLO
A sand bar linking an island with the shore.

SPIT
Waves carry sediment along the shore, building a spit where the land changes direction.

SALT MARSH
Mud flats that form behind barriers.

BAY-MOUTH BAR
Waves sweep sand and stones across the mouth of a bay.

DUNES
Formed when wind-blown sand is trapped by plants.

WAVES AT WORK *The Pacific Ocean has carved stacks and arches on the Oregon coast of the United States (above). The delicate Porte d'Aval arch and L'Aiguille rock needle (left) were shaped by the Atlantic Ocean, from chalk cliffs in northern France.*

SAND BARRIER *A spit across the mouth of a small river at Drakes Beach, California, is built of sand pushed by waves along the coast.*

up, their levels will rise, flooding coastal plains and river valleys. The rise in water level will be made even worse by the extra water pouring into the sea from melting ice caps. If the ice sheets on Antarctica and Greenland melted completely, the world's oceans could rise by about 165ft (50m).

Currents in the sea are another powerful force that shapes coastlines. A current may sweep stones and sand along beaches and across the sea floor, building up sand spits along the coast. A spit may continue to grow until it stretches across the mouth of a bay. A salt marsh is likely to form behind it, making an ideal habitat for birds. As the marsh builds up, the land may become part of the mainland as on the coasts of Massachusetts and north-west Germany.

Silt that is carried down by a river may build up at the river mouth to form a delta which can spread far out into the sea. The largest delta in the world, formed by the combined Ganges and Brahmaputra rivers, covers 30,000sq miles (78,000km^2).

HIGH CLIFFS
Usually made of hard rock such as granite or hard limestone. Not easily damaged by the sea.

HEADLAND
Usually made of stronger rock than the rest of the shoreline.

SEA STACK
Left standing when a sea arch collapses under constant attack by the sea.

SEA ARCH
When the sea attacks a headland, a cave is formed and is eventually cut right through.

CAVE
Produced when a weakness in the rock is attacked by the waves.

CONTINENTAL SHELF
Area of submerged land, gently sloping towards the deeper parts of the ocean.

WHITE CLIFFS *In southern England, the Seven Sisters present a sheer chalk face to the sea.*

How rivers carve patterns in the land

THE RELENTLESS FLOW OF WATER FROM MOUNTAIN TOPS TO THE SEA CREATES RIVER VALLEYS AND TRANSPORTS ENORMOUS AMOUNTS OF ROCK AND SOIL

In every country on Earth, rivers have helped to carve the shape of the landscape. Some rivers, such as those in the dry lands of southern Europe, the American south-west and inland Australia, only flow in the rainy season. Some may not have flowed for thousands of years, such as the Wadi Hadramaut in Arabia. Other rivers, such as the Tiber and the Thames, have flowed, flooded and dwindled for as long as stories have been told.

The longest river in the world is the Nile, which flows for 4160 miles (6695km) from the mountains of central Africa to the Mediterranean Sea. The shortest is the D River in Oregon, USA, which flows for 120 feet (37m) from Devils Lake to the Pacific Ocean. Despite their length, all rivers have much the same life cycle.

As rain and snow falls on the land, it is drawn downwards by gravity until it reaches the lowest point, usually a lake or the sea. As the water flows it wears away rock, and moves the sediment downhill. Rivers are ceaselessly wearing away the world's mountains. In its upper reaches, the river usually flows quickly, eroding the ground as it goes.

The carving process happens in three ways. When a river is flowing very strongly, perhaps during a flood, the bigger stones and boulders are moved. They roll and bounce along the

THE WORLD'S LONGEST RIVERS

NILE, AFRICA
4160 miles (6695km)

AMAZON, SOUTH AMERICA
4000 miles (6440km)

CHANG JIANG (YANGTZE), CHINA 3915 miles (6300km)

MISSISSIPPI-MISSOURI, USA 3740 miles (6019km)

OB'IRTYSH, RUSSIA
3460 miles (5570km)

ZAIRE (CONGO), AFRICA
2900 miles (4670km)

HUANG HE, CHINA
2900 miles (4670km)

AMUR (HEILONG JIANG), RUSSIA/CHINA
2800 miles (4510km)

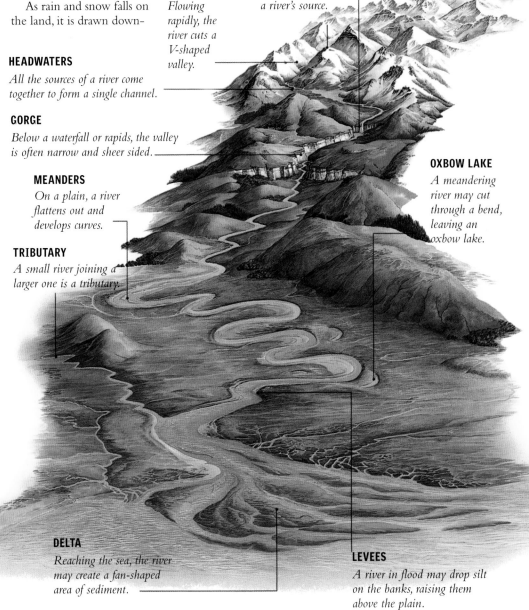

HEADWATERS

All the sources of a river come together to form a single channel.

GORGE

Below a waterfall or rapids, the valley is often narrow and sheer sided.

MEANDERS

On a plain, a river flattens out and develops curves.

TRIBUTARY

A small river joining a larger one is a tributary.

UPPER VALLEY

Flowing rapidly, the river cuts a V-shaped valley.

SOURCE

Water from a glacier, lake or spring can be a river's source.

WATERFALL

Soft rock in the bed wears away quicker than hard rock. A waterfall may occur.

OXBOW LAKE

A meandering river may cut through a bend, leaving an oxbow lake.

DELTA

Reaching the sea, the river may create a fan-shaped area of sediment.

LEVEES

A river in flood may drop silt on the banks, raising them above the plain.

river bottom as the 'bed load'.

Pieces of mud, silt and clay are picked up and carried along as 'suspended load'.

Some of the chemicals in the rocks are dissolved in the water and moved in solution – the 'dissolved load'. Limestone is often worn away like this.

The quantity of sediment carried by some rivers is enormous. In northern China the Huang He (Yellow River) each year carries 1600 million tons of silt from the uplands

of China to the Yellow Sea. The amount of silt is so great that the river banks have built up above the level of the surrounding farmland, so that the river flows above the land. In years of heavy rainfall the river can break through the banks (or levees), causing devastating floods. In 1887, when it burst its banks near the city of Zhengzhou, more than a million people died from drowning and from the starvation and disease that followed. In other years, low rainfall has brought famine from drought. It is not surprising that the Huang He is also known as 'China's Sorrow'.

The speed of the water is not the only way a river carves its valley. Rivers flow over different kinds of material – some hard like granite and basalt, some soft like clay or alluvium. The strength of the rock influences the shape of the valley. Harder rocks usually produce narrow,

CHANGE OF PACE *In Provence, the Regalon River (above left) cuts through a gorge. In Venezuela (left), a river meanders through rainforest.*

steep-sided valleys, whereas softer material gives a softer, concaved shape.

If a band of hard rock cuts across a valley, the river will erode the softer rock above and below it more quickly. The river bed will become uneven and rapids will develop. If the downstream soft rock erodes very quickly, a waterfall will develop. At Niagara Falls and Victoria Falls, deep gorges have been eroded by the enormous power of water plunging over hard rock beds.

THE SEA'S ROLE

When a river reaches the sea, its energy is reduced to zero. Then the sea may take over. If there are strong currents or tides, the silt carried by the river is swept away to form part of the sea bed or perhaps a beach further along the coast.

However, if the river flows into a sea that has only gentle currents and tides, like the Nile in the Mediterranean and the Mississippi in the Gulf of Mexico, the river's load is dumped at the shoreline and builds up banks of sand and mud. These become deltas, vast networks of streams winding slowly between shoals. The fine material that makes up a delta is some of the most fertile land on Earth and some deltas are among the most densely populated places. But because a delta is low-lying it is also highly vulnerable to flooding and

winds. The delta of the Ganges and Brahmaputra makes up most of the country of Bangladesh with its population of more than 100 million people. The vast delta is often devastated by river flooding, as well as tidal surges and hurricanes, causing great loss of life.

THE WORLD'S HIGHEST WATERFALLS

ANGEL, VENEZUELA
3212ft (979m)

TUGELA, SOUTH AFRICA
3110ft (948m)

UTIGÅRD, NORWAY
2625ft (800m)

MONGEFOSSEN, NORWAY
2540ft (774m)

MTARAZI, ZIMBABWE
2500ft (762m)

YOSEMITE, USA
2425ft (739m)

MARDALSFOSSEN, NORWAY
2154ft (656m)

TYSSESTRENGANE, NORWAY
2120ft (646m)

CUQUEÑAN, VENEZUELA
2000ft (610m)

(All figures are for the total drop)

FLAT AND HIGH *The Sacramento River in California (left) ends in a farm-patterned delta. Kegon Falls (right) is one of Japan's best-loved beauty spots.*

The brief lives of lakes

LAKES CAN BE FORMED BY SHIFTING CONTINENTS, COLLAPSING VOLCANOES, GLACIERS AND EVEN METEORS. BUT FEW OF THEM HAVE A LONG FUTURE

If the age of the Earth were shown as a one-year calendar, only a few lakes on the planet would be older than two or three minutes. The long, narrow lakes of northern Italy or the English Lake District are a little older, barely 30 minutes – in reality about 15,000 years old. The huge Great Lakes of North America are a little older still, maybe an hour or so.

On the same scale, people have lived on the planet about three hours. Only Lake Baikal in central Asia, some of the African Rift Valley lakes, and the world's biggest lake, the Caspian Sea, would have existed for longer.

A lake is born when water fills a hollow in the land. The

A LAKE IN A VOLCANO'S CRATER MAY BE SO HOT IT GIVES OFF STEAM

movement of the continents around the Earth's surface gives birth to lakes in a number of ways. When two continents collide they buckle, and water collects in the downfolds. When this happened in western Asia 250 million years ago the Caspian Sea was the result.

Moving plates can also drift apart. In East Africa and the Middle East, long lakes form a chain-like pattern running from Lake Malawi in the south to the Dead Sea

in the north, following the Rift Valley. Where the crust has split apart, steep valley sides – marking the fault lines of the rift – drop down to the lake basins.

The world's deepest freshwater lake, Lake Baikal in Russia, which is 25 million years old, is also located in a rift valley.

Many extinct or dormant volcanoes have a funnel-shaped hollow in the top which becomes filled by rain or melted snow, forming an often circular lake called a crater lake. The water may be warm and may even give off steam if the volcano is active.

If the lake is large, like Lake Toba in Sumatra which is 56 miles (90km) long, it has probably formed in a huge volcanic cavity called a caldera. When a volcano erupts, an empty space may be left under the cone which then collapses, creating a large hollow that eventually fills with water.

Similar large lakes can be formed in the few craters that have been blasted into the face of the Earth by a colliding meteor. One is the Cratère du Nouveau Québec in Canada which is about a quarter of a mile (400m) across.

Most of the world's lakes were formed by glaciers during the last 2 million years – the time of the Ice Ages, when great ice sheets, miles thick, spread down from the polar regions. As they moved they scoured the rocks beneath them. Then as the climate grew warmer again,

the ice began to retreat, leaving behind debris (moraine).

In many deep glacial valleys, piles of moraine dammed up the rivers to form long, narrow 'finger' lakes such as Lakes Maggiore, Como and Garda in northern Italy, and Windermere, Coniston and Wast Water in the Lake District of England.

High up in some mountains are armchair-shaped hollows carved by ice. Many have a roughly circular lake in

the bottom. In France they are called cirques, in Wales cwms, in Scotland they are corries and in England tarns. Today many of these names are used all over the world, but they all refer to the same kind of lake.

As the ice sheet scraped the vast, flat areas of landscape, known as shields, in Canada and the Baltic, they hollowed out some parts and dumped moraine on others. When the ice retreated, irregular sheets of moraine were left behind and the bare surface of the rocky shield was often left exposed.

MOUNTAIN TARN *Grisedale Tarn lies high up in the English Lake District in a hollow gouged out of the rock by ice.*

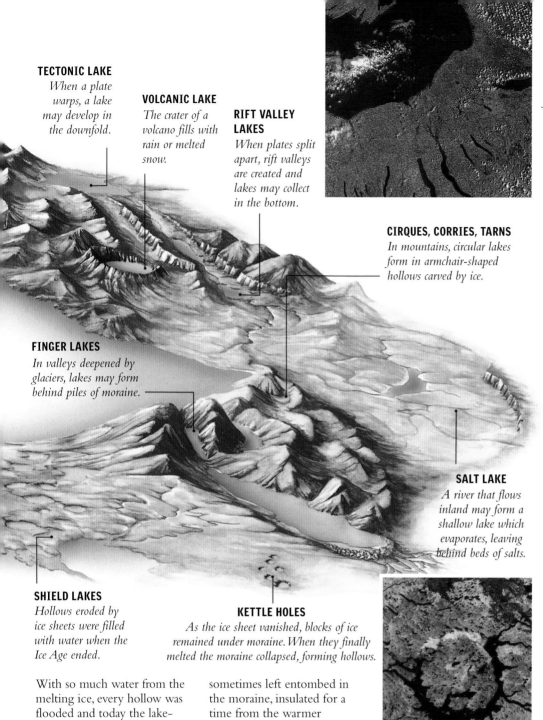

TECTONIC LAKE
When a plate warps, a lake may develop in the downfold.

VOLCANIC LAKE
The crater of a volcano fills with rain or melted snow.

RIFT VALLEY LAKES
When plates split apart, rift valleys are created and lakes may collect in the bottom.

GLACIAL STRIPS
Finger lakes stretch from Lake Ontario in New York State.

CIRQUES, CORRIES, TARNS
In mountains, circular lakes form in armchair-shaped hollows carved by ice.

FINGER LAKES
In valleys deepened by glaciers, lakes may form behind piles of moraine.

SALT LAKE
A river that flows inland may form a shallow lake which evaporates, leaving behind beds of salts.

SHIELD LAKES
Hollows eroded by ice sheets were filled with water when the Ice Age ended.

KETTLE HOLES
As the ice sheet vanished, blocks of ice remained under moraine. When they finally melted the moraine collapsed, forming hollows.

METEOR LAKE *Manicouagan Lake in Quebec, Canada, lies on the edge of a meteor crater.*

With so much water from the melting ice, every hollow was flooded and today the lakelands of Canada and Finland have a multitude of lakes of every shape and size.

When the ice sheets melted, blocks of ice were sometimes left entombed in the moraine, insulated for a time from the warmer climate. Slowly the ice melted and the moraine fell in to leave muddy hollows. These filled up with water to become small lakes or ponds called kettle holes, named after the large number in the Kettle Range of Wisconsin.

Rivers are also creators of lakes. Not all rivers have outlets to the sea, but drain into internal basins. The rivers carry salts dissolved from the rocks they have travelled over.

SALT FLATS *At Great Salt Lake, Utah, evaporated minerals form hard salt flats.*

If evaporation from the lake is high, the concentration of the salts gradually increases, producing a salt lake. Lake Eyre in Australia, Lake Chad in central Africa and the Great Salt Lake, USA, are among the biggest salt lakes.

Lakes are brought to the end of their usually short lives by a variety of causes. They may be filled with mud deposited by rivers. Or the natural dam that holds back the water may be breached or may collapse, allowing the water to drain away. Earth movements may make the lake so shallow it dries out. And a lake in the vent of an old volcano may even be blown away by the next eruption.

The awesome power of glaciers to sculpt the landscape

THE GRINDING AND QUARRYING BY GLACIERS IS ONE OF THE MOST SPECTACULAR WAYS THAT VALLEYS ARE CARVED AND ROCKS ARE MOVED FROM THE MOUNTAINS

 A glacier is one of the most powerful erosive forces in all nature. A great river of ice, compacted snow, boulders and rock fragments moves slowly but remorselessly downhill under the pressure of its own weight. The stones and other debris that it picks up on its journey turn it into a gigantic pan-scrubber that scours and gouges rock from the valleys down which it flows, often leaving them with a characteristic steep-sided U-shape.

Glaciers have left this 'signature' in mountain areas all over northern Europe, northern Eurasia and much of North America. For in the last Ice Age, which ended some 10,000 years ago, these lands lay buried under great ice sheets, some of which were more than half a mile (1km) thick.

Today, the ice is restricted to the polar regions and to the mountain tops, but it still covers about a tenth of the world's land surface.

The vast icefields in Greenland and Antarctica are known as continental glaciers, or ice sheets. They constantly flow from their centres to their edges, where the ice either melts or breaks off into the sea, forming icebergs.

A GLACIER FORMS

Where snow gathers in mountainous areas, the weight eventually overcomes the friction that was holding it stationary, and it begins to slide downhill. It has become a glacier.

Glaciers can form anywhere that snow accumulates on a slope and persists for year after year. A patch of snow soon becomes so heavy that pressure at the base of the patch causes melting, and the whole mass slides on its base, slowly cutting out a rounded hollow known as a cirque. As the snow continues to accumulate, the overflow eventually begins to move downhill under its own weight, flowing as a river of ice within a valley.

Over the steeper parts of its course, a valley glacier may have an icefall – a mass of broken ice blocks. Cracks, known as crevasses, develop in the surface. Crevasses can be covered by ice bridges and snow so that they are invisible, and are treacherous places for climbers. The Khumbu Icefall below Everest's South Col is a major hazard which has killed many climbers.

While most glaciers travel no more than a few inches a day, some almost race along. The fastest known major glacier is the Quarayaq Glacier in northern Greenland which moves at a rate of 65–80ft (20–24m) a day.

As the glacier moves, it picks up fragments from the rock over which it travels. Other material released by frost and water action from the valley sides drops onto it as well and may become incorporated in the ice. This grinding, abrasive material carried in the glacier's base is its main means of carving landscapes.

Glaciers have the power to wear away rock ten to twenty times faster than rivers. They can scour up to ⅛ in (3mm) from a rock surface in a year. Glaciers also move rocks, large and small, bodily from the mountains and redistribute them on the plains.

Whereas a mountain stream cuts a valley that is V-shaped in cross-section, a glacier typically creates a steep-walled U-shaped valley.

THE 'SNOUT'

Sunshine, especially in the summer, can be strong and hot in the rarefied air of the mountains, and ice sheets and glaciers lose ice by melting. At the point where the melting rate exceeds the rate at which the glacier can replace the ice, the glacier comes to an end as a terminus, or 'snout'.

The snouts of ice sheets and glaciers rarely remain in the same position for long. They are constantly advancing and retreating.

As the ice melts, the glacier sheds the debris along the valley sides and floor. Some of it reaches the glacier snout, and if this remains stationary for any time, a curved ridge of debris is left across the valley floor.

Valleys carved by glaciers provide spectacular scenery. One of the best known is the Yosemite Valley in California. There are many in the European Alps, and New Zealand's Southern Alps and Norway's mountains also have their share. In Norway, some U-shaped valleys have been flooded to form fjords.

TONGUES OF ICE *Two glaciers (above) flow from the ice sheet that covers most of Greenland to a depth of up to 1¾ miles (3km). On Mont Blanc (right), twin glaciers loom over a French village in the Chamonix Valley.*

DEATH OF A BERG *Born in Antarctica, this iceberg's journey is over. Weakened by waves, it collapsed moments after the picture was taken.*

ARÊTE
Sharply pointed mountain ridge formed when glaciers erode both sides of the ridge.

HORN, SPITZE OR PYRAMIDAL PEAK
Mountain spike formed when cirques cut back into a peak.

FIRN OR NÉVÉ
Snow which accumulates and compacts under its own weight to form the ice of the glacier.

MEDIAL MORAINE
When two glaciers meet, their lateral moraines merge in the centre of the combined glacier.

TRUNCATED SPUR
Mountain or hill spur whose tip has been removed by a glacier.

LATERAL MORAINE
Rock debris that falls from the valley sides accumulates along the edge of the glacier.

HANGING VALLEY
Side valley left stranded high above the floor of a main valley.

CIRQUE, CORRIE OR CWM
Armchair-shaped rock basin formed by the eroding ice.

GLACIAL LAKE
Small lake whose drainage is impeded by end moraine.

END MORAINE
Ridge of debris deposited by the glacier at its terminus.

POST-GLACIAL CIRQUE
This rock basin was formed by a glacier, but is now unoccupied.

THE WORLD'S LONGEST GLACIERS

LAMBERT, AUSTRALIAN ANTARCTIC TERRITORY
Length: 250 miles (402km).
Width: Up to 40 miles (64km)

PETERMAN, NORTHERN GREENLAND
Length: 125 miles (200km)

BEARDMORE, NEW ZEALAND ANTARCTIC TERRITORY
Length: 125 miles (200km)

HISPAR-BIAFO, KARAKORAM RANGE, PAKISTAN
Length: 75 miles (120km).
Width: Up to 2 miles (3.2km)

HUBBARD, ST ELIAS MOUNTAINS, ALASKA, USA
Length: 71 miles (114km)

HUMBOLDT, NORTH-WEST GREENLAND
Length: 71 miles (114km).
Width: About 59 miles (95km) near end

KOETTLITZ, ROYAL SOCIETY RANGE, NEW ZEALAND ANTARCTIC TERRITORY
Length: 53 miles (85km)
Width: About 8 miles (13km) near end

Deserts: changing landscapes sandblasted by the wind

SANDSTORMS COMBINE WITH HEAT AND COLD AND OCCASIONAL CLOUDBURSTS TO CREATE THE WORLD'S MOST DESOLATE REGIONS

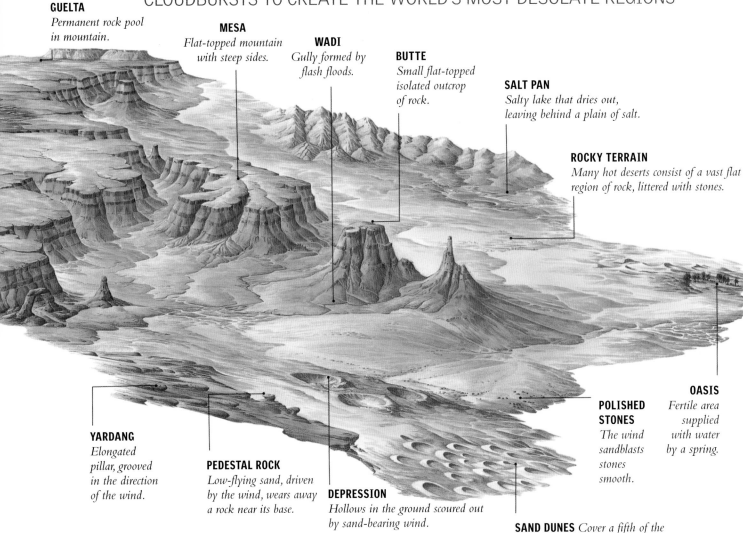

GUELTA
Permanent rock pool in mountain.

MESA
Flat-topped mountain with steep sides.

WADI
Gully formed by flash floods.

BUTTE
Small flat-topped isolated outcrop of rock.

SALT PAN
Salty lake that dries out, leaving behind a plain of salt.

ROCKY TERRAIN
Many hot deserts consist of a vast flat region of rock, littered with stones.

YARDANG
Elongated pillar, grooved in the direction of the wind.

PEDESTAL ROCK
Low-flying sand, driven by the wind, wears away a rock near its base.

DEPRESSION
Hollows in the ground scoured out by sand-bearing wind.

POLISHED STONES
The wind sandblasts stones smooth.

OASIS
Fertile area supplied with water by a spring.

SAND DUNES *Cover a fifth of the world's hot deserts.*

The traditional image of the desert as a sea of sand dunes – the abode of nomads riding camels – does exist, but it is only one of many desert landscapes. The most common type of desert is stony – a vast flat terrain of rock littered with stones, and extending to the horizon. To the traveller, it is an almost frightening scene of emptiness and desolation.

Deserts are not easy to define. Rainfall figures are deceiving because some of the rain may fall in a few torrential downpours every few years. An average of less than 6in (150mm) a year may mean there is little rain for a few years, then a tremendous downpour in one day.

The French geographer Robert Capot-Rey, in the 1930s, reckoned he had reached desert when the burrs of the cram-cram plant started to stick to his socks.

Plant life is still used to identify deserts. Once lack of water has caused plants to cover less than a third of the land, the soil and rocks become exposed to intensive erosion, creating a desert landscape.

The world is encircled by two belts of hot desert. The Northern Hemisphere has the Sahara, the Empty Quarter of Arabia, the deserts of central Asia, and the American deserts. The Southern Hemisphere has the Kalahari and Namib Deserts in Africa, the Atacama Desert in South America and the Australian deserts.

SANDSTONE CARVINGS *In Canyonlands National Park, Utah, mesas and buttes have been carved from sandstone by the weather.*

These barren regions have been created by global movements of the air. Hot air above the Equator rises, losing much of its moisture as rain. Then it moves either north or south and descends to form areas of high pressure along the Tropics of Cancer in the north and Capricorn in the south. Hot, dry winds flow from these high-pressure areas, searing the landscape and whipping up sand and dust into thick sandstorms.

Sand-laden wind is a powerful abrasive. Stones and pebbles that lie on the surface of the land are sandblasted so that they become flattened and smooth, even polished. Desert pebbles can sometimes be extraordinarily beautiful.

Because the wind carries most of the sand close to the ground, large rocks receive the onslaught near their base, wearing them away and eventually leaving them perched precariously on narrow, eroded necks.

Hard and soft rocks wear away at different rates to create weird shapes – yardangs like upturned hulls of ships, typical flat-topped desert mountains called mesas, and smaller remnants known as buttes.

As sand is blown across flat desert plains, it may scour out hollows where the rocks are softer, as in the Qattara Depression in Egypt. The depth of these depressions is restricted by underground water. If a water-soaked layer is reached, the particles of sand will bind together, and will be too heavy to be picked up by the wind. Plants will start to grow, creating that other classic desert scene, the oasis.

Desert temperatures can rise and fall dramatically during a single day. In the daytime the sun beats down from a cloudless sky and can push the temperature above 55°C (130°F). But at night the heat escapes upwards because there are no clouds to keep it in, and the temperature, even in the central Sahara, can fall below freezing point. Rocks which have baked under the sun during the day, and have then cooled rapidly, may crack, just as a plate will crack if it is moved from a hot oven to a cold surface. If dew enters a crack, it will expand as it freezes, forcing the crack

to widen. If this happens continually, fragments of rock will splinter off, to be broken down further as they collide in the wind.

DESERT WATER

Water can also be a powerful force in shaping the landscape. Occasional torrents of water rush over the parched desert floor as a flash flood and cut gullies called wadis. People have drowned in deserts. While crossing or camping in wadis they have been caught by the torrent from a rainstorm in nearby mountains.

Once the flooded land has dried out again, material loosened by water is quickly picked up by the wind, to play its part in the abrasive onslaught.

Deserts tend to collect salt. Streams and rivers often flow inland from the mountains and end up as shallow lakes where the water evaporates. All river water contains traces of salt that has been dissolved out of the ground. So when desert lakes dry up, they leave behind traces of salt which builds up over the years. Sometimes desert plains will flood and dry out again and again, leaving parched wastelands of salt, such as the Chott Djerid of Tunisia and the Great Salt Lake of the USA.

GUELTA *Plants grow around a pool, or guelta, in the Sahara.*

THE WORLD'S COLD DESERTS

Not all deserts are hot. A few are cold, such as the high-altitude Gobi Desert of Asia which lies outside the tropics at a height of up to 6500ft (2000m).

It owes its dryness to its remoteness from the sea and to the 'rain shadow' effect of mountains. Winds blowing from the south-west pick up moisture over the Indian Ocean. But as they rise over the Himalayas, they cool and the moisture condenses and falls as rain. By the time the winds reach the Gobi they have lost all their moisture and blow cold and dry across the desolate plateau of northern China and Mongolia.

DESERT BOULDERS *Shaped by extreme temperatures and fierce winds, rounded boulders litter the Tibesti Massif in Chad.*

Oceans of drifting sand

SAND DUNES COVER A FIFTH OF THE WORLD'S HOT DESERTS, OFTEN MOVING RELENTLESSLY ACROSS THE LANDSCAPE AND SWAMPING EVERYTHING IN THEIR PATH

Perfectly proportioned sand dunes, with their sinuous lines of knife-edge crests, are some of the world's most elegant landforms.

Dunes begin to form when grains of sand collect together. A small pile attracts more and more grains, like a magnet. In fact, the attraction happens because of changes in wind speed over very small areas. It might be due to an obstacle, such as a plant or a cluster of stones, or a meeting of two wind currents. As the wind slows down it drops some of the sand it is carrying. Once a small pile has accumulated, it becomes an even larger obstacle and attracts more drifting sand.

Growing in this way, dunes can reach astonishing proportions. Some dunes in the Grand Erg Occidental in Algeria, part of the Sahara Desert, are higher than the Empire State Building.

One-fifth of the world's hot desert is covered with a sea of sand, one dune merging into another. Many of these huge oceans are stationary, any movement kept in check by changes of wind direction. Others are slowly but unstoppably on the move, swamping everything in their path – isolated trees, roads, oases and even whole villages. They travel in the direction of the wind. The tiny grains of sand roll and bounce up the gradual slope of the windward side and

drop over the crest to roll down the steep leeward side.

Travelling dunes take on a crescent shape and are called barchans. They may occur singly or in swarms, smaller ones travelling faster than larger ones. During a dust storm you can watch a small dune no more than the height of your shoe cross the smooth surface of a tarmac road in a matter of minutes. Larger dunes are slower, moving at no more than 20yds (18m) a year.

Long straight dunes called seifs often occur in parallel groups. Each one can be as much as 12 miles (20km) long and up to 1 mile (1.5km) wide. Large, isolated 'whale-back' dunes build up in the lee of a mesa or large rock.

In the sandy desert nothing is permanent – footprints made in the morning will have vanished by the afternoon, the outline of the dunes changes from day to day. There are no landmarks.

The prospect of a traveller becoming totally lost in the wilderness is very real indeed.

IS THE SAHARA ON THE MOVE?

The southern fringe of the Sahara, known as the Sahel, is believed by some scientists to be advancing by as much as 9 miles (15km) a year. Reports of drought, starvation and death in Ethiopia, Somalia and Sudan have shocked the world. But is the Sahara really moving southwards or are the devastating crop failures being caused by politics and by bad management of land?

Global warming caused by increased carbon dioxide in the atmosphere from human activities is often blamed for the Sahel famines, but there is little proof. There is, however, plenty of evidence that the

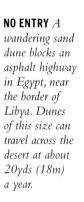

NO ENTRY *A wandering sand dune blocks an asphalt highway in Egypt, near the border of Libya. Dunes of this size can travel across the desert at about 20yds (18m) a year.*

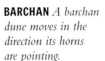

BARCHAN *A barchan dune moves in the direction its horns are pointing.*

BUTTER DUNES *Cold winds blow sand from deserts in central Asia south into the Gez Valley of the Chinese Pamir Mountains.*

STAR DUNE *Buttresses of sand radiate from the centre of a star dune in the Namib Desert. The wind constantly changes its shape.*

climate has fluctuated in long cycles over the past 2 million years. Stone Age paintings depict antelopes, elephants and lions at Tassili N'Ajjer in the Algerian Sahara. And Roman cities all over North Africa once ruled over the granaries of the Roman Empire where fields grew grain – without any need for irrigation – to be exported to Rome. Now the former farms are dusty plains of semi-desert. This is part of the natural climatic cycle – each cycle taking thousands of years – that is brought about by changes in the Earth's orbit around the Sun. It is the same cycle that caused the Ice Ages, and could now be at work to cause the Sahara to march into the Sahel.

However, the growth of deserts can also be blamed on man's treatment of the land. Cutting down trees and scrub to open up land for farming can expose soil to the ravages of erosion. Bad management of land on slopes, such as ploughing furrows up and down a hill instead of around it, can cause soil to be washed down or blown away. Bad farming practice in the American Midwest during the 1930s reduced an area of farm land nearly the size of

SEAS OF SAND *Rolling expanses of sand make up a fifth of the world's largest desert, the Sahara.*

England to a dust bowl. This type of soil erosion happens on the edges of the Sahara when grassland with poor soil is ploughed up to grow crops.

Over-grazing by farm animals is also alleged to cause erosion, but the evidence is inconclusive. Animals can actually encourage plant growth by fertilising the soil with their manure. Nomadic farmers, who have roamed and flourished in the deserts for thousands of years, never stay in one place for long. They move their flocks frequently, giving grass time to grow again. Only if they are stopped from moving on will their animals over-graze land.

In the short term, politics are probably as strong a factor as climate change in causing the Sahel famines. Wars in Ethiopia and Somalia have forced refugees to migrate into semi-arid land that cannot support them. Social and economic pressures, such as government settlement policies, have also forced people to give up traditional nomadic farming and adopt static Western farming methods not suited to the land and climate, and so lead to 'dust bowls'.

Climatic change is an easy scapegoat for countries suffering from famine, but the case has not yet been proved.

THE WORLD'S BIGGEST DESERTS

SAHARA, NORTH AFRICA
Area: 3,500,000sq miles
(9,100,000km²)

GREAT AUSTRALIAN, AUSTRALIA
Area: 1,480,000sq miles
(3,830,000km²)

GOBI, ASIA
Area: 500,000sq miles
(1,295,000km²)

RUB AL KHALI, ARABIAN PENINSULA Area: 251,000sq miles (650,000km²)

KALAHARI, SOUTHERN AFRICA Area: 200,000sq miles (520,000km²)

KARAKUM, TURKMENISTAN, WESTERN ASIA
Area: 130,000sq miles
(340,000km²)

Index

Acknowledgments

Photographs that are Reader's Digest copyright are given in *italics*.

T=top; ***C***=centre; ***B***=bottom; ***R***=right; ***L***=left.

Front cover GEO/Uwe George; (insets) ***L*** Paul Wakefield, ***R*** Explorer/Katia Krafft, **Back cover** Ashok Rodrigues/iStockphoto, **2-3** Digital Vision, **4-5** istockphoto.com, **12** The Image Bank/ Keone, **13** Explorer/Bruno Guiter, **14 *CL*** Colorific/Pierre Boulat, ***CR*** Bruce Coleman/Giorgio Gualco, **15 *B*** Colorific/Sylvain Grandadam, **16 *TL*** Jean-Marc Durou, ***C*** Syndication International, **17-19** (*all*) Philippe Lafond, **20-21** Daniele Pellegrini, **22-23** Odyssey Images/Colorific/J.L. Manaud, **23 *TR*** Colorific/J.L.Manaud, **24-25** Chris Johns, **26-27** AllStock/ Chris Johns, **28** (*all*) AllStock/Chris Johns, **29** John Hillelson/Georg Gerster, **30** AllStock/Chris Johns, **31 *T*** AllStock/Chris Johns, ***C*** Patrick Frilet, **32 *C*** Osterreichische National Bibliothek, ***R*** Douglas Botting, **33** Colorific/Mirella Ricciardi, **34 *B*** GEO/Uwe George, **35** Guy Yeoman, ***TL*** Colorific/© James Sugar/Black Star, **37 *B*** Allstock/Chris Johns, **38** Planet Earth Pictures/Sean Avery, **39 *L*** Gerald Cubitt, ***BR*** Magnum/ George Rodger, **40-41** Planet Earth Pictures/A & M Shah, **42-43** National Geographic Society/Robert Caputo, **43** *Stanley* The Mansell Collection, ***BR*** The Hulton Picture Company, **44-45** John Hillelson/Georg Gerster, **45** Royal Geographical Society, **46-47** Minden Pictures/Frans Lanting, **47** Minden Pictures/Frans Lanting, **48** Chris Johns, **49** AllStock/Chris Johns, **50-51** AllStock/Chris Johns, **51** Magnum/Michael K. Nichols, **52 *T*** Colorific/© James Sugar (Black Star), **53 *B*** Minden Pictures/ Jim Brandenburg, **54-55** Gerald Cubitt, **55 *BL*** Minden Pictures/Jim Brandenburg, **56 *TL*** Anthony Bannister Photo Library, ***C*** Bruce Coleman/ Eckart Pott, **57 *B*** Anthony Bannister Photo Library, **58 *TL*** John Hillelson/ George Gerster, **58-59** Anthony Bannister Photo Library, **60-61** Minden Pictures/Frans Lanting, **61** Robert Estall/David Coulson, **62 *T*** Anthony Bannister Photo Library, ***B*** Minden Pictures/Frans Lanting, **63 *T*** NHPA/ Peter Johnson, ***B*** Anthony Bannister Photo Library, **64 *TL*** Courtesy of Dept. of Library Services, American Museum of Natural History Neg. No. 410988, Photo: Shackelford, ***CL*** Impact/Alain Le Garsmeur, **64-65** *Background Vernon Morgan*, ***C*** Doug Scott, ***B*** Royal Geographical Society, **65 TL** Fondation Alexandra David Neel, **TR** Mountain Light/© Galen Rowell, ***CR*** Planet Earth Pictures/Howard Platt, **66 *B*** Minden Pictures/Frans Lanting, **67** Aspect/Antoniette Jaunet, **68-69** Network/ Herman Potgieter, ***BC*** The Hulton Picture Company, ***B*** Johan W Elzenga, **72-73** National Geographic Society/James L. Stanfield, **73 *BL*** Royal Geographical Society, ***BC*** Gerald Cubitt, ***B*** Gerald Cubitt, **76 *TL*** & ***TC*** Peter Newark's Pictures, **77** Photo Access/David Steele, **78 *TR*** Bruce Coleman/ Gerald Cubitt, ***CR*** Art Publishers, Durban/John Hone, ***B*** Photo Access/ Walter Knirr, **80** Walter Knirr, **80-81** Walter Knirr, **83** Minden Pictures/ Frans Lanting, **84-85** Minden Pictures/Frans Lanting, **85** After a photograph by Frans Lanting, **88-89** Photographers Aspen/Paul Chesley, **89 *T*** Robert Harding Picture Library/L. Giraudou, ***C*** Samfoto/Kim Hart, **90-91** Explorer/Katia Krafft, **91 *BR*** Private Collection/University of Heidelberg, **93** Samfoto/Pal Hermansen, **94-95** Paul Wakefield, **96 *TR*** Ulster Museum, Belfast, ***CR*** National Maritime Museum, London, ***B*** Ulster Museum, Belfast, **97** Paul Wakefield, **98-99** Paul Wakefield, **100-1** Slide File, **102-3** Jon Wyand, **103 *C*** Ronald W. Clark, ***BR*** John Cleare/Mountain Camera, **104 *T*** Images Colour Library, **105** Patricia Macdonald, **106 *B*** David Noton, **107 *B*** Colorific/Mike Yamashita, **108-9** Martti Rikkonen, **110-11** Husmofoto, **111** Werner Forman Archive/Statens Historiska Museum, Stockholm, **112-13** Patrick Frilet, **113** Explorer/Jean Loup, **114 *T*** Library of Congress (USF34-4052-E), ***CL*** Thomas Stephan, ***CR*** John Hillelson/ Georg Gerster, ***B*** The Image Bank/Guido Alberto Rossi, ***114-15*** *Background Vernon Morgan*, **115 *T*** ZEFA/Rossenbach, ***C*** Aspect/Geoff Tompkinson, ***BL*** Thomas S. Lang, ***BR*** Roger-Viollet, **116-17** Odyssey Productions/Robert Frerck, **118 *L*** Network/Silvester/Rapho, **119 *T*** Network/ Silvester/Rapho, **120-1** Network/Silvester/Rapho, **122-3** Odyssey Productions/ Robert Frerck, **124 *BL*** Scope/Jacques Sierpinski, **125 *L*** John Cleare/ Mountain Camera, **126 *TR*** The Mansell Collection, **127 *T*** & ***C*** Eisriesenwelt, **128 *B*** Images Colour Library, **129 *TC*** & ***TR*** Ronald W. Clark, **130 *BC*** Overseas/E. Gavazzi, **130-1** Gerhard & Waltraud Klammert, **132-3** Helga Lada Fotoagentur/Ernst Wrba, **133** Bildarchiv Huber/ R. Schmid, **134-5** Explorer/Katia Krafft, **135** *Etna Violet* After photograph by E. Poli Marchese, **136-7** Daniele Pellegrini, **138-9** Ric Ergenbright, **139** Daniele Pellegrini/Dottore Lino Pellegrini, **140-1** Network/Klaus D. Francke (Bilderberg), **141** NHPA/David Woodfall, **144-5** Colorific/© 1992, Lee Day (Black Star), **145** Robert Harding Picture Library/Nicolas Thibaut, **146** Explorer/R. Mattes, **147 *R*** Colorific/Richard Nowitz, **148-9** Aspect/Peter Carmichael, **150** John Hillelson/Georg Gerster, **151** Robert Harding Picture Library/J. Edwardes, **152-3** Aspect/Barrie Christie, **153 *BL*** Aspect/Barry Christie, **154 *B*** Agence de Presse/Vadim Gippenreiter, **155 *T*** ZEFA/Vadim Gippenreiter, ***BR*** Agence de Presse/ Vadim Gippenreiter, **156 *T*** NHPA/John Hartley, **157** Wolfgang Kaehler, **158-9** Daniele Pellegrini, **160-1** Novosti/Piotr Malinovskij, **161 *BR*** Tyne and Wear Museums, **162-3** NHPA/John Hartley, **164-5** Ric Ergenbright, **165 *B*** Explorer/P. Montbazet, **166** Mountain Light/© Galen Rowell, 1986, **168-9** Novosti/A. Lyskin, **170-1** John Cleare/Mountain Camera, **172-3** Mountain Light/© Galen Rowell, **174 *T*** The Aerial Display Company/ Mandy Dickinson, ***CL*** The Aerial Display Company/Leo Dickinson, **175 *T*** Colorific/Lee E. Battaglia, **176** Magnum/H. Hamaya. **176-7** Bruce Coleman/Orion Press, **177 *TR*** Courtesy of the Trustees of the Victoria and Albert Museum, London, ***C*** The Bridgeman Art Library/Private Collection, **178-9** Aspect/Tom Nebbia, **180 *B*** ET Archive/National Palace Museum, Taiwan, **180-1** China Travel & Tourism Press, **182-3** Lu Kai Di, **184-5** Aspect/Peter Carmichael, **186 *L*** & ***BR*** AJ Eavis, **187 *T*** John Hillelson/ Georg Gerster, ***B*** Explorer/Jean-Louis Gaubert, **188 *TL*** Frank Spooner/ Greg Lowe, ***C*** Christian Bonington, **188-9** Colorific/© James Balog (Black Star), *Background Vernon Morgan*, **189 *TL*** Mary Evans Picture Library, ***TR*** Explorer/Katia Krafft, ***BL*** Yosemite National Park Research Library/George Fiske, ***BR*** Network/Serraillier (Rapho). **190-1** The Image Bank/Nevada Wier, **192** Robert Harding Picture Library/A.C. Waltham, **193 *R*** Bruce Coleman/John Waters, **194 *B*** Taroko National Park, **195** Taroko National Park, **196-7** Robert Harding Picture Library/Robert Francis, **198-9** Robert Harding Picture Library/Robin Hanbury-Tenison, **199 *CR*** Robert Harding Picture Library/A.C. Waltham, **200** ZEFA/DAMM-ZEFA, **201 *L*** Bruce Coleman/Dieter & Mary Plage, **202-3** John Hillelson/ Georg Gerster, **204** Explorer/Katia Krafft, **205 *B*** Bruce Coleman/Dieter & Mary Plage, **206-7** A. Compost, **210-11** Bill Bachman, **212-13** R. Woldendorp, **213** Bill Bachman, **214 *R*** Bill Bachman, **215 *B*** Photo Index/R. Woldendorp, **216 *B*** Photo Index/R. Woldendorp, **217** Bill Bachman. **218-19** John Hillelson/ Georg Gerster, **220-1** Robin Morrison, **222-3** Auscape/Reg Morrison, **223 *BC*** From a photograph by I.R. McCann/Australasian Nature Transparencies, **224 *TL*** David Muench Photography, ***CL*** Photograph courtesy of Hirschl & Adler Galleries, Inc., New York/The Collection of Mr & Mrs. C. Kevin Landry, ***CR*** Royal Geographical Society, ***BR*** Colin Monteath/ Hedgehog House, NZ, **224-5** *Background Vernon Morgan*, ***T*** Lent by U.S. Department of the Interior, Office of the Secretary, **225 *TR*** Michael D. Yandell, ***CL*** The Bridgeman Art Library/Pushkin Museum, ***CR*** Yale Center for British Art/Paul Mellon Collection, ***BL*** Colorific/Patrick Ward, ***BR*** Bruce Coleman/ Geoff Dore, **226-7** John Hillelson/Georg Gerster, **228-9** Auscape/Gunther Deichmann, **230** Auscape/Jean-Paul Ferrero, **231 *TL*** Auscape/Jean Paul Ferrero, ***TR*** JohnHillelson/Georg Gerster, **232-3** Photo Index/R. Woldendorp, **234 *T*** Auscape/Jean-Paul Ferrero, **235 *CL*** Auscape/D. Parer & E. Parer-Cook, **236-7** Auscape/Reg Morrison, **238 *L*** Bill Bachman, **239 *T*** Bill Bachman, **240** David Austen, **240-1** Bill Bachman, **242-3** AllStock/Art Wolfe, **243** Auscape/J.M. La Roque, **244-5** Auscape/Jean-Paul Ferrero, **246 *T*** Bill Bachman, ***B*** After a photograph by A.P. Smith/Australasian Nature Transparencies, **247 *B*** Photo Index, **248 *CR*** & ***BR*** Auscape/L. Newman & A. Flowers, **248-9** Colorific/ Penny Tweedie, **250 *T*** Auscape/Kevin Deacon, ***B*** Auscape/L. Newman & A. Flowers, **251 *B*** Auscape/Jaime Plaza van Roon, **252 *C*** & ***R*** Auscape/ Reg Morrison, **253** R. Armstrong, **254 *T*** David & Anne Doubilet, **258-9** Explorer/Katia Krafft, **259** Alexander Turnbull Library, NZ/ Auckland Star Collection, **260-1** Bruce Coleman/Frances Furlong, **261 *CR*** Brian Enting Projects, *Greenstone figure* Bruce Coleman/J. Fennell, **262** John Hillelson/ Brian Brake, **263 *T*** Auscape/Kevin Deacon, ***C*** Alexander Turnbull Library, NZ/Gifford Collection, **264 *BR*** Colin Monteath Hedgehog House, NZ/Pat Barrett. **264-5** Bruce Coleman/ G. Egger, **266-7** Bill Bachman, **268** John Hillelson/Brian Brake, **269 *T*** The Image Bank/List Dennis, **270-1** The Image Bank/Margarette Mead, **272 *TL*** NHPA/Stephen Krasemann, ***TR*** The Hulton Picture Company, ***B*** David Muench Photography, **273 *B*** Minden Pictures/ Frans Lanting, **274-5** The Image Bank/Don King, **275 *B*** Minden Pictures/Frans Lanting, **276-7** Network Hans-Jurgen Burkard (Bilderberg), **280-1 *T*** DRK/ Krasemann, ***B*** Planet Earth Pictures/Jim Brandenburg, **282 *BL*** National Geographic Society/Collection Robert E. Peary, ***BC*** Reed Consumer Books Picture Library, **283** Tom Bean, **284-5** Jeff Gnass Photography, **286-7** Tom Bean, **287** Science Photo Library/Jack Finch. **288-9 *T*** Network/© 1991 Sarah Leen (Matrix), ***B*** Colorific/© James Balog (Black Star), **290-1** Tim Thompson Photography, **291 *C*** National Geographic Society, **292-3** Colorific/Erich Spiegelhalter, **293** Fred Bruemmer, **294 *T*** Colorific/Erich Spieglehalter, **295 *B*** Matt Bradley, **296-7** Matt Bradley, **298 *T*** & ***CL*** Matt Bradley, **299 *BR*** Yva Momatiuk/John Eastcott, **300 *B*** The Image Bank/ William A. Logan, **300-1** Ric Ergenbright, **302 *TL*** The Ronald Grant Archive Diamond Films Ltd (Paramount), ***CL*** Cinema Bookshop/ Colombia Pictures, ***C*** Camera Press/Snowdon, ***BR*** The Kobal Collection/Colombia Pictures, **302-3** *Background Vernon Morgan*, ***B*** The Kobal Collection/MGM, **303 *TL*** British Film Institute/ Universal, ***C*** The Ronald Grant Archive, ***CR*** The Kobal Collection, **304-5** ZEFA/S. Dauner, **305 *BL*** The Mansell Collection, **306-7** Larry Ulrich Photography, **308 *T*** Peter Newark's Pictures, **309 *BR*** Sierra Club/William E. Colby Memorial Library, ***B*** Planet Earth Pictures/Robert A Jureit, **310** Jeff Gnass Photography, **311 *C*** University of California/The Bancroft Library, ***R*** Owner unknown, Poster in Yosemite National Park Collection/ Photograph by Bob Woolard, ***B*** David Muench Photography, **312 *TL*** David Muench Photography, ***R*** Planet Earth Pictures/John Downer, **313** Photographers Aspen/Paul Chesley, **314-15** National Geographic Society/W.A. Allard, **316 *TL*** David Muench Photography, **316-17** Ric Ergenbright, **317 *BL*** Jeff Gnass Photography, **318-19** Mountain Light/© Galen Rowell, **319 *C*** National Park Service, **320 *B*** David Muench Photography, **321 *T*** NHPA/John Shaw, **322 *R*** Bruce Coleman/Michael Freeman, **323** Lloyd Smith, **324-5** Colorific/Michael J. Howell, **326-7** Jeff Gnass Photography, **327 *T*** Tom Bean, **328 *T*** The Image Bank/James H. Carmichael Jr, ***BL*** David Muench Photography, **329 *R*** Magnum/Michael Nichols, **330** Magnum/Michael Nichols, **331 *CR*** & ***B*** Magnum/Michael Nicols, **332-3** Dietrich Stock Photos, Inc, **334 *T*** David Muench Photography/Marc Muench, ***B*** David Muench Photography, **335 *CL*** Smithsonian Institution (1,591) ***CR*** Private Collection, ***B*** Tom Bean, **336 *CL*** Magnum/ Bruno Barbey, BL National Geographic Society/E.C. Erdis, ***BR*** Loren McIntyre, **336-7** *Background Vernon Morgan*, ***T*** Svenska Aero-Bilder AB/G. Soderberg, **337 *TR*** Aerofilms, ***CL*** John Hillelson/Brian Brake, ***CR*** Richard Alexander Cooke III, ***B*** Slide File, **338-9** Woodfin Camp & Associates/Jonathan Blair, **339** Courtesy of Dept. of Library Services, American Museum of Natural History, Negative no. 329148, **340-1** David Muench Photography, **341 *TR*** National Archives, Washington, Neg. no. 75-BAE-2421B-6, ***BR*** David Muench Photography/Bonnie Muench, **342 *T*** Peter L. Kresan Photography, ***C*** David Muench Photography, **343 *L*** David Muench Photography, **344 *CL*** Colorific/Michael Melford, **344-5 *L*** Ric Ergenbright, **345 *CR*** John Hillelson/Georg Gerster, **346 *TR*** Bruce Coleman/Charlie Ott, **347** Jeff Gnass Photography, **348 *BL*** David Muench Photography, ***BR*** Library of Congress Neg. no. 300195 LC-262 78279, **349 *R*** DRK/Marty Cordano, **350** David Muench Photography, **350-1** Carr Clifton, **352-3** Warren Marr, **354-5** Eduardo Fuss, **356 *L*** David Muench Photography, ***BR*** Courtesy of The Scheinbaum & Russek Gallery of Photography/Photo by David Scheinbaum, **357** Photographers Aspen/David Hiser, ***B*** Colorific/© John Running (Black Star), **358-9** Colorific/Michael Melford, **359** Loren McIntyre, **362** *Kinkajou* After a photograph by Loren McIntyre, ***T*** Loren McIntyre, **363** NHPA/George Bernard, **364 *CL*** Loren McIntyre, **364-5** Loren McIntyre, **366-7** GEO/ Charles Brewer-Carias, **368-9** GEO/Uwe George, **370-1 *B*** The Lost World Balloon Society/Michael Lawton, **371 *C*** National Portrait Gallery, London, ***CR*** John Murray (Publishers) Ltd./Sir Arthur Conan Doyle, *The Lost World*, **372-3** Ardea, London/Adrian Warren, **374** GEO/Uwe George, **375 *B*** Loren McIntyre, **376-7** Nigel Press Associates Ltd, **377 *BR*** Loren McIntyre, **378-9** NHPA/Martin Wendler, **379 *C*** Explorer/Jose Moure, **380 *TL*** Photographers Aspen/Nicholas Devore III, ***TR*** Bruce Coleman/ Gunter Ziesler, **381 *T*** Loren McIntyre, **382-3** Loren McIntyre, **384-5** Loren McIntyre, **385** Magnum/F. Scianna, **386-7** Rex Features Ltd/Michael Friedel, **388** Loren McIntyre, **388-9**, Loren McIntyre, **390 *T*** Loren McIntyre, **391 *B*** South America Pictures, **392-3** Loren McIntyre, **394 *B*** Trustees of the British Museum (Natural History), **394-5** Explorer/Revel, **395 *BR*** Aspect/ Julia Bergada, **396-7** Colin Monteath Hedgehog House, NZ, **397 *CR*** The Mansell Collection, **B** Colorific/© Olaf Soot (Black Star), **398-9** Daniele Pellegrini, **402-3** Jim Snyder, **404** National Geographic Society/George Mobley, **405 *T*** Colin Monteath Hedgehog House, NZ, **406-7** Colin Monteath Hedgehog House, NZ, **408 *BL*** & ***BC*** Popperfoto, **409** Colin Monteath Hedgehog House, NZ/Pat Tinnelly, **410-11** Thomas Ives, **412 *T*** Images Unlimited, Inc./Al Giddings, ***B*** Biofotos, **412-13** National Geographic Society/ Emory Kristol, **414 *T*** Icelandic Photo & Press Service/Mats Wibe Lund, ***B*** Bildarchiv Preussischer Kulturbesitz, **415** Ardea, London/Francois Gohier, **416 *TL*** & ***BC*** Explorer/Katia Krafft, **416-17 *B*** Explorer/Katia Krafft, **417 *TL*, *TC*, *TR***, © Gary Rosenquist, 1980. The Publishers have been unable to contact the photographer, **418-19 *T*** Andreas Stieglitz, **419 *TC*** Colorific/P. Maitre (Odyssey), ***TR*** Entheos/Steven C. Wilson, ***B*** Daniele Pellegrini, **420 *BL*** Colorific/© James Sugar (Black Star), ***BR*** Icelandic Photo & Press Service/Mats Wibe Lund, **421 *T*** Colorific/© James Balog (Black Star), ***BL*** Natural Science Photos/A.J. Sutcliffe, ***BR*** Photo Researchers, Inc./Ronny Jaques, **422 *BL*** Rob Lewine, ***BC*** John S. Shelton, **423 *TL*** Guillermo Aldana, **424** Explorer/K. Krafft, **425** Ric Ergenbright, **426** Telegraph Colour Library, **426-7** Geoscience Features, **427 *TR*** Aerofilms, ***C*** Robert Harding Picture Library/A.C. Waltham, ***BR*** Mountain Camera/John Cleare, **429 *T*** John Cleare (Mountain Camera), ***BL BR*** Network/H. Silvester (Rapho), **430 *TL*** & ***C*** David Gasser, **430-1 *T*** Minden Pictures/Frans Lanting, ***B*** John Hillelson/Georg Gerster, **431 *TR*** DRK/Stephen J. Krasemann, ***BR*** Landscape Only/Images Colour Library Limited Roger Moss, **432 *BL*** David Muench Photography, **432-3 *B*** Peter Dombrovskis/West Wind Press, **433 *TL*** Geoscience Features, **434 *TL*** Robert Harding Picture Library/Daphne Pochin-Mould, ***TR*** Bruce Coleman/Geoff Dore, ***C*** Robert Harding Picture Library/N.A. Callow, **435** Photo Index/R. Woldendorp, **436 TL** DRK/Stephen J. Krasemann, **436-7 *T*** David Muench Photography, **437 *TR*** The Image Bank/Steve Proehl, ***CL*** The Image Bank/Alain Choisnet, ***BR*** Sheila & Oliver Mathews, **439 *TL*** Geoscience Features/Dr. B. Booth, ***CL*** Ardea, London/Adrian Warren, ***BL*** The Image Bank/Barrie Rokeach, ***BR*** The Image Bank/Tom Mareschal, **440** Aspect/Rob Moore, **441 *TC*** Satellite image data processing by Environmental Research Institute of Michigan (ERIM), Ann Arbor, Michigan, ***C*** National Air Photo Library, Canada, ***BL*** David Muench Photography, **442 *TR*** Kort-OG Matrikelstyrelsen, Copenhagen, ***BL*** Colin Monteath Hedgehog House, NZ/Mark Jones, **443 *TL*** Photographers Aspen/Paul Chesley, **445 *TL*** David Muench Photography, ***TR*** Colorific/ Koene, ***B*** GEO/Uwe George, **446** Impact/Yann Arthus-Bertrand (Altitude), **446-7** The Image Bank, **447 TL** Mountain Light/© Galen Rowell, ***TC*** John Hillelson/Georg Gerster, ***TR*** Loren McIntyre. **Endpapers** PhotoDisc.

40/345/05